The Nineteenth Century Periodical Press and the Development of Detective Fiction

This book re-imagines nineteenth-century detective fiction as a literary genre that was connected to, and nurtured by, contemporary periodical journalism. Whilst 'detective fiction' is almost universally-accepted to have originated in the nineteenth century, a variety of widely-accepted scholarly narratives of the genre's evolution neglect to connect it with the development of a free press.

The volume traces how police officers, detectives, criminals, and the criminal justice system were discussed in the pages of a variety of magazines and journals, and argues that this affected how the wider nineteenth-century society perceived organised law enforcement and detection. This, in turn, helped to shape detective fiction into the genre that we recognise today. The book also explores how periodicals and newspapers contained forgotten, non-canonical examples of 'detective fiction', and that these texts can help complicate the narrative of the genre's evolution across the mid- to late nineteenth century.

Samuel Saunders holds a PhD in English from Liverpool John Moores University, which he obtained in 2018 after defending a thesis that examined nineteenth-century crime and detective fiction and its connections with Victorian journalism and print culture. He has published research in numerous peer-reviewed journals such as the *Journal of Popular Culture*, the *Wilkie Collins Journal, Law, Crime and History*, and the journal of the *Open Library of the Humanities*, and has co-edited a collection on sidekicks in crime fiction. Samuel has taught English at both LJMU and the University of Chester, has acted as a guest professor for the Ohio State University, and is a Fellow of the Higher Education Academy (FHEA).

Routledge Studies in Nineteenth Century Literature

For more information about this series, please visit: https://www.routledge.com/Routledge-Studies-in-Nineteenth-Century-Literature/book-series/RSNCL

The Nineteenth Century Periodical Press and the Development of Detective Fiction

Samuel Saunders

Routledge
Taylor & Francis Group

NEW YORK AND LONDON

First published 2021
by Routledge
605 Third Avenue, New York, NY 10158

and by Routledge
2 Park Square, Milton Park, Abingdon, Oxon OX14 4RN

Routledge is an imprint of the Taylor & Francis Group, an informa business

Library of Congress Cataloging-in-Publication Data
A catalog record for this title has been requested

ISBN: 978-0-367-02961-6 (hbk)
ISBN: 978-0-367-76907-9 (pbk)
ISBN: 978-0-429-01978-4 (ebk)

Typeset in Sabon
by Taylor & Francis Books

For Emma

Contents

Figures

Acknowledgements

My overwhelming thanks go firstly to Dr Jonathan Cranfield, who was my master's and subsequent PhD supervisor between 2014 and 2018. This book would not have been possible without his support, guidance, advice, and, above all, his seemingly endless supply of patience, which never wavers no matter how much it is tried. I'd also like to thank Professor Glenda Norquay for acting as second supervisor, and for providing a stream of wonderfully-directed advice.

My gratitude also to the entire School of English at Liverpool John Moores University for providing funding, support, and teaching opportunities across my PhD and beyond. A better institution at which to do a PhD does not exist. I'm also grateful to the Department of English at University Centre Shrewsbury, for more recent teaching and continued library access.

My thanks to all of the staff at the Museum of Policing in Cheshire, the National Library of Scotland and at the Parliamentary Archives in Westminster for all of their help and support to a researcher who was often a little lost, didn't quite know what he was doing, or who wasn't sure how to use the photocopier.

Thank you to my entire family for their continued support and their resolute optimism, and to my very patient and understanding in-laws, who housed me throughout my PhD.

For all of the above, and for everything else, I thank my wife Emma, without whom I would never have gotten started.

Introduction

Victorian Policing and Victorian Periodicals

This book originally began life as a PhD thesis completed in the School of English at Liverpool John Moores University between 2015 and 2018. Despite numerous amendments, edits, and rearrangements since that time, its purpose has remained the same: to explore and reveal a hitherto-understudied relationship between the evolution of 'detective fiction' and British periodical and magazine journalism published between circa 1840 and 1900.

There are two distinct gaps in scholarship concerning Victorian detective fiction that the volume resolves. The first is that broad studies of generic development (especially those that look at such a contentiously-defined genre as this)[1] tend to be insular, and insecurely connect sporadically-published texts together through various shared characteristics in order to present a viable literary chronology. The second is that, quite simply, detective fiction is (perhaps surprisingly) rarely explored in the context of its connection to contemporary perceptions of actual law enforcement. To combat both oversights, this book uses a historicist model to examine nineteenth-century journalistic representations of police officers, detectives, crimes, and criminals alongside fiction, to establish more concrete connections between detective literature and the prevalent ideologies that surrounded it.

The study is organised into three parts, each with two chapters and each with their own particular focus, designed to guide the reader through detective fiction's constantly-shifting literary landscape in both thematic and chronological terms from the mid-nineteenth century to the *fin-de-siècle*. Chapters 1 and 2, which form Part I, reveal and solidify the connection between periodicals, law enforcement and crime. Chapter 1 establishes the relationship between 'police' and 'periodical', arguing that while the press had been mildly interested in the regulation of society from as early as the eighteenth century, it was in the mid-Victorian era that it began to more openly critique the police as an institution.[2] Periodicals became keenly interested in policing in this period, and direct commentary on the force was often shaped by titles' own political or partisan allegiances – leading to disagreement on the remit, expense and overall effectiveness of the police. Despite this conflict, however, Chapter 1 also highlights how the varied journalistic coverage of the police was actually all connected in that it a) simply helped to entrench the force as part of the Victorian social fabric whether supportive or not, and b) helped to construct an image of the police as operating on the fringes of society, located somewhere between criminality and the rest of the 'respectable' public.

Chapter 2 switches perspective to highlight how Victorian periodical commentary on the police was largely separate from their coverage of crime. This was at least partly due to a well-established historic tradition on which periodical crime reporting was built, that had emerged long before the police had been established. The eighteenth and early nineteenth century witnessed the development of a wide variety of written forms that reported criminal activity, including popular execution broadsides and chap-books, prison chaplains' records such as the *Ordinary of Newgate's Accounts*, and the earliest issues of the infamous *Newgate Calendar*, all of which were precursors to later crime 'round-up' features that appeared in Victorian-era periodicals. The police, however, remained largely absent from these periodical crime reports, because earlier forms of crime-writing had constructed an entrenched methodology of reporting which left little room for their involvement. This, the chapter goes on to suggest, further demonstrates how the police were socially indistinct, as they were usually completely invisible in periodical crime reports and only appeared whenever they were required to perform a certain function before disappearing again. Chapter 2 then switches perspective to argue that crime journalism was also designed, right from its earliest roots, to figuratively transport curious readers into often-inaccessible spaces and moments associated with the criminal justice system, such as court rooms, prisons, executions, and the domestic scenes where crimes had taken place. This interest was, alongside the social invisibility of the police officer, transposed into periodical crime 'round ups', and came to have a significant impact on the development of the first forms of 'detective literature'.

Part II, formed by Chapters 3 and 4, takes the contextual journalistic landscape constructed in Part I and applies it to various kinds of 'detective fiction' that appeared across the mid-nineteenth century. The third chapter details how 'police criticism' (as explored in Chapter 1) and 'crime journalism' (as explored in Chapter 2) began to mesh together to create new forms of writing, including the first genre of fiction to be contemporarily described as 'detective literature'.[3] It firstly suggests that the police's social invisibility meshed with the pseudo-voyeuristic interests of crime reporting, causing the police to naturally evolve into useful guides and protectors for journalists performing 'social exploration' into supposedly-inaccessible criminal spaces. Journalists, famously including Charles Dickens, began to accompany police officers on their duties, and officers themselves began to be represented in articles that were interested in entering, exploring, and revealing for curious readers the criminal underworld which was perceived to lurk just beneath society's visible surface.[4] Chapter 3 then moves on to discuss how this 'social exploration' journalism mutated into new forms of writing – including fiction. Unlike journalism, fiction did not need to adhere to the restriction of presenting the truth, and authors could therefore be much more inventive in their approach, especially when performing targeted social criticism.[5]

'Social exploration' journalism thus sparked the appearance of 'police memoir fiction': cheap texts marketed as 'true' recollections of (usually retired) police officers or detectives and which performed the same task of figuratively transporting a reader into the world of the urban criminal.

Chapter 4 branches out sideways from Chapter 3, to highlight how the police officer's quality as a guide, protector, or (occasionally) invader was also transposed into other forms of writing. It focuses on popular 'sensation fiction', and discusses characters such as Dickens's Inspector Bucket (1853), Wilkie Collins's Sergeant Cuff (1868) or Mary Elizabeth Braddon's Joseph Peters (1860) and Robert Audley (1862) to show how the police were actively used in sensation writing in similar ways and for similar purposes to police memoirs. There were some slight differences; in sensation fiction, the scene largely shifted away from the criminal underworld of the city to the more bourgeois domestic spaces of the middle or upper classes, often an isolated country manor-house. However, the purpose of the police officer to penetrate and reveal secrets of private spaces for the benefit of the reader remained largely the same. Thus, by highlighting how both police memoirs and sensation fiction used the police officer in comparable fashions, the chapter cements *both* genres' positions in the chronology of detective fiction, and highlights how the evolution of the genre can be understood as not merely linear, but instead as multifaceted.

Part III, consisting of Chapters 5 and 6, moves the volume into the late-nineteenth century, to demonstrate how the literary landscape of 'detective fiction', largely constructed by the periodical press's engagement with crime and policing, destabilised as the Victorian era drew to a close. The fifth chapter represents a turning point in the volume's narrative, and examines how the various public opinions of the police, which had been turbulent but generally-accepting across the mid-Victorian era, took a turn for the worse as the age entered the 1870s.[6] In 1877, it reached perhaps its lowest point of the nineteenth century, as four detective inspectors and a solicitor were indicted on charges of corruption and collusion with convicted criminals. Three of the detectives (and the solicitor) were convicted and sentenced to two years imprisonment, sparking a substantial response in the press concerning the status of British policing. This chapter traces these reactions and highlights the changes in public perceptions of the force. These included the perspective that the police were inefficient, corrupt, and lazy; that the detective department had been too free from governmental scrutiny since its inception; and that the police's reputation simply may never recover.

Chapter 6, the final chapter, continues the narrative begun by Chapter 5. It highlights how the police's damaged reputation caused by the 1877 scandal persisted into the 1880s, as a series of incidents such as the Irish Republican Brotherhood bombing campaign and the 1888 Whitechapel murders prevented the police from recovering their reputation. The chapter argues that the changed perception of the police, from necessary social protectors to undesirable and/or inefficient blunderers, affected the way they were represented in fiction. The police were no longer seen as trusted and powerful guides into criminal or inaccessible spaces, and thus the reign of the police memoir as a 'standard' incarnation of detective literature, built on the maintenance of public trust or confidence in the police, ended. Subsequently, the *private* detective came to dominate 1880s and 90s detective fiction, with official police officers now depicted as incompetent, bumbling, and foolish, while private detectives were shown to take on cases that the police had failed to solve, and had a much greater degree of success. The chapter, and volume, ends by connecting this discussion to the meteoric rise of the most famous private detective of all, Arthur Conan Doyle's Sherlock Holmes, who appeared towards the end of the 1880s and who epitomised the connection between periodicals and detective fiction. The final sections thus examine how Holmes and his occasional collaborator, Inspector Lestrade, fit into the narrative of the effective private detective and the incompetent, bumbling police officer, particularly after the character appeared in the pages of the *Strand Magazine*.

Context and Methodological Frameworks

The previous outline of this volume is designed to orientate the reader with the book's structure and to highlight the strengths of approaching the exploration of a literary genre's evolution through paratextual contexts. However, it also raises a number of methodological and theoretical issues and questions that must be addressed before any analysis can begin.

As this study traces the evolution of a literary genre by focusing on *other* forms of literary production that appeared around and alongside it, it quite naturally situates itself in and amongst both new historicist and (to a lesser extent) cultural materialist schools of critical thought. The volume subscribes to the idea that there is a complicated yet close relationship between literature, society, and history, and Stephen Greenblatt, widely regarded as an originator of new historicist thinking, summarises this idea as:

> The work of art is itself the product of a set of manipulations, some of them our own [and] many others undertaken in the construction of the original work. That is, the work of art is the product of a negotiation between a creator or class of creators, equipped with a complex communally shared repertoire of conventions, and the institutions and practices of society.[7]

Put slightly more simply, John Brannigan argues in *New Historicism and Cultural Materialism* (1998) that 'new historicist and cultural materialist critics [...] break down the simplistic distinction between literature and history and open up a complex dialogue between them'.[8] In 2000, Greenblatt, alongside Catherine Gallagher, revisited new historicism and argued that their original intention was

> not to aestheticize an entire culture, but to locate inventive energies more deeply interfused within it [and] to imagine that the writers we love did not spring up from nowhere and that their achievements must draw upon a

whole life-world and that this life-world has undoubtedly left other traces of itself.[9]

This complex approach to studying literature, through the perspective of the influence of *other* forms of cultural production, has produced some excellent studies that have generated complex re-readings of a great deal of established material. Indeed, Matthew Rubery's book *The Novelty of Newspapers: Victorian Fiction After the Invention of the News* (2009) is a particularly good example of this, which takes the idea of using the press as an influence on literary production and applies it to various kinds of Victorian fiction, from the Brontës to Bram Stoker. Rubery argues that:

> [T]he transformation of news during the nineteenth century profoundly influenced literary narrative in ways that have yet to be recognized. The English novel during the era of the commercial press drew on news as a rival practice of realistic representation and as an authoritative form of public knowledge.[10]

The present volume takes this same approach, but uses it in a more targeted way to present a complicated and hitherto under-examined connection between a specific genre – detective fiction – and periodical discussion of a specific sociocultural development – the growth of nationwide policing. It subscribes to Gallagher and Greenblatt's assertions that '[it is] crucially important to [...] to delve as deeply as possible into the creative matrices of particular historical cultures' and that 'the relative positions of text and context often shift, so what has been the mere background makes a claim for the attention that has hitherto been given only to the foregrounded and privileged work of art [...]'.[11] In short, this book deliberately uses 'literary texts as equal sources with other texts in the attempt to describe and examine the linguistic, cultural, social and political fabric of the past in greater detail'.[12]

From a cultural materialist perspective, which focuses on the ideological tensions contained *within* cultural artistic products,[13] this volume rejects contemporary assertions regarding the canonicity of specific examples of 'detective fiction', which has hitherto limited our understanding of the genre's evolution. Instead, it focuses on texts that demonstrate value to the study through their observable connections to relevant non-literary, paratextual material. It also analyses institutions of state power in relation to how they were ideologically presented to the public. This was itself an act with its own ideological intentions, and the book explores how cultural productions surrounding the police were affected by wider, often invisible or silent political motivations. Events such as the 1877 'Great Detective Case', for example, were presented to the reading public within periodicals which often had their *own* agendas and which directly helped to shape public opinion as a result. These agendas, as the book argues, were almost naturally transposed into *fictional* representations of the police.

With all of that established, it is important to clarify that this volume does not use a concrete or linear 'history' (or set of histories) made of up that which Brannigan terms 'secure knowledge' to explore the development of detective fiction. Rather, it explores how 'history' was both constructed and presented to the contemporary public through *other* forms of material production.[14] The histories that periodicals presented to their readers were, again, affected by titles' own politics and ideologies. As Brannigan also suggests:

> [New historicists and cultural materialists] refuse to see literary texts against an overriding background of history or to see history as a set of facts outside the written text [...] history is not objective knowledge which can be made to explain a literary text.[15]

As such, this volume is aligned with some of the key tenets of these theoretical fields. In the introduction to his 1989 edited volume *The New Historicism*, Harold A. Veeser argues that, among other things, the characterising features of new historicism is that, firstly, 'every expressive act is embedded in a network of material practices'; secondly; that 'literary and non-literary "texts" circulate inseparably'; and finally that '[t]he New Historicists combat empty formalism by pulling historical considerations to the center [sic] stage of literary analysis'.[16] Veeser's idea that artistic productions are always placed within a wider network of material practices is a central concept to this study, as it argues that detective fiction was itself created and nurtured by the material practices of periodical journalism and the corresponding production of non-fiction explorations into policing, detection, and crime. Naturally, therefore, this volume agrees with Veeser's statement that both literary and non-literary texts constantly orbit each other, and demonstrates this by connecting non-fiction journalistic writing with the production of fiction, and highlights how they circulated and affected each other's production. The book also shows this by actually linking together different forms of *fiction*, which have retrospectively been subsequently labelled 'literary' and 'non-literary' by scholarly criticism. In short, this study performs Veeser's precise act of 'pulling historical considerations to the center [sic] stage of literary analysis', and is broadly an exploration into the impact of wider material and cultural practices such as the development of nationwide policing, changes to the criminal justice system, and how these innovations were explored in a rapidly-changing periodical press.[17]

This description of where this volume is situated in terms of a critical or theoretical framework leads rather well into the first methodological issue that requires discussion: the question of generic definition. 'Detective fiction' has historically been difficult to define, as scholars tend to arrive at their own conclusions as to exactly what constitutes the genre according to their individual purpose of study, or, indeed, the individual aspects of a particular text which the critic consciously chooses to look for. As such, both histories and definitions of the genre tend to look inwardly at texts' own textual features, rather than by situating them in a wider historical narrative or context. 'Detective fiction', 'crime fiction' 'mystery fiction', or 'police fiction' are all terms used to describe different iterations of the genre that focus more strongly on one or another aspect of the text, be they 'detectives', 'crimes', 'mysteries', or 'the police'. Julian Symons claims that these sub-genres all constitute 'the same kind of literature', which he simply terms 'sensational literature' in an attempt to provide a catch-all, umbrella term (which, seemingly, never really caught on):

> The truth is that the detective story, along with the police story, the spy story and the thriller, all of them immensely popular in the past twenty years, makes up part of the hybrid creature we call sensational literature. [...] [H]owever unlike Sherlock Holmes and Philo Vance may be to Sam Spade and Superintendent Maigret, they all belong to the same kind of literature. [...] The tree is sensational literature, and these are among its fruits.[18]

Some have attempted to identify common features across different textual examples to help identify potential overarching connections between these sub-genres and thus provide other ways of categorising lots of kinds of fiction together under one larger term. Alma Murch, for example, argues that the common feature across different strands of the genre is a puzzling mystery: '[b]asically [...] a detective story [...] may be defined as a tale in which the primary interest lies in the methodical discovery, by rational means, of the exact circumstances of a mysterious event or series of events'.[19] Similarly, Stephen Knight argues that there is 'always a crime (or very occasionally just the appearance of one)' and thus he opts for the broad term 'crime fiction'.[20]

There are, however, some problems with both these definitions in the context of the present volume. Murch's definition preoccupies itself with the presence and solution of a mystery, but perhaps a little conversely the question of whether or not a puzzle is resolved at the end of a narrative is actually not a concern for the kinds of fiction under examination here. Similarly, Knight's definition is predicated on the presence of a crime in a text; but again, the presence of criminality in fiction is again not necessarily a prerequisite for inclusion in this study. Charles Rzepka brings us slightly closer to a useful way of defining the detective genre, by claiming that it is 'any story that contains a major character undertaking the investigation of a mysterious crime or similar transgression [...]'.[21] This focus on the presence of a 'detective' character is a useful definition for Rzepka's specific purpose of identifying examples of 'detective' fiction (indeed, his book is titled, simply, *Detective Fiction*). However, it is rather narrow. As Rzepka himself admits, not all 'detective fiction' necessarily contains a crime, and similarly not all 'crime fiction' necessarily contains a detective.[22] Indeed, to make things even more complicated, 'mystery' fiction, an archetypal category purported by John G. Cawelti in 1976,[23] need not contain either crime *or* detective.[24]

Rzepka's definition also suffers from another complication when one questions exactly what constitutes a 'detective'. Must the detective figure in a narrative necessarily be officially employed by the police? Or must they self-identify as a 'detective' in order for them to be labelled as one? True to the broad nature of this study, the answer here would be an unequivocal 'no', as several characters discussed here are neither official police detectives, nor do they consider themselves to be 'detectives' even in an amateur sense. Nevertheless, Rzepka's approach of focusing on the presence of significant literary characters as a way of identifying examples of the genre is a useful starting point. As this volume explores representations of police officers or detectives in periodical journalism, it follows that it should look for the presence of the same police officers or detectives in periodical fiction. This volume's definition of the genre therefore combines both Rzepka's and Knight's approaches. It opts to use the term 'detective fiction', as the texts under study here loosely focus on the presence of characters in narratives which can be identified as 'detectives', in either official or amateur capacities. These characters attempt to elucidate the solution to a usually-present crime or mystery, which echoes Knight's approach to generic definition.

A second methodological question that requires answering stems from the nature of 'periodical studies' as a scholarly field and how it has changed in recent years. Using nineteenth-century periodicals as the primary resource for the study of a literary genre's development engages with a unique and under-explored connection between literature and nineteenth-century society, and demonstrates one of this volume's claims to originality. As Joanne Shattock and Michael Wolff correctly argue:

> [The periodical press] is worth study in its own right because it represents and articulates, as nothing else does, what was ordinary about Victorian Britain, and we cannot understand Victorian Britain without understanding the ordinary [...][25]

The convergence between periodicals and the everyday is fertile ground for exploration into the development of genre. Periodicals contained a highly-relevant mixture of fiction, socio-political criticism, and news, and provide perhaps the closest indication of what everyday people were reading and discussing across the Victorian era. This phenomenon is also almost exclusive to the nineteenth century; before this era, this was not the case due to a lack of diversity in the media market, whilst conversely after the *fin-de-siècle* new kinds of media, particularly radio and early cinematic broadcasting, began to supersede the periodical press as primary reflectors and shapers of public discussion, and the periodical press itself began to fragment and degrade. Thus, as Rosemary VanArsdel and J. Don Vann succinctly put it, '[n]ineteenth-century Britain was uniquely the age of the periodical'.[26] Periodicals and magazines were the forum in which Victorians both discussed pressing social issues and simultaneously received the bulk of their literary entertainment. In fact, as Michael Wolff argued in his landmark essay 'Charting the Golden Stream', a topic or social issue 'did not exist until it had registered itself in the 'press', and that a topic truly became prominent once a journal of its own study had been established.[27]

Despite their useful connection to everyday reading habits of the Victorians, periodicals are still an underutilised resource in the study of the development of literary genre, mainly due to the difficulty experienced by researchers using periodicals as their primary resource. Prior to the growth of 'periodical studies' throughout the last 20 years, embarking on a systematic study of the innumerable number of periodicals which constituted the 'first of the mass media' was far more difficult than it is today.[28] Organised study of periodicals only began in earnest in the latter half of the twentieth century, notably with Walter E. Houghton's landmark compilation of the *Wellesley Index to Victorian Periodicals* (1965–1988). However, even this substantial, five-volume endeavour only scratched the surface of potential material. Consequently, many studies of periodical or newspaper publications tended to focus on specific titles, authors, or publications, and the larger, more famous titles attracted more sustained scrutiny than smaller ones. As Shattock and Wolff elegantly put it, '[...] the trees prevent[ed] us from seeing the forest.'[29]

With the emergence of vast digital archives of material, however, 'periodical studies' has experienced something of a renaissance. It has progressed towards a rejection of the study of individual texts, authors, and titles in favour of explorations which cast a much wider net in order to identify broader patterns and trends. The creation of monumental, searchable repositories such as the *Gale Cengage 19ᵗʰ Century UK Periodicals* database, the *British Newspaper Archive*, or the even larger *ProQuest British Periodicals* database has enabled this approach to periodical study by making it much easier for scholars to quickly and easily access vast swathes of material.

This has generally been a positive development, but has also raised a number of problems, the most significant of which is perhaps the opposite to that which Shattock and Wolff raise, in that we can potentially no longer see the trees for the forest. Researchers are easily overwhelmed by the sheer amount of material available to them, which potentially leads to them finding it difficult to orientate themselves within an ocean of potentially useful (or potentially useless) resources. They can simply lose the ability to distinguish between different titles, authors or publishers, and could miss important, useful or even critical material to their studies. Even in 1971, far before the creation of these databases, Michael Wolff indirectly identified this potential issue when he suggested that periodicals contain an enormous amount of diverse information which can, in essence, go on forever:

> There is something both overwhelming and overwhelmingly attractive about periodicals research. It is not just "that untravell'd world, whose margin fades for ever and for ever as I move." It is that every new title investigated, almost every fresh page turned, is "[a] bringer of new things."[30]

This is the most significant problem which this study must overcome, and raises a number of difficult methodological questions. How is the study to gauge the importance of different publications which are given an equal presence in large digitised repositories? How is it to ensure that all of the relevant (or, indeed, the *most* relevant) material has been identified and captured? How it to ensure that nothing vital is missed? And how is it to make an orderly sense of this vast amount of material, once it has been identified?

The answer, conversely, lies within the final problem raised by the summary of the study. The chronological period which this volume covers is substantial, which means that the source material with which it is concerned is similarly broad. It addresses the years between approximately 1840 and 1900, which constitutes very nearly the entire Victorian period. Throughout this era, society itself went through a number of fundamental and permanent changes which make it impossible to characterise in simple or singular terms; Britain in the 1840s was unrecognisable compared to Britain in the 1890s. Whilst this may seem like a difficulty, some of the larger and more significant changes and events which occurred throughout this era can helpfully provide 'historic milestones' around which journalistic material tended to cluster. This clustered material, in turn, helped shape contemporaneously-published fiction, and so focusing on specific, galvanising events in this way becomes a useful methodology for the project to orientate itself. It also helps overcome both the problem of the project's lengthy timescale, and additionally addresses the issue of the sourcing and analysis of periodical matter.

In terms of orienting searches for primary material (and making sense of it once it has been gathered), an understanding of these historical markers helps to identify specific subjects with which periodical material was engaging. As a result, search-strings inputted into large digital repositories of material such as the *ProQuest British Periodicals* database or the *Gale Cengage Nineteenth Century UK Periodicals* database can be constructed using both key terms related to individual historical events or milestones, and filters to narrow down relevant material. For example, when searching for material pertaining to the 1877 'turf fraud' scandal, a combination of an advanced key-word search string such as ("detect*") AND ("trial" OR "Drusco*" OR "Meikle*"), and the use of filters to limit hits to those published between April 1877 and September 1879, returns, at the time of writing,[31] a largely-manageable 631 results.[32] This particular string's use of both wider concepts, such as the trial, but also the individual names of those involved in the case (specifically detectives 'Druscovich' and 'Meiklejohn') also ensures that results which mention the case but potentially not those involved by name are also captured. The use of the wildcard asterisk symbol (*) in the search string ensures that any variations on any of the words are captured. 'Detect*' captures words such as 'detective', 'detection' or 'detected'. The use of the wildcard asterisk on the names of those involved ensures that the specific (and distinctive) names of the detectives indicted in the case are captured, but also allows for any potential spelling mistakes. This balance between specificity and breadth ensures that a healthy-sized dataset is captured in the first instance, before analysis of individual articles or other material can be performed.

It is also worth clarifying that this is only one particular example of many different searches performed throughout the construction of this study, and also that this use of digital periodical material was not exclusive. The study also uses material gained from explorations of physical periodical material contained in physical archives, where appropriate or necessary. For example, the journalist and author William Russell, who wrote a great number of 'police memoirs' across the mid-Victorian era became a person of interest to this project after his work repeatedly appeared in searches of different online databases of periodical material. Much of this work appeared anonymously/ pseudonymously on digital databases; however when cross-referenced with Allen J. Hubin's *Crime Fiction 1749–1980: A Comprehensive Bibliography* (1984), Russell emerges as the most prolific author of police memoirs in this era.[33] A significant amount of Russell's fiction appeared in *Chambers's Edinburgh Journal,* and so this necessitated a visit to the National Library of Scotland, which holds an archive of material retained from the offices of William Chambers. This provided extra material on Russell's relationships with his editors and the proprietors of the magazine as well information on how much he was paid, where he lived and precisely which pieces he contributed to the magazine (and when he contributed them).

This multifaceted approach to gathering source material means that the project itself is organised around a number of different 'moments' that occurred throughout its period of study and that generated relevant source material. These 'moments' were both cultural (such as the popularity of 'sensation fiction' across the 1860s) and historic (such as the 1877 'turf fraud' scandal). The first such historic milestone which can be used to orientate searches for primary material was the simultaneous abolition of the 'taxes on knowledge' and the passage of the 1856 County and Borough Police Act. These two events were intertwined, and thus mark the beginning of this volume's field of study. It is therefore necessary to provide a brief historical overview of both in order to contextualise their convergence, describe how they intersected, and explore why this is relevant. The remainder of the volume can then use this backdrop to explore how the relationship between periodical and police remained aligned across the remainder of the nineteenth century, and how it affected the way that crime and detective fiction was constructed and received by an increasingly literate readership.

In summary, both developments were distinct facets of the overarching evolution which took place in early nineteenth-century Britain. The first Industrial Revolution had galvanised the growth of new urban centres, increased literacy rates among the growing professional working classes, and improved inter-city transportation links via canals, roads, and railways. A further effect, however, was the growth of a legitimate periodical press, which had been hitherto stifled by the punitive effects of the 'taxes on knowledge'. These, while fiercely defended by some, were slowly repealed across the early to mid-nineteenth century as society itself developed and governmental fears of political radicalism diminished. The development of a professional system of law enforcement was another facet of the same drastic evolution of early nineteenth-century society. The new urban centres were sprawling, densely populated, and naturally difficult to control, and the establishment of the police was, quite simply, a reaction to this. Early police forces largely focused on managing the growing cities, forming part of the march of professionalisation which came to characterise the early nineteenth century.[34]

The 'Taxes on Knowledge'

The 'taxes on knowledge' were pieces of legislation enacted to strangle the development of the cheap newspaper and periodical press, and to prevent the spread of what was perceived to be 'political radicalism'.[35] The first tax was a charge on printing paper which was established in 1712, and this began a long succession of charges on publishing material that was not to truly end until the mid-Victorian era.[36] The stamps were imposed on three main areas: advertisements in newspapers, printing, and a duty on printing paper,[37] and were placed on publications that carried informative or politically-oriented material (in other words, 'news') and advertisements.

As Britain entered a new phase of industrialisation in the late eighteenth and early nineteenth century the publishing industry began to grow, and as Patricia Anderson argues, this was the first phase of a broad cultural transformation of the cultural experiences of ordinary working people.[38] During the first Industrial Revolution, literacy rates increased, reading as a pastime grew in popularity, and the first wave of the 'professionalisation' of the working classes also meant that, for the first time, working people began to use their newly-acquired literacy skills in professional capacities. These 'professionalising working classes' occupied diverse areas of society such as science, which 'came to replace theology and philosophy as the supreme example of man's intellectual endeavours', as well as law, the military, public transport, advertising, retail, medicine and healthcare, and even sport.[39] Advances in printing technology also began to make reading material more accessible, and so the ability to read either for work or for pleasure was no longer the domain of the bourgeoisie. Indeed, by the middle of the nineteenth century, literacy had often become a precondition of employment.[40]

This spread of mass-literacy alarmed some political circles, who openly discouraged the growth of a 'mass-reading public' due to their fear that it would encourage political radicalism and eventually incite outright revolution. Throughout the early nineteenth century, these dissenting discourses permeated both Parliament and the aristocracy,[41] which was quickly offset by a contrasting political argument that suggested that mass public literacy *should* be encouraged as it would raise the general mental level and intelligence of the population as a whole. This, it suggested, would increase understanding of the dangers of radical and revolutionary politics, and thus prevent them.[42] These competing voices created strong political tension surrounding the maintenance of the 'taxes on knowledge', and some prominent figures such as Henry Brougham (1778–1868)[43] as well as a number of periodical proprietors and editors openly called for their abolition. In 1802, a petition was put before Parliament complaining about the effects that the 'taxes' were having on the publishing industry, and in response a report was commissioned to explore its complaints.[44] This addressed four areas: the alleged decline in the trade of books, the apparent causes of the decline, suggested relief measures, and finally objections to these relief measures.[45] Booksellers, publishers, and engravers provided accounts of their lost business, and ultimately the report concluded that the 'taxes on knowledge' were largely to blame for an unnecessary stranglehold on the entire publishing industry.

However, no charges were lifted, and publishers were forced to think more creatively to circumvent or negate the taxes' effects.[46] Some focused on monthly publication, which was cheaper than weekly or daily production and subject to less scrutiny.[47] Others began to print fiction by both professional and amateur writers, in lieu of publishing material of an informative nature.[48] However, things were to get even tougher; following a series of politically charged events, including the French Revolution in 1789, the Peninsular War (1807–1814), the Battle of Waterloo in 1815, the Peterloo Massacre in 1819, and the Cato Street Conspiracy in 1820, the 'taxes on knowledge' were intensified in an effort to stamp out perceived political radicalism in the legitimate press.[49] The notorious 'Six Acts', introduced in November 1819,[50] intensified the taxes already in place, and were meant to eradicate political radicalism by 'extending the already stiff powers given to the government [...] to search for arms, control meetings and prosecute on seditious libel charges'.[51] The Newspaper and Stamp Duties Act was particularly nasty, levying a 4*d.* tax on the publication of 'news or comments on the news', appearing at least once every 26 days and costing less than 6*d.*[52] As Altick suggests, this tax was not specifically aimed at news, but instead targeted politically radical views such as anti-governmental or anti-religious sentiments, and was directly aimed at underground radical magazines.[53] Indeed, publications that printed material specifically of a pious, religious or charitable nature were exempt, leaving no doubt as to the Act's purpose.[54]

The 'Six Acts' had a significant, immediate, and lasting effect. As Joel Wiener points out, many radical journalists 'either fled into exile or "legalized" [sic] their periodicals' by simply raising their prices and paying for a stamp,[55] and that across the 1820s 'a surface calm predominated in the field of journalism [and] [f]ew unstamped periodicals were published.'[56] In this era, most publications moved to operate within the law, and there were only a 'few flagrant attempts to violate the stamp laws. Only a handful of publications were prosecuted, and no ministry faced the problem of pronounced resistance to the press laws'.[57] That said, there were at least a small number of publications that continued to defy the taxes on knowledge. Leigh Hunt and his brother John, for example, were imprisoned for libel from 1812–1815 and John was incarcerated for a second time, again for libel, in 1821. Despite this, they continued to edit and publish their literary and informative magazine, the *Examiner.* [58]

The years 1830–1836 saw one of the most intense and concerted efforts by campaigners to abolish the 'taxes on knowledge'. Andrew King argues that the various duties were consciously relaxed in this era as fear of revolution and dissent brought about by earlier events had largely dissipated.[59] However, the story was actually more complicated than this. Joel Wiener suggests that the first concerted challenges to the stamp laws occurred in 1830: the publication of William Carpenter's successful[60] *Political Letters and Pamphlets* (eventually crushed by a prosecution against him in May 1831), and the appearance of the weekly *Penny Papers for the People, Published by the Poor Man's Guardian*, produced by radical printer Henry Hetherington (1792–1849).[61] Like Carpenter, Hetherington was prosecuted but refused to acquiesce, and instead began to publish even more vociferously.[62] His illegal (and inflammatorily-titled) newspaper the *Poor Man's Guardian: A Weekly Newspaper for the People, Established Contrary to 'Law' to Try the Powers of 'Might' Against 'Right'* appeared in July 1831, sparking that which was contemporarily-termed the 'war of the unstamped'.[63] This 'war' raged between 1830 and 1836, with Hetherington and several other prominent publishers such as James Watson (1799–1874) and John Cleave (born c.1790) leading the charge against the taxes on knowledge by publishing numerous illegal and politically radical publications and speaking out at every opportunity. The radical publishers were accompanied, though not actively assisted, by the activities of more moderate abolitionists such as Charles Knight and Henry Brougham, who formed the Society for the Diffusion of Useful Knowledge in 1826 as a deliberately less radical (and, as Alan J. Lee argues, more 'middle-class') driver of reform.[64] The state responded: as Hewitt points out, between 1830 and 1836 at least 1,130 cases of selling unstamped papers were brought before London magistrates, and by 1836 almost 800 people had been imprisoned.[65] The 'war' eventually became a war of attrition, with both sides suffering as a result. On one hand, illegal publishers motivated more by political idealism than by financial gain[66] almost continually made a loss on their activities, and suffered repeated prison sentences.[67] On the other, governmental opponents of abolition were unable to stop the spread of illicit publications, and prosecution often served more as an advertisement for illegal publishers than as a deterrent.[68] The relentless campaign of the underground press thus eventually had a, perhaps inevitable, effect; the stamp on pamphlets was repealed in 1834,[69] while in 1836, the newspaper stamp was reduced from 4*d.* per copy (at which it had been set since 1815) to 1*d.* per copy.[70] Similarly in 1836, the excise duty on printing paper was halved from 3*d.* per lb to 1½*d.* per lb, at which it had been set since 1802.[71] This easing had an effect on numerous kinds of writing; serialised fiction, for example was already commonplace, and as early as 1750, serialised novels numbered in their hundreds and some publications numbered copies into the thousands.[72] In the 1830s, however, the triumphant success of texts such as Charles Dickens's *The Posthumous Papers of the Pickwick Club* (1836–7) and its successors such as *Oliver Twist* (1837–9) demonstrated that part-issue fiction could be profitable as well as popular.[73] The relaxation also caused an increase in the production of low-cost, weekly penny and half-penny magazines.[74]

The political fear of mass uprising and radicalism somewhat re-emerged in the 1840s due to the demands of the Chartists and the spread of the 1848 revolutions across Europe. Political focus shifted back towards what people might be reading, as it could potentially be perceived as 'socially inflammatory'.[75] This was short lived, however; as Wiener suggests, after 1849 the movement to repeal the taxes gained momentum largely due to the ultimate failure of the Chartist movement.[76] By the early 1860s, the taxes on knowledge had all but vanished, and the landscape of the periodical press witnessed a dramatic shift towards mass production and quick-fire publication that was not to be echoed until the end of the nineteenth century. In 1853, the advertisement tax was rescinded. In 1855 the newspaper stamp was repealed, and finally the excise duty on printing paper, which made the printing and publishing process so expensive, was abolished in 1861.[77] The abolition of the 'taxes on knowledge' therefore allowed what Patricia Anderson has grandly termed a 'cultural transformation' to proliferate. As Warren Fox summarises:

> The abolition of these [...] "taxes on knowledge," along with technological improvements in production and a population which was increasingly literate and concentrated in urban centers [sic], produced dramatic increases in some newspapers' circulation rates and encouraged the launching of many others.[78]

The relaxation, leading up to the eventual abolition of the 'taxes on knowledge' was therefore tied closely to the broad socio-cultural changes taking place in the early to mid-nineteenth century. The taxes' repeal allowed the periodical, newspaper and other cheap presses to expand more freely, and this gave rise to a diverse, richly populated, and prolific cheap press that could now openly discuss politically-oriented material and, quite simply, print news. Indeed, Martin Wiener's assertion that '[i]n the nineteenth century, "media" meant newspapers' was largely untrue, as throughout the Victorian era a diverse range of printed media emerged and the media itself homogenised and went from a largely localised industry to a truly national one.[79] A roaring trade in magazines and periodicals designed for specific and diverse audiences, as well as other forms of writing such as cheaply-produced 'yellowback' books, serialised fiction, play-bills, pamphlets, advertisements, and other printed ephemera grew exponentially, 'from the serious to the comic, from the drab to the illustrated'.[80] Venerable titles including (but not limited to) Dickens's *Household Words* (1850), the *Leader* (1850), *Cassell's Illustrated Family Paper* (1853), the *Daily Telegraph* (1855), the *Saturday Review* (1855) and the *Cornhill* (1860) all emerged in this era, directly benefitting from the slow but steady repeal of the 'taxes on knowledge'.[81] In short, as John Drew eloquently summarises:

> From the 1860s onwards [...] with the repeal of the 'Taxes on Knowledge' and the widespread introduction of rotary presses, the stage was set for a dramatic expansion of what can now genuinely be considered a mass media market.[82]

The Development of British Policing

In much the same way as the periodical press, the evolution of the police in Britain was also closely connected to the broad socio-cultural changes that took place in the early-to-mid nineteenth century. Indeed, the police formed part of the 'emergent professionalism [...] in nearly all walks of life' described by Don Vann and VanArsdel, both through becoming a distinct 'profession' in of itself but also in that it was designed to manage and regulate steadily-growing urban centres filled with the new, professionalising working-classes.[83]

Consequently, it is worth detailing how the police force evolved into a nationwide organisation in much the same way (and at the same time) as the periodical press. I suggest that these two seemingly separate historical strands were actually closely tied, as both the police and periodical press simultaneously homogenised and evolved from 'local' to 'national' entities. Eventually, in the mid-century, they intersected and combined to create an environment where new periodical writing concerning new policing could proliferate.

In the eighteenth century, before the establishment of an official police force, a number of volunteer constables or night-watchmen were appointed to maintain law and order in localised areas such as individual towns or parishes. These were usually ordinary citizens, who performed the role alongside their main occupation and who were paid either only in expenses or not at all. Several unofficial, largely private attempts at establishing organised law enforcement also occurred in this era, including Henry Fielding's now-infamous Bow Street Runners, formed in 1749; and the Liverpool Dock Police, established in 1811, among others. Whilst these were relatively privatised, there were at least some cursory legislative aspects to law enforcement. It was often enshrined in law that areas maintained a certain amount of volunteer watchmen, and the Constables Protection Act was passed in 1750, designed to officially protect both constables and justices of the peace in the performance of their duties under the authority of the law itself.[84] In 1756, an additional Act was passed, designed to increase the number of these constables in order to maintain peace in Westminster, as well as to recruit specifically 'reputable' people to become members of juries when required.[85]

The official police force as a uniformed and recognisable entity was established in 1829. The Metropolitan Police Act, dated 19 June 1829, was the brainchild of Tory politician Sir Robert Peel[86] combined with the efforts of a group of political reformers including Edwin Chadwick, who felt that the old system of volunteer constables and night-watchmen was inadequate.[87] With this Act, the first official Metropolitan Police department was formed to police Westminster. This also created the Commissioner of Police rank, which from 1829 to 1856 was jointly filled by two officers, initially Sir Richard Mayne (1796–1868) and Sir Charles Rowan (1782–1852). The rank was merged into one position as a result of the Metropolitan Police Act 1856, and this remains the head of the Metropolitan Police (and all UK police forces) today. The passage of the 1829 Act was directly discussed in a number of periodicals despite the imposition of the 'taxes on knowledge' stifling informative news. Several publications described the new police for interested readers and offered their support. The *Examiner*, for example, reprinted a brief article from the *Times* on 16 August 1829, which outlined the jurisdictional areas, appearance, expense and scale of the new Metropolitan Police force.[88] In July 1829 the *New Monthly Magazine* published 'The New Police', which pragmatically suggested that the new police were a 'beneficial innovation' that were, at least, an improvement on the old system of parochial volunteer constables and night-watchmen.[89]

The 1829 Act was actually designed to be a first, tentative step towards establishing a nationwide set of police forces. Slightly less well-known is the fact that an additional Act was passed three weeks prior, on 1 June 1829, which formed an equivalent force in the rural county of Cheshire. This was designed and operated as an experiment into rolling out the concept of policing into non-urban environments,[90] however it was largely seen as a failure due to a lack of central control and lack of officers (although the model may have been utilised for later rural county forces).[91] Despite the experiment's lack of success, steps towards rolling the concept of policing out on a country-wide scale proceeded relatively quickly. Government went to great efforts to find the most effective way of creating regional forces, using the knowledge gained from the trial in Cheshire as well as the experience of the Metropolitan Police. As the rural Cheshire experiment had failed, the broadest concern remained with how to manage the quickly-growing cities, and focus understandably remained on urban centres where it was believed crime was more commonplace and policing more urgently required. A succession of smaller 'local' Acts thus followed 1829, which established and maintained similar forces in urban centres across Britain, using the Metropolitan Police as a model.[92]

A further step towards police centralisation occurred as part of the Municipal Corporations Act, passed in 1835. This included several clauses that required reformed local authorities to appoint a sufficient number of constables and create a framework of operation for them if not already present.[93] However, this left a 'significant legacy' for established local administrators, as it did not strongly affect parish constables in rural counties.[94] A renewed focus on policing the rural community followed, and in 1836 a report was commissioned to explore the most efficient ways of establishing rural police forces, to be authored by prominent social reformer Edwin Chadwick (1800–1890), politician Charles Shaw-Lefevre (1794–1888), and the aforementioned Charles Rowan. This sought to summarise the current state of crime throughout the country by contacting regional Justices of the Peace, and then to make recommendations as to how crime levels could be lowered.[95] It took three years to compile and was published in 1839.[96] The report argued that the state of law enforcement in the country was largely limited to use of the military, and that this was inadequate. It also suggested that rural areas suffered from crime in the same way as urban areas despite their less dense population, and recommended that regional police forces be established. It also argued that public information and records regarding levels of crime in the UK were erroneous,[97] and that unpaid and randomly-appointed community constables kept no records of habitual criminals' crimes so they were known by reputation only.[98]

A proposed solution was to recommend that policing be centralised, so that records of crime and criminals could be collected to prevent the problem of habitual criminals simply moving to a location where they were not recognised. This had the effect of binding the police into bureaucratic trends of centralised governance which came to characterise the Victorian era, and the report ultimately concluded that 'from the want of an efficient preventative force, the peace and manufacturing prosperity of the country are exposed to considerable danger'.[99]

Chadwick's report sparked a concerted effort to improve the police force in rural areas. In 1839 the County Police Act was passed, with an amended version a year later, designed to improve the established system and to pave the way for counties to set up their own police forces.[100] However, while a significant step, the County Police Acts of 1839 and 1840 did not make their establishment *mandatory*, by 1853, only 28 out of 56 eligible areas had done so,[101] and many were still reluctant.[102] Even among those who did set up a system of policing across the 1840s, the processes by which this was achieved were individualised and disjointed. Clive Emsley notes that '[t]here was no common pattern to implementation' and that in some areas the rural police acts were adopted in largely piecemeal ways, often as reactionary measures to particularly heinous crimes.[103] Local taxpayers were also resistant, and numerous areas produced petitions to remove newly set up, publicly-funded forces which were condemned as expensive and inefficient.[104] Indeed, the Parish Constables Act 1842 was directly designed to combat this complaint.

The 1840s were thus a turbulent time for the establishment of regional offices of police. Although the idea had taken hold quite widely, it had been implemented largely haphazardly. However, this was to change between 1853 and 1856, with Lord Palmerston (1784–1865), appointed Home Secretary in 1852, as the apparent driving force behind it.[105] In 1853, Edward Rice (1790–1878), MP for Dover, moved to establish a select committee to explore 'the expediency of adopting a more uniform system of police in England and Wales'.[106] This committee published its report in July 1853, and echoed Chadwick's earlier conclusions in his 1839 report that the extant system of incoherent forces was ineffective, and that they should be 'consolidated with districts or counties for Police purposes'.[107] A series of riots in Wigan and Blackburn in the early 1850s expedited matters by shedding even further light on the weak state of small and isolated borough police forces and this, when combined with the absence of much of the armed forces due to the Crimean War (1853–1856), acted as a further catalyst for the final compulsory establishment of nationwide civilian law enforcement. Despite some initial resistance, the County and Borough Police Act passed in 1856, which legislated for the rapid and compulsory establishment of county-wide police forces across Britain. Forces set up under this act were required to be county-wide, and smaller ones that already existed in certain areas were merged with new, larger ones.[108] However, small 'police districts' could still exist if they were deemed necessary, allowing distinctions between inner-city forces and larger, rural county ones (this arrangement still operates in some areas today). There was also a large movement towards centralising the police's power into the county-towns, and small, local forces now uncomfortably found themselves accountable to powers residing in distant locations. The 1856 Act additionally created a national Inspectorate of Constabulary (HMIC) in order to maintain professional standards across the country through the provision of 'certificates of efficiency' to provincial police forces which matched the standards of London's Metropolitan Police.[109] A parallel act which set up the Inspectorate of Constabulary in Scotland (HMICS) was also passed in 1857.[110] Both offices remain operational, and in 2017 HMIC was expanded to include oversight of Fire and Rescue services.

After 1856, then, the police force as it is recognised today was fully established across the country. The image of the police officer became universally recognised by the general public, as the uniform, powers, and structure of the police became nationally standardised and administered. As Emsley notes, '[t]he example of London provided [the rest of the country's police forces] a degree of uniformity'.[111] However, the universal image of the uniformed police officer gestures towards another important point: the formation of the plain-clothes 'detective department' as a separate arm of the Metropolitan Police, a narrative that proceeded slightly differently to the rest of the force. The department was first set up in 1842, and the first named 'detectives' were appointed for the purpose of solving already-committed crimes and catching those responsible. It was established as a very small department and remained so across most of the nineteenth century, consisting of just six constables and two sergeants at the time of its formation, rising only to around 15 permanent officers by the 1870s.[112]

Interestingly, the detective department itself was established, at least partially, due to a public outcry manifested in the press. A series of failings by the force to apprehend criminals had shaken public confidence in the police. The most prominent of these was the failure to apprehend a murderer named Daniel Good who, in 1842, eluded capture for several days before being apprehended by a civilian in a public-house in Tonbridge Wells. Public dissatisfaction found expression in the media; the *Examiner*, for example, reflected:

> Now that the preliminary investigation into the facts of the murder at Roehampton have been brought to a close [...] public attention has become directed to [...] the important question, whether or not the metropolitan police [sic] are at all effective as a detective police. [...] we think quite enough has been shown to prove that the existing system of police is not a detective one, and that unless some most important alterations are made by the appointment of a detective police [...] the perpetrators of crimes, however horrid and revolting in their nature, will, in nine cases out of ten, escape the hands of justice.[113]

Despite disapproval surrounding the police's failings, the formation of the detective department was not widely publicised in the press, and the department actually appeared under a cloud of relative obscurity.[114] Even the establishment press, including publications such as the *Spectator* and the *Times*, did not report on the department's formation. This was potentially due to contemporary mistrust in plain-clothes policing which was seen as threatening to civil liberties,[115] or may have been simply because the department itself was designed to operate in secrecy, and thus it was felt that its existence should not be publicly broadcast. Regardless of its motivation, the decision to keep the department's existence quiet was to lead to some complex issues in later years, as will be explored further on in this volume.

The liberation of the periodical press from the taxes on knowledge and the emergence of a nationwide, uniformed, and professionalised form of policing were therefore closely intertwined with each other, and this moment marks the opening of this study's research period. Both movements were connected to the development of wider nineteenth-century industrialised and urbanised society, and both formed part of the era's so-called 'march of professionalism'. The process of industrialisation had caused public literacy to substantially increase, and had led to the growth of new urban centres which required a new form of regulation – realised in the form of professional law enforcement. Both periodical publishing and nationwide policing thus became professional working spheres in of themselves throughout the mid-Victorian era.[116] Indeed, an article titled 'The New Police', from the *New Monthly Magazine* in July 1829, consciously connected the growth of law enforcement and the proliferation of the periodical press:

> But these matters have been already touched upon in the newspapers, to the police reports of which, when confined to the substantial matter, it is incredible how much the country is indebted. [...] Let the newspapers be dumb respecting an offender, as the lawyers wish them to be, and he escapes. Reverse the thing. The police reports fly into every corner of the provinces: the strange comer to every country village and town is watched, and people have their conjectures about him. His case is read before his face: perchance he is confused, or soon flies to some other spot, and induces suspicion; there the fatal newspaper meets him again. He is arrested, found to be the "true man," and delivered over to justice.[117]

The 1856 County and Borough Police Act and the repeal of the 'taxes on knowledge' were thus both homogenising moments that took their respective concerns from a largely localised scale to a national one. They both contributed to a growing sense of national identity, and established themselves as uniquely 'Victorian' institutions that can help characterise the era. Finally, the abolition of the 'taxes on knowledge' meant that periodical publishers' fears about producing politicised commentary were diminished at a time when the politicised ideas regarding policing, law enforcement and crime would have been at the forefront of public consciousness. The 1856 County and Borough Police Act had made it compulsory for all regions in Britain to establish county-wide police forces, and thus, the idea of policing, detection and criminality would be an easy and popular subject for newly-liberated periodicals to address. This, in turn, had significant ramifications for the development of detective fiction between 1850 and 1895, and so it is from this angle which this volume begins its exploration into periodicals and detective fiction.

Notes

1 Charles Rzepka, *Detective Fiction* (Cambridge: Polity, 2005), p. 9.
2 Particularly in the wake of the 1856 County and Borough Police Act.
3 Samuel Saunders, '"To Pry Unnecessarily into Other Men's Secrets": Crime Writing, Private Spaces and the mid-Victorian Police Memoir', *Law, Crime and History*, 8, 1 (2018), 76–90 (p. 84).
4 Anthea Trodd, 'The Policeman and the Lady: Significant Encounters in Mid-Victorian Fiction', *Victorian Studies*, 24, 4 (1984), 435–460 (p. 437).
5 Jessica Valdez, 'Dickens's "Pious Fraud": The Popular Press and the Moral Suasion of Fictional Narrative', *Victorian Periodicals Review*, 44, 4 (2011), 377–400 (p. 378).
6 Clive Emsley, 'A Typology of Nineteenth-Century Police', *Crime, Histoire et Sociétés/Crime, History and Societies*, 3, 1 (1999), 29–44 (p. 30).
7 Stephen Greenblatt, 'Towards a Poetics of Culture', in *The New Historicism*, ed. by Harold A. Veeser (Oxon: Routledge, 1989), p. 12.
8 John Brannigan, *New Historicism and Cultural Materialism* (Basingstoke: Macmillan, 1998), p. 3.
9 Catherine Gallagher and Stephen Greenblatt, *Practicing New Historicism* (Chicago, University of Chicago Press, 2000), pp. 12–13.
10 Matthew Rubery, *The Novelty of Newspapers: Victorian Fiction After the Invention of the News* (Oxon: Oxford University Press, 2009), p. 4.
11 Gallagher and Greenblatt, p. 17.
12 Brannigan, p. 12.
13 Brannigan, p. 12.
14 Brannigan, p. 3.
15 Brannigan, p. 3.
16 Harold A. Veeser, 'Introduction', in *The New Historicism*, ed. by Harold A. Veeser (Oxon: Routledge, 1989), p. xi.
17 Veeser, 'Introduction', in *The New Historicism*, ed. by Veeser, p. xi.
18 Julian Symons, *Bloody Murder: From the Detective Story to the Crime Novel* (London: Faber and Faber, 1972; repr. Basingstoke: Papermac, 1992), pp. 15–16.
19 Alma Murch, *The Development of the Detective Novel* (London: Peter Owen, 1958; repr. 1968), p. 11.
20 Stephen Knight, *Crime Fiction 1800–2000: Detection, Death, Diversity* (Basingstoke: Palgrave Macmillan, 2004), p. xii.
21 Rzepka, p. 12.
22 Rzepka, p. 9.
23 See John G. Cawelti, *Adventure, Mystery and Romance: Formula Stories as Art and Popular Culture* (Chicago and London: University of Chicago Press, 1976).
24 Rzepka, p. 9.
25 Joanne Shattock and Michael Wolff, 'Introduction', in *The Victorian Periodical Press: Samplings and Soundings*, ed. by Joanne Shattock and Michael Wolff (Leicester: Leicester University Press, 1982), pp. xiii–xix (p. xiii).
26 Rosemary VanArsdel and J. Don Vann, 'Introduction', in *Victorian Periodicals and Victorian Society*, ed. by. Rosemary VanArsdel and J. Don Vann (Toronto: University of Toronto Press, 1994), pp. 3–8 (p. 7).
27 Michael Wolff, 'Charting the Golden Stream: Thoughts on a Directory of Victorian Periodicals', *Victorian Periodicals Newsletter*, 4, 3 (13) (1971), 23–38 (p. 26).

28   Shattock and Wolff, 'Introduction', in *The Victorian Periodical Press*, ed. by Shattock and Wolff, p. xiii.
29   Shattock and Wolff, 'Introduction', in *The Victorian Periodical Press*, ed. by Shattock and Wolff, p. xiii.
30   Wolff, pp. 23–38 (p. 24).
31   Naturally, these databases are consistently updated with new material, and results may now differ.
32   This search was conducted on the *ProQuest British Periodicals* database.
33   Allen J. Hubin, *Crime Fiction 1749–1980: A Comprehensive Bibliography* (New York and London: Garland Publishing, 1984), p. 416. Hubin's reference book lists William Russell's work under his pseudonym 'Waters'.
34   VanArsdel and Don Vann, 'Introduction', in *Victorian Periodicals and Victorian Society*, ed. by. VanArsdel and Don Vann, p. 5.
35   Richard Altick, *The English Common Reader: A Social History of the Mass Reading Public 1800–1900* (Ohio: Ohio State University Press, 1957), p. 321.
36   Joel Wiener, 'Newspaper Taxes, Taxes on Knowledge, Stamp Taxes', in *Dictionary of Nineteenth Century Journalism*, ed. by Laurel Brake and Marysa Demoor (London and Ghent: Academia Press, 2009), p. 454.
37   Martin Hewitt, *The Dawn of the Cheap Press in Victorian Britain: The End of the 'Taxes on Knowledge', 1849–1869* (London: Bloomsbury, 2014), p. 6.
38   Patricia Anderson, *The Printed Image and the Transformation of Popular Culture: 1790–1860* (Oxford: Clarendon Press, 1991), p. 1.
39   VanArsdel and Don Vann, 'Introduction', in *Victorian Periodicals and Victorian Society*, ed. by. VanArsdel and Don Vann, pp. 5–6.
40   David Mitch, *The Rise of Popular Literacy in Victorian England* (Philadelphia: University of Pennsylvania Press, 1992), p. 11.
41   Stanley Harrison, *Poor Men's Guardians: A Survey of the Struggles for a Democratic Newspaper Press, 1763–1973* (London: Lawrence and Wishart, 1974), p. 54.
42   Andrew King, *The London Journal: 1845–83* (Aldershot: Ashgate Publishing, 2004), pp. 23–24.
43   Michael Lobban, 'Brougham, Henry Peter', in *Oxford Dictionary of National Biography* <http://www.oxforddnb.com/view/article/3581> [accessed 30 November 2015] (2008).
44   William Young, *Report from the Committee on the Booksellers and Printers Petition*, <https://parlipapers.proquest.com/parlipapers > [accessed 25 November 2015] (1802), p. 164.
45   Young, p. 164.
46   Young, p. 167.
47   Graham Law, *Serializing Fiction in the Victorian Public Press* (Basingstoke: Palgrave Macmillan, 2000), p. 10.
48   Law, p. 14.
49   Joel Wiener, *The War of the Unstamped: The Movement to Repeal the British Newspaper Tax, 1830–1836* (New York: Cornell University Press, 1969), p. 3.
50   Harrison, p. 53.
51   Harrison, p. 53.
52   Altick, pp. 327–328.
53   Altick, p. 328.
54   Altick, p. 328.
55   Wiener, J., *The War of the Unstamped*, p. 6.
56   Wiener, J., *The War of the Unstamped*, p. 7.
57   Wiener, J., *The War of the Unstamped*, p. 138.
58   Leora Bersohn, '*Examiner* (1808–1881)', in *Dictionary of Nineteenth Century Journalism*, ed. by Laurel Brake and Marysa Demoor (London and Ghent: Academia Press, 2009), p. 211. The *Examiner* is an excellent example of how some

magazines were forced underground by the 'taxes on knowledge'. Stifled in the 1810s and 20s, especially in the wake of Waterloo, Leigh Hunt fits into Wiener's category of a journalist entering 'exile' after he left for Italy in 1821. His brother John subsequently managed the magazine from 1821 to 1828, when he passed it on to his son.

59 King, p. 24.
60 Wiener notes that *Political Letters and Pamphlets* reached an estimated circulation of around 10,000 (p. 138).
61 Wiener, J., *The War of the Unstamped*, p. 138.
62 Wiener, J., *The War of the Unstamped*, p. 139.
63 Wiener, J., *The War of the Unstamped*, pp. 137–139. This particular citation is taken from these pages of Wiener's book, however the term 'war of the unstamped' is referred to both in the title of the volume itself and also repeatedly throughout it.
64 Alan J. Lee, *the Origins of the Popular Press, 1855–1914* (London: Croom Helm, 1976), p. 26.
65 Hewitt, p. 5.
66 Wiener, J., *The War of the Unstamped*, p. 183.
67 Hewitt, p. 5.
68 Wiener, J., *The War of the Unstamped*, p. 195.
69 Hewitt, p. 5.
70 Wiener, J., *The War of the Unstamped*, p. xii.
71 Law, p. 10.
72 Law, p. 3.
73 King, p. 24.
74 Deborah Wynne, *The Sensation Novel and the Victorian Family Magazine* (Basingstoke: Palgrave, 2001), pp. 15–16.
75 King, p. 25.
76 Wiener, J., *The War of the Unstamped*, p. xii.
77 Hewitt, p. xiv.
78 Warren Fox, 'Murder in Daily Instalments: The Newspapers and the Case of Franz Müller (1864)', *Victorian Periodicals Review*, 31, 3 (1998), 271–298 (p. 273).
79 Martin Wiener, 'Convicted Murderers and the Victorian Press: Condemnation vs. Sympathy', *Crime and Misdemeanours*, 1, 2 (2007), 110–125 (p. 110).
80 Lee, pp. 70–71.
81 Laurel Brake and Marysa Demoor, 'Chronology', in *Dictionary of Nineteenth Century Journalism*, ed. by Laurel Brake and Marysa Demoor (London and Ghent: Academia Press, 2009), pp. ix–xxiii (pp. xv–xvi).
82 John Drew, 'The Newspaper and Periodical Market', in *Charles Dickens in Context*, ed. by. Sally Ledger and Holly Furneaux (Cambridge: Cambridge University Press, 2011), pp. 109–117 (p. 110).
83 VanArsdel and Don Vann, 'Introduction', in *Victorian Periodicals and Victorian Society*, ed. by. VanArsdel and Don Vann, p. 5.
84 'The Constables Protection Act 1750 (24 Geo II, c. 44)', *legislation.gov.uk* <http://www.legislation.gov.uk/apgb/Geo2/24/44/contents> [accessed 21 January 2016].
85 'Public Act, 29 George II, c. 25', *UK Parliamentary Archive Portcullis* <http://www.portcullis.parliament.uk/CalmView/Record.aspx?src=CalmView.Catalog&id=HL%2fPO%2fPU%2f1%2f1756%2f29G2n124&pos=3> [accessed 21 January 2016].
86 Peel was a staunch advocate for uniformed law enforcement, and had previously been involved with efforts to establish centralised and state-controlled systems of policing, not in the least his involvement in the creation of the Peace Preservation Force in Ireland in 1814, while he was serving as Chief Secretary for Ireland.
87 Emsley, 'A Typology of Nineteenth-Century Police', pp. 29–44 (p. 30).
88 'Metropolitan New Police', *Examiner*, 16 August 1829, p. 518.

89   'The New Police', *New Monthly Magazine*, July 1829, p. 426.

90   Charles Lefevre, Charles Rowan and Edwin Chadwick, *First Report of the Commissioners Appointed to Inquire as to the Best Means of Establishing an Efficient Constabulary Force in the Counties of England and Wales* (London: Charles Knight and Co, 1839), p. 210.

91   R. W. James, *To the Best of our Skill and Knowledge: A Short History of the Cheshire Constabulary 1857–1957* (Cheshire: Museum of Policing in Cheshire, 2005), pp. 10–11.

92   For example, Bristol Constabulary was set up in 1835, Dublin's police force (the Dublin Metropolitan Police) was brought into line in 1836, alongside Liverpool's City Police and Newcastle-Upon-Tyne's City Police, which both also appeared in 1836. Manchester and Birmingham's forces appeared in 1839.

93   Carolyn Steedman, *Policing the Victorian Community: The Formation of English Provincial Police Forces, 1856–80* (London: Routledge, 1984), p. 14.

94   Steedman, p. 14

95   Lefevre, Rowan, and Chadwick, pp. 1–3.

96   Lefevre, Rowan, and Chadwick, pp. ix–1.

97   Lefevre, Rowan, and Chadwick, p. 343.

98   Lefevre, Rowan, and Chadwick, p. 344.

99   Lefevre, Rowan, and Chadwick, p. 345.

100 'Metropolitan Police', *UK Parliament* <http://www.parliament.uk/about/living-her itage/transformingsociety/laworder/policeprisons/overview/metropolitanpolice/> [accessed 19 November 2015].

101 Richard Cowley, Peter Todd, and Louise Ledger, *The History of HMIC: The First 150 Years 1856–2006* <https://www.justiceinspectorates.gov.uk/hmic/media/the-his tory-of-hmic-the-first-150-years.pdf> [accessed 4 February 2016], pp. 9–10.

102 Clive Emsley, *The English Police: A Political and Social History* (London: Routledge, 2014 (orig. 1991)), p. 43.

103 Emsley, *The English Police: A Political and Social History*, pp. 43–44.

104 Emsley, *The English Police: A Political and Social History*, p. 44.

105 Emsley, *The English Police: A Political and Social History*, p. 49.

106 House of Commons, *Hansard's Parliamentary Debates: The Official Report*http s://api.parliament.uk/historic-hansard/commons/1853/apr/26/national-police# S3V0126P0_18530426_HOC_6 [accessed 7 September 2019], vol. 126, cc. 545–52.

107 *Second Report of the Select Committee on Police*, July 1853, p. iv.

108 County and Borough Police Act 1856 (19 & 20 Victoria, c. 69), accessed via Parliamentary Archive, 2 September 2016, p. 361.

109 Emsley, 'A Typology of Nineteenth-Century Police', pp. 29–44 (p. 33). See also Cowley, Todd, and Ledger, *The History of HMIC: The First 150 Years 1856–2006* for a more comprehensive history.

110 'Creating the Nation's Police Force', *UK Parliament*, <http://www.parliament.uk/a bout/living-heritage/transformingsociety/laworder/policeprisons/overview/nationsp oliceforce/> [accessed 4 February 2016].

111 Emsley, 'A Typology of Nineteenth-Century Police', pp. 29–44 (p. 33).

112 Trodd, pp. 435–460 (p. 438).

113 'Efficiency of the Metropolitan Police,' *Examiner*, 30 April 1842, pp. 283–284.

114 Trodd, pp. 435–460 (p. 439).

115 Haia Shpayer-Makov, *The Ascent of the Detective: Police Sleuths in Victorian and Edwardian England* (Oxford: Oxford University Press, 2011), p. 33.

116 VanArsdel and Don Vann, 'Introduction', in *Victorian Periodicals and Victorian Society*, ed. by. VanArsdel and Don Vann, p. 5.

117 'The New Police', *New Monthly Magazine*, July 1829, pp. 426–427.

Bibliography

Primary Periodical Material

'Efficiency of the Metropolitan Police,' *Examiner*, 30 April 1842, pp. 283–284.
'Metropolitan New Police', *Examiner*, 16 August 1829, p. 518.
'The New Police', *New Monthly Magazine*, July 1829, pp. 426–432.

Secondary Material

Altick, Richard, *The English Common Reader: A Social History of the Mass Reading Public 1800–1900* (Ohio: Ohio State University Press, 1957).

Anderson, Patricia, *The Printed Image and the Transformation of Popular Culture: 1790–1860* (Oxford: Clarendon Press, 1991).

Bersohn, Leora, 'Examiner (1808–1881)', in *Dictionary of Nineteenth Century Journalism*, ed. by Laurel Brake and Marysa Demoor (London and Ghent: Academia Press, 2009), p.211.

Brake, Laurel and Marysa Demoor (eds.), *Dictionary of Nineteenth Century Journalism* (London and Ghent: Academia Press, 2009).

Brannigan, John, *New Historicism and Cultural Materialism* (Basingstoke: Macmillan, 1998).

Cawelti, John G., *Adventure, Mystery and Romance: Formula Stories as Art and Popular Culture* (Chicago and London: University of Chicago Press, 1976).

The Constables Protection Act 1750 (24 Geo II, c. 44), legislation.gov.uk <http://www.legislation.gov.uk/apgb/Geo2/24/44/contents> [accessed 21 January 2016].

County and Borough Police Act 1856 (19 & 20 Victoria, c. 69), accessed via Parliamentary Archive, 2 September 2016.

Cowley, Richard, Peter Todd, and Louise Ledger, *The History of HMIC: The First 150 Years 1856–2006* <https://www.justiceinspectorates.gov.uk/hmic/media/the-history-of-hmic-the-first-150-years.pdf> [accessed 4 February 2016].

Creating the Nation's Police Force, UK Parliament, <http://www.parliament.uk/about/living-heritage/transformingsociety/laworder/policeprisons/overview/nationspoliceforce/> [accessed 4 February 2016].

Drew, John, 'The Newspaper and Periodical Market', in *Charles Dickens in Context*, ed. by. Sally Ledger and Holly Furneaux (Cambridge: Cambridge University Press, 2011), pp.109–117.

Emsley, Clive, 'A Typology of Nineteenth-Century Police', *Crime, Histoire et Sociétés/ Crime, History and Societies*, 3, 1 (1999), 29–44.

Emsley, Clive, *The English Police: A Political and Social History* (New York: St. Martin's Press, 1991 (repr; London: Routledge, 2014)).

Fox, Warren, 'Murder in Daily Instalments: The Newspapers and the Case of Franz Müller (1864)', *Victorian Periodicals Review*, 31, 3 (1998), 271–298.

Gallagher, Catherine and Stephen Greenblatt, *Practicing New Historicism* (Chicago: University of Chicago Press, 2000).

Greenblatt, Stephen, 'Towards a Poetics of Culture', in *The New Historicism*, ed. by Harold A. Veeser (Oxon: Routledge, 1989).

Harrison, Stanley, *Poor Men's Guardians: A Survey of the Struggles for a Democratic Newspaper Press, 1763–1973* (London: Lawrence and Wishart, 1974).

Hewitt, Martin, *The Dawn of the Cheap Press in Victorian Britain: The End of the 'Taxes on Knowledge', 1849–1869* (London: Bloomsbury, 2014).

House of Commons, Hansard's Parliamentary Debates: The Official Report https://api.parliament.uk/historic-hansard/commons/1853/apr/26/national-police#S3V0126P0_18530426_HOC_6 [accessed 7 September 2019], vol. 126, cc. 545–52.

Hubin, Allen J., *Crime Fiction 1749–1980: A Comprehensive Bibliography* (New York and London: Garland Publishing, 1984).

James, R. W., *To the Best of our Skill and Knowledge: A Short History of the Cheshire Constabulary 1857–1957* (Cheshire: Museum of Policing in Cheshire, 2005).

King, Andrew, *The London Journal: 1845–83* (Aldershot: Ashgate Publishing, 2004).

Knight, Stephen, *Crime Fiction 1800–2000: Detection, Death, Diversity* (Basingstoke: Palgrave Macmillan, 2004).

Law, Graham, *Serializing Fiction in the Victorian Public Press* (Basingstoke: Palgrave Macmillan, 2000).

Lee, Alan J., *The Origins of the Popular Press, 1855–1914* (London: Croom Helm, 1976).

Lefevre, Charles, Charles Rowan, and Edwin Chadwick, *First Report of the Commissioners Appointed to Inquire as to the Best Means of Establishing an Efficient Constabulary Force in the Counties of England and Wales* (London: Charles Knight and Co, 1839).

Lobban, Michael, 'Brougham, Henry Peter', in *Oxford Dictionary of National Biography* <http://www.oxforddnb.com/view/article/3581> [accessed 30 November 2015] (2008).

Metropolitan Police, UK Parliament <http://www.parliament.uk/about/living-heritage/transformingsociety/laworder/policeprisons/overview/metropolitanpolice/> [accessed 19 November 2015].

Mitch, David, *The Rise of Popular Literacy in Victorian England* (Philadelphia: University of Pennsylvania Press, 1992).

Murch, Alma, *The Development of the Detective Novel* (London: Peter Owen, 1958; repr. 1968).

Public Act, 29 George II, c. 25, UK Parliamentary Archive Portcullis <http://www.portcullis.parliament.uk/CalmView/Record.aspx?src=CalmView.Catalog&id=HL%2fPO%2fPU%2f1%2f1756%2f29G2n124&pos=3> [accessed 21 January 2016].

Rubery, Matthew, *The Novelty of Newspapers: Victorian Fiction After the Invention of the News* (Oxon: Oxford University Press, 2009).

Rzepka, Charles, *Detective Fiction* (Cambridge: Polity, 2005).

Saunders, Samuel, '"To Pry Unnecessarily into Other Men's Secrets": Crime Writing, Private Spaces and the mid-Victorian Police Memoir', *Law, Crime and History*, 8, 1 (2018), 76–90.

Second Report of the Select Committee on Police, July 1853.

Shattock, Joanne and Michael Wolff (eds.), *The Victorian Periodical Press: Samplings and Soundings* (Leicester: Leicester University Press, 1982).

Shattock, Joanne and Michael Wolff, 'Introduction', in *The Victorian Periodical Press: Samplings and Soundings*, ed. by Joanne Shattock and Michael Wolff (Leicester: Leicester University Press, 1982), pp.xiii–xix.

Shpayer-Makov, Haia, *The Ascent of the Detective: Police Sleuths in Victorian and Edwardian England* (Oxford: Oxford University Press, 2011).

Steedman, Carolyn, *Policing the Victorian Community: The Formation of English Provincial Police Forces, 1856–80* (London: Routledge, 1984).

Symons, Julian, *Bloody Murder: From the Detective Story to the Crime Novel* (London: Faber and Faber, 1972; repr. Basingstoke: Papermac, 1992).

Trodd, Anthea, 'The Policeman and the Lady: Significant Encounters in Mid-Victorian Fiction', *Victorian Studies*, 24, 4 (1984), 435–460.

Valdez, Jessica, 'Dickens's "Pious Fraud": The Popular Press and the Moral Suasion of Fictional Narrative', *Victorian Periodicals Review*, 44, 4 (2011), 377–400.

VanArsdel, Rosemary and J. Don Vann, *Victorian Periodicals and Victorian Society* (Toronto: University of Toronto Press, 1994).

VanArsdel, Rosemary and J. Don Vann, 'Introduction', in *Victorian Periodicals and Victorian Society*, ed. by. Rosemary VanArsdel and J. Don Vann (Toronto: University of Toronto Press, 1994), pp.3–8.

Veeser, Harold A. (ed.), *The New Historicism* (Oxon: Routledge, 1989).

Veeser, Harold A., 'Introduction', in *The New Historicism*, ed. by Harold A. Veeser (Oxon: Routledge, 1989).

Wiener, Joel, 'Newspaper Taxes, Taxes on Knowledge, Stamp Taxes', in *Dictionary of Nineteenth Century Journalism*, ed. by Laurel Brake and Marysa Demoor (London and Ghent: Academia Press, 2009), p.454.

Wiener, Joel, *The War of the Unstamped: The Movement to Repeal the British Newspaper Tax, 1830–1836* (New York: Cornell University Press, 1969).

Wiener, Martin, 'Convicted Murderers and the Victorian Press: Condemnation vs. Sympathy', *Crime and Misdemeanours*, 1, 2 (2007), 110–125.

Wolff, Michael, 'Charting the Golden Stream: Thoughts on a Directory of Victorian Periodicals', *Victorian Periodicals Newsletter*, 4, 3 (13) (1971), 23–38.

Wynne, Deborah, *The Sensation Novel and the Victorian Family Magazine* (Basingstoke: Palgrave, 2001).

Young, William, Report from the Committee on the Booksellers and Printers Petition, <https://parlipapers.proquest.com/parlipapers > [accessed 25 November 2015] (1802).

Part I
Policing and Crime in Periodicals

1   Periodical Discourse on Policing
c. 1850–1875

The Universal Concept of Uniformed Policing

Between 1829 and 1856, the sight of a patrolling police officer outside of Britain's urban centres would likely have been relatively rare, as efforts to set up centrally-controlled forces had hitherto been contained mostly to inner-city environments. However, after the 1856 County and Borough Police Act, every region around the country, rural or urban, became obligated to establish a force. These were visually and ideologically based on London's (by this point relatively well established and influential)[1] Metropolitan Police, and held largely the same authority and responsibility.

Naturally, the new police, and its socio-political and economic implications, moved quickly into public discussion, with commentators debating its merits and potential drawbacks. A substantial amount of this took place in periodicals, as the police's transformation into a nationwide organisation coincided with almost the exact moment of the abolition of the 'taxes on knowledge'. Publications revelled in the ability to publish on a variety of informative subjects without reproach and, as Barbara Korte argues, a broad theme in newly-liberated mid-Victorian magazines was engagement with socio-political debates that responded to the needs and problems of the public.[2] Discussion of law enforcement and criminal justice thus experienced an observable 'groundswell' in popularity in non-fiction criticism.[3] Even today, however, Victorian attitudes towards the police have not been fully examined, leading to some incorrect and oversimplified views of police evolution. This is succinctly highlighted by Clive Emsley, who suggests that the pervading view of the police's growth still remains something along the lines of the following:

> [T]he pre-police system of parish constables and night watchmen was inefficient and incapable of dealing with the problem of rising crime [...] Fortunately, a group of far-sighted reformers, including Chadwick, came up with the solution – the modern police. First established in London in 1829, the 'police idea' rapidly showed its worth, was adopted across the whole country, and was perceived as a model by others elsewhere.[4]

Emsley quickly shows this to be a simplistic narrative that does not cater for the nuances in the history of police development, and even suggests that it is still used as the 'official' version often promoted by the force itself.[5] In this he is correct; the narrative certainly does not account for the complex and often-virulent reception of the new police in the press. A study of a variety of journalistic criticism can therefore help better illustrate how the mid-Victorian community reacted to the new presence of nationwide policing, and the conclusions it reaches can then be subsequently applied to other areas of Victorian cultural development, including the production of fiction. Indeed, as Caroline Reitz contends, non-fictional debate presented in periodicals can (and should) be explored in conjunction with contemporary fiction to reveal what she terms a 'coherent dialogue' between the two.[6]

This opening chapter therefore looks at a variety of mid-Victorian periodical discourses, to show that the debate concerning the police was far from universally agreed upon. It makes two arguments that can then be applied to the history of 'detective fiction': firstly, that the periodical press was instrumental in both improving and disseminating public understanding of the police, solidifying them as part of the social fabric. Secondly, that periodical discussion of the police helped to nurture a growing ideology that police officers themselves occupied an indistinct social position, located somewhere between 'criminality' and 'respectability'.

Politics, the Police, and the Periodical Press

Perhaps predictably, exploring 'the police' through mid-Victorian periodical discussion is a complex operation. As this book's introduction discussed, *any* organised study of a broad range of mid-nineteenth-century periodicals has historically been difficult, and has necessitated the construction of careful methodologies with which to approach the enormous amount of primary material available. The growth of the press, coupled with the progression of social change (not in the least vast improvements in public literacy) also means that any study of periodicals must also necessarily link itself to the development of nineteenth-century society,[7] as the boost the press experienced allowed it to embed itself as both a shaper and a reflector of public ideology. This complex connection between the press and society means that, while the press is a rich source of information on the police, it must be tempered by an effective methodological framework that organises the vast amounts of information, while simultaneously navigating the socio-political ideologies of journalists and publications themselves.

One way of doing this is through exploring the subject through different titles' self-ascribed political leanings. In fact, this is a particularly relevant way of organising this part of the study, as both the police and the press shared a strong connection with contemporary politics. As Aled Jones argues, the diversification of the press in the mid-Victorian era was actually structured by newly-forged connections with contemporary politics, and the impressive variety of publications was actually constrained by 'strict political limitations'.[8] It was the moment of the repeal of the taxes on knowledge that had catalysed this politicisation of the press; as Stephen Koss summarises:

> No sooner had legislative trammels been lifted from them than newspapers proudly affixed to themselves the labels Tory, Whig, or Radical, which broke down into such sub-categories as Peelite or Disraelian, Russellite or Palmerstonian, Cobdenite or Gladstonian.[9]

Given the extant connection between the press and politics, a relatively simple way of categorising titles by political allegiance is immediately appealing. However, it is also worth pointing out that it there are greater complexities that should be considered. Firstly, establishing exactly which publications can be ascribed which (or indeed any) political label is complex.[10] As Martin Hewitt argues, many papers often had aims of their own and some were sustained by considerable political subsidy in exchange for open support.[11] These back-alley antics obscured political motives, as it is often unclear whether periodical titles were offering their support for genuine ideological or for simply financial reasons. Indeed, some titles (particularly those who disagreed with this practice and others like it) became deliberately anti-political.[12] Koss also notes that newspapers and periodicals occasionally amended their allegiances as the plate-tectonics of Victorian politics shifted, and publications became increasingly reluctant to flaunt their political alignment through fear of alienating potential readers – even more so when they were in receipt of party-related funds.[13]

Secondly, this kind of high-level categorisation cannot tell us much about readership, as it is virtually impossible to conclude exactly who read what, or whether the reader's political views aligned in any way with what they were reading. Proof of a periodical's purchase (itself hard to obtain on an individual level) also does not necessarily prove that it was read by the purchaser alone and, as Richard Altick suggests, this complicates the often-present narrative surrounding the class status of readers:

> Whatever newspapers and other periodicals a household took in would, in the normal course of events, filter down to the servants' quarters. In estimating the numbers of hands through which a given copy of a middle-class paper, or even a cheap book, might pass, one must not forget that the Victorian household contained not only a sizable family but also one or more servants with whom the paper wound up its travels.[14]

In fact, we should remember that proof of a magazine's purchase does not necessarily prove that it was read by the purchaser *at all*. It may simply have been bought for someone else, or it could even have been immediately mislaid and forgotten about (perhaps unlikely, but nevertheless possible).

Thirdly, it almost goes without saying that 'political', or more accurately 'partisan', publications naturally did not constitute the entire press. Other, more 'popular' titles emerged that had interests other than politics some of which were quite specific. The lack of political interest on the part of some titles meant that these magazines often dealt with crime, policing, and punishment in different ways (though it should be noted that they could have just as strong an impact on the *political* sphere).[15] The 'popular' press, which for the purposes of this chapter consists of largely non-partisan aligned magazines, is more difficult to organise and has a much murkier history, with some – such as Rosalind Crone – even suggesting there was not really a 'popular press' at all until after the repeal of the taxes on knowledge.[16]

Nevertheless, the way that Koss categorises periodicals according to politics is, at least, a useful initial approach to explore how the police were discussed in the mid-Victorian press. It sidesteps the issues surrounding readership by focusing on the target, rather than the actual, audience, and allows the chapter to explore how law enforcement was represented rather than how it was actually received. Again, Koss's politically-driven model is also an especially relevant way to approach periodical commentary on the police, as criticism of the force was politicised particularly heavily. Openly partisan periodicals often used discussion of the police as a somewhat thin veil to promote their own ideologies and, as both Anthea Trodd and Martin Wiener argue, many began to make more concerted efforts to influence their readers' opinions on matters concerning crime.[17]

It is worth iterating two final caveats; firstly, that publications aligned with all (or no) sides of the political spectrum had little motivation to engage with the practical methods of detection. Secondly, and most importantly, the enormous number of surviving articles that commented on the police contained within an impressive variety of publications, means that this opening chapter barely scratches the surface of potential material on this subject. Rather it presents a necessarily high-level analysis of broad trends in the ongoing debate on the police, by using what it perceives to be good representative examples of articles that approached it from a variety of perspectives, to establish a contextual landscape for the remainder of the book.

From 'the perfection of efficiency' to 'notoriously inferior': The Police in Victorian Partisan Periodicals

Victorian 'conservatism' was characterised by several factors, such as the defence of tradition; of the monarchy and aristocracy; the preservation of the union between church and state; maintenance of the status quo; the idea that political strength could be defined in social, rather than individual terms; and the idea that every member of society was individually obligated to uphold it.[18] Throughout the nineteenth century, conservative ideologies stressed the importance of defending property, tradition, and protecting against political revolution,[19] which accounted for many conservatives' support for protectionist laws (such as the 'taxes on knowledge') and for many withholding their support for the repeal of the Corn Laws in 1846.

Robert Peel, the politician responsible for the formation of the Metropolitan Police in 1829, presented the Tamworth Manifesto in 1834 and the Conservative Party itself was born out of the old Tories between 1834 and 1835.[20] Across the mid-Victorian era, the Conservatives maintained a significant but turbulent presence in British politics. Peel's convincing majority of 1841 was obliterated by his mismanagement of his decision to repeal the Corn Laws, which caused a three-way split in his party between the Peelites who supported Peel, the 'Free Traders' who felt that the repeal did not go far enough, and traditional conservatives who did not want to repeal the Laws at all. This moment had a substantial legacy; the Peelites went on to join the Whigs to form the new Liberals in 1859, and after 1846 the Tories did not taste majority power again until 1874. That said, they did hold a succession of short-lived minority governments between 1852 and 1868 under figures such as Edward Smith-Stanley (1852, 1858, and 1866) and Benjamin Disraeli (1868), usually brought about by prominent opposing Whig/Liberal resignations such as Lord John Russell in 1852, Lord Palmerston in 1858, and Russell again in 1866. Disraeli's Conservatives lost the 1868 election (despite believing they would be assisted by newly-enfranchised voters after the 1867 Reform Act), won a resounding victory in 1874, but were ousted again in 1880.[21] The final years of the Victorian era saw a significant increase in fortune for the Tories; they won a substantial majority in 1886, their largest since 1841 (though they lost it again in 1892), and after William Gladstone's final retirement in 1894 took advantage of the political disinterest of his replacement, Lord Rosebery. Rosebery's ministry was brought down in 1895, and the Marquess of Salisbury's Conservatives took over – initially as a minority and then under a majority won in 1895. The final election of the Victorian era took place in 1900, and Salisbury won convincingly.

Despite their inconsistent electoral performance, particularly across the mid-Victorian era, the Tories enjoyed substantial support in the periodical press. Well-established and venerable titles such as *Blackwood's Edinburgh Magazine* (1817–1980),[22] the *New Monthly Magazine* (1814–1884),[23] the *Quarterly Review* (1809–1967),[24] and *Fraser's Magazine for Town and Country* (1830–1882)[25] all leant towards political and social conservatism. This grew stronger as the Tories themselves did towards the end of the Victorian era, with some newer magazines such as the *National Review* (1883–1960) established purely as platforms for the party voice.[26] Indeed, as Aled Jones and Matthew Taunton point out, by the 1890s the Conservatives maintained largely dominant position in the periodical press.[27]

Throughout the eighteenth century the old Whig party laid the foundations for Victorian concepts of liberalism, where they had drawn support from rapidly-growing industrial interests and opposed the absolute rule of the monarchy. As the nineteenth century progressed, the Whigs became an official voice of reform and often sided with the more outspoken Radicals – occasionally attempting to guide them back towards pragmatic political practicality.[28] The Whigs (later the Liberals) enjoyed more majority governments than the Conservatives across the Victorian era. They won a small majority in 1837, though they were soundly beaten by Peel's Conservatives in 1841. However, as the repeal of the Corn Laws spectacularly brought Peel's ministry down, the consequent three-way Tory split allowed the Whigs numerous opportunities to repeatedly enter government. They formed a minority in 1847, and despite losing in 1852 to Smith-Stanley's protectionists, quickly regained a controlling voice in Parliament after his ministry collapsed in the December of the same year. A Whig/Peelite coalition was formed under Lord Aberdeen, which was a precursor to the formation of the Liberal Party. In 1857, the Whigs won a resounding majority under Palmerston, and this marked the beginning of a new age of British Liberalism. Palmerston resigned in 1858 and Derby's Conservatives took over until 1859, but in the same year the Peelites merged with the Whigs and semi-officially rebranded themselves the Liberals. The 1859 election saw Palmerston return and win another majority, governing to 1865. Palmerston won again in 1865, but died in the same year and the premiership was handed to Lord John Russell, who promptly resigned in 1866 and the Conservatives took power under Smith-Stanley and (subsequently) Disraeli until 1868. However, the 1868 election saw the first premiership of William Gladstone (now officially under the Liberal name), who increased their majority again and who remained Prime Minister until the Conservative victory of 1874. Gladstone returned in 1880 and governed for another five years before resigning in early 1885, which paved the way for the Tory resurgence in 1886 that characterised the final years of the nineteenth century.

Liberal free-trade economic principles lent themselves well to the development of the periodical press, which led to substantial reciprocal support from publishers for both party and ideology. Jones and Taunton argue that:

> Liberals, who had already adopted a free trade position in relation to popular communication, were arguably the most aggressive in their overtures to editors and journalists. Many of the key editors of the century [...] were not only firm supporters of the Liberal Party but also became MPs and established political dynasties.[29]

Additionally, a variety of magazines quite simply shied away from supporting what they perceived to be forms of authoritarianism, again leading to support for liberal politics which opposed absolute rule. The press, in fact, had a historic relationship with anti-authoritarianism, as a number of earlier radical magazines, such as Hetherington's infamous *Poor Man's Guardian* (1831–35) or John Cleave's *Cleave's Weekly Police Gazette* (1834–36) had already actively opposed and deliberately flouted what it had perceived to be oppressive laws during the 'war of the unstamped'.[30] Consequently, some of the most long-lasting titles of the nineteenth century leant towards political liberalism that was ideologically friendlier to a free press. The *Edinburgh Review* (1802–1929),[31] the *Fortnightly Review* (1865–1954),[32] the *Contemporary Review* (1866–1988),[33] *Macmillan's Magazine* (1859–1907),[34] and the *Nineteenth Century: A Monthly Review* (1877–1901) all aligned themselves towards the liberal end of the political spectrum, and both the *Contemporary Review* and the *Nineteenth Century: A Monthly Review* counted Gladstone – by this point a prominent Liberal – among their regular contributors.[35]

Many of these magazines had observable connections with each other. Both the *Quarterly Review* and *Blackwood's Edinburgh Magazine* were set up as direct conservative rivals to the 'dangerously unpatriotic' and vehemently Whig *Edinburgh Review*,[36] whilst the *New Monthly Magazine* was 'founded [...] as a Tory counter to the more liberal periodicals of the period'.[37] The conservative *Fraser's Magazine* was set up in 1830 as a direct competitor to its also-conservative counterpart, *Blackwood's*, and took it as its model as well as its chief rival.[38] Consequently, this section is organised thematically rather than by title or orientation, because these inter-title connections are difficult to navigate and because the perspectives from which partisan-aligned journalism approached the police were all surprisingly similar, even if the conclusions they reached were wildly different. Conservative-leaning magazines tended to support uniformed policing, and defended its public expense by arguing that the police were a manifestation of the state's responsibility for the respectable public who effectively protected property, capital, people, and the established status quo.[39] By contrast, publications that were more liberal-leaning had a stronger vested interest in criticising the police, as they were both at the opposite end of the political spectrum from that which had been responsible for the force's establishment, and they had a historic tendency towards anti-authoritarianism.[40] More liberal or radical criticism was thus naturally more suspicious, viewing the police as ineffective, oppressive, expensive, and as invasive representatives of the state. Three largely-common themes therefore emerge in *both* sides of the discussion through which the remainder of this section is organised: the police's effectiveness, their connection to the state, and their public expense.

Overall Effectiveness

The discussion that centred on the police's effectiveness in their mandate to protect the public and to prevent crime is the most obvious place to start. This was a universal and often fierce debate, with all sides of the political spectrum examining the force's efficiency through either drawing comparisons with the older parochial system, or by examining various statistical results of the new one.

As the conservative-leaning press was broadly aligned with the side of the political spectrum that had been responsible for the force's creation and roll-out,[41] articles that appeared in these magazines tended to argue that the police were indeed effective, and attempted to persuade readers to think the same. The Tory-leaning publications *Blackwood's Edinburgh Magazine* and *Quarterly Review* can help demonstrate this, as both provide some useful examples of it in action. In May 1844, a piece in *Blackwood's* argued that the police force's expansion from 1829 onwards had been a largely positive development because its efficiency was now markedly improved over the old system of night-watchmen:

[A] police force is [now] more extensively established, and [it] is more efficient than it formerly was; [...] the vast concourse from all parts of the empire unavoidably forced upon government, fourteen years ago, the establishment of a central police, since found to be attended with such admirable effects [...].[42]

Similarly, in 1856 the *Quarterly Review* produced 'The Police and the Thieves'; an enormous essay that explored almost every aspect of the new force. Like *Blackwood's*, it criticised the old system of parochial constables and presented it as simply inferior to the one that had replaced it:

At night [...] the authorities provided [the night-watchman] with a watch-box in order that he might enjoy his snooze in comfort, and furnished him with a huge lantern in order that its rays might enable the thief to get out of his way in time. [...] Up to the year 1828, and indeed for ten years later, in the City these men were the sole defence by night of the first metropolis in the world [and] it is well known that they 'winked hard,' when required to do so by people who could afford to pay them for it. It is not astonishing that crimes under such a police flourished apace, or that robberies increased to an extent which alarmed all thoughtful people.[43]

In fact, this article went on to argue that the old system was *so* terrible that Peel's efforts to introduce a professional organisation of uniformed police were 'immediately adopted' by the House of Commons.[44] The remaining sections provided a lengthy description of the new police's divisions, duties, training, methodologies and responsibilities, and attempted to highlight the benefits of having such a dedicated, disciplined and highly-trained force.[45] It ultimately concluded that the police's conduct was nothing less than 'exemplary',[46] and that their methodologies were so effective that, simply, '[t]hieves will no longer be able to get away with their plunder'.[47]

Other articles took a less comparative approach, but were still openly supportive of the police's efficiency. Another piece of interest appeared in *Blackwood's* in 1858, which praised the police in more methodological terms by praising their apparent skill at recognising criminals hiding in crowds. It argued that officers' confidence in their ability to spot these criminals was so extensive that they would willingly risk making a wrongful arrest in order to make a quick apprehension. More often than not, the piece contended, the police's instincts turned out to be correct:

The detective officer knows the thief, not only individually but generically. [...] the accomplished detective will mark his man among the thousands of faces in a full night in Covent Garden, with such precision that he does not hesitate to run the risk of immediately apprehending him without a warrant.[48]

By 1870, the comparative approach with the old, defunct system of night-watchmen and volunteer constables had largely disappeared to be replaced by open support of the uniformed police and their ability to prevent crime and protect the public. In the July, for example, the *Quarterly Review* produced 'The Police of London' that emphatically argued:

> For the same reason that the lawless classes arrayed against society are weak, the constabulary forces arrayed in defence of society are strong. [...] A comparatively small number of honest, steady, active men [...] acting under the direction of skilled and experienced officers, will always have an immense advantage over the heterogeneous mass of roughs, thieves, and desperate characters which constitute the scoundrelism [sic] of great cities. And such a body London unquestionably possesses in its Metropolitan Police Force [...] for a more carefully-selected, well-conducted, and efficient body of men [...] probably does not exist in any country.[49]

A final, quite late-Victorian conservative-leaning example, in 1886 an article titled 'The City of London Police' by Tory barrister Alexander Innes Shand (1832–1907) appeared in *Blackwood's*, which essentially summarised the conservative-leaning view of the police's overall competence. While musing on the distinctions between the Metropolitan Police and the City of London Police, Shand boldly claimed that the efficiency of the police (in either the wider Metropolis or in the City of London) had caused ordinary people to largely forget their own security and safety:

> Citizens have come to take the comparative security of their persons and property, with the regulation of traffic in overcrowded thoroughfares, as simple matters of course. [...] [a]s a matter of fact, the City police has arrived at pretty nearly the perfection of efficiency [...].[50]

Perhaps slightly predictably, more liberal-leaning publications presented the opposite view to their conservative counterparts, arguing that the police were inefficient, corrupt, and susceptible to the same temptations and failings as the criminals whom they were meant to apprehend. In May 1869, for example, the *Contemporary Review* published a review of a pamphlet entitled *The Police Force of the Metropolis in 1868* anonymously written by an author named 'Custos'. This argued, quite simply, that:

> Crime is on the increase, and the vigilance of the police is notoriously inferior to the skill of our professional thieves.[51]

Elsewhere, one of the most vocal publications in its attacks on the police's efficiency was the *Saturday Review*. Established in 1855 and directly benefiting from the repeal of the Stamp Act, the magazine was 'cautiously liberal' in its editorial line and positioned itself between established quarterlies such as the 'vigorously Whig' *Edinburgh Review* [52] and the more conservative *Blackwood's* or *Quarterly Review*. [53] Despite its political hedge-betting, however, it was one of the most interested periodicals in criticising the police, and frequently published articles that questioned its competence. In April 1870, it produced the rather bluntly titled 'Inefficiency of the London Police Force', where it mused on a recent spate of riots and rough behaviour:

> The law is openly defied and its guardians confess themselves powerless to vindicate its majesty [...]. The ordinary policeman is not quick enough for the work [...] The Metropolitan police performs many and various duties satisfactorily, but it is hardly strong enough for all the work it has to do, and in mobility it is more deficient than in numbers. [54]

A month later, the magazine produced 'The Jewel Robberies', which pragmatically argued that victims of burglaries would do well to remember that the police were perhaps not omniscient. [55] However this generous view was short lived; far from defending the police's ability to track criminals, the article went on to argue that the police should at least have *some* leads on most crimes and that its largest problem was simply laziness:

> As we are not behind the scenes, we of course cannot speak with confidence upon the matter, but if the police are as acute [...] as they ought to be on a reasonable computation, they should surely have some suspicions [...] from which we may infer either that they have been wanting in energy and ingenuity [...]. [56]

Finally, in 1873 the *Saturday Review* printed another article that argued that the police's inefficiency should be blamed squarely on the force's apparently poor management. It suggested that the ordinary constable was actually largely well-meaning, but that it had been improper management at higher levels that had led to the police's apparent lack of efficiency and poor behaviour:

> [...] a force of this kind must necessarily contain a proportion of black sheep. [...] They are certainly not all bullies and perjurers, but it is difficult to resist the evidence that bullying and perjury are increasing, and that the police are in some degree becoming danger, instead of a protection, to the public. [...] the chiefs of the force have [...] been weak and vacillating in dealing with internal discipline [...]. [57]

In short, discussion of the police's effectiveness in its mandate to prevent crime was largely polarised along political battle lines. Conservative-leaning titles tended to support the police and argued that they were at least better than that which had come before, and that they were generally effective protectors of the public. However, more critical publications maintained that the police were inefficient, ill-managed and lazy. There were, obviously, exceptions to this general rule of thumb; in 1852 for example, the Whig-aligned *Edinburgh Review* produced a piece titled 'The Police System of London' which was enormously in favour of police expansion across the country.[58] For the most part, however, it remained largely the case.

The Police and the State

A second theme observable in much periodical criticism concerned the force's connection with the state. Both conservative and liberal-aligned criticism helped to create and nurture a close ideological link between the police and the institution that had both created and continued to control it. Naturally, like the discussions on their effectiveness, this was viewed from largely polarised partisan perspectives. Conservative-leaning critics, for example, argued that the police were a representation of the state's responsibility for protecting the public, and who upheld the laws that the government created by acting as a visible symbol of the crown. They also often ridiculed opposing ideas that the force was actually invasive and threatening to civil liberties; indeed, in June 1856 the article 'The Police and the Thieves' from the *Quarterly Review* openly referenced these contrasting arguments:

> That stalking horse, 'the liberty of the subject,' which in truth meant the liberty of rogues to plunder, was immediately paraded before the public. [...] Those accustomed only to the slow pace of the constitutional watchman [...] believed so powerful a force concentrated under a single head might be turned to political purposes.[59]

The article's response to these claims was to deride the notion as simply alarmist and to argue that the police were no doubt experienced and wise enough to use their state-imbued power responsibly. It skated over the fact that an inquiry had taken place into the force's overzealous behaviour at a physical clash between it and a group of protestors in Coldbath Fields in 1833, and again after the Sunday Trading Bill riots in Hyde Park in 1855. Instead, the piece argued that the fact that the public had taken up arms against a force that represented the state should have been, but was not, perceived as the actual reprehensible act:

> [I]n 1833, an actual collision took place between [the police] and the great unwashed in Coldbath Fields. [...] It might have been thought that the very fact of a mob coming thus armed, with the express purpose of resisting a *constituted authority*, would have excited the indignation of the more respectable classes of the citizens; the contrary was the fact. [...] Such was the ferment that a commission was held to inquire into the conduct of the police, and they were exonerated from the charge of having as a body acted with greater violence than was necessary. From that period, with the exception of the investigation during the present year into the charge of

having dispersed a gathering in Hyde Park with undue severity – a charge which was not at all substantiated – their conduct has been so exemplary as to have removed the original dislike [my italics].[60]

This perceived connection between the police and the state also appeared in other conservative-leaning discourse across the Victorian period. In January 1870, *Fraser's Magazine* produced an article titled 'Laissez-Faire', attributed to 'R. W.'. This openly rejected the concept of state interference in society and argued that, in short, '[m]en are the best judges of their own interests'.[61] However, despite this overarching belief, it was also forced to admit that the state did have at least some responsibility for protecting the physical welfare of its citizens, and that the police were an essential part of this:

> All that is requisite on the part of the State is that it should protect the persons and the property of its members. [...] a nation is a body of individuals, who are bound together by a common organisation, taking the shape of [...] *a police force to repress assault and robbery* [my italics].[62]

Indeed, the same article went on to argue that the police actually manifested *all* necessary areas of state influence in society, to be used in places where individuals either required assistance or where no single person had individual responsibility. It quoted a summary of a small part of Hegel's *The Philosophy of Right* (1820), penned by Thomas Collett Sandars (1825–1894), to suggest:

> I cannot refrain from quoting *in extenso* the following passage: – 'There are many actions which under some circumstances are wrong, and others not; and as individuals cannot estimate their true character, they require that it should be estimated for them. These functions are discharged by what [...] we may term "the Police." [...] the Police has to regulate all such things as roads or bridges, the construction of which benefits all, but does not fall under the province of any one.'[63]

In 1863, *Blackwood's Edinburgh Magazine* also made a connection between the police and the state, in a piece titled 'The Wigtown Martyrs' by barrister, magistrate, and regular contributor John Paget (1811–1898). Paget analysed the case of two Scottish women, Margaret McLachlan and Margaret Wilson, who were executed by drowning in 1685 for refusing to acknowledge James VII as head of the Church. The piece leapt to the defence of the enforcers of the judicial system, who it termed 'agents' of the government:

> Much sympathy has been claimed for these women, on the supposition that they were the victims of a novel and unusual mode of death. All capital punishments must be revolting; new and strange modes of death are peculiarly so [...] In 1685, drowning was the ordinary mode of executing capital sentences upon females in Scotland [...] Neither the Government *nor its*

agents can therefore be justly held answerable for the mode of execution [my italics] [...][64]

The phrase 'nor its agents' is particularly relevant here; Paget suggests that the agents of the law, which in 1863 certainly included the police, were also the agents of the state, representing the government and helping it to both manifest its power over its citizens and exercise its ability to uphold the law. Thus, they themselves were blameless in the conduct of their duty, even when that conduct was backed by morally-questionable principles.

As conservative periodical support for the police solidified, so too did the apparent connection between the police and the crown. In July 1870, the article from the *Quarterly Review* titled 'The Police of London' produced perhaps the most explicit example of this in action, where it highlighted the power which the crown provided the force to protect the respectable public. Here, the police manifested the will, apparent moral incorruptibility and physical force of the nation-state, and the article connected the police with unwavering patriotism bordering on jingoism:

> The baton may be a very ineffective weapon of offence, but it is backed by the combined power of the Crown, the Government, and the Constituencies. Armed with it alone, the constable will usually be found ready, in obedience to orders, to face any mob, or brave any danger. The mob quails before the simple baton of the police officer, and flies before it knowing the moral as well as the physical force of the Nation whose will, as embodied in law, it represents.[65]

This summarised the attitude of much conservative-leaning criticism; that the police manifested the will, moral incorruptibility, and physical arm of the nation itself. On the other side of the debate, however, more overtly-critical perspectives tended to link the police force with the state through the lens of oppressive governmental interference in everyday society. Commentators approaching the force from this perspective frequently argued that the police were a state-operated tool that was fundamentally designed to keep the lower echelons of society as downtrodden as possible. This suspicious view was, as Warren Fox asserts, purported by some particularly radical publications such as *Reynold's Newspaper*, founded in 1850 (initially as *Reynolds's Weekly Newspaper*) by the famously radical pressman G.W. M. Reynolds (1814–1879). In July 1864, *Reynolds's* wrote:

> [T]he police of London are taught to look upon a really liberal politician as a more "dangerous character" than a burglar or a murderer – as a being who is to be more closely watched and more severely dealt with than a Bill Sykes, a Manning, or a Greenacre.[66]

The article, in slightly alarmist terms, suggested that the police were being systematically taught to innately reject liberal politics and to view them as untrustworthy – indeed, more untrustworthy even than the reprehensible Bill Sykes from Dickens's *Oliver Twist* or the infamous murderers, Frederick and Maria Manning, hanged for the murder of Maria's lover Patrick O'Connor in 1849. *Reynolds's*, and apparently at least some of its readership maintained this sceptical view of the police as methodically indoctrinated against liberal ideologies in other pieces, too. In 1861, a letter to the editor of the paper signed only from 'Northumbrian' appeared, which accused the police of 'scandalous behaviour' and argued that officers were regularly abusing their powers by 'trumping up false charges of assault and disorderly conduct against unoffending citizens' in order to politically silence them.[67] It went on to ultimately recommend that the connection between the police and the state should be reconsidered, and power over the force passed to local authorities that represented the public, rather than the crown:

> The time is rapidly nearing when the Magisterial office must be made elective, as in the United States, and the supreme control of the police forces must be vested in the local authorities representing the public.[68]

This idea that the police were a state-controlled force for political oppression was also displayed in other slightly less radical but certainly liberal-leaning publications than *Reynolds's*. The *Fortnightly Review*, a magazine hailed by Mark W. Turner as 'the vanguard of change in mid-century periodical publishing', can help highlight this.[69] This was a free-thinking and experimental publication which 'sought to combine the opinion-forming, serious journalism of the quarterlies, with the more responsive criticism of the weeklies, together with the entertainment value of a shilling monthly.'[70] Indeed, even fortnightly publication was an untested frequency, which certainly highlights the periodical's innovative nature.[71] In 1868, it published an article titled 'The Transit of Power' by jurist and radical thinker Frederic Harrison (1831–1923), which argued that the police were a weapon of the government which could conceivably be used against the masses (though it also believed that it would not go well for the force when tested):

> Our Executive has nothing to fall back on. There are practically no reserves. The few bayonets and sabres here and there are perfectly powerless before the masses, if the people really took it into their heads to move [...]. There are only the police, hardly a match for the "roughs," as we know to our cost. The Government would be mad which seriously attempted to face an angry people on the strength of several thousand police staves.[72]

The *Fortnightly Review* also demonstrated this rather critical link between police and state through other, quite complex explorations of criminality. In 1865 it published 'Civilisation and Crime' by another jurist, Sheldon Amos (1835–1886), which argued that the condition of law enforcement in any country was directly related to the level of 'civilisation' that nation had attained.[73]

Crime, and consequently its prevention and punishment, was thus a gauge of
the state of society as a whole; the greater number of violent or deviant acts
that were considered 'criminal', then the further 'evolved' a given society was.
Thus, when society was in a more 'primitive' state, fewer offences were considered 'crimes'.[74] Predictably, the article then went on to discuss the role of the
police in maintaining this state of 'civilisation':

> With respect to the effective execution of the criminal law, it is obvious, that
> inasmuch as the whole fabric of society rests in the last resort on the strength
> of its sanctions, any prevalent laxity or indolence in apprehending and pun-
> ishing offenders is a sure token of national prostration. [...] Such was the
> case not so long ago in England, when armed highwaymen infested every
> thoroughfare, and the executive authorities tried to atone for the inefficiency
> of the police by savage and indiscriminate cruelty in punishment.[75]

The effectiveness of the police thus became a measurable gauge of social evolution. The piece argued that the inefficiency of the police in its mandate to
apprehend criminals was balanced out by 'indiscriminate cruelty' on the part of
the state in its treatment of criminals that the police actually *had* managed to
capture. In other words, the police caught fewer criminals than they otherwise
should, and the state treated these more brutally in order make up for their lack
of effectiveness.

The Economics of Policing and the Treatment of Criminals

From a slightly different perspective, a variety of partisan-leaning magazines also
discussed uniformed, state-controlled law enforcement through their economic
impact. This was not merely limited to a discussion on the public expense of
maintaining a police force, but also examined their wider financial and sociological
aspects. Some conservative discourse, for example, maintained that the police
benefited the economy because they acted as protectors for middle-class financial
and cultural capitals, and protected businesses and traders. In January 1868, for
example, *Fraser's Magazine* printed an article written by prominent social reformer Edwin Chadwick, titled 'On the Consolidation of the Police Force and the
Prevention of Crime'. In this, Chadwick referred to his own report into the state of
policing and crime in Britain produced in collaboration with Charles Lefevre and
Charles Rowan and published in 1839.[76] He revisited the methodology of this
report to ultimately link the requirement for country-wide policing to crimes
committed against trade and commerce (particularly by striking trade unions), and
argued that manufacturers and workers suffered without the existence of adequate
law-enforcement authorities to protect them:

> The protection of the individual workman and the manufacturer from
> personal violence is loudly declared to be a matter of imperative necessity.
> [...] Everywhere, however, we found that due means of executing the law

were wanting. The local constabulary or police forces were inefficient [...]
The Government decided upon introducing [...] a permissive measure for
the appointment new county police forces [...].[77]

The police, according to Chadwick, were thus actually set up as an effort to
help protect not only the people, but particularly businesses and economic
stability. This attitude seemingly stuck; in 1861 the Tory-leaning *Blackwood's*
published an article titled 'Uncivilised Man' by George Henry Lewes (1817–1878)
that discussed the merits of 'civilisation' as juxtaposed with 'barbarism'. It firstly
explored the difficulties that ethnologists had in reconstructing societies before the
'commercial age [of the nineteenth century],[78] and went on to describe various
indigenous customs in detail. However, the sentence of particular interest here
stated:

> Although there are no police [...] to protect the trader [in these 'barbaric
> societies'], it very rarely happens that a trader is attacked for the sake of
> booty [...][79]

This statement gestures towards the perspective that the police were a force for
economic protection, as it intimates how other societies held different values
from their own, and placed less importance on the material worth of goods and
commerce. 'Traders', therefore, were at less of a risk of attack than they were
in capitalist Victorian society – which fortunately had a police dedicated to
protecting them. This idea was echoed in the *Quarterly Review* in October
1874, when it published a piece titled 'Criminal Statistics', attributed to Angli-
can priest Robert Gregory (1819–1911). This was a compilation of statistics of
criminals committed for trial, imprisoned or convicted of capital offences
between 1805 and 1873,[80] and the article attempted to make sense of this data
by building an overarching narrative on the national state of crime, and to
enhance it by spotting loopholes in it.[81] However, it also engaged directly with
the role of the police suggesting, quite simply, that their responsibility was to
protect economic interests:

> Let us look next at the means used to *protect property* and to discover
> crime. For these we naturally turn to the strength and efficiency of the
> police force kept on foot at the different periods [my italics].[82]

However, the discussion of the police force's economic impact could hardly fail to
eventually examine the cost of the police to the taxpayer. Conservative discourses
were particularly concerned by the ever-increasing expense of both crime and the
police. Indeed, Gregory's article actually provides a good example of this, where it
by highlighted the economic cost of the police in detail:

> Since the passing of this Act [the 1856 County and Borough Police Act], the
> strength of the police force has been steadily growing, its efficiency has

been tested, and its general utility acknowledged. At the census of 1861 the total police and constabulary force gave one for every 937 of the population; at the census of 1871 there was one for every 828; last year there was one for every 795. In 1871 there were 27,425 men engaged in this work [...] and the expenditure was almost two and a quarter millions; last year the number had risen to 28,550 and the cost to 2,567,491*l*. [83]

From a similar perspective, Chadwick (still writing in *Fraser's*) also contended that further centralisation of the police into a wholly-national system, as opposed to a series of disjointed or individualised constabularies operated at county level, would be even more economically efficient than it already was:

In respect to two separate county police forces, it was proved that the expense was not greater than of the old and comparatively inefficient and in many cases the so-called 'unpaid' system of parochial constables, and if all the borough forces had been included, the expense would have been less and the efficiency greater. It may be averred that, under a proper administration the services of a united and systematised force of twenty-five or twenty-six thousand men, including Scotland, may be had for nothing; that is to say, at no greater expense than the total expense of the existing disconnected forces; and two millions of expenditure now squandered on an ineffective system of repression would be largely economised.[84]

Indeed, Chadwick was a lifelong advocate of further centralisation of the police force right up until his death in 1890, and consistently argued in other articles that it would be more economically practical, and would also improve police efficiency in the long run.[85]

From a slightly different perspective, it should also be pointed out that some commentary also critiqued the economic expense of *criminals* as well as that of the police. In a particularly strong example from 1863, *Fraser's Magazine* openly criticised the way that criminals were handled as a public expense. John Ruskin (1819–1900), writing for *Fraser's*, commented on the expense of keeping prisoners in prisons and made what seems to be quite a startling suggestion:

All criminals should at once be set to the most dangerous and painful forms of [manual labour], especially to work in mines and at furnaces, so as to relieve the innocent population as far as possible [...][86]

By today's standards this attitude seems reprehensible and seemingly helps confirm Christopher Casey's assertion that the mid-Victorian era saw a return to the 'more brutal forms of punishment' due to widespread anxiety concerning an apparent lack of effectiveness in the criminal justice system.[87] However, while true to a point, this should be considered in context. Transportation, which grew steadily more unpopular after 1840,[88] was abolished in 1857 by the Penal Servitude Act, and the Offences Against the Person Act 1861 had reduced the number of offences that carried capital sentences from hundreds to four. Imprisonment as a form of punishment consequently increased dramatically in the wake of these reforms and, predictably, prisons quickly became overwhelmed. There was thus increasing concern about what to do with growing numbers of prisoners, leading to a substantial programme of nationwide prison reform across the mid-Victorian years.[89] Indeed, the pervading anxiety over what to do with convicted felons was even gestured towards in some examples of mid-Victorian fiction, including the looming presence of the prison-hulk ships in the opening pages of Dickens's *Bleak House* (1853). Prison-work details such as bakeries and carpenter workshops also became popular, alongside the more feared treadmills and other menial tasks, designed to keep prisoners economically functional. A schematic of Coldbath Fields prison from 1884 after it was rebuilt following a fire in 1877 shows evidence of increased capacity, as well as presence of systematic work-details including a carpenter's workshop, an oakum-picking house, a paper-making workshop, and a treadwheel house.[90] Additionally, as Rosalind Crone has shown, some prisons, notably Reading Gaol, were transformed into religiously-oriented learning environments for prisoners, in an effort to improve their prospects when they were released and prevent them from reoffending.[91] A return to forms of corporal punishment was, therefore, perhaps the case because it allowed a criminal to be punished immediately and then released, without their taking up room or consuming resources in already-overstretched prisons.

Predictably, some liberal-leaning magazines also chose to critique the police's economic expense, and often broadly questioned whether the benefits of organised law enforcement were worth its cost. In May 1869, the *Contemporary Review*'s review of 'Custos's' pamphlet *The Police Force of the Metropolis in 1868* accurately (and quite helpfully) summarised much of the liberal-aligned critical opinion on the economic implications of mid-Victorian policing:

> Our property is notoriously insecure, our persons by no means safe, and our police force certainly quite as large as the British payer of taxes is likely to tolerate.[92]

Liberal commentaries on the police's economic impacts were actually quite complex in places. In August 1865, the *Fortnightly Review* published an article by Herbert Graham titled 'Public and Private Prosecutors'. Graham lamented that there was no centralised and publicly funded system for prosecuting offenders in Britain once their crimes had been detected and the offender apprehended. The article detailed the judicial processes that occur after a criminal had been caught, and argued that

> Many criminals go unpunished because the person injured has no wish to incur trouble and expense, and other people have no desire to mix themselves up in a matter with which they have no personal connection, and for their trouble in regard to which they would receive no adequate

remuneration, but, on the contrary, run the risk of being involved in subsequent litigation, and, it may be, compelled to pay heavy damages.[93]

Thus, many simply could not afford justice (or could not afford to pay for damages if the case ended up going against them). However, the indirect argument here was that the police, despite their best efforts, were often wasting their time, energy, and (crucially) public money in their pursuit of offenders because it was likely that they were often never going to be prosecuted anyway because the victims simply could not afford the legal fees.

From a slightly different perspective, some liberal-aligned commentary also often explored the physical and psychological treatment of criminals who had been apprehended by the police. As we have seen, many conservative commentators discussed on the expense and upkeep of convicts in the light of the abolition of transportation and a reduction in the number of capital offences, and their broad concern was with how to keep the imprisoned contributing to society and to the economy in some form. From the other side, more liberal periodicals also frequently addressed the same problem, with some directly responding to the idea of keeping prisoners working. In 1870, for example, the *Contemporary Review* produced 'The Employment of Criminals' by prominent radical politician and trade unionist George Odger (1813–1877), which argued that giving prisoners work to do would actually damage the free market because it would create unnecessary competition and ultimately reduce prices for honest working people.[94] Elsewhere, other liberal-leaning voices explored the impacts that the criminal justice system had on the people who had been convicted and released. In 1865 the venerable and Liberal-supporting[95] *Edinburgh Review* published 'Our Convicts', an article that explored the way that becoming a 'criminal' affected those branded with this label and caused fundamental, irreparable changes to their identities. It also looked at how the more centralised, bureaucratic system of law-enforcement affected how the public perceived criminals, and how these perceptions created a marginalised identity from which they could not escape even if they had paid their social debt:

> A blind man is thought of not as a man who is blind, but as one separated from the rest of mankind by his blindness. A man addicted to liquor, becomes to all but his household connexions, a drunkard and there's an end. So a man who has once transgressed the boundaries of the criminal law, is thenceforward a *criminal*, and in that term we seem, as it were, to drown many of the common attributes of human nature, though it is by the temptations of human nature itself that he has fallen [original italics].[96]

The concern of this article was therefore not the political implications of establishing a police, but instead the effect that centralised, state-controlled, and bureaucratic systems of law enforcement had on the population as a whole. Even the article's title, '*Our* Convicts', implied a sense of social inclusion of the criminal portion of society, and was naturally a gentle reminder to readers that even the criminal population were still society's responsibility, even if they were now hidden from view by the police.

Overall, then, we can see how 'the police' were examined through numerous socio-political lenses in the pages of partisan-aligned periodicals across the entire mid-to-late Victorian era. Publications that were allied to political orientations often used the police to promote or exemplify their own ideologies, with contributors from both sides of the debate using the force as a catalyst for commenting on various aspects of society and the regulation of crime. However, as was mentioned earlier in this chapter, the partisan press did not constitute the *entire* press, and thus it remains to explore how *non*-partisan (or indeed non-political) publications explored the police, to complete the picture of how the force was depicted in periodicals across this volume's research period.

Scrutiny of the Police in Non-Partisan Periodicals

Across the mid-Victorian era, specific-interest periodicals on a variety of eclectic subjects all saw increases in volume and frequency. Publications which concerned themselves with topics such as literature, art, music, and religion, as well as those targeted at either certain socio-political movements[97] or certain social groups such as children, women and the elderly, all sprang up, keen to take advantage of the liberated market and carve out new audiences for themselves. Samuel Beeton's *Boy's Own Magazine*, for example, which was one of the first boy's magazines to achieve commercial success, appeared in 1855.[98] There was also an increase in magazines aimed at those working in specific professions (or even just 'working' in general). The *British Workman* and *British Workwoman* appeared in 1855 and 1863 respectively, seemingly benefiting directly from the recent abolition of the various taxes on knowledge.[99]

Despite their apparent lack of interest in participating in party-political debate, the wider periodical press was just as interested in scrutinising the concept of nationwide law enforcement. Naturally, there were differences in the way that they could (and did) critique it, and this had different corresponding effects. While ideologically-aligned periodicals used the police to present commentary which was largely in line with their own viewpoints, non-partisan periodicals were not bound by such restrictions. Consequently, scrutiny of the police force in what we might term the 'popular' press was more ambiguous, complex, and less organised, though it certainly helped to cement the police firmly in the mid-Victorian social fabric and in public consciousness. Some magazines were sceptical of the police, others vaguely curious, and still others, such as Charles Dickens famously writing in *Household Words*, were actively interested.

Chambers's (Edinburgh) Journal, published between 1832 and 1956 under various names, examined the police extensively and can thus help to exemplify this. It was a popular magazine aimed at both young people and the lower-to-middle classes as an accessible, general interest publication.[100] It particularly praised the police force and the way it operated. In January 1860, for example, it published

'Criminal Statistics', which argued that the police were 'conservators of life, limb and property' and stated that the 'labours of the police are by no means light'.[101] This rather pragmatic attitude was relatively common in *Chambers's*; in 1864, the magazine returned to the topic of the police's effectiveness in 'The Metropolitan Police and what is Paid for Them', where it argued that it was understandable that an entity so widespread and essential incurred considerable financial expense:

> So valuable an organisation as the police force, so essential to the social order of this great metropolis and the comfort of its denizens, cannot be maintained without considerable aggregate cost. Few, however, who fairly examine the various items of expenditure for the metropolitan police, will find much to criticise.[102]

Not all publications shared *Chambers's* optimistic outlook, however. The politically-minded but non-partisan *Examiner*, for example, frequently commented on crime and policing, and the conclusions it reached were wildly different. The magazine was founded by brothers John and Leigh Hunt in 1808 as a literary publication, which Leora Bersohn argues was the lens through which they wished to approach political critique.[103] In an August 1866 article simply titled 'The Police', the *Examiner* mused on the police's failings when it came to using physical force in the midst of rioting, where innocent bystanders had found themselves on the receiving end of unwarranted blows, yet subsequently had their complaints dismissed:

> In one instance of great unprovoked violence, the magistrate said the officer was justified in breaking the complainant's head by mistake. That the mistake could be excused we admit, but we cannot see how a knock on the head of A., deserved and intended for B., can be justified.[104]

This rather contemptuous attitude was intensified in a number of other articles which appeared in the *Examiner*. In 1869, the magazine ran a story titled 'Capital Punishment Without Trial', which related the case of Hannah Saunders, a poor lady driven insane after she was evicted from her home and who attempted suicide by throwing herself into a canal. She was picked up by a local police officer who, the magazine lamented, instead of conveying her to a hospital or infirmary, placed her unceremoniously in a cell and left her unattended for several days. Saunders did not survive this ordeal, and the paper furiously attacked the police's incompetence and cruelty at refusing her bail and neglecting to seek medical attention, and blamed it for her 'execution':

> When asked what ground he had for making a charge of attempted suicide, the constable flippantly answered, none whatever; so that if Mrs Saunders had lived until Monday morning, she would either have been "turned out," [...] without any charge having been made, or upon the summary breaking down of the wretched accusation. But if no proof or even charge was

possible, how comes it that she was done to death in the midst of a civilised and so-called Christian community [...]?[105]

Furthermore, in an article titled 'The London Police' from 1872, the *Examiner* (slightly more pragmatically) argued that the police force's incompetence may actually have been due to dissatisfaction in the force itself. Intolerable working conditions led to a mutiny among the force in the early 1870s, and several officers were consequently dismissed.[106] The article suggested that this was perhaps not without justification:

> That the police had serious grounds for disaffection hardly any one now appears to doubt. Their work was very hard. Their pay was miserably small. Even at present [...] it is far from liberal. But the scanty pay was the least grievance. One very sore point with the force was that duties had been put upon it which tended to make it ridiculous and even unpopular. To say nothing of the new Licensing Act [...] gave the force an infinitude of trouble, and made the men very dissatisfied with their duty [which] under Colonel Henderson the life of a policeman has become almost intolerable.[107]

Perhaps some of the most striking images of the police in non-partisan magazines from this mid-Victorian period came from the deliberately satirical press. Like many magazines which took a satirical line, the 'Victorian institution'[108] *Punch, or, the London Charivari*, tended to lean towards outright mockery. In March 1856, for example, it produced an article which directly commented on the spread of the police into rural areas as a result of the County and Borough Police Act and, given the state of the police in the city, remarked that this was perhaps ill-advised:

> The policemen, disgusted at the accusation that has so long been hurled at them, that they are never to be found when wanted in the Metropolis, are about to throw themselves on the Country.[109]

Punch's published attacks also occasionally centred on the police's overall ability to prevent and solve crime. In January 1856 it produced 'Policeman's Logic', which colourfully argued that police officers seldom displayed the ability to think rationally:

> We find [...] from a recent police case at Marylebone, that the reasoning powers of a metropolitan constable are occasionally used by himself to supply a want of actual knowledge, as may be seen in the following brief dialogue:–
> "MAGISTRATE. Do you think the pork was stolen?"
> "POLICEMAN. I have no doubt of it, or she would not have let it drop."
> [...] This species of circumstantial evidence must be received with considerable caution, for there are many articles that one might very innocently

drop [...] which one would not like to be accused of stealing, unless one was prepared to burn one's fingers. The policeman [...] should be careful to avoid such nonsense [...][110]

A third remarkable depiction of the police emerged in *Punch* in April 1863, when it printed a large image of two police officers in the guise of Gog and Magog. These were famously the colloquial names of two effigies of giants displayed at London's Guildhall and locally known as the city's guardians. Far from depicting them as protectors of the masses, however, *Punch* depicted the two giants as beset by them, generally accused of uselessness and incompetence.[111]

Away from *Punch*, other satirical magazines similarly attacked the competence of the police force throughout its lifespan. *Fun*, as Brian Maidment argues, was one of the more successful of *Punch*'s imitators,[112] and followed its style so closely that Thackeray was reputed to have dubbed it 'Funch'.[113] In March 1873, the magazine published 'Police!', which bluntly presented the apparent idiocy of police officers, by describing an officer who insists that residents of a particular street clear their doorways of snow in the middle of a blizzard. When suggested to him that the task should perhaps wait until the blizzard has ceased so as to not make it a pointless endeavour, the officer responds aggressively, much to the bemusement of local residents:

> [I]t was suggested by one taxpayer that it would be time enough to clear away the snow when it had ceased to fall, a suggestion which elicited an objectionable reply and the threat of a summons from the active and intelligent officer.[114]

In even starker terms, in 1869 *Fun* produced a contemptuous comic-strip titled 'The Idiot Detective, or, the Track! The Trial! and The Triumph!', which depicted a hapless police officer following incorrect scents after a criminal. He arrests another officer (who had actually managed to apprehend the *real* criminal), before assaulting a child, much to the appreciation of an overfed magistrate with a hair-style that resembles devil-horns. The magistrate labels the child's resistance '[...] one of the most brutal and *unmanly* assaults ever committed on the police'. The 'idiot detective' is then pensioned for life for his 'services', and is depicted as 'triumphant' in the final panel of the strip, drawn in a pose that resembles the statue of Lady Justice, peering out from underneath a blindfold over his eyes, truncheon in one hand and scales in the other, striking others down before him (see Figure. 1.1).[115]

There is certainly a lot to unpack here. The incompetent detective, naturally, represented all police officers who, the piece suggested, regularly apprehended the wrong suspects and made poor (and occasionally outrageous) decisions in the execution of their duties. The fact that the incompetent detective peers out from underneath the blindfold when arranged like the statue of Justice also intimated at corruption within the force. The fat, devil-horned magistrate

Figure 1.1 'The Idiot Detective, or, the Track! The Trial! and the Triumph!'
Source: *Fun*, 2 January 1869, p. 13. Image published with permission of ProQuest. Further reproduction is prohibited without permission.

represented the bureaucratic and similarly corrupt arm of the justice system, accepting and even rewarding the police's inadequacies and spinning them to the public as somehow admirable qualities.

There are vast numbers of other articles from other periodicals that could be quoted in this section, but space constraints mean that it must end here. However, these brief examples of depictions of the police in the wider periodical press demonstrate a singular, rather important conclusion. Unlike the partisan press, which naturally drew its criticism of the police along ideological line, the non-partisan press was more disorganised, varied and multifarious simply *because* it was often not bound by political restrictions.[116] This, in far broader terms, these magazines and their often conflicting viewpoints on the force helped to cement the police ever more firmly as part of the social fabric, given that all the perspectives on the force – critical or supportive, all accepted them as a part of everyday life. Even commentary such as that which was presented in satirical magazines that largely attacked the police and their efficiency helped to solidify the police's presence as part of wider society, permeating a universal (sometimes literal) image of the uniformed officer and subsequently accepting them as a permanent, if occasionally unwelcome, institution.

Positioning the Police Officer

In spite of their frequently-polarised and multifarious representation in various areas of the periodical press, it is now worth clearly iterating that there was a singular, unifying, common perspective on the police present in almost all mid-Victorian commentary. In short, the press discussions of the force helped to create and cultivate the idea that the police officer was a figure who occupied a transitional, fringe or somehow threshold social space, located somewhere in between the criminal and the rest of society. Criticism of the police consistently suggested – either directly or indirectly – that they operated largely on the boundaries of respectable civilization, and this notion appears repeatedly in a variety of periodicals and articles of almost all persuasions. It is thus the unifying feature which ties *all* of this journalistic criticism on the police together, and it is to become very significant in the context of the later parts of this volume.

This theme is therefore worth exploring in its own right in order to make it abundantly clear, and we shall return to some of our earlier examples in order to do it effectively. The 'The Police of London' article from the July 1870 issue of the *Quarterly Review*, for example, provides a particularly strong route in. I quoted this piece earlier when exploring periodical perceptions of the force's overall effectiveness; however, it also has some relevance here:

> For the same reason that the lawless classes arrayed against society are weak, the constabulary forces arrayed in defence of society are strong. [...] take any man from [the] mob, place a baton in his hand and a blue coat upon his back, put him forward as a representative of the law, and he too will be found equally ready to face the mob from which he was taken, and exhibit the same steadfastness and courage in defence of constituted order.[117]

The statement that the 'constabulary forces' were 'arrayed in defence of society' clearly positions the police *between* society and the 'mob' of criminals, and this codifies the force as socially external, somewhere between the respectable public and acting as a barrier or metaphorical shield against the dangers of crime. The 'mob', so to speak, threatened the existence and safety of the social order, and so the police were deployed along its frontier to protect society from the threat that criminals apparently posed. Thus, the police's role as defenders of the social order actually caused them to become separated them from it. Indeed, the police are specifically presented here as *in defence* of society which, naturally, leads to an implication that they were not part of it themselves.

The largely 'external' social position of the police officer outside of extant class structures is also evident in the 1858 article from *Blackwood's Edinburgh Magazine*, titled 'Our Convicts – Past and Present'. This highlighted the police officer's powers of observation in a proto-Foucauldian sense,[118] noting their ability to spot discrepancies within the social fabric that the ordinary member of the public would likely have missed:

> The detective officer knows the thief, not only individually but generically. [...] the accomplished detective will mark his man among the thousands of faces in a full night in Covent Garden [...][119]

The piece argued that police officers possessed the ability to understand, observe, and interact with those perceived to be the 'criminal classes' on their own level. This, I again suggest, demarcated the police from the wider public who could *not* spot latent criminality in the same way, pushing them to the boundaries of society and largely out of the everyday person's field of view. In fact, the same article went on to highlight this apparently-*conscious* social separation of the police even more clearly, when it argued:

> *Kept in its proper place*, an increased force will be an eminent boon to the honest portion of the community [my italics].[120]

The phrase 'kept in its proper place' is naturally significant, as this gestures towards the idea that some critics, while supportive of the police's abilities and presence, preferred to maintain their support for them from a distance, and therefore did not see the police as part of their own social sphere. They were happy to reap the benefits offered by the existence and protection of the police and were even willing to praise the force for its efforts when it was successful, but at the same time they repeatedly placed the force in a fringed, peripheral position that was largely separate from themselves.

From a slightly more complicated perspective, other commentary on the police (particularly that which was slightly more sceptical regarding its effectiveness) also positioned the police officer as distinct or separate from respectable society. However, unlike more supportive discourse that presented the force as a protective shield, this kind of commentary isolated the police by tying the figure of the police officer to that of the *criminal*, thereby presenting them as somehow socially undesirable and therefore socially demarcated. The review of Custos's *The Police Force of the Metropolis* that appeared in the *Contemporary Review* in 1869 can highlight this at work, when it suggested that the work of the police force inherently linked it to the criminals it was meant to apprehend:

> Of course the question which the general public has been for some time repeating is, not, Why don't the police succeed in recovering our property and bringing the criminal to justice? but, How is it that thousands of notorious criminals are allowed to live in our midst, and carry on their practices under our very eyes, when the police know them, their vocation, and their abodes?[121]

The second rhetorical question in this quotation, in particular, placed responsibility for managing society's criminals squarely on the police through its suggestion that it was the force that was directly responsible for 'knowing' society's criminal element. The police were thus tied to the criminal through their daily interaction with criminals, and their knowledge of their 'vocation' and 'abodes' essentially criminalised them just enough for them to be perceived as separated from the rest of the 'un'-criminalised general population. In short, the police operated with criminals on the periphery of society, and this operation was both undesirable and almost always out of the view of the rest of the public. Even pieces that were supportive of the police recognised this pervading link between police and criminal; in 'The Police and the Thieves' from the *Quarterly Review*, for example, the author attempted to portray this relationship as both pseudo-professional and somehow mischievous:

> Between the detective and the thief there is no ill blood: when they meet they give an odd wink of recognition to each other – the thief smiling, as much to say, 'I am quite safe, you know;' and the detective replying with a look, of which the interpretation is, 'We shall be better acquainted, by and by.' They both feel, in short, that they are using their wits to get their living, and there is a sort of tacit understanding between them that each is entitled to play his game as well as he can.[122]

A particularly strong and critical example of the police's pseudo-criminalised and peripheral social position appeared in the *Saturday Review* in October 1872. An article titled 'Where are the Police?' was included in this issue, and the title itself is quite useful in the context of this argument as it gestures nicely towards the police's perceived socially indistinct nature. The simple answer to the rhetorical question it poses is that, much of the time, we simply do not know where they are. The article itself examined a conviction of a woman operating in violation of the Licensing Act by illegally selling alcohol when she should not have been. However, the piece focused its attention on two police officers who were seen drinking and fraternising with barmaids whilst on duty. The officers claimed that they were simply there to spy on (and apprehend) those who were contravening the law, but the *Saturday Review* was understandably sceptical:

> Next night he went to the same house, accompanied by a constable, and taking with him a sovereign derived from some unexplained source, to be expended in treating the young ladies of the establishment to "fizz." We must suppose that the sergeant sat on one sofa with a girl, and that the constable sat on another sofa with another girl, until they had drunk all the "fizz" and *completed the evidence in the case.*[123]

Once more, then, we see evidence of the police's positioning outside of respectable society, somewhere between the public and criminality. This article suggested that the police operated on the periphery of respectable society and outside of everyday class distinctions, by interacting with criminals, inhabiting the same spaces as them, and often succumbing to the same temptations. In addition, aside from rather sarcastically suggesting that the police were essentially criminals themselves, the piece also indirectly highlighted how the police were *supposed* to act barrier for the public against society's criminal element. It pointed out that while the police officers were off enjoying themselves with barmaids, other criminals would naturally take advantage of their absence:

We hope that while in the strict performance of duty they are sitting upon sofas with girls and drinking "fizz," garrotters and burglars may not improve the occasion thus presented.[124]

In short, *all* sides of the debate surrounding the police in periodicals, consciously or unconsciously, contributed to the idea that the police were largely separated from the general public that they were supposed to protect. Almost all critical perspectives on the police either saw them as excellent protectors of a society to which they did not wholly belong, or saw their constant connection to criminality as reason for them to be kept at arm's length. In *either* case, the police were repeatedly demarcated away from the core public, and were thus viewed to operate on the very outer edges or frontiers of society. This, as we will see in later chapters, had extensive ramifications for the construction of other kinds of writing which developed alongside criticism of the police force.

The Police and the Periodical Press: Chapter 1 Conclusions

An enormous variety of periodicals and magazines published between 1850 and 1870 were concerned with the social, economic, and political implications of nationwide policing, right from its inception. The discussion that took place in the pages of periodicals helped to cement the police firmly as part of the social fabric, and I argue that this improved public understanding of law enforcement could not have been achieved without the influence of extensive periodical discussion. In fact, 'The Police and the Thieves' from the *Quarterly Review* made this abundantly clear, when it argued that '[the police] are now looked upon as a constitutional force, simply because we have gotten accustomed to them'.[125]

Consequently, as an early section in this chapter pointed out, the vast surviving numbers of articles and images of the police force available from a huge variety of periodicals means that this opening chapter has barely touched the surface of potential periodical commentary on law enforcement and the management of crime. Instead, it has merely endeavoured to present good, representative examples of articles that commented on the police from a variety of socio-political backgrounds and from a variety of cultural or economic perspectives. It has done this so that later parts of the volume can highlight how interest in the police shown in such an eclectic variety of publications had a profound impact on other forms of cultural production, such as other kinds of journalism and, of course, fiction.

The differences in periodical criticism of the police came largely from external influences on publications themselves. In the politically-minded press, for example, explorations of nationwide policing were distorted by each publication's own political ideologies or allegiances, while in the partisan press these external influences surrounded the publication's individual cultural interest. However, it is again worth pointing out that magazines of *all* persuasions helped to cultivate the idea that the police occupied a transitional or indistinct space between the criminal classes and the rest of society and that they operated on the outskirts of respectable civilisation. A final, particularly clear example of this can be taken from the *National Review*, which in 1883 published the first in a series of articles titled 'Homes of the Criminal Classes' by politician Hugh E. Hoare (1854–1929). This rather nicely highlights the politically-universal nature of the view of the police as socially-liminal; the *National Review* was an openly Tory magazine, while Hoare himself was eventually a Liberal MP. Hoare identified a distinct 'criminal' class that inhabited its own urban space that was segregated by the presence of the police:

> [...] a street in the East End, which I knew by repute as having the best claim to the title of the worst street in London. I had only twice walked through the street, and the first time I was warned by a policeman, as I turned down into it, to "look out where I was going to."[126]

Naturally, the most interesting figure here is that of the police officer, depicted as physically stood on the street corner at the pseudo-'entrance' to the criminal area of the city of which he has knowledge, and the author does not. He is thus both literally and figuratively placed in a space somewhere between the 'criminal world' and the rest of respectable society, keeping the two separate and operating somewhere along the periphery, out of the sight of the general public.

Notes

1 Clive Emsley, *The English Police: A Political and Social History* (London: Routledge, 2014 (orig. 1991)), p. 43.
2 Barbara Korte, 'On Heroes and Hero Worship: Regimes of Emotional Investment in Mid-Victorian Popular Magazines', *Victorian Periodicals Review*, 49, 2 (2016), 181–201 (p. 181).
3 Anthea Trodd, 'The Policeman and the Lady: Significant Encounters in Victorian Fiction', *Victorian Studies*, 27, 4 (1984), pp. 435–460 (p. 440).
4 Clive Emsley, 'A Typology of Nineteenth-Century Police', *Crime, Histoire & Sociétés (Crime, History & Societies)*, 3, 1 (1999), pp. 29–44 (p. 30).
5 Emsley, 'A Typology of Nineteenth-Century Police', pp. 29–44 (p. 30).
6 Caroline Reitz, 'Colonial "Gwilt": In and Around Wilkie Collins's *Armadale*', *Victorian Periodicals Review*, 33, 1 (*Cornhill Magazine Special Issue II*) (2000), 92–103 (p. 93).
7 Richard Altick, *The English Common Reader: A Social History of the Mass-Reading Public*, 2nd Edition (Ohio: Ohio State University Press, 1998), pp. 81–82.
8 Aled Jones, 'Local Journalism in Victorian Political Culture', in *Investigating Victorian Journalism*, ed. by Laurel Brake, Aled Jones and Lionel Madden (Basingstoke: Macmillan, 1990), pp. 63–70 (p. 63).
9 Stephen Koss, *The Rise and Fall of the Political Press in Britain: The Nineteenth Century* (London: Fontana Press, 1990), p. 4.
10 Martin Hewitt, *The Dawn of the Cheap Press in Victorian Britain: The End of the 'Taxes on Knowledge', 1849–1869* (London: Bloomsbury, 2014), p. 11.
11 Hewitt, p. 11.
12 Hewitt, p. 11.
13 Koss, p. 4.
14 Altick, p. 83.

15 Aled Jones and Matthew Taunton, 'Politics and the Press', in *Dictionary of Nineteenth Century Journalism*, ed. by Laurel Brake and Marysa Demoor (London and Ghent: Academia Press, 2009), p. 500.

16 Rosalind Crone, 'Popular Press', in *Dictionary of Nineteenth Century Journalism*, ed. by Laurel Brake and Marysa Demoor (London and Ghent: Academia Press, 2009), p. 501.

17 Trodd, pp. 435–460 (p. 445). See also Martin Wiener, 'Convicted Murderers and the Victorian Press: Condemnation vs. Sympathy', *Crime and Misdemeanours*, 1, 2 (2007), pp. 110–125 (p. 122).

18 Sally Mitchell, *Victorian Britain* (Abingdon: Routledge, 1988; repr. 2012), p. 188.

19 Mitchell, p. 189.

20 Mitchell, p. 189.

21 Mitchell, p. 189.

22 David Finkelstein, '*Blackwood's Edinburgh Magazine* (1817–1980)', in *Dictionary of Nineteenth Century Journalism*, ed. by Laurel Brake and Marysa Demoor (London and Ghent: Academia Press, 2009), p. 60.

23 Damian Atkinson, '*New Monthly Magazine* (1814–1884)', in *Dictionary of Nineteenth Century Journalism*, ed. by Laurel Brake and Marysa Demoor (London and Ghent: Academia Press, 2009), p. 443.

24 David Ian Morphet, '*Quarterly Review* (1809–1967)', in *Dictionary of Nineteenth Century Journalism*, ed. by Laurel Brake and Marysa Demoor (London and Ghent: Academia Press, 2009), p. 522.

25 Mark W. Turner, '*Fraser's Magazine for Town and Country* (1830–1882)', in *Dictionary of Nineteenth Century Journalism*, ed. by Laurel Brake and Marysa Demoor (London and Ghent: Academia Press, 2009), p. 228.

26 The *National Review* included a quotation from Lord Beaconsfield (Disraeli) in its masthead: 'What is the Tory Party, unless it represents national feeling?'.

27 Aled Jones and Matthew Taunton, 'Political Parties and the Press', in *Dictionary of Nineteenth Century Journalism*, ed. by Laurel Brake and Marysa Demoor (London and Ghent: Academia Press, 2009), p. 499.

28 See the relationship between the radical press and organisations such as Charles Knight's/Henry Brougham's Society for the Diffusion of Useful Knowledge for a good representation of this.

29 Jones and Taunton, 'Political Parties and the Press', in *Dictionary of Nineteenth Century Journalism*, ed. by Brake and Demoor, p. 499.

30 David Magee, ''Unstamped' Press', in *Dictionary of Nineteenth Century Journalism*, ed. by Laurel Brake and Marysa Demoor (London and Ghent: Academia Press, 2009), p. 648.

31 Joanne Shattock, '*Edinburgh Review* (1802–1929)', in *Dictionary of Nineteenth Century Journalism*, ed. by Laurel Brake and Marysa Demoor (London and Ghent: Academia Press, 2009), pp. 190–191 (p. 190).

32 Mark W. Turner, '*Fortnightly Review* (1865–1954)', in *Dictionary of Nineteenth Century Journalism*, ed. by Laurel Brake and Marysa Demoor (London and Ghent: Academia Press, 2009), pp. 227–228 (p. 228).

33 Anthony Cummins, '*Contemporary Review* (1866–1988)', in *Dictionary of Nineteenth Century Journalism*, ed. by Laurel Brake and Marysa Demoor (London and Ghent: Academia Press, 2009), p. 139.

34 Merion Hughes, '*Macmillan's Magazine* (1859–1907)', in *Dictionary of Nineteenth Century Journalism*, ed. by Laurel Brake and Marysa Demoor (London and Ghent: Academia Press, 2009), p. 389.

35 Gladstone contributed over 60 articles to the *Nineteenth Century: A Monthly Review*. Mark W. Turner, '*Nineteenth Century: A Monthly Review* (1877–1901)', in *Dictionary of Nineteenth Century Journalism*, ed. by Laurel Brake and Marysa Demoor (London and Ghent: Academia Press, 2009), p. 456.

36   Morphet, '*Quarterly Review* (1809–1967)', in *Dictionary of Nineteenth Century Journalism*, ed. by Brake and Demoor, p. 522.

37   Atkinson, '*New Monthly Magazine* (1814–1884)', in *Dictionary of Nineteenth Century Journalism*, ed. by Brake and Demoor, p. 443.

38   Turner, '*Fraser's Magazine for Town and Country* (1830–1882)', in *Dictionary of Nineteenth Century Journalism*, ed. by Brake and Demoor, p. 228.

39   Wiener, pp. 110–125 (p. 124).

40   In fact, liberal-aligned publications also had a historic precedent for particularly railing against law enforcement, as even throughout the early nineteenth century a number of publications had already begun to criticise the idea as an unwanted, corrupt, untrustworthy and continental invention. The fact that the French system of policing had predated the British meant that a number of British publications were already sceptical of the police far before the idea was floated in Britain. This was especially the case during (and in the aftermath of) the Napoleonic Wars. For a good example of this in action, see 'The French Police (Cautions to all British Travellers)', *Weekly Entertainer*, 2 December 1816, pp. 971–972.

41   Robert Peel had famously been responsible for the passage of the 1829 Metropolitan Police Act, and at the time of the passage of the 1856 County and Borough Police Act it was a coalition of Peelite Conservatives and Whigs, under the premiership of the conservative Lord Aberdeen, in government.

42   'Imprisonment and Transportation I: The Increase of Crime', *Blackwood's Edinburgh Magazine*, May 1844, pp. 535–536.

43   'The Police and the Thieves', *Quarterly Review*, June 1856, pp. 160–200 (p. 160).

44   An erroneous claim; Peel's efforts to establish a uniformed system of policing had historically been met with resistance in the Commons until the eventual approval of the 1829 Metropolitan Police Act.

45   'The Police and the Thieves', *Quarterly Review*, June 1856, pp. 160–200 (p. 160).

46   'The Police and the Thieves', *Quarterly Review*, June 1856, pp. 160–200 (p. 164).

47   'The Police and the Thieves', *Quarterly Review*, June 1856, pp. 160–200 (p. 166).

48   'Our Convicts – Past and Present', *Blackwood's Edinburgh Magazine*, March 1858, p. 299.

49   'The Police of London', *Quarterly Review*, July 1870, pp. 90–91.

50   Alexander Innes Shand, 'The City of London Police', *Blackwood's Edinburgh Magazine*, November 1886, p. 594.

51   'Review of Books: The Police Force of the Metropolis by Custos, London: Ridgway', *Contemporary Review*, May 1869, p. 477.

52   Shattock, '*Edinburgh Review* (1802–1929)', in *Dictionary of Nineteenth Century Journalism*, ed. by Brake and Demoor, p. 190.

53   Elizabeth Tilley, '*Saturday Review of Politics, Literature, Science, and Art* (1855–1938)', in *Dictionary of Nineteenth Century Journalism*, ed. by Laurel Brake and Marysa Demoor (London and Ghent: Academia Press, 2009), pp. 557–558.

54   'Inefficiency of the London Police', *Saturday Review*, 30 April 1870, p. 575.

55   'The Jewel Robberies', *Saturday Review*, 14 May 1870, p. 640.

56   'The Jewel Robberies', *Saturday Review*, 14 May 1870, p. 640.

57   'Police Rule', *Saturday Review*, 15 November 1873, p. 625.

58   'The Police System of London', *Edinburgh Review*, July 1852, pp. 1–33.

59   'The Police and the Thieves', pp. 160–200 (pp. 162–164).

60   'The Police and the Thieves', pp. 160–200 (pp. 162–164).

61   'Laissez-Faire', *Fraser's Magazine for Town and Country*, January 1870, p. 72.

62   'Laissez-Faire', *Fraser's Magazine for Town and Country*, January 1870, p. 72.

63   'Laissez-Faire', *Fraser's Magazine for Town and Country*, January 1870, p. 76.

64   John Paget, 'The Wigtown Martyrs', *Blackwood's Edinburgh Magazine*, December 1863, p. 743.

65   'The Police of London', *Quarterly Review*, July 1870, p. 90.

66   'The Progress of Murder', *Reynolds's Newspaper*, 17 July 1864, p. 1. Cited in Warren Fox, 'Murder in Daily Installments: The Newspapers and the Case of Franz Müller (1864)', *Victorian Periodicals Review*, 31, 3 (1998), 271–298 (p. 281).

67   'Our Perjured Police', *Reynolds's Newspaper*, 6 September 1861, p. 2.

68   'Our Perjured Police', *Reynolds's Newspaper*, 6 September 1861, p. 2.

69   Turner, '*Fortnightly Review* (1865–1954)', in *Dictionary of Nineteenth Century Journalism*, ed. by Brake and Demoor, p. 227.

70   Turner, '*Fortnightly Review* (1865–1954)', in *Dictionary of Nineteenth Century Journalism*, ed. by Brake and Demoor, pp. 227–228.

71   The experiment failed; after 20 months it actually became a monthly (though the name '*Fortnightly*' stuck). See Turner, '*Fortnightly Review* (1865–1954)', in *Dictionary of Nineteenth Century Journalism*, ed. by Brake and Demoor, p. 228.

72   Frederic Harrison, 'The Transit of Power', *Fortnightly Review*, April 1868, p. 384.

73   Sheldon Amos, 'Civilisation and Crime', *Fortnightly Review*, 15 September 1865, p. 320.

74   Amos, p. 320.

75   Amos, p. 328.

76   See 'Introduction', this volume.

77   Edwin Chadwick, 'On the Consolidation of the Police Force and the Prevention of Crime', *Fraser's Magazine*, January 1868, pp. 7–11.

78   George Henry Lewes, 'Uncivilised Man', *Blackwood's Edinburgh Magazine*, January 1861, p. 27.

79   Lewes, p. 35.

80   Robert Gregory, 'Criminal Statistics', *Quarterly Review*, October 1874, pp. 527–529. The tables in these pages begin showing statistics from 1834, however the same pages state that records began in 1805.

81   Gregory, 'Criminal Statistics', pp. 533–534.

82   Gregory, 'Criminal Statistics', p. 532.

83   Gregory, 'Criminal Statistics', p. 533.

84   Chadwick, 'On the Consolidation of the Police Force and the Prevention of Crime', p. 15.

85   Chadwick wrote at least one other piece making this argument, which appeared in the *Contemporary Review* in 1884. In an article titled 'London Centralized', Chadwick repeated his suggestion that 'complete unity' of disjointed police forces would not increase their expense, but would substantially augment their efficiency. See Edwin Chadwick, 'London Centralized', *Contemporary Review*, June 1884, p. 801.

86   John Ruskin, 'Essays on Political Economy', *Fraser's Magazine*, April 1863, p. 442.

87   Christopher Casey, 'Common Misperceptions: The Press and Victorian Views of Crime', *Journal of Interdisciplinary History*, 41, 3 (2011), 367–391 (p. 368).

88   Hamish Maxwell-Stewart and Emma Watkins, 'Transportation', *The Digital Panopticon* <https://www.digitalpanopticon.org/Transportation> [accessed 26 March 2020].

89   Neil R. Storey, *Prisons and Prisoners in Victorian Britain* (Cheltenham: The History Press, 2010), pp. 12, 17.

90   Ground Plan of HM Prison Cold Bath Fields, *National Archives* <http://www.nationalarchives.gov.uk/wp-content/uploads/2014/03/a-victorian-prison-source-1.jpg> [Accessed July 2020] (1884).

91   Rosalind Crone, 'The Great "Reading" Experiment: An Examination of the Role of Education in Nineteenth-Century Gaol, *Crime, Histoire & Sociétés/Crime, History and Societies*, 16, 1 (2012), 47–74 (pp. 47–50).

92   'Review of Books: The Police Force of the Metropolis by Custos, London: Ridgway', *Contemporary Review*, May 1869, p. 477.

93   Herbert Graham, 'Public and Private Prosecutors', *Fortnightly Review*, 1 August 1865, p. 676.

94 George Odger, 'The Employment of Criminals', *Contemporary Review*, August 1870, pp. 465–466.
95 Shattock, '*Edinburgh Review* (1802–1929)', in *Dictionary of Nineteenth Century Journalism*, ed. by Brake and Demoor, pp. 190–191.
96 'Our Convicts.', *Edinburgh Review*, October 1865, p. 338.
97 A good example of this includes the *Ragged School Union Magazine*, published by the Ragged Schools Union between 1849 and 1875.
98 Christopher M. Banham, '*Boy's Own Magazine* (1855–1874)', in *Dictionary of Nineteenth Century Journalism*, ed. by Laurel Brake and Marysa Demoor (London and Ghent: Academia Press, 2009), p. 70.
99 Frank Murray, '*British Workman* (1855–1921)', in *Dictionary of Nineteenth Century Journalism*, ed. by Laurel Brake and Marysa Demoor (London and Ghent: Academia Press, 2009), p. 80 and Margaret Beetham, '*British Workwoman* (1863–1896)', in *Dictionary of Nineteenth Century Journalism*, ed. by Laurel Brake and Marysa Demoor (London and Ghent: Academia Press, 2009), p. 80.
100 E. Foley O'Connor, '*Chambers's (Edinburgh) Journal* (1832–1956)', in *Dictionary of Nineteenth Century Journalism*, ed. by Laurel Brake and Marysa Demoor (London and Ghent: Academia Press, 2009), p. 106.
101 'Criminal Statistics', *Chambers's Journal*, 11 February 1860, p. 84.
102 'The Metropolitan Police and what is Paid for Them', *Chambers's Journal*, 2 July 1864, p. 424.
103 Leora Bersohn, '*Examiner* (1808–1881)', in *Dictionary of Nineteenth Century Journalism*, ed. by. Laurel Brake and Marysa Demoor (London and Ghent: Academia Press, 2009), p. 211.
104 'The Police', *Examiner*, 11 August 1866, p. 498.
105 'Capital Punishment Without Trial', *Examiner*, 9 January 1869, p. 19.
106 'The London Police', *Examiner*, 23 November 1872, p. 1148.
107 'The London Police', *Examiner*, 23 November 1872, p. 1148.
108 Brian Maidment, '*Punch* (1841–2002)', in *Dictionary of Nineteenth Century Journalism*, ed. by Laurel Brake and Marysa Demoor (London and Ghent: Academia Press, 2009), p. 517.
109 'The Rural Police', *Punch, or, the London Charivari*, 15 March 1856, p. 107.
110 'Policeman's Logic', *Punch, or, the London Charivari*, 5 January 1856, p. 10.
111 This image was originally included as an image in an early draft of this volume, however tight copyright restrictions have sadly prevented it from being reprinted here.
112 Brian Maidment, '*Fun* (1861–1901)', in *Dictionary of Nineteenth Century Journalism*, ed. by Laurel Brake and Marysa Demoor (London and Ghent: Academia Press, 2009), p. 237.
113 Alvin Sullivan, *British Literary Magazines: The Victorian and Edwardian Age, 1837–1913* (London: Greenwood Press, 1984), p. 135.
114 'Police!', *Fun*, 8 March 1873, p. 106.
115 'The Idiot Detective, or, the Track! The Trial! and the Triumph!', *Fun*, 2 January 1869, p. 13. Image produced by ProQuest as part of *British Periodicals*. www.proquest.com.
116 This is not to suggest that non-partisan periodicals did not have political viewpoints; they often did so, however it is to suggest that they were not inherently or consistently tied by them.
117 'The Police of London', *Quarterly Review*, July 1870, pp. 90–91.
118 See Michel Foucault, *Discipline and Punish: The Birth of the Prison* (New York: Vintage, 1977).
119 'Our Convicts – Past and Present', *Blackwood's Edinburgh Magazine*, March 1858, p. 299.
120 'Our Convicts – Past and Present', *Blackwood's Edinburgh Magazine*, March 1858, p. 299.

121   'Review of Books: *The Police Force of the Metropolis* by Custos, London: Ridgway', *Contemporary Review*, May 1869, p. 477.
122   'The Police and the Thieves', *Quarterly Review*, June 1856, pp. 160–200 (p. 176).
123   'Where are the Police?', *Saturday Review*, 12 October 1872, p. 465.
124   'Where are the Police?', *Saturday Review*, 12 October 1872, p. 465.
125   'The Police and the Thieves', *Quarterly Review*, June 1856, pp. 160–200 (p. 164).
126   Hugh E. Hoare, 'Homes of the Criminal Classes', *National Review*, April 1883, p. 224.

Bibliography

Primary Periodical Material

Amos, Sheldon, 'Civilisation and Crime', *Fortnightly Review*, 15 September 1865, pp. 319–328.

'Capital Punishment Without Trial', *Examiner*, 9 January 1869, p. 19

Chadwick, Edwin, 'London Centralized', *Contemporary Review*, June 1884, pp. 794–810.

Chadwick, Edwin, 'On the Consolidation of the Police Force and the Prevention of Crime', *Fraser's Magazine*, January 1868, pp. 1–18.

'Criminal Statistics', *Chambers's Journal*, 11 February 1860, pp. 84–86.

Graham, Herbert, 'Public and Private Prosecutors', *Fortnightly Review*, 1 August 1865, pp. 675–684.

Gregory, Robert, 'Criminal Statistics', *Quarterly Review*, October 1874, pp. 526–542.

Harrison, Frederic, 'The Transit of Power', *Fortnightly Review*, April 1868, pp. 374–396.

Hoare, Hugh E., 'Homes of the Criminal Classes', *National Review*, April 1883, pp. 224–239.

'Imprisonment and Transportation I: The Increase of Crime', *Blackwood's Edinburgh Magazine*, May 1844, pp. 533–545.

'Inefficiency of the London Police', *Saturday Review*, 30 April 1870, pp. 574–575.

'Laissez-Faire', *Fraser's Magazine for Town and Country*, January 1870, pp. 72–83.

Lewes, George Henry, 'Uncivilised Man', *Blackwood's Edinburgh Magazine*, January 1861, pp. 27–41.

Odger, George, 'The Employment of Criminals', *Contemporary Review*, August 1870, pp. 463–478.

'Our Convicts – Past and Present', *Blackwood's Edinburgh Magazine*, March 1858, pp. 291–310.

'Our Convicts', *Edinburgh Review*, October 1865, pp. 337–371.

'Our Perjured Police', *Reynolds's Newspaper*, 6 September 1861, p. 2.

Paget, John, 'The Wigtown Martyrs', *Blackwood's Edinburgh Magazine*, December 1863, pp. 742–748.

'Police Rule', *Saturday Review*, 15 November 1873, pp. 623–625.

'Police!', *Fun*, 8 March 1873, p. 106.

'Policeman's Logic', *Punch, or, the London Charivari*, 5 January 1856, p. 10.

'Review of Books: *The Police Force of the Metropolis* by Custos, London: Ridgway', *Contemporary Review*, May 1869, pp. 477–478.

Ruskin, John, 'Essays on Political Economy', *Fraser's Magazine*, April 1863, pp. 441–462.

Shand, Alexander Innes, 'The City of London Police', *Blackwood's Edinburgh Magazine*, November 1886, pp. 594–608.

'The French Police (Cautions to all British Travellers)', *Weekly Entertainer*, 2 December 1816, pp. 971–975.

'The Idiot Detective, or, the Track! The Trial! and the Triumph!', *Fun*, 2 January 1869, p. 13

'The Jewel Robberies', *Saturday Review*, 14 May 1870, pp. 639–640.

'The London Police', *Examiner*, 23 November 1872, pp. 1148–1149.

'The Metropolitan Police and what is Paid for Them', *Chambers's Journal*, 2 July 1864, pp. 423–426.

'The Police and the Thieves', *Quarterly Review*, June 1856, pp. 160–200.

'The Police of London', *Quarterly Review*, July 1870, pp. 87–129.

'The Police System of London', *Edinburgh Review*, July 1852, pp. 1–33.

'The Police', *Examiner*, 11 August 1866, p. 498.

'The Progress of Murder', *Reynolds's Newspaper*, 17 July 1864, p. 1.

'The Rural Police', *Punch, or, the London Charivari*, 15 March 1856, p. 107.

'Where are the Police?', *Saturday Review*, 12 October 1872, pp. 464–465.

Secondary Material

Altick, Richard, *The English Common Reader: A Social History of the Mass-Reading Public* (Ohio: Ohio State University Press, 1957; repr. 1998).

Atkinson, Damian, 'New Monthly Magazine (1814–1884)', in *Dictionary of Nineteenth Century Journalism*, ed. by Laurel Brake and Marysa Demoor (London and Ghent: Academia Press, 2009), p. 443.

Banham, Christopher M., 'Boy's Own Magazine (1855–1874)', *in Dictionary of Nineteenth Century Journalism*, ed. by Laurel Brake and Marysa Demoor (London and Ghent: Academia Press, 2009), p. 70.

Beetham, Margaret, 'British Workwoman (1863–1896)', in *Dictionary of Nineteenth Century Journalism*, ed. by Laurel Brake and Marysa Demoor (London and Ghent: Academia Press, 2009), p. 80.

Bersohn, Leora, 'Examiner (1808–1881)', in *Dictionary of Nineteenth Century Journalism*, ed. by Laurel Brake and Marysa Demoor (London and Ghent: Academia Press, 2009), p. 211.

Brake, Laurel and Marysa Demoor (eds.), *Dictionary of Nineteenth-Century Journalism* (London and Ghent: Academia Press, 2009).

Brake, Laurel, Aled Jones and Lionel Madden (eds.), *Investigating Victorian Journalism* (Basingstoke: Macmillan, 1990).

Casey, Christopher, 'Common Misperceptions: The Press and Victorian Views of Crime', *Journal of Interdisciplinary History*, 41, 3 (2011), 367–391.

Crone, Rosalind, 'Popular Press', in *Dictionary of Nineteenth Century Journalism*, ed. by Laurel Brake and Marysa Demoor (London and Ghent: Academia Press, 2009), p. 501.

Crone, Rosalind, 'The Great "Reading" Experiment: An Examination of the Role of Education in Nineteenth-Century Gaol', *Crime, Histoire & Sociétés/Crime, History and Societies*, 16, 1 (2012), 47–74.

Cummins, Anthony, 'Contemporary Review (1866–1988)', in *Dictionary of Nineteenth Century Journalism*, ed. by Laurel Brake and Marysa Demoor (London and Ghent: Academia Press, 2009), p. 139.

Emsley, Clive, 'A Typology of Nineteenth-Century Police', *Crime, Histoire & Sociétés (Crime, History & Societies)*, 3, 1 (1999), pp. 29–44.

Emsley, Clive, *The English Police: A Political and Social History* (New York: St. Martin's Press, 1991 (repr; London: Routledge, 2014)).

Finkelstein, David, 'Blackwood's Edinburgh Magazine (1817–1980)', in *Dictionary of Nineteenth Century Journalism*, ed. by Laurel Brake and Marysa Demoor (London and Ghent: Academia Press, 2009), p. 60.

Foley O'Connor, E., 'Chambers's (Edinburgh) Journal (1832–1956)', in *Dictionary of Nineteenth Century Journalism*, ed. by Laurel Brake and Marysa Demoor (London and Ghent: Academia Press, 2009), p. 106.

Foucault, Michel, *Discipline and Punish: The Birth of the Prison* (New York: Vintage, 1977).

Fox, Warren, 'Murder in Daily Installments: The Newspapers and the Case of Franz Müller (1864)', *Victorian Periodicals Review*, 31, 3 (1998), 271–298.

Hewitt, Martin, *The Dawn of the Cheap Press in Victorian Britain: The End of the 'Taxes on Knowledge', 1849–1869* (London: Bloomsbury, 2014).

Ground Plan of HM Prison Cold Bath Fields, National Archives <http://www.nationalarchives.gov.uk/wp-content/uploads/2014/03/a-victorian-prison-source-1.jpg> [accessed July 2020] (1884).

Hughes, Merion, 'Macmillan's Magazine (1859–1907)', in *Dictionary of Nineteenth Century Journalism*, ed. by Laurel Brake and Marysa Demoor (London and Ghent: Academia Press, 2009), p. 389.

Jones, Aled and Matthew Taunton, 'Political Parties and the Press', in *Dictionary of Nineteenth Century Journalism*, ed. by Laurel Brake and Marysa Demoor (London and Ghent: Academia Press, 2009), p. 499.

Jones, Aled and Matthew Taunton, 'Politics and the Press', in *Dictionary of Nineteenth Century Journalism*, ed. by Laurel Brake and Marysa Demoor (London and Ghent: Academia Press, 2009), p. 500.

Jones, Aled, 'Local Journalism in Victorian Political Culture', in *Investigating Victorian Journalism*, ed. by Laurel Brake, Aled Jones and Lionel Madden (Basingstoke: Macmillan, 1990), pp. 63–70.

Korte, Barbara, 'On Heroes and Hero Worship: Regimes of Emotional Investment in Mid-Victorian Popular Magazines', *Victorian Periodicals Review*, 49, 2 (2016), 181–201.

Koss, Stephen, *The Rise and Fall of the Political Press in Britain: The Nineteenth Century* (London: Fontana Press, 1990).

Magee, David, 'Unstamped' Press', in *Dictionary of Nineteenth Century Journalism*, ed. by Laurel Brake and Marysa Demoor (London and Ghent: Academia Press, 2009), p. 648.

Maidment, Brian, 'Fun (1861–1901)', in *Dictionary of Nineteenth Century Journalism*, ed. by Laurel Brake and Marysa Demoor (London and Ghent: Academia Press, 2009), p. 237.

Maidment, Brian, 'Punch (1841–2002)', in *Dictionary of Nineteenth Century Journalism*, ed. by Laurel Brake and Marysa Demoor (London and Ghent: Academia Press, 2009), p. 517.

Maxwell-Stewart, Hamish and Emma Watkins, 'Transportation', *The Digital Panopticon* <https://www.digitalpanopticon.org/Transportation> [accessed 26 March 2020].

Mitchell, Sally, *Victorian Britain* (Abingdon: Routledge, 1988; repr. 2012).

Morphet, David Ian, 'Quarterly Review (1809–1967)', in *Dictionary of Nineteenth Century Journalism*, ed. by Laurel Brake and Marysa Demoor (London and Ghent: Academia Press, 2009), p. 522.

Murray, Frank, 'British Workman (1855–1921)', in *Dictionary of Nineteenth Century Journalism*, ed. by Laurel Brake and Marysa Demoor (London and Ghent: Academia Press, 2009), p. 80.

Reitz, Caroline, 'Colonial "Gwilt": In and Around Wilkie Collins's Armadale', *Victorian Periodicals Review*, 33, 1 (*Cornhill Magazine Special Issue II*) (2000), 92–103.

Shattock, Joanne, 'Edinburgh Review (1802–1929)', in *Dictionary of Nineteenth Century Journalism*, ed. by Laurel Brake and Marysa Demoor (London and Ghent: Academia Press, 2009), pp. 190–191.

Storey, Neil R., *Prisons and Prisoners in Victorian Britain* (Cheltenham: The History Press, 2010).

Sullivan, Alvin, *British Literary Magazines: The Victorian and Edwardian Age, 1837–1913* (London: Greenwood Press, 1984).

Tilley, Elizabeth, 'Saturday Review of Politics, Literature, Science, and Art (1855–1938)', in *Dictionary of Nineteenth Century Journalism*, ed. by Laurel Brake and Marysa Demoor (London and Ghent: Academia Press, 2009), pp. 557–558.

Trodd, Anthea, 'The Policeman and the Lady: Significant Encounters in Victorian Fiction', *Victorian Studies*, 27, 4 (1984), pp. 435–460.

Turner, Mark W., 'Fornightly Review (1865–1954)', in *Dictionary of Nineteenth Century Journalism*, ed. by Laurel Brake and Marysa Demoor (London and Ghent: Academia Press, 2009), pp. 227–228.

Turner, Mark W., 'Fraser's Magazine for Town and Country (1830–1882)', in *Dictionary of Nineteenth Century Journalism*, ed. by Laurel Brake and Marysa Demoor (London and Ghent: Academia Press, 2009), p. 228.

Turner, Mark W., 'Nineteenth Century: A Monthly Review (1877–1901)', in *Dictionary of Nineteenth Century Journalism*, ed. by Laurel Brake and Marysa Demoor (London and Ghent: Academia Press, 2009), p. 456.

Wiener, Martin, 'Convicted Murderers and the Victorian Press: Condemnation vs. Sympathy', *Crime and Misdemeanours*, 1, 2 (2007), pp. 110–125.

2   A Condemned Cell with a View
Crime Journalism c. 1750–1880

Introduction: From the Execution Broadside to the Crime 'Round Up'

As this book's first chapter explored, the police received extensive, often politicised criticism in a huge variety of periodicals between around 1850 and 1875. In the aftermath of the 1856 County and Borough Police Act, commentators became interested in the social and political implications of nationwide uniformed law enforcement and used their medium to discuss the force at length. However, perhaps a little surprisingly, journalistic discussion of the police remained almost completely separate from mid-Victorian periodical reporting of crime.

'Crime' was, to put it simply, a far older phenomenon, and was thus already well-established as a topic of both criticism and reporting. Alongside their fierce discussion of the police, therefore, a substantial number of mid-Victorian periodicals, magazines, and newspapers ran feature regular columns that summarised recent criminal events and printed them for the reader's interest – features that are hereafter termed 'crime round ups'. These reported interesting, scandalous, or particularly heinous crimes, often from far-flung locations across Britain and beyond, and helped the press to more actively influence the criminal justice process and played into an ever-increasing public appetite for criminality.[1] Indeed, Judith Knelman quotes Richard Altick to suggest that:

> The policy of the new aggressive, circulation-hungry journalism was to give the broadening public what it wanted; and high on the list of what it wanted was Murder.[2]

The mid-Victorian 'crime round up' evolved out of much older forms of popular reporting.[3] Indeed, crime journalism is widely thought to have originated in the eighteenth century, where it established for itself a diverse literary tradition by appearing in a variety of innovative forms.[4] Perhaps one of its best-known early incarnations was as the cheaply-peddled execution broadside, pamphlet, or chapbook. 'Broadsides' generally consisted of 'an unfolded sheet of paper with printed matter on one side only – a proclamation, poster, handbill, or ballad-sheet',[5] and the form had actually appeared as far back as the sixteenth century.[6] Those that specifically focused on public executions were especially popular between around

1750 and 1840, and were made up of single-page, highly-sensationalised accounts of the lives of criminals and their crimes and punishments, and were frequently accompanied by (occasionally crude but sometimes detailed) woodcut illustrations. They were largely designed to instil fear of judicial vengeance on potential offenders and to provide readers with a grisly form of entertainment, and were sold by street-peddlers directly to the public gathered in crowds at executions themselves, typically for 1d. (or less).[7]

The chaplains of prisons, with the physical and spiritual responsibility for those condemned to death, quickly realised the lucrative potential of publishing their own experiences with criminals and sought to supplement their own income by jumping on the 'crime reporting' bandwagon.[8] They began producing records of their interactions with prisoners awaiting the gallows, and a 'brisk trade in chaplains' accounts of a prisoner's last hours before their execution took shape.[9] These were less sensationalised than execution broadsides, and were more expensive given their supposed ability to provide readers with privileged information from inside the prison that broadsides could not replicate.[10] In 1770, for example, a typical chaplain's pamphlet would cost potential readers 6d., compared to an execution broadside's comparatively-cheap 1d. price tag. Especially popular were those which emerged from inside the infamous Newgate Prison, which became known collectively as the *Ordinary of Newgate's Accounts*, the first of which appeared in 1676 and which continued to be published frequently throughout almost the entire eighteenth century.

Both execution broadsides and prison chaplains' accounts enjoyed considerable popularity with readers, and so it was perhaps only a matter of time before they were given a more permanent form of publication. This took the form of what Knelman terms 'compendiums of criminal careers', the most famous of which was the *Newgate Calendar*.[11] The first *Newgate Calendar* appeared in 1773,[12] however they remained popular throughout almost the entire nineteenth century and were continuously republished under various similar titles, including the *Chronicles of Crime, or, the New Newgate Calendar* and the *Modern Newgate Calendar*.[13] Knelman also helpfully identifies various other 'compendiums' that sought to emulate the *Calendars'* popularity, including Paul Lorraine's *Numerical Account of All Malefactors* (1812); George Borrow's *Celebrated Trials* (1825); *The Calendar of Horrors* (1836); *Poisoners and Slow Poisoning: A Narrative of the Most Remarkable Cases of Poisoning* (1865); *The Life and Recollections of Calcraft, the Hangman* (1871) and *The Groans of the Gallows, in the Past and Present Life of William Calcraft, the Living Hangman of Newgate* (1882).[14] As with the broadsides and chaplains' accounts before them, the *Calendars* and their imitators were designed to simultaneously entertain readers and to steer them away from perceived criminality. Many opted not to focus exclusively on contemporary criminals, but published accounts of historic crimes alongside more recent ones for both entertainment value and to demonstrate how far society had progressed in the way it managed various forms of social deviance.[15] They also helped demonstrate the sheer power of the law and, as

Stephen Knight argues, evidence how society was thought to manage and regulate its own system of law enforcement through ideological means prior to the emergence of the official police.[16]

As we can see, then, the early market for crime journalism was diverse, with different publications presenting their material in different forms, for different purposes, for different prices, and targeting different readerships with different levels of literacy.[17] However, by the mid-Victorian era, almost all of these forms of crime writing had been 'largely supplanted by the popular press'.[18] New articles that reported on recent criminal occurrences began to circulate in magazines. Indeed, as Judith Rowbotham, Kim Stevenson, and Samantha Pegg argue, newspapers and periodicals actually began to constitute the largest medium through which 'crime intelligence' was related to readers in this era.[19]

This second chapter examines the history of crime reporting by looking at how mid-nineteenth century periodical crime 'round ups' were connected with its various older forms through a variety of literary characteristics. It moves away from the politically-focused approach Chapter 1 took[20] in favour of a more thematic methodology, because there were multiple shared themes in both eighteenth- and nineteenth-century crime journalism that helpfully tie them all together. Indeed, as Anne Rodrick argues, crime reports linked new journals and newspapers to traditional modes of popular culture, including chapbooks, broadsides, and the 'scandalous journalism of the early nineteenth century'.[21] The chapter firstly explores the inconsistent presence of the police officer, highlighting how the police's assumption of responsibility for maintaining law and order allowed crime journalism to diversify away from acting as a deterrent to readers by recounting crimes with the most spectacular punishments. It then uses this to build on the argument made in the preceding chapter regarding the position of the police, as the haphazard and often-invisible presence of the police officer in crime reporting further exemplifies how they occupied an unclear space in Victorian social consciousness. Finally, the chapter then switches perspective to explore how crime reporting, in both its mid-Victorian and older incarnations, was quasi-voyeuristic in nature. Crime reporting consistently catered for readers' desires to peek inside criminalised spaces such as court rooms, condemned cells, executions or even convicted criminals' domestic arrangements. This, when coupled with the pervading view of the police as socially-indistinct, had a significant impact on the development of mid-Victorian detective *fiction*, as the collision of these journalistic perspectives, namely the police officer's invisibility and the curiosity of crime reporting, generated new forms of writing – including the first genre to be labelled 'detective literature'.

Mid-Victorian Crime Reporting and the Police Officer

A large number of mid-Victorian periodicals published regular crime 'round ups' that described the latest criminal happenings from up and down the country, designed to furnish the reader with digestible snippets of information on the latest and most interesting crimes. Rather helpfully, in 1851 the *Leader* commented on the purpose of these narratives, arguing that '[t]he records of the assizes and of the police courts sometimes furnish stories as dramatic and extravagant as any detailed by the novelist',[22] and Knelman provides a useful list of newspapers that became interested in printing crime reports around the 1840s and 50s:

> [...] *Lloyd's Weekly Newspaper* and the *Illustrated London News*, founded in 1842, the *News of the World* (1843), the *Daily Express* and the *Daily News* (1846), the *Weekly Times* (1847), and *Reynolds's Newspaper* (1850) [...] pushed the established papers [such as] the *Times,* the *Observer,* the *Advertiser,* the *Chronicle,* the *Herald,* the *Post,* the *Standard,* the *Globe,* and the *Sun* [...] to publish more and more about crime.[23]

It was not only newspapers that produced these features; periodicals and magazines also began to regularly publish crime round ups, including *John Bull,* the *Sixpenny Magazine, Bell's Life in London,* the *Lady's Magazine,* the *Leader,* the *London Review, Once a Week* and the *Spectator,* to name a few. They appeared as regular columns with titles such as 'Law and Police' (*John Bull*), 'Police Intelligence' (*Bell's Life in London*), 'Criminal Record' (the *Leader*), or 'Law and Crime' (the *Sixpenny Magazine*). They were often prominently placed and long-running; *John Bull's* 'Law and Police' column was published weekly throughout the 1860s and well into the 1870s. The features were so common, in fact, that satirical magazines like *Punch* also published mock-versions of their own.[24] A typical example can be seen in Figure 2.1:[25]

At their core, crime round ups were designed to help publications to sell more copies. Indeed, Anne Rodrick cites the radical publisher Henry Hether-ington (of *Poor Man's Guardian* fame)[26] musing on the idea of publishing crime reports in his newspaper the *Twopenny Dispatch* (1834–6):

> Even the ultra-Radical pressman Henry Hetherington, setting out on a new publishing venture [the *Twopenny Dispatch*], catalogued the "sort of dev-ilment that will make it sell": "Police Intelligence, [...] Murders, Rapes, Suicides, Burnings, Maimings, Theatricals, Races, [and] Pugilism".[27]

Hetherington's list of crimes also helpfully highlights the diversity of these narratives even across different issues of the same publication, and this was to become even more pronounced in the mid-Victorian years due to a number of socio-cultural changes catalysed by the presence of the new police. Historical crime reporting in the form of the chap-book, broadside, or compendium had tended to focus on serious crimes such as murder, treason, or piracy, all of which were punished capitally. This was at least partially because they had manifested a form of 'law enforcement' themselves[28] by either instilling fear of judicial or divine retribution in readers or by attempting to create among readers a communal feeling of contempt for criminals who were to suffer the

Figure 2.1 'Criminal Record'
Source: *Leader*, 7 August 1858, p. 767. Image published with permission of ProQuest. Further reproduction is prohibited without permission.

law's ultimate punishment.[29] However, as the police grew, they steadily took on responsibility for managing society's crime, driving both a physical and ideological 'wedge' between criminality and the public.[30] In essence, it was no longer the responsibility for increasingly self-identified 'respectable' readers to engage with crime as the police would manage it for them, and so they became increasingly distanced from it. The police therefore naturally supplanted the historic necessity for crime *journalism* to actively attempt to prevent further crime, and consequently the press was afforded greater freedom to report on more varied cases than simply those with spectacular punishments. Mid-century periodical crime 'round ups' were thus far more diverse in terms of the kinds of crimes they reported and more sanitised in the way they presented them. For example, the 'Police Intelligence' column contained in the July 7 1866 issue of *Bell's Life in London* included such varied cases as 'horse coping', 'cruelty to a dog', and 'throwing vitriol' – a contemporary term for an acid-attack.[31] In August 1861, the *Sixpenny Magazine* even reported a highly complicated case of libel in great detail in its 'Law and Crime' column.[32]

The police's assumption of responsibility for crime, and the consequent distancing of the public away from it, also contributed to the growing rejection of the public execution which, like crime reporting itself, became less necessary as a deterrent. Distaste for public hangings steadily increased in public discourse, and a number of legislative measures culminated in the eventual abolition of public capital punishment across the mid-Victorian era.[33] William Makepeace Thackeray, for example, openly criticised public executions in his essay 'Going to See a Man Hanged', which described his experiences watching the execution of François Courvoisier and which appeared in *Fraser's Magazine for Town and Country* in August 1840. Thackeray argued that public executions were ineffective deterrents as they frequently elicited the opposite feelings in spectators to those which they were designed to instil:

> We asked most of the men [...] whether the sight of [public hangings] did any good? "For that matter, no; people did not care about them at all; nobody ever thought of it after a bit." [...]There is some talk, too, of the terror which the sight of this spectacle inspires [...] I fully confess, that I came away down Snow Hill that morning with a disgust for murder, but it was *the murder I saw done* [original italics].[34]

By far the most interesting aspect of this piece, however, is how Thackeray positioned the *police* as the entity that physically distanced the public from criminality:

> Soon came a squad of policemen; stalwart, rosy-looking men, saying much for city-feeding; well-dressed, well limbed and of admirable good humour. *They paced about the open space between the prison and the barriers which kept the crowd from the scaffold* [my italics].[35]

By placing the police between the crowd and the scaffold, Thackeray inadvertently gestured towards their purpose of physically and ideologically separating the public from crime and occupying the space in between. Their presence prevented a greater degree of interaction between the crowd and the condemned, and actually increased the physical space between the crowd and the scaffold, moving them further apart. Other prominent members of society also railed against public executions; Charles Dickens wrote a series of letters on the subject, to the *Daily News* in 1846 (which also described Courvoisier's execution), and to the *Times* in 1849 (describing the execution of Frederick and Maria Manning at Horsemonger Lane). Dickens particularly focused on the behaviour of the crowd in the face of such a terrible spectacle, and argued that it should become a 'private solemnity within the prison walls'.[36] In fact, the behaviour of the crowd gathered underneath the scaffold was a common point for discussion in reformist periodical commentary on public hangings. Whilst musing on Franz Müller's execution in 1864, the *Examiner* presented a frequent argument that public executions attracted the very criminal classes from which the public were seeking to distance themselves:

> The execution was well attended as all executions are, by all the worst characters with all their worst conduct. The neighbourhood was a pandemonium from Sunday night to Monday morning. Robbery was the least offensive part of that horrid night's work, for it seemed only a due penalty for the presence of any person pretending to respectability at such a spot.[37]

The notion of 'pretence at respectability' is of particular note here, as it further evidences the 'distancing' away from criminality experienced by the public in the wake of the police's proliferation. Rather than encouraging people to attend executions to instil fear or moral guidance, as was the purpose of earlier forms of crime journalism, this instead highlighted the undesirability of doing such a thing in a more 'modern' age where 'respectable' people kept away from such unpleasantness. Perhaps even more interestingly, crime reporting's progression away from providing accompaniment to a supposedly-moralising spectacle was directly referenced in some mid-century periodical commentary, as if it were a conscious change. Indeed, some openly rejected the idea that crime journalism *itself* was meant to furnish readers with gory details and argued, essentially, that they had moved on from such barbarity. In December 1862, for example, the *National Magazine* suggested:

> [...] were "sensation" our object, it would not be difficult to cull from the Newgate Calendar [sic.] scenes and actions sufficiently terrible and startling.[38]

The new presence of the police in society thus helped bring about changes in a number of areas, including in the ways that journalists reported crimes, the kinds of crimes they reported, pervading ideological perspectives on crime itself, and the overall purposes behind the production and dissemination of crime reporting. The police had taken over responsibility for managing society's crime, allowing both publishers and the public to become increasingly distanced from it. Thus, crime reports diversified in content, and increasingly saw both crime itself and extant forms of public punishment as distasteful, as mid-Victorian social divisions solidified and the police grew to occupy the space between the 'respectable' public and 'criminality' that they had actively helped create.

However, despite the observable impacts of the police on periodical crime reporting and discussion, it is interesting to note that *visual* depictions of police officers were almost completely absent from crime round ups and reports. One might be forgiven for assuming that, once the police had been established and (perhaps grudgingly) accepted as a nationwide organisation, they would begin to appear in crime reports, yet this was largely not the case for a number of reasons. As we have seen already, periodical crime 'round ups' had evolved out of earlier literary influences so that, by 1856, 'crime-journalism' was well-established and had no need for the presence of a police officer in order to function. Secondly, despite contemporary rejection of the idea that crime reporting manifested a form of law enforcement in and of itself through describing gruesome punishments, an evolved form of Stephen Knight's argument concerning eighteenth and early nineteenth century social regulation still persisted. Knight contends that crime writers depicted society as self-regulating, and that criminals would always be caught by a vigilant public.[39] Correspondingly, mid-century crime 'round ups' largely assumed that criminals would be apprehended with or without the police's intervention, and often depicted police officers as manifesting 'the law' as a concept. Furthermore, there was almost no literary precedent for the printing of a narrative that explicitly focused on the exploits of the police or a detective in the tracking and apprehension of a criminal. Indeed, the fact that the criminal had been caught already was usually the reason for the narrative's printing in the first place. Finally, and most importantly, the police's perception as occupying a space somewhere between criminals and the public, separating and distancing the two, caused them to remain largely invisible in crime narratives. Police officers present in crime reports were usually only there to assume responsibility for criminals and to remove them from public sight, ensuring that the distance between the respectable public and the criminal remained constant. In a variety of periodical crime round ups, therefore, police officers were seen to operate on the periphery of society, 'popping up' whenever they were needed to make an arrest, and then disappearing again once their duties were complete.

These points are perhaps best illustrated through examples. In 1860, the *Examiner* published an account of a crime in which the detective appears only at the end in order to validate the criminal's arrest, and who is connected more closely with the criminal than with any of the narrative's other 'characters':

> Mr. Bevan, solicitor [...] obtained the services of Spittle, the city detective, went in search of the prisoner Gilson, whom they found at a small coffee-house in Brewer street [...][40]

As we can see, the police officer, Spittle, appeared only when he was required to provide the member of the public, Mr Bevan, with physical and social protection and distance from the criminal. Spittle was there simply to perform the arrest as Bevan could not do this himself, and this moment occurred right at the end of the narrative after the actual search for the criminal's identity was complete. For the rest of the time, Spittle remained completely unmentioned. Additionally, it is interesting to note that neither detective nor prisoner were *titled* in this article, but were instead simply referred to by surname: Spittle and Gilson. This associated them with each other, and further distanced them both from the solicitor, *Mr* Bevan.

A second, similar example of this comes from the January 1860 issue of the *Examiner*, where a criminal had apparently fled Britain for Australia:

> J. Brett, city detective, deposed that a warrant for the apprehension of the prisoner was placed in his hands in April last, and he proceeded to Melbourne and found him at a place called South Yarrow [...][41]

Again, the officer acted as little more than a *deus ex machina* who appeared at the end of the narrative simply to make the arrest, but who remained invisible to the reader for the rest of the article and quickly disappeared back into obscurity once their purpose was complete. In fact, it was the case that police officers or detectives were invisible in crime 'round ups' even when they themselves were central to the narrative. In January 1858, for example, the *Leader* reported the case of a murdered detective, but the detective himself is only mentioned in the piece's opening line.[42] The remainder discussed the criminal's motive, which was based on vengeance against the officer rather than an attempt to escape the law. Yet information explaining what actually happened between the criminal and the officer and *why* the criminal was seeking revenge in the first place is (disappointingly) omitted, again suggesting that this was a world that the public was never meant to see.

Police officers in mid-Victorian periodical crime round ups were also often depicted as receiving information from other members of society, before they disappeared from the narrative to perform their duties out of sight. This is perhaps the clearest connection to Knight's argument that society was a united, self-regulating force from a law-enforcement perspective, from which a felon could not possibly escape no matter where they turned.[43] However, it also helps to further demonstrate how the police operated on the periphery of society, out of general view. In December 1862, for example, a piece in the magazine *John Bull* wrote:

> Holding told this to the Blackburn police on Saturday, and on Sunday the men were apprehended.[44]

In this instance, a member of society, Holding, informed the police of an offender's location, and within 24 hours they were apprehended. However the reader does not receive information as to exactly how this was done, but is instead required to trust to the fact that the police would go and do their job, and that justice would prevail – which it invariably did. This process allowed Holding, a respectable member of society, to maintain his distance from the criminal justice process; by telling the police, he shifted responsibility away from himself and onto them, allowing himself to stay clear of that separate, undesirable world. In another example of this in action, taken from an October 1862 issue of *John Bull*, the police again received information from a member of the public:

> She gave information to the police, but heard nothing of the prisoner until the night before, when she was taken to the station-house and identified her.[45]

Again, a character provided the police with information, and again the police apprehended the criminal out of sight. Neither the reader nor the informant were given a view into the methodology of the offender's apprehension, but were instead asked to simply assume that it was guaranteed, allowing them to stay clear of the criminal world that existed separately to their own. In a final example, taken from *John Bull and Britannia* in June 1860, a priest supplied the police with information that directly led to an offender's arrest, and once more it was not specified exactly how the offender was captured:

> The Rev. Mr. Hodgson, on learning the flight of young Vansittart, took steps to have him apprehended by the police.[46]

In some periodical crime 'round ups', the police were seen as an instrument whose purpose was merely to validate information that the reader already knew to be true, which provides an alternative viewpoint to how police officers appeared in these narratives only when necessary and to act as 'officially' responsible for criminals. In January 1860, for example, in their regular feature titled 'Police' the *Examiner* reported how the lady of a house apprehended a burglar herself, and the police quickly arrived to simply provide an official presence and to remove the criminal:

> Mrs Snell [...] said: Between nine and ten o'clock on the previous night I had occasion to go up stairs, and found the prisoner coming out of my bed-room. I called him a thief, and laid hold of him by the throat and held him. [...] The police proved, finding the missing brooch, a wax taper, a jemmy, some skeleton keys, and lucifer matches on the prisoner's person.[47]

The police were squeezed into the final two sentences of the narrative, with the officer depicted as an agent that merely provided authoritative confirmation of that which was already known, namely the fact that a criminal has violated the law and has been caught. In a second example of this, in August 1859 the *Leader* wrote:

> A burglary was committed on the premises of Messrs. Greer and Sons, Newgate-street, when a large quantity of cutlery was carried off.

Subsequently upwards of 200 packets of the stolen property was discovered by the police, in the house of a man named Richard Tucker, a type-founder.[48]

The police were, again, present in this narrative only to validate the property as matching that which had been stolen and to identify the criminal, while the actual process of discovery remained completely absent. In a third, quite succinct example also taken from the *Leader* – this time from October 1858 – the sole reference to the police was simply:

Inquiries which have been made by the police confirm the poor creature's statements.[49]

Obviously, there was no elaboration of the 'inquiries' made by the police in order to establish the truthfulness of the victim's statements, how they went about them, or what the final results were. Instead, the police were required here to officially confirm the truth of the evidence. These passing mentions of methodology remained a tantalising aspect of these narratives, and were almost never elaborated on. In one final (and quite clear) example, in 1860 *John Bull and Britannia* wrote:

The prisoner was very cleverly caught by a detective, just as he was about to take his departure for America [...][50]

The fact that the prisoner was said to have been 'very cleverly' tracked leaves the option open for the narrative to discuss exactly how this was done, but (predictably) the article disappointingly does not elaborate.

Overall, then, crime 'round up' features and reports were produced largely separately from the earlier police criticism discussed in this volume's first chapter owing to their largely separate literary history. However, this is not to suggest that crime 'round ups' were not *affected* by the growth of (and discussion of) the police. Historically, crime journalism had focused on gruesome or violent forms of crime and punishment in an attempt to maintain law and order through the direct application of terror or appeals to religious sentiment. However as the police took over responsibility for maintaining law and order as part of the early to mid-nineteenth century 'march of professionalism', periodical crime round ups were able to diversify in retelling much more varied crimes and their punishments.

A secondary effect of the police's assumption of responsibility for maintaining society's law and order was their steady creation of, and transition into, the indistinct, threshold social space we saw in Chapter 1. The police's growth drove both a physical and ideological wedge between criminality and the rest of society, and created a neutral space that they themselves came to directly occupy. In popular crime round ups, therefore, the police officer was often depicted as a figure who appeared only when it was necessary, who existed to validate pre-existing information, and who operated invisibly on society's periphery to keep the public as far away from criminals as possible in order to reinforce rigid social distinctions.[51] This idea has extensive ramifications for the development of mid-Victorian detective fiction, as a variety of fictional writings made use of the apparently ambiguous and often marginalised social position of the police officer as a useful characteristic when constructing their narratives, even when the officer themselves manifested a central figure to the plot.[52]

Crime Journalism and the Criminal Space

In order to explore *how* the socially-blurred police officer was used in the construction of fiction, there is a final, highly important trend within the history of crime reporting that must be turned to first. Crime journalism in all of its incarnations discussed in this chapter so far possessed an interest in projecting the private spaces and moments of crime for the entertainment and amusement of its readers. Mid-nineteenth century periodical crime reports were often centred on acts of revealing the details of usually-private criminal spaces or moments for their readers' interest and curiosity. 'Reality' was naturally a central concern to crime reporting across its history, because it needed to allow readers to believe what they were seeing – and to believe that the information was privileged. Confessions of criminals were frequently deemed to be 'real' or 'true', events that took place behind closed doors were asserted to be accurately presented, and even images of disgraced criminals upon the dissecting table were presented as true likenesses of what they actually looked like.[53] As Alyce Von Rothkirch suggests, the 'criminals' in crime round ups were always grounded in reality, as articles themselves were manifestations of contemporary social and cultural anxieties and it was thus necessary for them to be both believable and accessible.[54]

From its beginnings as the humble broadside, crime reporting was interested in providing the reader with views inside various often-impenetrable spaces and moments associated with crime, including court-rooms, prisons, the moments before executions, and domestic spaces which had become crime scenes. Indeed, execution broadsides even allowed a grisly form of 'vicarious participation' in the crime on the part of witnesses to the execution, by printing both a textual narrative of what happened and also occasionally producing images of crime scenes, criminals, and the precise moments of crimes taking place.[55] As Heather Worthington elegantly summarises:

> [...] broadsides made their appeal to the voyeuristic interests of the masses, exposing the gory and sometimes salacious details of the crimes and making public what had been private.[56]

Execution broadsides also complemented the grisly spectacle of a public hanging by enhancing their level of interactivity. As Michel Foucault famously argues, spectators were required to actively participate in a public execution on some level, in order to both view the 'law's triumph' and to validate that justice had been done.[57] Martin Wiener also correctly argues that the public execution *itself* was a 'pornographic invasion of the integrity of the body',[58] and by extension the broadside helped to publicise another moment usually desired to be kept private – the precise moment of death. Broadsides that accompanied executions thus enabled witnesses to participate in it and, as Knelman argues, 'encouraged the public to [...] poke sticks through the cage' at those convicted of murder.[59] They also provided valuable contextual information on the condemned through the inclusion of penitent verses that warned others away from criminality, which were often marketed as written by the condemned themselves (even if they were not). As a result, broadsides helped the reader gain a clearer window into the crime and execution by allowing them to supposedly see 'inside' the criminal's mind.

Prison chaplains' accounts were similarly quasi-voyeuristic, but they had an obvious edge over the broadside. Chaplains had direct access to condemned criminals and they could obtain information far beyond the broadside's reach.[60] Even if their account was completely fictional, the fact that the prison chaplain had written it (or was *said* to have written it) gave their account a degree of legitimacy which could not be manufactured through alternative means, no matter how hard the broadside tried. The bulk of the writing in chaplains' accounts was thus naturally reserved for a condemned prisoner's last hours inside the prison – a privileged space to which the chaplain alone had access. They often depicted heartfelt moments of farewell, repentance or confession, or in some cases defiance or even attempted suicide to escape the humiliation of the gallows. A good example of this from 1760 reads:

> [...] two or three gentlemen [...] wanted to see Tilling [the condemned]. At his own earnest request, they were admitted to him [...] One of the gentlemen [...] was so nearly touched and so much overcome [...] that he could scarce be supported, had thought to have stayed and attended prayers with the convicts, but could not bear it.[61]

There was a difference in ideological purpose, however; these scenes of farewell were at least partially designed to be didactic, and this was a different pedagogical approach to the broadside. Broadsides motivated readers away from criminality largely through fear, whilst chaplains' accounts appealed less to the reader's sense of terror and more to their conscience. They usually depicted the condemned as penitently accepting of their sentence, and in some cases 'reprinted' letters in which they expressed sorrow and their desire for forgiveness. In one example from 1772, the criminal William Siday wrote to his father, and requested that the Ordinary of Newgate publish his letter so that others would 'take warning' in a manner which he himself had not.[62] Aside from attempted pedagogy however, these scenes simply made for sensational reading and figuratively 'opened up' the condemned ward for the reader to peer inside. In an example from 1767, the Ordinary of Newgate described a close, intimate moment of farewell with the infamous Elizabeth Brownrigg:

[...] she appeared to be much affected [...] we went up to chapel; where her husband and son were again permitted to be with her, and joined in receiving the holy sacrament. After which she prayed with the utmost fervency [...] She seemed quite composed and resigned, and continued in prayer with her husband and son upwards of two hours, when she took leave of them, which exhibited a scene too affecting for words to describe, and which drew tears from all present.[63]

Criminal compendiums such as the famous *Newgate Calendar*s were also quasi-voyeuristic, in that they allowed readers to feel what Charles Rzepka dubs, 'smug condemnation of [...] despicable villains.'[64] However, these gave less attention to the criminal's punishment and instead focused on the criminal's domestic life and the moment of the crime. They often depicted private scenes or moments within domestic spaces, and included detail from before the crime and the precise moment of the crime taking place. For example, the 1824 edition of the *Newgate Calendar* detailed a bitter domestic battle between a man named Robert Hallam and his wife:

She sat, partly undressed, on the side of the bed, as if afraid to go in [...] At length she ran down stairs, and he followed her, and locked the street-door to prevent her going out. On this she ran up into the dining-room, whither he likewise followed her, and struck her several times. He then went into another room for his cane, and she locked him in. Enraged at this, he broke open the door, and, seizing her in his arms, threw her out of the window, with her head foremost, and her back to the ground, so that, on her falling, her back was broken, her skull fractured, and she instantly expired.[65]

No prior form of crime writing had gone into such detail surrounding the domestic arrangements of the criminal before their apprehension. However, it should be noted that this is not to suggest that the established courtroom or prison cell scenes were wholly abandoned. On the contrary, the *Newgate Calendar* often replicated prison chaplains' accounts, in that it depicted the criminal's experiences in both Newgate and inside the courtroom. They were, however, much less pronounced.

Predictably, then, mid-Victorian crime 'round ups' published in periodicals were closely linked with these older forms of crime writing through this particular thematic strand. The interest in presenting views inside criminalised spaces and moments was directly transferred from older forms of crime reporting and into crime round ups. As Jessica Valdez suggests, 'the goal of news [was] not to be discriminative but simply to produce enough to satiate the public's "constant craving[s]" [...]' or in other words, to appeal to the desires of those interested in reading about the latest criminal occurrences and to be figuratively transported into the spaces and moments that came with them.[66] Knelman also makes this point, and quotes an excellent and highly relevant article from an 1849 issue of *Punch* which suggested that exposing the usually-private details of criminals for readers to eagerly consume was perhaps the largest purpose of mid-Victorian crime journalism:

> [...] we notoriously spare no pains to furnish the nation with [a criminal's] complete biography; employing literary gentlemen, of elegant education and profound knowledge of human nature, to examine his birthplace and parish register, to visit his parents, brothers, uncles and aunts, to procure intelligence of his early school days, diseases which he has passed through, infantile (and more mature) traits of character, etc. [...] we employ artists of eminence to sketch his likeness as he appears at the police court, or views of the farm-house or back-kitchen where he has perpetrated the atrocious deed [...] we entertain intelligence within the prison walls with the male and female turnkeys, gaolers, and other authorities, by whose information we are enabled to describe every act and deed of the prisoner, the state of his health, sleep and digestion, the changes in his appearance, his conversation, his dress and linen, the letters he writes, and the meals he takes [...][67]

This desire to furnish readers with the criminal's biographical history, as well as the details surrounding their crimes, can be directly observed in action in a variety of mid-century periodical crime round ups. This rather lengthy passage is used here as a representative example, and is taken from an article from the March 1862 issue of the *Examiner*:

> On Saturday last a short, dark, thick-set young man, named Belsey, made an attempt to shoot Louisa King, cook to Mr D'Alquen, of Brighton. It appears that Belsey was to have been married to Lucy Walder, house maid at Mr D'Alquen's, on that morning. He then appeared to be on the most affectionate terms with her, and they all proceeded to St. Nicholas's Church, Belsey walking with Lucy Walder's mother, and the rest following. All at once, Belsey said he had forgotten his gloves, and that he must go back and get them, adding that he should be with them in a few minutes. He went back, and the party proceeded to church, where they waited for his arrival about an hour. No bridegroom appearing, they left. [...] Nothing was seen of Belsey till about half-past one o'clock, when he knocked at Mr. D'Alquen's door [...] Belsey asked to see Lucy Walder, and Mr. D'Alquen, jun., told him he could not see her, upon which he presented a six-barrel revolver at the breast of Mr D'Alquen, sen. Louisa King, the cook [...] went to assist her master in closing the door against the prisoner. [...] King put her head out of the door too far, not knowing that Belsey had a pistol, when he fired [...][68]

The narrative format of this excerpt certainly recalls the interest in domestic arrangements of stories published in the earlier *Newgate Calendars*. As before, the reader obtained an insight into the criminal's domestic life and circumstances, as well as the particular situation that led them to commit the crime – in this case, a disagreement between the criminal, his fiancée, and his father-in-law to be. The narrative then provided a detailed account of the crime itself, before eventually going on to discuss the situation that the prisoner found himself in after he had been apprehended. In a second example, in 1858 the *Leader*, as part of the column 'Criminal Record', detailed the domestic arrangements between the criminal and his contemporaries which led to a murder:

> Atkinson is the son of a flax-spinner, and he has been intimate with the young lady since they were both children; but the mother of Miss Scaife and the father of Atkinson did not approve the match, and it was broken off for a time, during which interval Miss Scaife received the attentions of a Mr. Gill. But that intimacy was also put an end to, and the young lady again accepted Atkinson as her suitor. On Tuesday week, however, Atkinson saw Miss Scaife at a gala talking with Gill, and this appears to have awakened a strong feeling of jealousy.[69]

This provision of contextual information not only gave insights into the details surrounding why the murder was committed, but also into the intimate domestic relationships between the people involved. I have selected this example because the murder (itself an intimate and 'private' moment) was retold in close detail using testimony *from the murderer himself* to paint a public portrait of a private scene:

> Atkinson was examined before the county magistrates at Knaresborough, and he then made a verbal confession of his guilt. The girl had refused to marry him [...] He then threatened to murder her, and ultimately clutched her round the throat. She cried out, and he released his hold [...] but soon pulled out a knife, and showed it her. "She cried out, 'let's go home, Jim – let's go home, Jim!' Then I seized her and cut her throat [...]"[70]

The fact that the testimony came from Atkinson himself was an attempt to provide a guarantee for the reader that the tale they were reading was true and accurate. In fact, this use of a figure that was physically, psychologically, or emotionally close to the principle characters in these narratives to provide as many private and privileged details as possible became a common trope in mid-Victorian periodical crime reporting. A second example taken from the *Leader* also highlights this:

> On Thursday morning early a young woman went to her sister's house in Little-Lever-street. She knew that her sister and her husband had not been living comfortably together, and was taking her some bread and butter. She looked through the kitchen window before opening the door, and saw her sister lying with her head on the floor [...][71]

The fact that the article's source of information was the victim's *sister* legitimised the insider-information the piece provided the reader. It was not hearsay or rumour, but fact told by one close to the story. The domestic arrangements that led to the murder quickly followed this, again using a figure perceived to be close to the principle characters in the narrative:

> At the inquest a neighbour said that the deceased and her husband were drinking and fighting every night. About three o'clock that morning witness was awoke by a great noise in the prisoner's house. She heard three successive heavy falls down the stairs, and then a female cried out. [...][72]

This time, the source of information was a neighbour of the deceased, thereby presenting the sense that their information was both legitimate and confidential. The inclusion of the neighbour's testimony thus opened up the closed world of the domestic sphere to the reader, using those characters as close as possible to the crime as a window through which readers could figuratively enter it. Finally, the *London Review* provides another, slightly different example of reprinting evidence given by those close to the case in order to produce the illusion of truthful representation of private areas associated with the crime. In 1866, it published 'The Cannon Street Murder', which reproduced evidence given by a witness:

> It appears from the evidence of Terry that he had been instrumental in procuring for Mrs. Milson a loan of money from a Mrs. Webber, and that he had entered into some sort of arrangement with Smith for acting as his "adviser" in endeavouring to recover the sum. Smith, according to the statement of Terry, went at his request one day to Messrs. Bevington's warehouse, and got fourteen shillings from the deceased.[73]

This article used the testimony of the housekeeper at a neighbouring property to, again, produce the insider information vital to the narrative to give the effect of providing the reader with truthful and privileged information. In this case, however, the magazine expressed exasperation that the neighbour's testimony was less reliable. This frustrated the purpose of the narrative, which was forced to rely on it despite its apparent vagueness:

> The testimony of Mrs. Robbins, the housekeeper at a neighbouring ware-house in Cannon-street, was most unsatisfactory. She said that on the night of the murder she heard Messrs. Bevington's door shut violently at about ten minutes past ten, and saw a man come from the door whom she subsequently recognised at the station-house in the person of the prisoner, who was placed with a number of others. But it appears that on the previous day Smith [the prisoner] was taken past the house by the police, and that Mrs. Robbins, though told beforehand what was going to be done, could not recognise the man.[74]

The word 'unsatisfactory' has a double meaning here. It both highlights how the evidence is not enough to secure a conviction, but it also laments the fact that it does not provide accurate enough insider information to the reader. The fact that 'Mrs. Robbins' was merely the 'housekeeper at a neighbouring warehouse' was not a close enough relationship to the crime or the criminal, and it is disappointed in the quality and quantity of 'insider information' which she can present.

In short, then, crime reporting in its numerous forms (and from its earliest origins) was consistently interested in presenting the reader with an 'insider view' of the privileged and private moments and spaces associated with criminals and their misdeeds. Execution broadsides allowed readers to vicariously participate in both the crime and the execution, augmenting a spectacular display of justice with privileged information that was often claimed to have come from the criminals themselves. Prison chaplains' accounts took the reader inside the condemned cells of the prisons in their charge, allowing them to witness final moments of penitence and farewell before the condemned ascended the fatal platform. Elsewhere, crime compendiums focused more on domestic spaces and the life of the criminal, providing both a window into the life of the criminal and rhetorically asking how a member of society could go so badly astray. However, *all* of these different perspectives were absorbed into periodical crime reports, which used new journalistic techniques (such as the provision of expert witnesses and testimony from those closest to the crime) to continue the tradition of providing readers with detailed pictures of the life, crimes and punishments of criminals.

Looking Ahead to 'Detective Literature': Chapter 2 Conclusions

As this chapter has demonstrated, there was an observable distinction between non-fiction critique of the police and contemporarily published crime round up features in mid-Victorian periodicals. However, this is not to suggest that crime reporting in mid-Victorian periodicals was not influenced by the police's establishment across Victorian Britain. In fact, it had a substantial impact; thanks to the police's assumption of responsibility over criminals and managing crime, the kinds of crime which crime reporting could relate to readers diversified exponentially across this era as crime reporting was no longer needed to influence its readers into obeying the law through the application of fear or appeals to morality. Additionally, a secondary effect of the establishment of the police was the growth in distaste for reporting on violent or gruesome crimes and punishments, as the force increased the distance between criminality and the respectable public and, as we have repeatedly seen, came to occupy this growing space themselves. This was directly visible in periodical crime round ups, as the police were often relegated to a marginal and invisible position in the narratives, appearing only when necessary to make an arrest or to validate a crime, and to ensure that both readers and the innocent figures within the reports remained as separate as possible from society's criminal element. Secondly, mid-Victorian periodical 'crime round up' features were thematically connected to earlier forms of crime writing through their shared interest in quasi-voyeuristically exposing the private or secret world of criminality.[75] Crime reporting had a historically observable desire to take private spaces and moments associated with criminal justice and make them publicly viewable for readers to both witness and, on some levels, experience for themselves. These included the moment of execution and the last words of the criminal before they died; the scenes inside the condemned cell prior to execution; and the domestic and social arrangements of the criminals themselves.

All of these aspects of periodical journalism, from police criticism to crime reporting, had significant consequences for the development of other forms of writing and, crucially, the first form of so-called 'detective fiction'. As the next chapter will explore in detail, the steadily-growing perception of the police as socially indistinct (and on some level 'undesirable') *combined* with the journalistic interest in the revealing the private details of diverse crimes and criminals reported in periodicals. This created a situation where *new* narratives began to be constructed that purposefully explored criminality, using the police officer as a guide and protector in order to delve deeper and deeper into the criminal world.

Notes

1 Martin Wiener, 'Convicted Murderers and the Victorian Press: Condemnation vs. Sympathy', *Crime and Misdemeanours*, 1, 2 (2007), 110–125 (p. 110).

2 Richard Altick, *Victorian Studies in Scarlet: Murders and Manners in the Age of Victoria* (London; W. W. Norton and Co., 1970), p. 66, cited in Judith Knelman, *Twisting in the Wind: The Murderess and the English Press* (Toronto: University of Toronto Press, 1998), p. 35.

3 See both Anne Rodrick, 'Only a Newspaper Metaphor: Crime Reports, Class Conflict and Social Criticism in Two Victorian Newspapers, *Victorian Periodicals Review*, 29, 1 (1996), 1–18 (p. 2) and Christopher Casey, 'Common Misperceptions: The Press and Victorian Views of Crime', *Journal of Interdisciplinary History*, 41, 3 (2011), 367–391 (p. 375).

4 Knelman, p. 25. See also Vic Gatrell, *The Hanging Tree: Execution and the English People, 1770–1868* (Oxford: Oxford University Press, 1994).

5 Heather Worthington, *The Rise of the Detective in Early Nineteenth Century Popular Fiction* (Basingstoke: Palgrave Macmillan, 2005), p. 6.

6 Judith Rowbotham, Kim Stevenson and Samantha Pegg, *Crime News in Modern Britain: Press Reporting and Responsibility, 1820–2010* (Basingstoke: Palgrave Macmillan, 2013), p. 14.

7 Gatrell, p. 159.

8 Worthington, p. 7.

9 Knelman, p. 27.

10 Worthington, p. 7.

11 Knelman, p. 27.

12 Stephen Knight, *Form and Ideology in Crime Fiction* (Basingstoke: Macmillan, 1980), p. 9.

13 Knelman, p. 27.

14 Knelman, pp. 27–28.

15 For example, in the 1824 edition, the first story detailed the criminal career and execution of Reverend Thomas Hunter, executed for murdering two of his pupils in 1700. For more information, see Andrew Knapp and William Baldwin, *The Newgate*

Calendar: Comprising Interesting Memoirs of the Most Notorious Characters who Have Been Convicted of Outrages on the Laws of England Since the Commencement of the Eighteenth Century; with Occasional Anecdotes and Observations, Speeches, Confessions, and Last Exclamations of Sufferers (London: J. Robins and Co, 1824).

16 Knight, p. 12.

17 Knelman, p. 25.

18 Knelman, p. 35.

19 Rowbotham, Stevenson, and Pegg, p. 17.

20 This is not to suggest that reporting on crime in periodicals was not politicised. In fact some, such as Edward Jacobs, suggest that crime writing in newspapers and periodicals engaged with politics more than has been recognised, and that scholars tend to avoid observing political debates in crime journalism in favour of arguing that sensationalism was designed to distract readers from politics. See Edward Jacobs, 'Edward Lloyd's Sunday Newspapers and the Cultural Politics of Crime News, c. 1840–1843', *Victorian Periodicals Review*, 50, 3 (2017), 619–649 (p. 620).

21 Rodrick, pp. 1–18 (p. 2).

22 'Criminal Conversation, Divorce, etc.', *Leader*, 26 January 1851, p. 700.

23 Knelman, p. 36.

24 A good example was the 'Police Intelligence' feature published in *Punch*, the title of which acted as a *double entendre* to suggest that the police possessed, in actuality, very little intelligence. For a good representative example, see 'Police Intelligence', *Punch, or, the London Charivari*, 21 January 1865, p. 29.

25 'Criminal Record', *Leader*, 7 August 1858, p. 767. Image produced by ProQuest as part of *British Periodicals*. www.proquest.com.

26 Malcolm S. Chase, 'Hetherington, Henry (1792–1849)', in *Dictionary of Nineteenth Century Journalism*, ed. by Laurel Brake and Marysa Demoor (London and Ghent: Academia Press, 2009), p. 281.

27 Rodrick, 1–18 (p. 2).

28 Samuel Saunders, '"Were sensation our object, it would not be difficult to cull from the *Newgate Calendar*": Periodical Journalism and Distaste for Public Executions, c. 1830–1870', in *From Public Spectacle to Hidden Ritual: Execution Culture in Nineteenth Century Britain* ed. by Patrick Low, Helen Rutherford and Clare Sandford-Couch, (Oxon: Routledge, 2020/21), pp. 121–135 (p. 124). This volume is currently in print.

29 Knelman, p. 21.

30 Saunders, '"Were sensation our object [...]"', in *From Public Spectacle to Hidden Ritual*, ed. by Low, Rutherford and Sandford-Couch, pp. 125–126.

31 'Police Intelligence', *Bell's Life in London*, 7 July 1866.

32 'Law and Crime', *Sixpenny Magazine*, August 1861, p. 251.

33 The Offences Against the Person Act 1861 reduced the number of crimes punishable by death from hundreds to four, yet continued simmering resentment towards public executions sparked governmental investigations into the execution of capital punishment. A dedicated commission, The Royal Commission on Capital Punishment, was set up in 1864, and published its report in 1866 which made various recommendations based on evidence provided by figures working within the criminal justice system. It suggested, among other things, that 'an Act be passed putting an end to public executions, and directing that sentences of death shall be carried out within the precincts of the prison, under such regulations as may be considered necessary to prevent abuse, and satisfy the public that the law has been complied with' (pp. 50–51). The Capital Punishment (Amendment) Act followed in 1868, and legislated exactly that which the Commission had recommended – that prisoners under death sentences were to be executed within the prison walls rather than in public view For full details, see Charles Henry et al., *Report of the Capital Punishment Commission; Together with the Minutes of Evidence* (London: George E. Eyre and William Spottiswoode (HMSO), 1866). See

also the Capital Punishment Amendment Act 1868, (31 & 32 Vict., c. 24), *legislation. gov.uk*, <http://www.legislation.gov.uk/ukpga/Vict/31-32/24> [accessed 25 July 2017].

34 William Makepeace Thackeray, 'Going to See a Man Hanged', *Fraser's Magazine for Town and Country*, vol. 22, July–December 1840, p. 155 and p. 158.

35 Thackeray, p. 154.

36 Charles Dickens, 'Mr. Charles Dickens and the Execution of the Mannings', *Times*, 13 November 1849.

37 'Public Execution', *Examiner*, 19 November 1864, p. 737.

38 'Recent Trials for Murder', *National Magazine*, December 1862, p. 81.

39 Knight, p. 12.

40 'Law', *Examiner*, 4 February 1860, p. 76.

41 'Law', *Examiner*, 7 January 1860, p. 12.

42 'Gatherings from Law and Police Courts', *Leader*, 30 January 1858, p. 104.

43 Knight, p. 12.

44 'Law and Police', *John Bull*, 6 December 1862, p. 781.

45 'Law and Police', *John Bull*, 4 October 1862, p. 637.

46 'Law and Police', *John Bull and Britannia*, 16 June 1860, p. 381.

47 'Police', *Examiner*, 14 January 1860, p. 28.

48 'Law, Police and Casualties', *Leader*, 20 August 1859, p. 954.

49 'Gatherings from Law and Police Courts', *Leader*, 2 October 1858, p. 1022.

50 'Law and Police', *John Bull and Britannia*, 28 January 1860, p. 61.

51 D. A. Miller, *The Novel and the Police* (California, University of California Press, 1988), pp. 17–18.

52 Miller, pp. 2–3.

53 For example, a broadside that was given away freely to those who bought the *Weekly Dispatch* on August 11 1828 depicted the likeness of the head and upper body of William Corder (perpetrator of the 'Red Barn Murder' of Maria Marten and executed in 1828) on the dissecting table, captioned with 'The Head of CORDER as is appeared on the disecting [sic] table'.

54 Alyce Von Rothkirch, 'His face was livid, dreadful, with a form at the corners of his mouth': A Typology of Villains in Classic Detective Stories, *Modern Language Review*, 108, 4 (2013), 1042–1063 (p. 1043).

55 Worthington, p. 7.

56 Worthington, p. 7.

57 Michel Foucault, *Discipline and Punish* (New York: Vintage, 1977) pp. 57–58.

58 Martin Wiener, *Reconstructing the Criminal: Culture, Law and Policy in England, 1830–1914* (Cambridge: Cambridge University Press, 1990; repr. 1994), p. 96.

59 Knelman, p. 21.

60 Worthington, p. 7.

61 'Ordinary's Account, 28th April 1760', *Old Bailey Online* <https://www.oldbaileyon line.org/browse.jsp?name=OA17600428> [accessed 20 March 2017], (1760).

62 'Ordinary's Account, 8th July 1772', *Old Bailey Online* <https://www.oldbaileyon line.org/browse.jsp?name=OA17720708> [accessed 20 March 2017], (1772).

63 'Ordinary's Account, 14th September 1767', *Old Bailey Online* <https://www.oldba ileyonline.org/browse.jsp?div=OA17670914> [accessed 2 February 2017], (1767).

64 Charles Rzepka, *Detective Fiction* (Cambridge: Polity, 2005), p. 52.

65 Knapp and Baldwin, p. 311–312.

66 Jessica Valdez, 'Dickens's "Pious Fraud": The Popular Press and the Moral Suasion of Fictional Narrative', *Victorian Periodicals Review*, 44, 4 (2011), 377–400 (p. 377).

67 'The Proper Time for Public Executions', *Punch, or, the London Charivari*, 1 December 1849, p. 214. Quoted in Knelman, pp. 21–22.

68 'Murders and Murderous Crimes', *Examiner*, 29 March 1862, p. 201.

69 'Criminal Record', *Leader,* 7 August 1858, p. 767.

70 'Criminal Record', *Leader,* 7 August 1858, p. 767.

71 'Criminal Record', *Leader*, 2 October 1858, pp. 1021–1022.
72 'Criminal Record', *Leader*, 2 October 1858, p. 1022.
73 'The Cannon Street Murder', *London Review*, 16 June 1866, p. 669.
74 'The Cannon Street Murder', *London Review*, 16 June 1866, p. 669.
75 Rodrick, pp. 1–18 (p. 2).

Bibliography

Primary Periodical Material

'Criminal Conversation, Divorce, etc.', *Leader*, 26 January 1851, p. 700.
'Criminal Record', *Leader*, 2 October 1858, pp. 1021–1022.
'Criminal Record', *Leader*, 7 August 1858, p. 767.
Dickens, Charles, 'Mr. Charles Dickens and the Execution of the Mannings', *Times*, 13 November 1849.
'Gatherings from Law and Police Courts', *Leader*, 2 October 1858, p. 1022.
'Gatherings from Law and Police Courts', *Leader*, 30 January 1858, p. 104.
'Law and Crime', *Sixpenny Magazine*, August 1861, pp. 251–254.
'Law and Police', *John Bull and Britannia*, 16 June 1860, p. 381.
'Law and Police', *John Bull and Britannia*, 28 January 1860, p. 61.
'Law and Police', *John Bull*, 4 October 1862, p. 637.
'Law and Police', *John Bull*, 6 December 1862, p. 781.
'Law, Police and Casualties', *Leader*, 20 August 1859, p. 954.
'Law', *Examiner*, 4 February 1860, p. 76.
'Law', *Examiner*, 7 January 1860, pp. 11–12.
'Murders and Murderous Crimes', *Examiner*, 29 March 1862, pp. 200–201.
'Police Intelligence', *Bell's Life in London*, 7 July 1866.
'Police Intelligence', *Punch, or, the London Charivari*, 21 January 1865, p. 29.
'Police', *Examiner*, 14 January 1860, p. 28.
'Public Execution', *Examiner*, 19 November 1864, p. 737.
'Recent Trials for Murder', *National Magazine*, December 1862, pp. 81–84.
Thackeray, William Makepeace, 'Going to See a Man Hanged', *Fraser's Magazine for Town and Country*, vol. 22, July-December 1840.
'The Cannon Street Murder', *London Review*, 16 June 1866, p. 669.
'The Head of CORDER as is appeared on the disecting [sic] table', *Weekly Dispatch*, 11 August 1828, n.p.
'The Proper Time for Public Executions', *Punch, or, the London Charivari*, 1 December 1849, p. 214.

Secondary Material

Altick, Richard, *Victorian Studies in Scarlet: Murders and Manners in the Age of Victoria* (London: W. W. Norton and Co., 1970).
Brake, Laurel and Marysa Demoor (eds.), *Dictionary of Nineteenth Century Journalism* (London and Ghent: Academia Press, 2009).
Capital Punishment Amendment Act 1868, (31 & 32 Vict., c. 24), legislation.gov.uk, <http://www.legislation.gov.uk/ukpga/Vict/31-32/24> [accessed 25 July 2017].

Casey, Christopher, 'Common Misperceptions: The Press and Victorian Views of Crime', *Journal of Interdisciplinary History*, 41, 3 (2011), 367–391.

Chase, Malcolm S., 'Hetherington, Henry (1792–1849)', in *Dictionary of Nineteenth Century Journalism*, ed. by Laurel Brake and Marysa Demoor (London and Ghent: Academia Press, 2009), p. 281.

Foucault, Michel, *Discipline and Punish* (New York: Vintage, 1977).

Gatrell, Vic, *The Hanging Tree: Execution and the English People, 1770–1868* (Oxford: Oxford University Press, 1994).

Henry, Charles, et al., *Report of the Capital Punishment Commission; Together with the Minutes of Evidence* (London: George E. Eyre and William Spottiswoode (HMSO), 1866).

Jacobs, Edward, 'Edward Lloyd's Sunday Newspapers and the Cultural Politics of Crime News, c. 1840–1843', *Victorian Periodicals Review*, 50, 3 (2017), 619–649.

Knapp, Andrew and William Baldwin, *The Newgate Calendar: Comprising Interesting Memoirs of the Most Notorious Characters who Have Been Convicted of Outrages on the Laws of England Since the Commencement of the Eighteenth Century; with Occasional Anecdotes and Observations, Speeches, Confessions, and Last Exclamations of Sufferers* (London: J. Robins and Co., 1824).

Knelman, Judith, *Twisting in the Wind: The Murderess and the English Press* (Toronto: University of Toronto Press, 1998).

Knight, Stephen, *Form and Ideology in Crime Fiction* (Basingstoke: Macmillan, 1980).

Miller, D. A., *The Novel and the Police* (California: University of California Press, 1988).

'Ordinary's Account, 14th September 1767', *Old Bailey Online* <https://www.oldbaileyonline.org/browse.jsp?div=OA17670914> [accessed 2 February 2017].

'Ordinary's Account, 28th April 1760', *Old Bailey Online* <https://www.oldbaileyonline.org/browse.jsp?name=OA17600428> [accessed 20 March 2017].

'Ordinary's Account, 8th July 1772', *Old Bailey Online* <https://www.oldbaileyonline.org/browse.jsp?name=OA17720708> [accessed 20 March 2017].

Rodrick, Anne, 'Only a Newspaper Metaphor: Crime Reports, Class Conflict and Social Criticism in Two Victorian Newspapers', *Victorian Periodicals Review*, 29, 1 (1996), 1–18.

Rowbothmam, Judith, Kim Stevenson, and Samantha Pegg, *Crime News in Modern Britain: Press Reporting and Responsibility, 1820–2010* (Basingstoke: Palgrave Macmillan, 2013).

Rzepka, Charles, *Detective Fiction* (Cambridge: Polity, 2005).

Saunders, Samuel, '"Were sensation our object, it would not be difficult to cull from the Newgate Calendar": Periodical Journalism and Distaste for Public Executions, c. 1830–1870', in *From Public Spectacle to Hidden Ritual: Execution Culture in Nineteenth Century Britain* ed. by Patrick Low, Helen Rutherford and Clare Sandford-Couch, (Oxon: Routledge, 2020/21), pp. 121–135.

Valdez, Jessica, 'Dickens's "Pious Fraud": The Popular Press and the Moral Suasion of Fictional Narrative', *Victorian Periodicals Review*, 44, 4 (2011), 377–400.

Von Rothkirch, Alyce, '"His face was livid, dreadful, with a form at the corners of his mouth": A Typology of Villains in Classic Detective Stories', *Modern Language Review*, 108, 4 (2013), 1042–1063.

Wiener, Martin, 'Convicted Murderers and the Victorian Press: Condemnation vs. Sympathy', *Crime and Misdemeanours*, 1, 2 (2007), 110–125.

Wiener, Martin, *Reconstructing the Criminal: Culture, Law and Policy in England, 1830–1914* (Cambridge: Cambridge University Press, 1990; repr. 1994).

Worthington, Heather, *The Rise of the Detective in Early Nineteenth Century Popular Fiction* (Basingstoke: Palgrave Macmillan, 2005).

Part II

Memoirs and Sensation

3 '"Detective" literature, if it may be so called'

The Police Officer and the Police Memoir

Introduction: The Merging of 'Police Criticism' and the 'Crime Round-Up'

The forms of periodical writing discussed in this volume so far, namely police criticism and crime reporting, had profound impacts on the development of 'detective fiction'. To recap: the growth in the non-fiction debate created a wider, deeper, and more sophisticated understanding of the police, and repeatedly highlighted their perception as a physical and metaphorical shield against criminality. At the same time, periodical crime 'round ups' catered for readers' desires to know about local and national criminal occurrences, and built on a lengthy tradition of allowing readers to figuratively view inside private spaces, moments, and relationships associated with crime.

It naturally follows that the thematic interests of both of these kinds of writing meshed together to create new literary forms. The first was that which will hereafter be termed 'social exploration journalism'; articles designed to explore and reveal 'criminalised' urban spaces of growing cities that, it was often assumed, the respectable public would not have visited. By reading these, readers obtained similar 'insider views' of criminalised worlds as those in crime reporting. However unlike in crime reporting where the police officer was usually absent, the police officer's perceived position as between respectable and criminal was actively used in social exploration journalism to help journalists penetrate urban criminal spaces more effectively. In fact, they were to become an *obligatory* figure in this kind of writing to allow the author or journalist access to an otherwise inaccessible location without incurring physical or social consequences to themselves. Indeed, Anthea Trodd suggests that by the 1860s a pervading ideology that there was a 'subterranean world of [...] crime concealed just below the surface' of society had developed.[1] This world rejected the face-value of mid-Victorian culture and was difficult to access except for those who were either already a part of it – namely criminals – or those who possessed the authority to enter it – the police. Consequently, articles that explored the city's 'crime gardens', as one example eloquently put it, became common as society became more urbanised, chaotic, and difficult to navigate,[2] and almost always included a police officer to guide and protect the journalist. Eventually, as we will see, police officers themselves began to move steadily towards the centre of these narratives.[3]

The second literary form was an evolution of this 'social exploration journalism'. Across the mid-nineteenth century, a microgenre of fiction appeared that took the idea of the police officer's ability to enter and reveal the urban criminal space and essentially ran with it, focusing on the recollections of the experiences of retired, deceased, or (occasionally) still-serving officers. I have christened this 'police memoir fiction', and argue that this was a self-contained genre that consciously built on the ideas surrounding crime and the police present in various forms of periodical writing, and that it forms a concrete example of 'detective fiction'. Perhaps most interestingly, police memoir-fiction was directly described as 'detective literature' by some mid-Victorian authors and commentators, and it is perhaps the first fictional genre to be openly given this label. However, it remains under-discussed in genre models of detective fiction due to the perception that it was merely cheap trash and unworthy of critical attention, as well as the fact that its full impact on the detective genre's development is only fully revealed when studied in conjunction with the periodical press.

This chapter therefore explores both of these forms of writing in turn, to highlight how the pervading perception of the police officer as socially peripheral was transformed into a useful capacity, allowing journalists to move in their company and thereby invade and reveal the criminal space contained within the urban labyrinth of growing mid-century cities. It then goes on to argue that the act of performing 'social exploration' in the protective company of the police officer was transposed into fiction, forming one of the earliest genres of 'detective fiction' with a set of characteristics and hallmarks with which it can be identified, and which had a substantial legacy on later iterations of the genre.

'[W]e are made accurately acquainted by the copious chronicles of such events': Early Nineteenth Century 'Social Exploration Journalism'

In the early nineteenth century, there was already substantial journalistic interest in writing pieces dedicated to entering and exploring spaces deemed to be 'criminal'. As we have seen, contemporary crime reporting catered for readers' curiosity by allowing them an 'inside view' into crimes, prison cells, confessions and executions, and even Thackeray in 'Going to See a Man Hanged' commented that this was a common journalistic activity:

> While these things are going on within the prison (with which we are made accurately acquainted by the copious chronicles of such events which are published subsequently [...])[4]

It was perhaps natural, then, that there was also a substantial amount of writing dedicated to performing 'social exploration' of the city for the amusement of readers that usually included a 'criminal' element. Pierce Egan the Elder's famous *Life in London* (1821) is a good early example with which to begin. It depicts its protagonists, Corinthian Tom, Jerry Hawthorn, and Bob Logic, exploring the metropolis and describing their experiences directly to the reader. They pay a brief but memorable visit to the condemned yard (also known as the Press-Yard) of Newgate Prison, where they witness several prisoners being prepared for the gallows. This scene may itself have been influenced by earlier texts such as Daniel Defoe's *The History of the Press-Yard* (1717), which provided a startlingly similar account of the scene inside the condemned ward.[5] My quote from Egan's text refers directly to an image printed on the opposite page, and so the image itself is also included here for clarity (see Figure 3.1):[6]

> An opportunity presented itself to our TRIO to visit the Condemned Yard in NEWGATE. [...] The Plate represents the Morning of Execution, and the malefactors having their irons knocked off previous to their ascending the fatal platform that launches them into eternity. The Yeoman of the Halter is in waiting to put the ropes about them. The Clergyman is also seen administering consolation to these unfortunate persons in such an awful moment [and] neither the PEN nor the PENCIL, however directed by talent, can do it adequate justice, or convey a description of the *"harrowed feelings"* of the few spectators that are admitted into the Condemned Yard [...][7]

The connection to crime reporting here is quite clear; this passage could almost have been taken from a prison chaplain's recollection or even an early *Newgate Calendar*, as it figuratively 'opened up' the scene of confession, penitence and farewell that had been popularised by crime reporting. In fact, the expression to 'launch into eternity' was a common turn of phrase within contemporary crime reporting, which certainly intimates at the strong journalistic connection between it and this early kind of 'social exploration' writing.[8] The Ordinary of Newgate himself is even present in the image, depicted with his hand raised on the far-left as he ministers to one of the unhappy condemned (a figure referred to as 'Lively Jem').[9]

Life in London's colourful illustrations such were completed by George Cruikshank; his first major work as a book illustrator,[10] and Cruikshank went on to draw for a great number of other novels across a long career, famously including those by a young Charles Dickens. Dickens, considered by Walter Bagehot to be the 'quintessential reporter and writer of urban life', is an important figure to consider when examining the evolution of social exploration journalism across this period, as well as its evolving use of the police officer and its development into fictional versions of itself.[11] In his 1833–1836 work *Sketches by Boz*, Dickens produced another early example of writing designed to reveal the inner workings of a supposedly-criminal space that the ordinary public would not usually have been able to see. Originally, it appeared in a variety of publications between 1833 and 1836, including in the *Monthly Magazine*, the *Evening Chronicle* and *Bell's Life in London*, however it was collected together and published as two volumes in 1836, and again as a single volume in 1839. The 'sketches' contained two essays of interest that were

Figure 3.1 Isaac Richard and George Cruikshank, 'Symptoms of the Finish of "Some Sorts of Life" in London. Tom, Jerry and Logic in the Press Yard at Newgate'

Source: Pierce Egan, *Life in London, or, The Day and Night Scenes of Jerry Hawthorn, Esq. and his Elegant Friend Corinthian Tom in their Rambles and Sprees though the Metropolis* (London: Chatto and Windus, 1821; repr. 1881), p. 315. Public domain.

similar in both content and purpose to the previous scene from *Life in London*; namely 'Criminal Courts' and 'A Visit to Newgate'.

'A Visit to Newgate' is perhaps best examined first. It was actually not included in any of the periodical incarnations of the 'sketches' but written specifically for the 1836 collected edition. However, as Philip Collins argues, Dickens's purpose was to provide the reader with as detailed a picture of the prison's interior as possible:

> [...] as he explained to his publisher, Macrone, he would add a few pieces to fill out the two volumes. In particular, he was seeking permission to go over Newgate – 'I have long projected sketching its Interior, and I think it would tell extremely well.'[12]

In fact, 'A Visit to Newgate' itself explicitly states its purpose of revealing the prison's interior in as much detail as it could, in order to (figuratively) transport the reader inside:

> It was with some such thoughts that we determined not many weeks since to visit the interior of Newgate – in an amateur capacity, of course; and [...] we proceed to lay its results before our readers, in the hope [...] that this paper may not be found wholly devoid of interest.[13]

Some of the close, highly descriptive detail Dickens was consciously trying to provide the reader can be exemplified here. Immediately after he is admitted, Dickens provides the reader with an exceptionally-detailed passage which truly makes a conscious and valiant attempt to transport the reader inside the prison along with him:

> Leaving this room [...] we found ourself [sic] in the lodge which opens on the Old Bailey; one side of which is plentifully garnished with a choice collection of heavy sets of irons [...] From this lodge, a heavy oaken gate, bound with iron, studded with nails of the same material, and guarded by another turnkey, opens on a few steps [...] which terminate in a narrow and dismal stone passage, running parallel with the Old Bailey, and leading to the different yards, through a number of tortuous and intricate windings, guarded in their turn by huge gates and gratings, whose appearance is sufficient to dispel at once the slightest hope of escape that any new comer may have entertained: and the very recollection of which, on eventually traversing the place again, involves one in a maze of confusion.[14]

Not only is this detail already sufficient to allow the reader to picture the scene in their mind effectively, but it is also interesting to note that there is a hybridised mixture of journalistic and fictional writing techniques at work, foreshadowing Dickens's progression towards a long and successful career writing fiction. Dickens deliberately saves his description of Newgate's condemned cells for a later part of the essay, no doubt wishing to leave the reader waiting for that happy moment:

> These yards, with the exception of that in which prisoners under sentence of death are confined (*of which we shall presently give a more detailed description*) [...] [my italics][15]

Dickens certainly delivers on his promise, devoting the entire second half of the essay to a description of the prison's condemned ward. Particularly harrowing is the account of one of the condemned cells in which a prisoner is left languishing on the night prior to their execution:

> We entered the first cell! It was a stone dungeon, eight feet long by six wide, with a bench at the further end, under which were a common horse-rug, a bible, and prayer-book. An iron candlestick was fixed into the wall at the side; and a small high window in the back admitted as much air and light as could struggle in between a double row of heavy, crossed iron bars. It contained no other furniture of any description. [...][16]

Dickens follows this by asking his reader to '[c]onceive the situation of a man, spending his last night in this cell',[17] and there then follows a description of the hypothetical prisoner's last thoughts over his final night, flitting from panic, to helplessness, to disbelief. The article ends with the prisoner falling into an uneasy sleep, wishfully dreaming that he has escaped, only to be reawakened at 6:00am by the turnkey entering the cell. As Dickens himself bluntly puts it in the piece's final line, 'in two hours more he is a corpse'.[18]

Much of the atmosphere created in this scene is echoed in the final chapters of Dickens's 1837–9 novel *Oliver Twist*, where the career-criminal Fagin is depicted inside the condemned cells of Newgate awaiting his impending execution in terror, and some of the description of his last night are startlingly reminiscent of 'A Visit to Newgate'.[19] Indeed, George Cruikshank's famous illustration, titled 'Fagin in the Condemned Cell', certainly recalls the panicked description of the hypothetical condemned in the cell depicted in the latter half of 'A Visit to Newgate' (see Figure 3.2).[20]

Interestingly, the depiction of the condemned prisoner panicking in his cell in Newgate that Dickens colourfully projected to his readers was replicated by Thackeray in 'Going to See a Man Hanged', which could itself be placed under the umbrella-term 'social exploration journalism'. Thackeray presents a similar hypothetical description of a prisoner (albeit a real one, the condemned Courvoisier), and similarly muses on what his final night on earth might be like:

> [...] I could not help thinking, as each clock sounded, what is he doing now? – has he heard it in his little room in Newgate yonder? Eleven o'clock. He has been writing until now. The gaoler says he is a pleasant man enough to be with; but he can hold out no longer, and is very weary.

Figure 3.2 George Cruikshank, 'Fagin in the Condemned Cell'
Source: *The Adventures of Oliver Twist, or, the Parish Boy's Progress, Victorian Web*
<http://www.victorianweb.org/victorian/art/illustration/cruikshank/ot24.html> [accessed July 2 2018], scanned and uploaded by Philip V. Allingham (1839, uploaded 2014).

"Wake me at four," says he, "for I still have much to put down." From eleven to twelve the gaoler hears how he is grinding his teeth in his sleep. At twelve he is up in his bed, and asks, "Is it the time?" He has plenty more time yet for sleep; and he sleeps, and the bells go on tolling. Seven hours more – five hours more. Many a carriage is clattering through the streets, bringing ladies away from the evening parties; many bachelors are reeling home after a jolly night; Covent Garden is alive; and the light coming through the cell-window turns the gaoler's candle pale. Four hours more! "Courvoisier," says the gaoler, shaking him, "it's four o'clock now, and I've woke you, as you told me, but there's no call for you to get up yet." The poor wretch leaves his bed, however, and makes his last toilet; and then falls to writing, to tell the world how he did the crime for which he has suffered. This time he will tell the truth, and the whole truth.[21]

Returning to Dickens, the infamous Newgate was not the only prison which he wished to 'project' for the interest of his curious readers. As Collins also points out, he became close friends with the governors of Coldbath Fields and Tothill Fields prisons and openly wished to supplement 'A Visit to Newgate' with some comparative pieces, but quickly realised that his essay on Newgate had 'stolen all the thunder which the prison-theme could produce'.[22] However, he continued to write articles that were designed to allow readers to observe the interiors of unpleasant and inaccessible criminal spaces, often with a slight socio-political agenda attached. For example, another of his *Sketches* was titled 'Criminal Courts', which appeared in the *Morning Chronicle* in October 1834 under the title 'The Old Bailey'. The piece concerned itself with depicting the interior of the criminal court, and scathingly mocked the attending officials:

> There sit the Judges, with whose great dignity everyone is acquainted, and whom therefore we need say no more. Then, there is the Lord Mayor in the centre, looking as cool as a Lord Mayor *can* look, with his immense *bouquet* before him, and habited in all the splendour of his office. Then, there are the Sheriffs, who are almost as dignified as the Lord Mayor himself, and the Barristers, who are quite dignified enough in their own opinion, and the spectators, who having paid for their admission, look upon the whole scene as if it were got up especially for their amusement.[23]

Despite Dickens's ribbing of the pompous appearance and over-inflated sense of self-importance that the officials of the court (and the watching public) seem to possess, his focus moves sharply to the plight of the man in the dock. This has the effect of turning the scene from one of light-hearted amusement to a commentary on how the court system has enormous and potentially dangerous amounts of power over the people – a power barely acknowledged by those who were institutionalised by it:

> Look upon the whole group in the body of the Court – some wholly engrossed in the morning papers, others carelessly conversing in low whispers, and others, again, quietly dozing away an hour – and you scan scarcely believe that the result of the trial is a matter of life or death to one wretched being present. But [...] watch the prisoner attentively for a few moments, and the fact is before you, in all its painful reality. [...] a dead silence prevails as the foreman delivers in the verdict – 'Guilty!' A shriek bursts from a female in the gallery [...] The clerk directs one of the officers of the Court to 'take the woman out,' and fresh business is proceeded with, as if nothing had occurred.[24]

Dickens's discussion of social politics aside, the point to be drawn from these examples is that writing which explored, projected, and commented on the inaccessible spaces of criminality for their readers was steadily growing in popularity and frequency across the early years of the nineteenth century, influenced by the pseudo-voyeuristic interests of crime-reports such as prison chaplains' accounts or even early *Newgate Calendars*. However, it was also to develop substantially across the Victorian era. For example, writing which explored prisons and the operation of the criminal justice system more broadly, such as Henry Mayhew and John Binny's *The Criminal Prisons of London* (1862), became outspokenly reformist.[25] Within popular journalism that was designed to open up the world of crime, which remains our focus here, it was the introduction of the new police that fundamentally changed the way that the form of writing was constructed. As the next part of this chapter will highlight, the figure of the police officer became a useful presence within the narrative thanks to their positioning between criminals and the rest of the public and their constant 'access' to criminality.

'In company with detectives, he has visited beershops [...]': Social Exploration Journalism and the Police Officer in the Victorian Era

In the mid-Victorian era, 'social exploration journalism' interested in society's criminal element was to fundamentally change as the concept of popular journalism was rewritten and, crucially, knowledge of the police proliferated.[26] Crime and criminals was a common topic for discussion in mid-century periodicals, and Caroline Reitz suggests that this was due to a broad perception that the criminal justice system was going 'down and out' due to the expansion of the 'criminal classes' resulting in a journalistic fixation on criminals and their habitats.[27] However, I argue that mid-Victorian periodical writing that focused specifically on examining the haunts, activities, and 'hidden secret worlds' of crime and criminals was *also* a by-product of the interests of a) pseudo-voyeuristic reporting from crime reporting, b) knowledge of the police proliferated by periodical criticism, and c) the positioning of the police as a protective shield against criminality, all meshing together. In short, this kind of writing became a literary space where journalists could actively utilise the police officer as both a guide and a form of protection to delve further and further into criminal spaces, and to then project them for readers' interest or amusement.

The expansion of society itself meant that social exploration journalism also moved both out of static locations considered 'criminal', such as prisons or courtrooms, out onto the streets themselves. The growth of the city had been a factor in the establishment of the police, yet it also changed the way that social exploration was performed as the city evolved into a more chaotic and unmanageable state. As Paul Fyfe points out, this kind of writing grew *alongside* the city itself, and the sheer diversity of mid-century printed media actually shared the qualities of chaos and randomness with the metropolis it described.[28] The urban space grew almost alarmingly quickly throughout the early to mid-nineteenth century; for example, in 1806 the western border of London lay at the intersection between Oxford Street and Park Lane, yet by 1862 the entirety of Hyde Park and Kensington Gardens had been enveloped by the metropolis.[29] Not only this, but the growth of the urban environment actually created new, never before seen spaces such as suburban railway carriages, which could hide new kinds of criminality and which needed 'exploring' in order to iron out some of the public anxieties surrounding techno-logical change.[30]

Journalists thus naturally became increasingly interested in depicting the chaos of street-level activity to readers, particularly those deemed to be somehow dangerous or disreputable. Periodical descriptions of open street-environments became vividly detailed and meticulously accurate; in 1861, for example, *Blackwood's Edinburgh Magazine* published an article by John Paget discussing the case of Eliza Fenning, which opened with a description of a supposedly-dangerous part of London that, it assumed, its readers would not frequent:

> Immediately adjoining to High Holborn, and parallel with the southern side of Red Lion Square runs a long, narrow gloomy lane, called Eagle Street. Sickly children dabble in the gutters [...] Vendors of tripe and cat's-meat, rag and bottle dealers, marine-store keepers, merchants who hold out temptations in prose and verse, adorned with apoplectic numerals, to cooks and housemaids to purloin dripping, kitchen-stuff, and old wearing apparel, barbers who "shave well for a penny," shoe vampers, fried fish sellers, a coal and potato dealer, and a bird-stuffer, share the rest of the street, with lodging-houses of the filthiest description.[31]

This change in perspective from static locations of crime and out onto the streets immediately raises questions regarding the journalist's navigation, traversal, and comprehension of the urban space. As Christopher Pittard argues, the pedestrian's perspective of these streets was chaotic, undisciplined, and resistant to organisation,[32] and in suggesting this he echoes arguments regarding the pedestrian's street-level perspective famously posited by Michel de Certeau in *The Practice of Everyday Life* (1984). De Certeau suggests that a 'street-walking' pedestrian is inherently unable to 'read' the city that they inhabit, and thus they are consistently forced to traverse the streets blindly.[33] Authors of mid-century social exploration journalism certainly experienced this urban blindness; the 'down below' perspective of the journalist, as de Certeau puts it, prevented them from actually 'seeing' that which they wished to describe for their readers.[34] Journalists might have been able to wander the streets and knew where the supposed 'criminal' haunts were located, but they had little knowledge of them, no idea what it was they were actually looking for, or even when they had found it.

This is where the police officer enters the equation. The criminal has historically been seen as intrinsically tied to the urban space, operating within the subterranean world of criminality that was seen to exist just beneath the visible surface of society.[35] However, what is less recognised is that the *police officer* was just as closely tied to it. As knowledge of the police spread throughout public consciousness and the perception of them as a socially-indistinct shield against criminality proliferated, authors of social exploration journalism realised that the police officer could assist them perform their task of penetrating, understanding and revealing these criminalised locations. As Chapter 2 argued, the police essentially took over responsibility for the criminal element from society itself, distancing the public from criminals and occupying the space in between for themselves. Consequently, again as we have seen, the police effectively existed outside of rigid mid-Victorian class systems[36] in that they were seen as both respectable professionals, yet also as tainted by the fact that they were forced to associate with criminals on a daily basis and were thus on some levels 'criminalised'. In fact, Barbara Korte, when musing on the idea of hero-worship in mid-Victorian magazines, does not mention the police officer as a would-be heroic figure.[37] Instead, she lists other figures who received various forms of hero-worship for their actions, including orderlies, engineers, and (particularly) firemen, yet not police officers who were marred by their daily association with criminals and thus not singled out for hero-worship.[38] The pseudo-criminalised police officer thus helped to maintain the 'subterranean world of crime' to which Trodd refers, by keeping different classes of society separate from each other.[39] Indeed, as D. A. Miller puts it, the police created an 'enclosed world' of delinquency from which it was difficult to escape or to penetrate,[40] and a previously-quoted example from the *National Review* in 1883 helps to highlight this, as the author of the piece is warned away from a dangerous 'criminal' area by a police officer, apparently patrolling the 'borders' of the respectable part of the city:

> I had only twice walked through the street, and the first time I was warned by a policeman, as I turned down into it, to "look out where I was going to"[41]

However, the socially-peripheral nature of police officers also made them socially *mobile*. Unlike the general public, police officers were free to cross the boundaries between 'underworlds of crime and poverty' and the 'sunshine of bourgeois domesticity' at will – a right usually reserved, argues Susan Zlotnick, only for those with 'true' bourgeois identities.[42] The fact that the officer in this quotation warns the journalist to 'look out where [he] was going to', and the fact that the journalist was ignorant of the ramifications of doing so, demonstrates how the journalist *conforms* to Michel de Certeau's idea of the blind pedestrian, while the police officer, in fact, *challenges* it. The police officer shows knowledge and awareness of the urban maze, and could thus instead manifest what could be termed the 'knowledgeable pedestrian', who traverses the urban cityscape in full knowledge of both its seen and, crucially, its unseen aspects.[43]

Contemporary journalists, consciously blind to the secrets of the city and its criminal underworld, realised that they could accompany knowledgeable and socially-mobile police officers into undesirable and criminalised spaces that they themselves would otherwise not have been able to penetrate. In doing this, journalists could explore and learn about these locations more closely and, in turn, reveal and describe them for their curious readers. Interested journalists who made this connection thus began to perform social exploration in the direct company of police officers who, perhaps naturally, moved ever closer to the centre of these narratives.[44] The presence of the police officer as a figure that accompanied, guided, and protected the journalist in their explorations of urban criminal spaces, meant that a much more diverse spectrum of spaces were now open to explore, including the obvious poverty-stricken slums, but also internal city locations like public-houses, opium dens, gin-shops or dancing-houses.

It is Charles Dickens who again provides us with a good representative example of this in action. Building on his earlier work in *Sketches by Boz*, Dickens picked up on the fact that directly accompanying police officers afforded him the opportunity to expand his wanderings and enter into ever more dangerous and varied criminal spaces than the static prison. Accounts of his exploits in a multitude of urban locales, particularly St Giles-in-the-Fields, alongside police Inspectors Field and Whicher appeared in *Household Words* in 1850–51. This again highlighted his crossover between social criticism and fictional narratives, as Field himself famously became the inspiration for Inspector Bucket in *Bleak House* (1853).[45] Jessica Valdez also suggests that Dickens deliberately structured *Household Words* to mirror the chaos of mid-Victorian urban society to help the reader become more discerning of patterns and broader social trends,[46] and she echoes Pittard's sentiments that periodicals and their content directly mirrored the chaos of urban cities in which they were produced.[47]

Dickens's accounts specifically included 'A Detective Police Party' (1850), 'Three Detective Anecdotes' (1850) and 'On Duty with Inspector Field' (1851),[48] and each provided readers with an 'internal' view into the world of crime using the police officer as a knowledgeable literary protector and guide, occupying a social, as well as physical, space between Dickens and those he wished to observe. 'On Duty with Inspector Field', in particular, can highlight Dickens's interest in entering and revealing the realms of criminals to the reader:

> Saint Giles's church strikes half-past ten. We stoop low, and creep down a precipitous flight of steps into a dark close cellar. There is a fire. There is a long deal table. There are benches. The cellar is full of company, chiefly very young men in various conditions of dirt and raggedness. Some are eating supper. There are no girls or women present. Welcome to the Rat's Castle, gentlemen, and to this company of noted thieves![49]

The line '[w]elcome to the Rat's Castle, gentlemen, and to this company of noted thieves!' is particularly interesting, as it ambiguously suggested both Inspector Field speaking to Dickens, but also Dickens speaking directly to the reader, who thus figuratively accompanied him. However, Dickens had a number of ulterior purposes to producing this kind of writing other than simple social exploration of the urban criminal. Indeed, the idea that the police officer manifested a precarious class position is slightly less pronounced in Dickens's writing than in other examples. This is because, as Valdez also argues, Dickens's additional motive was actually to further highlight the positives in law enforcement, such as improvements in detection, as a response to contemporary criticism of the police – a motive which did not feature in other examples of this kind of writing.[50] Additionally, Dickens tended to highlight the nature of the crimes committed in these narratives as the result of poor moral or social choices, such as alcoholism, which perhaps gestured on some level back towards the idea that crime narratives were, at least on some basic (or perhaps pretended) level, aimed at the provision of social or moral instruction.[51] We witness this in action directly, as Dickens provides descriptions of who was being held inside the police-station, where several prisoners are depicted as having been apprehended for being intoxicated:

> [A] raving drunken woman in the cells, who has screeched her voice away, and has hardly enough power left to declare, even with the passionate help of her feet and arms, that she is the daughter of a British officer, and, strike her blind and dead, but she'll write a letter to the Queen! but who is soothed with a drink of water – in another cell [...] a meek tremulous old pauper man who has been out for a holiday "and has took but a little drop, but it has overcome him arter [sic] so many months in the house" [...][52]

'On Duty with Inspector Field' is described by Anthea Trodd as 'Dickens's most extravagant tribute to the new detective force', and she accurately suggests that Dickens himself operated within the narrative as a distinct figure from everything else contained within it – in other words, as a middle-class participant in, and observer of, police raids on the darkest areas of urban London.[53] D. A. Miller also argues that '[o]utside and surrounding the [closed] world of delinquency lies the middle-class world of private life',[54] and Dickens thus occupies the position of a middle-class journalist who used the police officer as his liminally-positioned guide and protector into the urban criminal world. For his part, Field's social ambiguity allowed him to protect Dickens both from physical danger, but also in a social sense by allowing him to retain his middle-class status. Indeed Field, argues Trodd, manifested the exact opposite qualities to Dickens himself, in that he was a 'model of courage, mental sharpness, and [possessed extensive] *knowledge of the urban labyrinth*'.[55] Field thus fits well into the idea of the police officer as the 'knowledgeable pedestrian', the street-walker with superior understanding of the complex urban landscape and who can help other, ignorant figures to traverse it successfully.[56]

It was not only Dickens who used the police in this protective fashion; this use of the police as a force for journalistic protection and urban knowledge began to appear in numerous other examples of mid-Victorian periodical journalism which was designed to penetrate, explore and reveal criminal spaces. In May 1869, for example, the *Ragged School Union Magazine* published an article describing how a journalist for the *Times* had recently spent a week exploring particular 'low areas' of London, under the apparently-necessary protection of a police officer:

> A well-known member of the "Times" staff has recently devoted about a
> week to the visitation of the "crime gardens" of London. In company with
> detectives, he has visited beershops, lodging-houses for travellers, and dolly
> shops in Tiger Bay, Kent Street, the Mint, and the other favourite haunts of
> our criminal classes.[57]

The use of the phrase 'crime gardens' colourfully highlights the journalist's
purpose. These areas were deemed to be spaces where criminal behaviour figuratively 'grew', and were thus spaces which respectable Victorians would not
have been able to visit under normal circumstances, without the protective presence and urban knowledge of a police officer. Again, the idea that the detective
was present for the journalist's 'safety' had a double-meaning, as they keep the
author 'safe' both from physical harm, but also from flouting unspoken restrictions on where respectable members of society could and could not go. The author
was thus careful to state that all of the journalist's explorations were 'in company
with detectives', as if this legitimised the activity as socially permissible. In another
example of this, in June 1865 an article by J. C. Parkinson and published in
Temple Bar wrote:

> From Stepney police-station, again, I have started – *always with the
> Inspector* [my italics] – to go the round of the cheap gaffs, squalid sal-
> oons, small music-halls, dancing taverns, and concert-rooms of the
> Ratcliffe Highway and Whitechapel. [...] where the shottishe [sic] is
> danced by foreign gentlemen and ladies [...] habitually carry knives, and
> occasionally use them.[58]

The phrase 'always with the Inspector' is, obviously, particularly significant, as
the presence of the police officer was again included to highlight how the author
would never have dreamed of 'going the round' in these criminal spaces without
their presence. In fact, in December 1874 the politician and later Liberal MP
John Burns (1858–1943), writing in *Good Words*, suggested that an entire *party*
of police officers needed to be present for the author to enter the haunts of the
criminal class:

> It was considerately arranged by the chief constable that everything should
> be shown to be in the worst haunts, and accordingly under the guidance of
> a lieutenant and picked escort of detectives, we made a sally from the
> Central Police Office [...][59]

In a final example, in 1851 the *Ragged School Union Magazine* wrote how a
police officer provided an escort to a group of determined journalists who had
travelled from Scotland to see the 'criminal underworld' of London. The
detective officer is, again, directly described as both a guide and protector of
this group, and the author argues that without the protection of the police the
entire operation would certainly not have been possible:

But we were anxious to get to the very bottom of the social fabric, to explore the lowest depths where human beings are to be found. Without the protection of the police such an enterprise would of course have been impossible; but on presenting a letter which we had brought from Scotland, we found the authorities ready to afford every facility, and as the best method of accomplishing our object, we were intrusted [sic] to the guidance of J. H. Sanders, an officer of the detective force.[60]

Interestingly, the use of a police officer as a companion by those who wished to explore criminalised or 'dangerous' urban spaces apparently extended beyond journalists to curious members of the public. A letter to the *London Review* published in January 1864 made a startling argument in respect to this practice:

One of the strangest pilgrimages that can be made among the wonderful sights of London used to be accomplished [...] by visitors who had the permission of the authorities and the aid of the police in "going the rounds" through the lowest haunts of crime. [...] A recent visit of this kind for many hours in company with officers *who could not be denied admittance anywhere, opened up large fields for observation* [my italics] [...][61]

According to the correspondent, the practice of using police officers to accompany people into slum areas was not limited to journalists interested performing social exploration, but was a possibility for anyone who wished to perform a form of what might be simply termed 'poverty tourism'. The police were thus a knowledgeable social institution which served to maintain the distinctions between respectable middle-class values and the chaos of criminality, which further highlights the fact that the police themselves occupied an indistinct social position somewhere in the middle. The author of this letter also points to the fact that this kind of practice 'opened' various closed, private, or dangerous spaces for exploration, as the police officer's power and influence allowed them an unprecedented level of access:

Here is the grand entrance of a huge theatre, with flaring gas, and a tide of people flowing in. But a few taps at a dark back door, and a magic word or two from our leaders, open the way [...][62]

The use of a theatre here is highly symbolic, as entering through the *back* door hinted at the idea that the distinction between visible front stage and hidden backstage mirrored wider society itself, which also contained a visible facade which masked a darker, 'backstage' area where ordinary spectators could not go. The 'criminal areas' of London and other cities were therefore spaces that were largely hidden from public view, where unknown activities took place, and which went unnoticed by the vast majority of people who only saw the visible part of the 'stage production' of Victorian society. Indeed, as the aforementioned article by John Burns, 'A Wild Night', suggested:

> Our neighbour the moon always shows her bright side: we never see that
> which is in the gloom, and so it may be said of most people who live in
> great cities. They know by report, but few practically have seen, the vicis-
> situdes of vast populations [...][63]

In short, these kinds of article where journalists used the presence of a
police officer to accompany them into urban spaces deemed to be 'criminal'
were an innovative form of writing which blended the various conventions
of both contemporary police criticism and crime journalism together. The
police officer, a figure which had been extensively discussed in periodicals,
had become socially blurred – both by their position as taking over the
active management of society's criminal element, and also by the tension
between their 'respectable' status as a uniformed professional and their
continuous association with criminals. However, the police officer was not
only socially external, but also socially *mobile*, and came to be perceived as
a figure that could understand the rapidly-developing urban sprawl and its
criminal aspects much better than the general public. They could physically
enter or exit supposed criminal areas at will, and subsequently assist others
who did not have that ability perform the same act, including journalists
who wished to reveal the criminal areas of growing cities for their readers.
This kind of social exploration journalism therefore catered for the same
pseudo-voyeuristic interests of readers of crime reporting, as journalists
entered criminal spaces in the company of the police, with the express
intention of finding out as much as possible about the people that inhabited
those spaces in order to render those spaces public for their amusement and
instruction of their curious readers, who could engage with the material
from a place of complete safety.

However, as the era progressed and as the periodical press developed, this
trope began to be transposed into more *creative* kinds of writing, as the
pretence at maintaining an 'illusion of truth' in these narratives gave way to
the desire to present more entertaining (and ultimately marketable) fiction to
readers. This, I suggest, directly influenced the appearance of the first genre
of fiction to be contemporarily ascribed the label 'detective literature' –
popular 'police memoir' fiction.

'"Detective" literature, if it may be so called': The Police Memoir as 'Detective Fiction'

Between approximately 1850 and 1870, a sizable amount of fiction marketed as
the 'memoirs' or 'recollections' of police officers was published. These were
(usually) fictional first person narratives told from the perspective of a police
officer directly to the reader, relating individual cases across their policing
career. The officer was often said to have been 'released' from secrecy, often
through retirement, and marketed their stories as previously-classified tales that
had not been able to be revealed before.

These fictional police memoirs were the natural culmination of the interests of all of the various forms of periodical writing this volume has examined so far meshing together. They utilised knowledge of the police from contemporary periodical criticism; catered for the quasi-voyeuristic interests of crime reporting; and – in particular – made the protective quality of the socially-marginalised police officer present in 'social exploration' journalism a central mechanic of the text. Indeed, as Erich Goode points out, the wider concept of the 'memoir' appealed to readers' sense of *inclusion* within a text, which particularly highlights police memoir fiction's connection to social exploration journalism that focused on revealing the haunts of the criminal classes in the figurative company of the police:

> What is the appeal of autobiography and memoir? Autonarrative is appealing to the extent that it permits the reader to enter the author's time and place, to see the world behind the author's eyes, to vicariously live another life – to both voyeuristically and experientially live the life of another person.[64]

Thus, like social exploration journalism, fictional police memoirs allowed readers to witness and experience both the dangerous world of criminality and, by extension, the exciting life and professional exploits of a police officer from a place of complete safety. This helps to answer a question posed by Catherine Nickerson, who rhetorically asks:

> The world of the detective novel is a place of untimely death, cruelty, suspicion and betrayal. If detective fiction is a literature of escape, why would anyone want to be transported to such anxious locales?[65]

Nickerson answers her own question by arguing that detective fiction's enduring popularity is almost always connected to the acceleration and public perception of true crime. Police memoir fiction certainly offered readers the 'truth', with individual texts marketing themselves as 'real' adventures of the police in 'real' places around the city. Presenting the 'truth' was also the central concern of the journalist – as we have seen already – but it did not always make for particularly entertaining reading, and this leads us to another reason for the growth in the police-memoir's popularity during the mid-Victorian era. In short, the fictional police memoir simply offered readers higher entertainment value than journalism.[66] As Warren Fox gestures towards when he discusses the Franz Müller case of 1864, some truthful stories of police officers tracking and apprehending true criminals actually lost their entertainment value as the criminals and detectives simply were not imaginative enough for readers' liking:

> It was with a certain derision, almost amounting to annoyance, that the newspapers reported the ease with which Müller had been taken: "It seems marvellous," the *Morning Star* commented, "how any man who had the

> evil ingenuity to plan and the wicked resolution to attempt a murder could
> have acted with such utter and abject imbecility when it became necessary
> to attempt an escape from the consequences of his crime." Some writers
> even began to wonder whether the police might not have pursued and
> arrested the wrong man, or at least a dim-witted accomplice rather than
> the mastermind behind the crime [...][67]

In cases such as this, the 'truthful' element to crime journalism was losing its
appeal in favour of the more sensational elements of fictional storytelling. In
addition, as Alyce Von Rothkirch has suggested, the *villain* of crime-storytelling
manifested 'contemporary social and cultural anxieties', and were representations of 'the public imagination about crime'.[68] Thus, the reality surrounding
actual criminals such as Franz Müller, namely that they were less interesting
than 'imagined' criminality, naturally gave way to more creative responses –
such as the fictional police memoir, which allowed the author's (and the reader's) imagination to wander more freely.

As well as higher entertainment value however, the production of fiction also
allowed authors a much greater degree of creative freedom, which in turn allowed
for more targeted social or political commentary as the necessity to maintain an
illusion of truth in a narrative was no longer an issue. This is perhaps explained
most succinctly by Jessica Valdez, who explores Charles Dickens's movement away
from journalism and into fictional story telling. Valdez suggests that Dickens's
move from *Household Words* to *All the Year Round* represented a 'hardening of
his views on journalism and a greater reliance on fictional narrative to provide
readers with an understanding of their positions in the Victorian social framework'.[69] Essentially, pesky reality sometimes obstructed the construction of writing
designed to critique specific areas of society which potentially needed reform, and
thus the production of fictional narratives were a natural move for journalists
looking to perform more targeted socio-political commentary.

The movement from 'social exploration journalism' to 'police memoir fiction'
is therefore understandable, as by writing fiction authors could do everything
that they would otherwise have been able to do by performing true journalism,
but more efficiently. They could present the urban underworld that readers
wished to view, in the figurative company of an interesting police officer who
did battle with intelligent and entertaining criminals who manifested contemporary sociocultural anxieties. Authors also had greater creative freedom to
choose what happened next to make their stories particularly targeted and to
help sell copies of their books to interested readers. All the while, authors
themselves remained safe, with no need to actually go out and explore the
criminal underworld like their journalist counterparts.

Despite its multifaceted cultural connections to other forms of popular writing
however, the influx of police memoirs which occurred across the mid-nineteenth
century is often dismissed today as unworthy of scholarly scrutiny, as it has
become characterised as little more than cheap and nasty hack fiction. Indeed, Ian
Ousby argues:

This cheap and cheerful reading, published in series such as Routledge's
Railway Library [...] included a flood of books presented as the reminiscences
of real policemen but actually fiction written by hacks.[70]

Others only glance towards police memoirs, only briefly acknowledging that
there was an increase in the genre's presence and popularity, but not offering
any real insights into its cultural relevance or literary significance. Many commentators simply prefer to focus instead on mid-Victorian 'sensation fiction'
and its relation to the development of the detective genre throughout the 1860s.
Indeed, Anthea Trodd ignores the influx of mid-Victorian police memoirs when
she contends that by 1862 the 'police detective [was] a character still in search
of a genre',[71] while Charles Rzepka acknowledges the presence of the police
memoir but quickly skates over it by opting to focus instead on the work of
Emile Gaboriau.[72] Rzepka does admit that police memoirs may have a place in
the genre's chronology, but is suspicious of the attribution of the title 'detective
fiction' to the genre when he suggests that detective fiction was still largely
contained within other forms of writing across the mid-Victorian years, and
that police memoirs were only a 'possible exception' to this rule:

> With the possible exception of the police 'recollections' and 'memoirs' of the
> 1850s and 1860s, detective novels and stories remained largely submerged in
> other types of Victorian literature [...][73]

Additionally, Stephen Knight similarly mentions several authors of police
memoirs, but remains unconvinced of the genre's codification as 'detective
fiction' because he sees the genre's procedural nature as a 'barrier' to the
development of 'detection' as a literary technique, and instead argues in
favour of texts which featured more amateur sleuths.[74]

Scholarly ambivalence towards the fictional police memoir has caused it to
remain largely unrecognised as a legitimate moment in the history of detective
fiction. Perhaps this is largely because the role of the periodical press, where
much of this material appeared, has not yet been properly examined in relation
to the development of the genre. There are very few studies which give explicit
focus to the rise and popularity of police memoirs, and those that do exist are
largely unsatisfactory. Indeed, *The Female Detective* by Andrew Forrester
(1864) and *Revelations of a Lady Detective* by William Stephens Hayward
(1864) are both examples of the genre, and thus form a part of a much wider
literary network, but they are almost always analysed simply because they feature female detectives.[75] Elsewhere, Haia Shpayer-Makov's chapter 'Explaining
the Rise and Success of Detective Memoirs in Britain' published in *Police
Detectives in History, 1750–1950* (2006) is a rare example of a scholarly piece
that focuses specifically on the memoir genre, but as it centres itself largely on
real detectives, its conclusions are limited. Shpayer-Makov concludes that actual
detectives had incentives to publish their experiences in the line of duty, as they
wished to present the police – and particularly the Criminal Investigations

Department – in a positive light.[76] Makov also suggests that the shift from reality towards fiction was due to the literary attraction of recounting detectives' experiences as a highly marketable form of writing.[77]

That said, there is a small amount of scholarly work which does recognise this form of writing as a significant literary moment. Heather Worthington, for example, argues that the mid-century police memoir was the first literary genre where the police officer or detective took centre stage,[78] and goes on to suggest that the influx of the genre was due to the 'professionalisation' and general acceptance of the police that allowed their stories to proliferate into periodicals alongside other 'anecdotes of professional men' that were common in early Victorian periodicals.[79] In fact, Worthington's exploration of police memoir texts is perhaps some of the most comprehensive yet completed, and she goes on to correctly argue that police memoirs 'offered their audience adventure and the excitement of a distanced contact with crime'.[80] Similarly, Haia Shpayer-Makov, in her monograph *The Ascent of the Detective: Police Sleuths in Victorian and Edwardian England* (2011), provides a much more satisfactory analysis than in her previously-mentioned chapter and suggests that the genre was important for raising awareness surrounding the use of detectives in literature:

> [T]he pseudo-memoirs of detectives [...] not only expanded the presence of the official detective figure in literature significantly, but also accorded him a central role in the plot.[81]

This point regarding the centralisation of the *detective* within the plot is particularly noteworthy, as it denotes the fact that journalism focused on crime had absorbed the understanding and interest in the police permeated by contemporary periodical criticism of the force, and had thus became a central focus of these narratives. Alyce Von Rothkirch makes this point succinctly, when she agrees with Shpayer-Makov that 'gradually [...] the detective assigned to a case attained parity with the criminal as a literary character, and in time replaced him as a dominant figure in aesthetic discourse.'[82] In other words, the rise of the fictional police memoir was part of the cultural progression away from focusing on the *criminal*, and a motion towards the *police officer* as the central figure within narratives. As Worthington argues, by the time police memoirs attained their zenith in popularity policing had come to be regarded as a profession and had been generally accepted as a necessity.[83]

The most important point, however, regarding the merit of police memoir fiction in terms of its contribution to the evolution of the detective genre is that mid-Victorian authors and periodical commentators *themselves* demonstrated an awareness of 'detective fiction' as an emerging, distinct literary genre, and directly associated police memoir fiction with it. In the first issue of 'Experiences of a Real Detective', a series of stories published in the *Sixpenny Magazine* throughout 1862 under the pseudonym 'Inspector F.', the journalist and prominent author of police memoirs William Russell argued that detective fiction itself was an emergent literary genre, which was directly characterised by the police memoir:

"Detective" literature, if it may be so called, appears to have acquired a wide popularity, chiefly, I suppose, because the stories are believed to be, in the main, faithfully-told, truthful narratives.[84]

There is much to unpack here. Russell's attempt at genre categorisation anticipates an argument made by Paul Fyfe, who suggests that the flood of cheap literature which emerged throughout the mid-Victorian era took commentators aback, and they naturally attempted to make sense of it using what he terms the 'classificatory rhetoric of natural history'.[85] The phrase, 'if it may be so called' certainly denotes a sense of hesitation. However whilst the label itself may only be tentatively ascribed, it was clearly necessary to distinguish police memoirs from other emergent literary forms. Russell suggested that the idea of 'detective literature' specifically *was* 'police memoir writing', because the point of 'detective literature' was to be 'faithfully-told, truthful narratives' of the experiences of police officers and their interactions with the criminal element of society. For all intents and purposes, therefore, I suggest that in the 1860s 'detective fiction' simply *was* 'police memoir fiction'. A review of Russell's work from the *Dublin Review* of May 1861 makes the point:

Just now books of narratives of detectives and ex-detectives are all the fashion. Diaries, note-books, and confessions issue from the press in shoals, and one would naturally expect to find amongst them a complete disclosure of an ingenious and successful system.[86]

Other journalists and writers also picked up on this. In December 1864, for example, a piece titled 'An Australian Detective's Story' appeared in *Once a Week*, which commented directly on police memoirs' contemporary popularity and suggested that 'detective literature' was designed to illustrate the 'science of crime discovery', or in other words, 'detection':

[...] the story I am about to tell [...] well deserves a place among those detective notabilia which of late years have furnished such curious illustrations of the science of crime-discovery.[87]

As the genre was contemporarily viewed, at least by some, as an emergent form of 'detective fiction', the police memoir became extremely important to the development of the genre. The ascription of the label 'detective literature' suggests that the genre was already distinctive, with its own characteristics separate from other emerging genres. Consequently, it is worth analysing the life-cycle of the genre itself some detail.

The 'Golden Age' of the Police Memoir

At this stage, it is important to point out that the wider 'fictional memoir' genre itself was not a mid-Victorian invention, and also that it was distinct from 'autobiography' in that memoirs focused on certain aspects of the protagonists' lives (such as their profession), rather than their entire experiences from birth. The late eighteenth and early nineteenth centuries were peppered with examples of would-be fictional 'memoirs' that dealt with a variety of subjects, which Worthington, musing on the common presence of this kind of writing, terms the 'anecdotes of professional men'.[88] At this point, there was *no* discernible trend in topics, and a short list of titles published in early nineteenth-century periodicals highlights this eclectic mixture of subject matter, including 'Memoirs of a Missionary' (the *Satirist*, 1810), 'Memoirs of a Recluse' (the *European Magazine*, 1816), 'Recollections of a Metropolitan Curate' (the *European Magazine*, 1819), 'Memoirs of a Misanthrope' (the *London Magazine*, 1822), 'The Memoir of a Hypochondriac' (the *London Magazine*, 1822), 'Real Scenes in the Life of an Actress' (the *Weekly Entertainer*, 1823), 'The Recollections of a Student' (the *New Monthly Magazine*, 1823), and 'Recollections of a Tour in France' (the *Weekly Entertainer*, 1824). There were also some more playful titles which could also potentially fit into the memoir genre, including 'Memoirs of a Haunch of Mutton', published in the *New Monthly Magazine* in 1823. These were published for a variety of different authorial purposes. There was firstly an apparent interest in representing the distant and occasionally dangerous experiences of the author to the reader. However crucially, as Worthington puts it, memoir fiction made 'public what had been private', and it is this aspect of the genre which connects memoirs with the broad interests of other forms of writing discussed already throughout this volume.[89]

The fictional 'memoir' genre became earnestly concerned with crime and law enforcement around the middle of the nineteenth century. However, rather interestingly there were some earlier proto-examples which somewhat foreshadowed this mid-century boom. Texts such as 'Diary of a Barrister during the Last Wexford Assizes', which appeared in January 1826 in the *New Monthly Magazine*, were marketed as direct excerpts from the private notebooks of law enforcement officials, and this particular example was marketed to be wholly separate from the official records of assizes.[90] It claimed that it provided readers with information on cases that contemporary crime reporting in newspapers and periodicals would have either missed or deliberately omitted, and the author asserted that readers could glean 'insider information', designed to 'gratify the[ir] curiosity'.[91] Secondly, the anonymous[92] novel *Richmond, or, Scenes in the Life of a Bow Street Runner* (1827) is also an early example of a fictional 'police memoir'. It is relatively unknown today, though it is occasionally recognised among scholarly circles which explore the chronology of detective fiction. Worthington suggests that *Richmond* was a 'teenage text'

> situated between the 'infancy' of policing in its semi-feudal form with parish constables and watchmen, and its 'coming of age' as the New Metropolitan Police.[93]

Outside of specialist scholarly discourse, however, *Richmond* is very rarely, if at all, remembered. Worthington is perhaps the most comprehensive, performing an extended comparison between *Richmond* and Russell's later work, and concluding that Russell's later work essentially highlighted how the genre had 'professionalised' in the intervening years.[94] Others are less interested, however. Haia Shpayer-Makov mentions the novel but almost instantly dismisses it, arguing that the author was 'most probably not a Runner himself, and that the book [...] did not prove a great success'.[95] Charles Rzepka also performs a cursory glance towards it, suggesting that it was a text 'ahead of its time', but he is suspicious of the assertion that *Richmond* be categorised as 'detective fiction' at all.[96] None of Ian Ousby's *The Crime and Mystery Book*, [97] John Scaggs's *Crime Fiction: A New Critical Idiom*, or Stephen Knight's *Crime Fiction 1800–2000* mention *Richmond* at all. However, it is worth at least some critical attention with regard to its connection with later, mid-Victorian police memoirs. The novel relates the experiences of 'Tom Richmond', a member of the Bow Street Runners (a loosely-organised group of law-enforcement officials working in London prior to the establishment of the Metropolitan Police, eventually closed in 1839). *Richmond* provides readers with insights into the Runners' experiences, and also into isolated or marginalised communities such as gypsies and circuses, where he spent much of his early life. Richmond himself thus acts as the reader's guide into these communities, allowing them a window into their society to which they would not otherwise have been privy. Richmond, much like his later literary descendants, thus occupies a transitional social position between communities, and actively uses this to his advantage. In one example, he questions his old friends in a gypsy encampment in order to obtain information and assistance in the capture of a criminal:

> Marshall showed me every disposition to assist me in the inquiry. I took care, indeed, not to let him know what authority I now possessed, nor give him any hint of my official situation; otherwise he might have been shy of renewing our old acquaintance.[98]

This, it need hardly be pointed out, curiously foreshadows later depictions of police officers, where they occupied a similar social position between criminality and respectability. As with the police officer in popular 'social exploration journalism', Richmond recognises the useful quality in occupying an almost invisible space between classes, and consciously uses it to his advantage.

A further proto-example of a police memoir was the satirical *Life of a Policeman by an Ex-Constable*, which appeared in the *Penny Satirist* in 1843. This is significant as it was apparently genuinely authored by a constable employed by the Liverpool Police in the late 1830s. It provides readers with a cheerful, half-fictional, half-truthful[99] view into the 'daily drudgery of the lowly police-constable on the beat'.[100] It is largely satirical, and offers a number of tongue-in-cheek views of the police, including officers sneaking off for a drink or hiding to avoid patrolling Inspectors:

Tom, in his usual hurry, came bang against me with the force of a thunderbolt; he fell, and I nearly fell upon him, which circumstance excited the unrestrained laughter of every constable present. Having received orders from the superintendent to appear before the commissioners [...] on the charge of being drunk on duty, Tom and I immediately afterwards resorted to our cousin's, where we formed a council of three, and adopted plans and resolutions necessary to bring us out of our disgrace before the commissioners.[101]

However, the fact that it was clearly a satire of the activities of the police force, coupled with its amusing description of the intoxicated police constables (and is thus designed more for gently mocking humour than to provide real insight)[102] somewhat separates this text from later police memoirs, which presented the police as incorruptible and highly professionalised members of a structured and powerful organisation, and as a literary window into the sensationalised criminal underworld.

The years 1850–1870 could perhaps be termed the 'golden age of the police memoir', as the genre reached the peak of its popularity during this period.[103] The potential of the police officer to act as a guide and protector for readers, which had been so useful for journalists performing 'social exploration' into dangerous urban areas, was transposed into an impressive amount of fictional narratives throughout this era. This, I suggest, was a natural evolutionary progression. Non-fiction criticism of the police in periodicals had created a wider awareness of their image, purpose, and remit, and thus allowed authors who had no direct connection with the police themselves to create realistic and convincing literary police officers. Simultaneously, the pseudo-voyeuristic interests of crime reporting, combined with the useful and generally-accepted socially-marginalised position of the police officer, were the drivers behind the *purpose* of these narratives. Numerous titles appeared that marketed themselves as the dangerous and exciting experiences of police officers, which readers were able to witness first-hand and share in directly. In essence, the mid-Victorian fictional police memoir was a successful literary blending of *all* of the kinds of writing from Chapters 1, 2 and the opening of Chapter 3 of this volume, and all of their associated textual purposes and ideologies.

William Russell, today largely forgotten, was perhaps the most prolific producer of police memoirs of the mid-Victorian era. Russell was a journalist living in London throughout the 1850s, contributing considerable amounts of fiction to periodicals and magazines, notably *Chambers's Edinburgh Journal* and the *Sixpenny Magazine*. Russell was an unsettled figure; a search through the *Chambers's Edinburgh Journal* business ledgers contained in the National Library of Scotland reveals that he had no fewer than nine different North-East London addresses between 1845 and 1856. However, he did list his occupation as 'Author Writer for Chief Periodicals' on the 1851 census, which certainly implies that his income was substantial enough for him to be able to make a living from his writing.[104] Russell made extensive use of that which Shpayer-

Makov terms an 'innovative and popular form', the fictional police memoir, and his published bibliography is impressive.[105] His earliest works in this area included 'Experiences of a Barrister' (1849) and 'Recollections of a Police Officer' (1849), which were both published in *Chambers's Edinburgh Journal*. 'Recollections of a Police Officer' proved popular enough to be republished as a novel in 1856, retitled *Recollections of a Detective Police Officer* (my emphasis), and a 'second series' of stories from this novel also appeared in 1859.[106] The process of publishing a single edition provided Russell with the opportunity to explain the idea behind his creation. In a new preface, Russell suggests that the text was originally written with the intention of providing the reader with a literary window into the exploits of the police:

> I [...] offer no apology, for placing these rough sketches of the police experience before the reader [...][107]

The apparent popularity of *Recollections of a Detective Police Officer* directly caused Russell to write and publish *Leaves from the Diary of a Law Clerk* a year later in 1857. Again, Russell used the preface to this to both highlight how the style of writing was a popular form of fiction, and that the form was a direct evolution of the journalistic purpose of exploring the private realms of criminality:

> The general favour with which the 'Recollections of a Detective Officer' have been received, induces the publishers to reprint, by permission, the following papers, by the same author, – who, in these sketches as in the 'Recollections,' has endeavoured to render as faithfully as might be, the *records of a real experience* [my italics].[108]

Leaves from the Diary of a Law Clerk was followed by 'Experiences of a Real Detective' and 'Undiscovered Crimes' in 1862, both published in the *Sixpenny Magazine*. Finally, Russell published *Autobiography of an English Detective* in two volumes in 1863. However, despite his impressive corpus of published fiction, Russell's work has been dismissed by some, particularly Ian Ousby, as a 'hack'.[109] However, it is premature and short-sighted to dismiss his writing and to suggest that it is of little historical or scholarly value merely because it was cheap and formulaic. Indeed, by the early 1860s, the police memoir genre had become 'all the fashion';[110] a review published in the *Dublin Review* in May 1861 directly acknowledged the police memoir's popularity, and went so far as to suggest that the genre was designed to give readers 'complete disclosure' of the dangerous experiences of the police. In fact, the review lamented that many of the recollections were not actually truthful *enough* to give readers the insider-information that they so ardently desired, which rather interestingly hearkened back to the idea that some periodical crime 'round-ups' complained that their sources of 'insider information' were sometimes not close enough to provide adequate detail.[111] The review argued:

> With, however, one or two exceptions, there is evidently no reality in any of these productions.[112]

The perceived truthfulness of these narratives was therefore apparently a factor that contributed to the texts' quality. In essence, the more truthful the narrative, the better it was deemed to be, as it gave a more realistic account of the police's exploits into dangerous criminal areas within the city.

Russell's earliest example of a memoir centred on the activities of the police was the popular 'Recollections of a Police Officer', which appeared in *Chambers's Edinburgh Journal* between 1849 and 1853.[113] The stories follow the career of an officer named 'Waters', who was not naturally inclined to join the police but instead was forced to do so after getting himself into a dire financial situation that left him with no alternative.[114] Worthington argues that Waters himself is positioned as a middle-class gentleman (particularly when compared to the rough-and-ready Tom Richmond), who had simply fallen on hard times and who was designed 'to ensure the restoration of property when the first line of defence has failed' and 'to maintain the social *status quo*' for the presumed middle class readers of *Chambers's Edinburgh Journal.* [115] She further goes on to argue that:

> The construction of Waters as middle-class figure, investigating the private affairs of the middle classes, requires that he is unobtrusive and unrecognisable as a police officer, but still someone whose actions are authorised by law. Acceptance of the police by the middle class was premised on the concept that the police policed criminals to protect, not police, the middle class.[116]

However, I suggest that it is not quite as straightforward as this. While it is true that many of Waters's cases show him interacting with middle-class victims, restoring the comfortable status quo for them, and reassuring victims (and by extension the reader) that he is aware of his strong sense of duty to protect middle-class values (as well as spare their embarrassments),[117] his own *social* position is not quite so clear. Indeed, the opening issue paragraphs of the first instalment establish Waters as a character with a potentially criminal past, which serves to highlight him instantly as a figure occupying an awkward, transitional space somewhere between respectability and criminality:

> 'I think I have met you before,' he [the Chief Police Officer] remarked with a meaning smile on dismissing me, 'when you occupied a different position from your present one? Do not alarm yourself: I have no wish to pry unnecessarily into other men's secrets. Waters is a name common enough in *all* ranks of society [...] At all events, the testimony of the gentlemen whose recommendation obtained you admission to the force [...] is a sufficient guarantee that nothing more serious than imprudence and folly can be laid to your charge.[118]

The chief officer's insinuation here is that he has met Waters on a previous occasion, and in a far different capacity. It is left up to the reader to decide what this capacity actually was, but it is heavily implied that it was in Waters's previous life as a criminal. As Worthington points out, police officers were originally deliberately taken from the lowest portions of society, and the original Commissioners of Police of the Metropolis, Charles Rowan and Richard Mayne, had actively prevented new recruits from being taken from the middle-classes (or 'gentlemen').[119] It is likely, therefore, that Waters was at least a petty criminal before economic necessity had forced him to join the police. However, as both firm police officer and only *implied* criminal, Waters is a perfect character to act as a literary guide and protector for the reader to enter the criminal underworld which was perceived to lurk just beneath the surface of society, and he thus perfectly manifests the socially-indistinct or liminal position of the police officer as occupying a space between respectable and criminal by actually being *both* simultaneously. This indirectly connects him to both social exploration journalism, which used the same indistinct position of the police to its own advantage, and also to older characters such as Tom Richmond, who similarly progresses from would-be criminal to officer of the law (albeit less professionally). In fact, Waters' literary purpose to enter the private realms of criminality (and for the reader to 'come along for the ride' under his protection) is explicitly mentioned in the text:

> 'Here is a written description of the persons of this gang of blacklegs, swindlers and forgers,' concluded the commissioner, summing up his instructions. 'It will be your object to *discover their private haunts*, and secure legal evidence of their nefarious practices [...]' [my italics].[120]

Waters regularly penetrates the invisible underworld of criminality lurking beneath the surface of society and reveals it for the reader, who figuratively accompanies him as he goes about his duties. In one example, he gains access to a house where a large group of criminals is hiding. As Waters has only just joined the force and is (as yet) unknown as a detective in London, he passes inside undetected. As events unfold, the perspective of the text makes it seem as if the reader is standing just over Waters's shoulder:

> We soon arrived before the door of a quiet, respectable-looking house in one of the streets leading from the Strand: a low, peculiar knock, given by Sandford, was promptly answered; then a password, which I did not catch, was whispered by him through the key-hole, and we passed in. [...] We proceeded up stairs to the first floor, the shutters of which were carefully closed, so that no intimation of what was going in could possibly reach the street. [...] a roulette table and dice and cards were in full activity: wine and liquors of all varieties were profusely paraded. [...] Play was proposed; and though at first stoutly refusing, I feigned to be gradually overcome by irresistible temptation, and sat down to a blind hazard with my foreign

friend for moderate stakes. I was graciously allowed to win and in the end found myself richer in devil's money by about ten pounds.[121]

This is startlingly reminiscent of the 'Rat's Castle' scene in Dickens's 'On Duty with Inspector Field', which also depicted the protagonist entering into a lowly urban haunt where criminals were lounging around, playing cards and dice.[122] The fact that Waters 'pretends' to play dice and cards and was 'graciously allowed to win' again highlights his position as between police officer and criminal; he apparently resists play, but ultimately (albeit somewhat unconvincingly) 'feigns' to be overcome by temptation.

As Waters manifests various aspects of both the police officer *and* the criminal, it follows that police memoir fiction consciously depicted the police officer and the criminal has possessing 'equal' knowledge of the urban space that they inhabited and traversed. In the November 1850 issue of 'Recollections of a Police Officer', a story appeared titled 'The Revenge', which depicted a tense meeting between Waters and an infamous criminal named Madame Jaubert, who is apparently known to Waters already. This meeting takes place on 'neutral' ground in a snowy Leicester Square, and the criminal world is thus shown to coexist simultaneously with that of the police, occasionally colliding with it:

> I was again passing along Leicester Square [...] with all my eyes about me. [...] Except myself, and a tallish, snow-wreathed figure [...] not a living being was to be seen. This figure, which was standing still at the further side of the square, appeared to be awaiting me, and as I drew near it, threw back the hood of a cloak, and to my great surprise disclosed the features of a Madame Jaubert. [...]
>
> "Madame Jaubert!" I exclaimed [...], "why, what on earth can you be waiting here for on a night such as this?"
>
> "To see you."[123]

Waters accompanies Jaubert into St Giles-in-the-Fields to capture a criminal – another reference to Dickens's own explorations into the same urban space. In this peculiar scene, criminal and police officer nervously go together through the labyrinth as tentative equals where, at 'the entrance of a dark blind alley, called Hine's Court,' Jaubert invites Waters 'to follow'.[124] As he possesses equal knowledge to Jaubert herself of the hidden world of criminality lurking beneath the visible surface of society, Waters (perhaps rather wisely) suspects a trap:

> "Nay, nay, Madame Jaubert," I exclaimed, "that wont [sic] do. You mean fairly, I daresay; but I don't enter that respectable alley alone at this time of night." [...]
>
> "What is to be done, then?" she added after a few moments' consideration. "He is alone, I assure you."
>
> "That is possible; still I do not enter that cul-de-sac to-night, unaccompanied save by you."[125]

The equality of knowledge which existed between the police officer and the criminal indirectly highlights the *lack* of knowledge of the subterranean world of crime on the part of the reader, who is often manifested in police memoir fiction as a member (or sometimes several members) of the general public. Waters's apparent knowledge of criminality thus also proves useful to reveal this criminal 'underworld' to readers themselves and to highlight how, much of the time, it hides in plain sight. For example, in a story titled 'Mary Kingsford' published in the May 1851 issue of *Chambers's*, Waters is forced off of a train by heavy snow, and ushered into a waiting room with a collection of other passengers. Immediately, the reader is provided with an example of his skill at 'reading' the appearance of other passengers and discovering the deviant hiding in plain sight. In this example, the devil is certainly in the detail:

> To an eye less experienced than mine in the artifices and expedients famil-
> iar to a certain class of 'swells,' they might have passed muster for what
> they assumed to be [...] but their copper finery could not for a moment
> impose upon me. The watch-chains were, I saw, mosaic; the watches, so
> frequently displayed, gilt; eye-glasses the same; the coats, fur-collared and
> cuffed, were ill-fitting and second hand; ditto of the varnished boots and
> renovated velvet waist-coats; while the luxuriant moustaches and whiskers,
> and flowing wigs, were unmistakeably *pieces d'occasion* – assumed and
> diversified at pleasure.[126]

This technique of analysing the appearance of members of the public and drawing conclusions surrounding their character or personality was famously replicated in later examples of popular detective fiction, where the detective possesses keen powers of observation which supersede those of either other characters in the narrative, or indeed the reader. However at this point it was designed to give readers a closer, personal, and privileged insight into the criminal underworld hiding in plain sight, under the literary 'protection' of Waters the detective, who manifests both criminal and police officer, who possesses the skill to assess people from a distance using his knowledge of the city which exceeds the reader's own, and who acts to protect 'true' respectability and middle-class values.

Waters therefore effectively exemplifies how the mid-Victorian fictional police memoir was a blend of a variety of other forms of contemporary journalism which this book has explored so far. It performed the task of periodical crime round-ups, as it catered for the curious interests of readers who wished to see 'inside' the closed worlds of criminals such as prisons, court-rooms, and the private moments before executions, and at this point it is also possible to add the inner workings of the police itself to this list. It also drew inspiration from periodical police criticism and social exploration journalism, as it utilised the figure of the police officer to 'protect' readers as they metaphorically ventured into dangerous criminal places around the city that they would not otherwise have frequented. For his part, Russell remained interested in the fictional police-memoir genre as it developed over the mid-nineteenth century, and continuously recycled stories and material and collated different parts of different publications into new titles. Indeed, *Recollections of a Detective Police Officer* was republished at least three times more: once in 1859 (which was marketed as a 'second series' of stories),[127] as well as again in 1878 with the addition of three short stories and the new title of *The Detective Officer and Other Tales*. It was published yet again in 1887, as *The Recollections of a Detective*. The latest and final reprint of *Recollections of a Detective Police Officer* appeared (relatively) recently, in 1972.

Other authors of cheap popular fiction quickly sought to capitalise on the genre's growing popularity which authors like Russell popularised. As Haia Shpayer-Makov argues, Russell's writing served as a 'direct model' for other authors of fictional police memoirs.[128] Interestingly enough, some were indeed the recollections of actual police detectives, including *Autobiography of a French Detective*, which was originally titled *Mémoires de Canler, anciens chef du service de sûreté* by M. Louis Canler. Both the French and English versions of this text appeared together in 1862. Additionally, in Scotland, James McLevy's *Curiosities of Crime in Edinburgh, Sliding Scale of Life* and *The Disclosures of a Detective* were all published throughout the 1860s, and cemented McLevy's reputation as both an effective sleuth and entertaining author. However, these factual reminiscences were largely in the minority, and for the most part the genre concerned cheap, formulaic fiction. Again, as the *Dublin Review* lamented, there was evidently 'no reality' in a great many police memoirs published in this era.[129]

There were numerous other examples of fictional police memoir fiction published between 1860 and 1875; indeed, far too many to analyse in close detail here, and the microgenre itself actually warrants an extended study of its own right in order to fully understand it and to completely re-insert it into the chronology of the evolution of detective fiction. Some particular texts worth noting to illustrate the genre's widespread nature include Charles Martel's *Diary of an Ex-Detective* (1860), 'Recollections of a New York Detective' published in *Twice a Week* (1862), 'An Australian Detective's Story' which appeared in *Once a Week* (1864), *The Female Detective* (1864) by Andrew Forrester Jr., *Revelations of a Lady Detective* (1864) by William Stephens Hayward, 'From a Detective's Note-Book' which appeared in the *Argosy* (1872) and 'My Detective Experiences' published in *Chambers's Edinburgh Journal* (1886).

This is merely a brief list of just some of the police memoirs published across the mid-Victorian era, however these specific texts are worth listing together, as they emphasise a final point that can be drawn surrounding the development of the police memoir across the mid-Victorian era. As Martin Kayman correctly suggests, these memoirs deliberately followed Russell's success in a search for new ingredients to liven up and diversify (without completely reforming) the growing genre.[130] This was done, essentially, in order to help individual texts 'stand out from the crowd'. In a particularly strong example, two police memoirs which consciously diversified away from Russell's format to make themselves 'stand out' appeared in 1864; namely Andrew Forrester's *The Female Detective* and William Stephen's Hayward's *Revelations of a Lady Detective*. These were 'unique' in that they used female protagonists, and consequently they have been extensively discussed in academic criticism which explores gender in relation to crime and detective fiction. Joseph Kestner, for example, argues that they diversified a male-dominated literary genre, but that they were threats to male power centres and were therefore crushed, which he suggests helps to explain why they have been largely forgotten today.[131] Elsewhere, Kathleen Gregory Klein dismisses both texts in terms of their importance to the genre's development, arguing that they were simply anomalies in a male-dominated genre.[132] Still others attempt to make sense of the appearance of female detectives, arguing that the change in domestic laws (such as the 1857 Matrimonial Clauses Act) caused an interest in the uncovering of a 'domestic secret' to appear, which helps to explain these texts' publication.[133]

The Female Detective and *Revelations of a Lady Detective* have thus been consistently viewed as literary milestones, as they are the first texts to feature professional female detectives, or feature female characters that collaborate professionally with the police force to solve crimes.[134] However, I suggest that these texts should actually be historicised alongside police memoirs, as this is the wider genre in which their narrative structures fit, and these texts actually form part of a much wider literary movement.[135] Indeed, Andrew Forrester also authored and published another police memoir, titled *Secret Service, or, Recollections of a City Detective* in the same year as *The Female Detective* in 1864, which suggests that he was more concerned with the memoir-genre than specifically with gender. Within this memoir context, I suggest that these texts were influenced by the contemporary popularity of the other police memoirs, but that they were written with the purpose of making them slightly different by including female detective protagonists. This was done in order to distinguish them from other examples of the genre and to perform a different task and, potentially, sell more copies.[136]

The concept of an official female detective protagonist was historically challenging, as women were not permitted to join the police as uniformed officers or detectives until the early twentieth century (although women were engaged with police work in a variety of other ways far before this). Both authors realised that this made ladies perfect for undercover detection, as they aroused next to no suspicion compared to their male counterparts. Female detectives were able to complete some of the duties of a detective more effectively, such as eavesdropping and infiltrating areas which were inaccessible to male detectives. Indeed, in *The Female Detective,* the detective Ms. Gladden suggested that 'the woman detective has far greater opportunities than a man of intimate watching, and of keeping her eyes upon matters near'.[137] Similarly, in *Revelations of a Lady Detective,* the principle detective, Mrs. Paschal, argued a similar point by suggesting that the practice of employing women as detectives was more widespread than was commonly known, and argued that they hid in plain sight in much the same way as the criminal underworld itself.[138]

This quality of lady detectives to pass unnoticed and unsuspected therefore allowed the reader to safely accompany the detective into even more diverse and inaccessible places than they had been able to in the company of male detectives. In a clear example of the author using a female detective to infiltrate (and thus 'open') a space inaccessible to men, Paschal was depicted as going undercover as an noviciate in a convent. Paschal discussed this point with her client, Alfred Wriniker:

> Colonel Warner told him [Wriniker] that, in his opinion, it was just the case for a Lady Detective [...] [Wriniker, to Paschal] "I like your plan very much. It is a clever conception, and worthy of a Lady Detective" [...] "You think so?" I replied, with a smile. [...] [Wriniker, to Paschal] "It is one of those cases that a man could not manage for any one whatever." [...] [Paschal, to Wriniker] "Certainly not. The appearance of a man in a convent would be like that of a wolf amongst a flock of sheep, or a hawk in a dovecot."[139]

As Paschal and her client Wriniker discuss, a male detective would be unable to infiltrate a convent, yet a female detective can do so quite easily. Through reading about Paschal's experiences, the reader again effectively infiltrates the convent along with her, under her guidance and her protection.

The Memoirs of a Detective: Chapter 3 Conclusions

The mid-Victorian fictional police memoir therefore constituted a blending together of a diverse range of earlier journalistic interests, and was a direct fictional counterpart to 'social exploration journalism'. The periodical commentary focused on the police discussed in Chapter 1 had provided wider understanding of the liminal social position of the police alongside greater understanding of how they operated. The nature of the police officer as occupying a social space somewhere between criminality and the rest of the general public combined with the quasi-voyeuristic interests of popular crime journalism, and this meant that authors sought to use the police as a tool to explore the criminal. This was initially done in reality, as in 'social exploration journalism', but it quickly gave way to fiction as this allowed much greater creative freedom and entertainment value, directly leading to the emergence of the fictional police memoir – a genre with a far greater significance to the evolution of 'detective fiction' than has been previously afforded to it, and which warrants a much larger study in of its own right.

The figure of the literary police officer therefore became a *necessary* literary tool through which authors could render these inaccessible or criminal spaces public and to act as a protector for the reader who accompanied them. This adds significant weight to both Worthington and Shpayer-Makov's suggestion that the police memoir genre was the first literary form in which the police officer or detective was afforded a central role.[140] In addition, it cements the importance of the police memoir genre as an early yet fully-formed genre of 'detective fiction'. As William Russell himself argued in 1862, police memoir writing was actually contemporarily considered to be an early, legitimate and recognisable form of formulaic 'detective fiction', and consequently I argue that it should be remembered as such within criticism today.

Notes

1   Anthea Trodd, 'The Policeman and the Lady: Significant Encounters in Mid-Victorian Fiction', *Victorian Studies*, 24, 4 (1984), 435–460 (p. 437).
2   'Haunts of Crime', *Ragged School Union Magazine*, May 1869, p. 104.
3   Alyce Von Rothkirch, '"His face was livid, dreadful, with a form at the corners of his mouth": A Typology of Villains in Classic Detective Stories', *Modern Language Review*, 108, 4 (2013), 1042–1063 (p.1042).
4   William Makepeace Thackeray, 'Going to See a Man Hanged', Fraser's Magazine for Town and Country, vol. 22, July-December 1840, p. 151.
5   Daniel Defoe, *The History of the Press-Yard: or, a Brief Account of the Customs and Occurrences that are put in Practice and to be met with in that Ancient Repository of Living Bodies, called, His Majesty's Gaol of Newgate* (London: T. Moor, 1717), pp. 8–9.
6   Isaac Richard and George Cruikshank, 'Symptoms of the Finish of "Some Sorts of Life" in London. Tom, Jerry and Logic in the Press Yard at Newgate', in Pierce Egan, *Life in London, or, The Day and Night Scenes of Jerry Hawthorn, Esq. and his Elegant Friend Corinthian Tom in their Rambles and Sprees though the Metropolis* (London: Chatto and Windus, 1821; repr. 1881), p. 315. Image is in the public domain.
7   Egan, *Life in London*, p. 315.
8   Vic Gatrell, *The Hanging Tree: Execution and the English People*, 1770–1868 (Oxford: Oxford University Press, 1994), p. 29.
9   Egan, p. 316.
10   Robert Patten, 'George Cruikshank', *Oxford Dictionary of National Biography* <http://www.oxforddnb.com/view/article/6843> [accessed 22 September 2017] (2006).
11   Jessica Valdez, 'Dickens's "Pious Fraud": The Popular Press and the Moral Suasion of Fictional Narrative', *Victorian Periodicals Review*, 44, 4 (2011), 377–400 (pp. 377–378). See also Walter Bagehot, *Literary Studies* (New York: Longman, Green, and Co., 1891).
12   Philip Collins, *Dickens and Crime* (London: Macmillan, 1962; repr. 1965), p. 27.
13   Charles Dickens, *Sketches by Boz* (London: John Macrone, 1836; repr. London: Penguin Classics, 1995), p. 235.
14   Dickens, *Sketches by Boz*, p. 236.
15   Dickens, *Sketches by Boz*, p. 236.
16   Dickens, *Sketches by Boz*, p. 246.
17   Dickens, *Sketches by Boz*, p. 246.
18   Dickens, *Sketches by Boz*, p. 248.
19   Charles Dickens, *Oliver Twist* (London: Richard Bentley, 1837–1839; repr. London: Penguin Classics, 2003), pp. 443–450.
20   George Cruikshank, 'Fagin in the Condemned Cell', in *The Adventures of Oliver Twist, or, the Parish Boy's Progress*, Victorian Web <http://www.victorianweb.org/victorian/art/illustration/cruikshank/ot24.html> [accessed July 2 2018], scanned and uploaded by Philip V. Allingham (1839, uploaded 2014).
21   Thackeray, p. 150.
22   Collins, pp. 52–53.

23 Dickens, *Sketches by Boz*, pp. 231–232.
24 Dickens, *Sketches by Boz*, p. 232.
25 Henry Mayhew and John Binny, *The Criminal Prisons of London and Scenes of London Life* (London: Griffin, Bohn and Co., 1862).
26 See Chapter 1.
27 Caroline Reitz, 'Colonial 'Gwilt': In and Around Wilkie Collins's Armadale, *Victorian Periodicals Review*, 33, 1 (2000), 92–103 (p. 95).
28 Paul Fyfe, 'The Random Selection of Victorian New Media', *Victorian Periodicals Review*, 42, 1 (2009), 1–23 (pp. 2–5).
29 This is drawn from a comparison between two contemporary maps of London: Edward Mogg's 'London in Miniature' (1806) and Reynolds's 'Map of Modern London' (1862) by James Reynolds. See also: Samuel Saunders, '"I was again passing along Leicester Square ... with all my eyes about me": Mapping Popular "Police Memoir" Detective Fiction', *Victorian Popular Fictions*, 1, 2 (2019), 100–109 (p. 102).
30 Warren Fox, 'Murder in Daily Instalments: The Newspapers and the Case of Franz Müller (1864)', *Victorian Periodicals Review*, 31, 3 (1998), 271–298 (p. 277).
31 John Paget, 'Judicial Puzzles – Eliza Fenning', *Blackwood's Edinburgh Magazine*, February 1861, p. 236.
32 Christopher Pittard, 'Cheap, Healthful Literature: The *Strand Magazine*, Fictions of Crime and Purified Reading Communities', *Victorian Periodicals Review*, 40, 1 (2007), 1–23 (p. 4).
33 Michael de Certeau, *The Practice of Everyday Life* (Berkeley and Los Angeles, CA: University of California Press, 1984), p. 93.
34 De Certeau, p. 93.
35 Saunders, 'I was again passing along Leicester Square...'", pp. 100–109 (p. 101).
36 D. A. Miller, *The Novel and the Police* (California, University of California Press, 1988), pp. 3–5 and p. 76.
37 Barbara Korte, 'On Heroes and Hero Worship: Regimes of Emotional Investment in Mid-Victorian Popular Magazines', *Victorian Periodicals Review*, 49, 2 (2016), 181–201 (p. 187).
38 Korte, 181–201 (p. 187).
39 Trodd, 435–460 (p. 437).
40 Miller, p. 5.
41 Hugh E. Hoare, 'Homes of the Criminal Classes', *National Review*, April 1883, p. 224
42 Susan Zlotnick, 'The Law's a Bachelor: *Oliver Twist*, Bastardy and the New Poor Law', *Victorian Literature and Culture*, 34, 1 (2006), 131–146 (p. 132).
43 Saunders, '"I was again passing along Leicester Square..."', pp. 100–109 (p. 104).
44 Von Rothkirch, pp. 1042–1063 (p. 1042).
45 Charles Rzepka, *Detective Fiction* (Cambridge: Polity, 2005), p. 90.
46 Valdez, 377–400 (p. 378).
47 Pittard, 'Cheap, Healthful Literature', pp. 1–23 (p. 4).
48 Heather Worthington, *The Rise of the Detective in Early Nineteenth Century Popular Fiction* (Basingstoke: Palgrave Macmillan, 2005), p. 164.
49 Charles Dickens, 'On Duty with Inspector Field', *Household Words*, 14 June 1851, p. 266.
50 Valdez, 377–400 (pp. 382–383).
51 Valdez, 377–400 (pp. 382–383).
52 Dickens, 'On Duty with Inspector Field', p. 265.
53 Trodd, 435–460 (p. 439).
54 Miller, p. 6.
55 Trodd, 435–460 (p. 439).
56 Saunders, '"I was again passing along Leicester Square..."', pp. 100–109 (p. 104).
57 'Haunts of Crime', *Ragged School Union Magazine*, May 1869, p. 104.
58 J. C. Parkinson, 'On Duty with the Inspector', *Temple Bar*, June 1865, p. 349.

59   John Burns, 'A Wild Night', *Good Words*, December 1874, pp. 211–212.
60   'The Low Haunts of London' *Ragged School Union Magazine*, January 1851, p. 200.
61   'A Visit to Low Haunts', *London Review*, 30 January 1864, p. 113.
62   'A Visit to Low Haunts', *London Review*, 30 January 1864, p. 113.
63   Burns, p. 211.
64   Erich Goode, *Justifiable Conduct: Self-Vindication in Memoir* (Philadelphia: Temple University Press, 2013), p. 27.
65   Catherine Nickerson, 'Murder as Social Criticism', *American Literary History*, 9, 4 (1997), 744–757 (p. 744).
66   Nickerson, 744–757 (p. 744).
67   Fox, 271–298 (pp. 282–283).
68   Von Rothkirch, 1042–1063 (p. 1043).
69   Valdez, 377–400 (p. 378).
70   Ian Ousby, *The Crime and Mystery Book: A Readers Companion* (London: Thames and Hudson, 1997), p. 34.
71   Trodd, 435–460 (p. 436).
72   Rzepka, pp. 90–92.
73   Rzepka, p. 99.
74   Stephen Knight, *Crime Fiction 1800–2000: Detection, Death, Diversity* (Basingstoke: Palgrave Macmillan, 2004), pp. 30–33.
75   See Joseph Kestner, *Sherlock's Sisters: The British Female Detective, 1864–1913* (London: Routledge, 2003) or Kathleen Gregory Klein, *The Woman Detective: Gender and Genre* (Illinois: University of Illinois Press, 1988) for examples of this in action.
76   Haia Shpayer-Makov, 'Explaining the Rise and Success of Detective Memoirs in Britain', in *Police Detectives in History, 1750–1950*, ed. by Clive Emsley and Haia Shpayer-Makov (Hampshire: Ashgate, 2006), pp. 103–134 (pp. 131–132).
77   Shpayer-Makov, 'Explaining the Rise and Success of Detective Memoirs in Britain', in *Police Detectives in History, 1750–1950*, ed. by Emsley and Shpayer-Makov, pp. 103–134 (p. 109)
78   Worthington, p. 4.
79   Worthington, p. 140.
80   Worthington, p. 156.
81   Haia Shpayer-Makov, *The Ascent of the Detective: Police Sleuths in Victorian and Edwardian England* (Oxford: Oxford University Press, 2011), pp. 232–233.
82   Von Rothkirch, 1042–1063 (p. 1042).
83   Worthington, p. 142.
84   William Russell, 'Experiences of a Real Detective', *Sixpenny Magazine*, March 1862, p. 325.
85   Fyfe, 1–23 (p. 3).
86   'Recollections of a Detective Police Officer, by "Waters"', *Dublin Review*, May 1861, p. 153.
87   'An Australian Detective's Story', *Once a Week*, 24 December 1864, p. 25.
88   Worthington, p. 140.
89   Worthington, p. 7.
90   'Diary of a Barrister During the Last Wexford Assizes', *New Monthly Magazine*, January 1826, p. 296.
91   'Diary of a Barrister During the Last Wexford Assizes', *New Monthly Magazine*, January 1826, p. 303.
92   Worthington, p. 104.
93   Worthington, p. 105.
94   Worthington, p. 140.

95   Shpayer-Makov, 'Explaining the Rise and Success of Detective Memoirs in Britain', in *Police Detectives in History, 1750–1950*, ed. by Emsley and Shpayer-Makov, pp. 103–134 (p. 108).

96   Rzepka, p. 66–68.

97   Although Ousby does mention *Richmond* in *Bloodhounds of Heaven: The Detective in English Fiction from Godwin to Doyle* (Cambridge, MA: Harvard University Press, 1976).

98   'Richmond' (attrib. T. S. Surr), *Richmond, or, Scenes in the Life of a Bow Street Runner* (London: H. Colburn, 1827; repr. New York: Dover Publications, 1976), p. 93.

99   Nick Foggo, 'Fact vs. Fiction: The Early Years of the Liverpool Constabulary Force', *Transactions of the Historic Society of Lancashire and Cheshire*, 167, 1 (2018), p. 94.

100   Foggo, p. 94.

101   'The Life of a Policeman, by an Ex-Constable', *Penny Satirist*, 28 October 1843.

102   Foggo, p. 97.

103   Martin Kayman, *From Bow Street to Baker Street: Mystery. Detection and Narrative* (Basingstoke: Macmillan, 1992), p. 122.

104   1851 UK Census, Ecclesiastical District of: West Hackney, Borough of: Tower Hamlets, entry 255: 9 Southgate Place, *ancestry.co.uk* <http://www.ancestry.co.uk> [accessed 24 November 2016].

105   Shpayer-Makov, *The Ascent of the Detective*, p. 234.

106   'Recollections of a Detective Police Officer, by "Waters"', *Dublin Review*, May 1861, p. 150.

107   William Russell, *Recollections of a Detective Police-Officer* (London: J & C Brown and Co., 1856), p. vi.

108   William Russell, *Leaves from the Diary of a Law Clerk* (London: J & C Brown and Co., 1857), p. 3.

109   Ousby, *The Crime and Mystery Book*, p. 34.

110   'Recollections of a Detective Police Officer, by "Waters"', *Dublin Review*, May 1861, p. 153.

111   See Chapter 2, 'Looking Ahead to 'Detective Literature': Chapter 2 'Conclusions'.

112   'Recollections of a Detective Police Officer, by "Waters"', *Dublin Review*, May 1861, p. 154.

113   Shpayer-Makov, *The Ascent of the Detective*, p. 234.

114   William Russell, 'Recollections of a Police-Officer', *Chambers's Edinburgh Journal*, 28 July 1849, p. 55.

115   Worthington, p. 149.

116   Worthington, pp. 150–151.

117   See, for example, the exchange between Waters and Mr Smith in the story titled 'X. Y. Z.' (November 1849), where Smith refers to Waters's sense of discretion in dealing with a family matter, and thus allows him 'behind the family curtain'. William Russell, 'Recollections of a Police-Officer: X. Y.Z.', *Chambers's Edinburgh Journal*, November 17 1849, p. 309.

118   Russell, 'Recollections of a Police-Officer', 28 July 1849, p. 55.

119   Worthington, p. 159.

120   Russell, 'Recollections of a Police-Officer', 28 July 1849, pp. 55–56.

121   Russell, 'Recollections of a Police-Officer', 28 July 1849, p. 57.

122   Dickens, 'On Duty with Inspector Field', p. 266.

123   William Russell, 'Recollections of a Police-Officer: The Revenge', *Chambers's Edinburgh Journal*, November 9 1850, pp. 294–295.

124   Russell, 'Recollections of a Police-Officer: The Revenge', November 9 1850, p. 295.

125   Russell, 'Recollections of a Police-Officer: The Revenge', November 9 1850, p. 295.

126 William Russell, 'Recollections of a Police-Officer: Mary Kingsford', *Chambers's Edinburgh Journal*, May 3 1851, p. 274.
127 'Recollections of a Detective Police Officer, by "Waters"', *Dublin Review*, May 1861, p. 150.
128 Shpayer-Makov, 'Explaining the Rise and Success of Detective Memoirs in Britain', in *Police Detectives in History, 1750–1950*, ed. by Emsley and Shpayer-Makov, pp. 103–134 (p. 109).
129 'Recollections of a Detective Police Officer, by "Waters"', *Dublin Review*, May 1861, p. 154.
130 Kayman, p. 122.
131 Kestner, pp. 229–230.
132 Klein, p. 29.
133 Dagni Bredesen, 'Conformist Subversion: The Ambivalent Agency in *Revelations of a Lady Detective*', *Clues: A Journal of Detection*, 25, 1, 20–32 (p. 20).
134 Kestner, p. 14.
135 Kayman, p. 122.
136 Samuel Saunders, '"To Pry Unnecessarily into Other Men's Secrets": Crime Writing, Private Spaces and the mid-Victorian Police Memoir', *Law, Crime and History*, 8, 1 (2018), 76–90 (p. 88).
137 Andrew Forrester, *The Female Detective* (London: Ward, Lock and Tyler, 1864; repr. London: British Library Publishing, 2012), p. 4.
138 William Stephens Hayward, *Revelations of a Lady Detective* (London: George Vickers, 1864; repr. London: British Library Publishing, 2013), p. 18.
139 Stephens Hayward, pp. 142–145.
140 Shpayer-Makov, *The Ascent of the Detective*, pp. 232–233.

Bibliography

Primary Periodical Material

'A Visit to Low Haunts', *London Review*, 30 January 1864, pp. 113–114.

'An Australian Detective's Story', *Once a Week*, 24 December 1864, pp. 24–28.

Burns, John, 'A Wild Night', *Good Words*, December 1874, pp. 211–216.

'Diary of a Barrister During the Last Wexford Assizes', *New Monthly Magazine*, January 1826, pp. 296–306.

Dickens, Charles, 'On Duty with Inspector Field', *Household Words*, 14 June 1851, pp. 265–270.

'Haunts of Crime', *Ragged School Union Magazine*, May 1869, pp. 104–107.

Hoare, Hugh E., 'Homes of the Criminal Classes', *National Review*, April 1883, pp. 224–239.

Paget, John, 'Judicial Puzzles – Eliza Fenning', *Blackwood's Edinburgh Magazine*, February 1861, pp. 236–244.

Parkinson, J. C., 'On Duty with the Inspector', *Temple Bar*, June 1865, pp. 348–358.

'Recollections of a Detective Police Officer, by "Waters"', *Dublin Review*, May 1861, pp. 150–194.

Russell, William, 'Experiences of a Real Detective', *Sixpenny Magazine*, March 1862, pp. 325–334.

Russell, William, 'Recollections of a Police-Officer: Mary Kingsford', *Chambers's Edinburgh Journal*, 3 May 1851, pp. 274–279.

Russell, William, 'Recollections of a Police-Officer: The Revenge', *Chambers's Edinburgh Journal*, 9 November 1850, pp. 294–298.

Russell, William, 'Recollections of a Police-Officer: X. Y.Z.', *Chambers's Edinburgh Journal*, November 17 1849, p. 309.

Russell, William, 'Recollections of a Police-Officer', *Chambers's Edinburgh Journal*, 28 July 1849, pp. 55–59.

Thackeray, William Makepeace, 'Going to See a Man Hanged', *Fraser's Magazine for Town and Country* 22, July-December 1840.

'The Life of a Policeman, by an Ex-Constable', *Penny Satirist*, 28 October 1843.

'The Low Haunts of London', *Ragged School Union Magazine*, January 1851, pp. 200–205.

Secondary Material

1851 UK Census, Ecclesiastical District of: West Hackney, Borough of: Tower Hamlets, entry 255: 9 Southgate Place, ancestry.co.uk <http://www.ancestry.co.uk> [accessed 24 November 2016].

Bagehot, Walter, *Literary Studies* (New York: Longman, Green, and Co., 1891).

Bredesen, Dagni, 'Conformist Subversion: The Ambivalent Agency in Revelations of a Lady Detective', *Clues: A Journal of Detection*, 25, 1, 20–32.

Collins, Philip, *Dickens and Crime* (London: Macmillan, 1962; repr. 1965).

de Certeau, Michael, *The Practice of Everyday Life* (Berkeley and Los Angeles, CA: University of California Press, 1984).

Cruikshank, George, 'Fagin in the Condemned Cell', in *The Adventures of Oliver Twist, or, the Parish Boy's Progress*, Victorian Web <http://www.victorianweb.org/victoria n/art/illustration/cruikshank/ot24.html> [accessed 2018], scanned and uploaded by Philip V. Allingham (1839, uploaded 2014).

Defoe, Daniel, *The History of the Press-Yard: or, a Brief Account of the Customs and Occurrences that are put in Practice and to be met with in that Ancient Repository of Living Bodies, called, His Majesty's Gaol of Newgate* (London: T. Moor, 1717).

Dickens, Charles, *Oliver Twist* (London: Richard Bentley; repr. London: Penguin Classics, 2003), pp. 1837–1839.

Dickens, Charles, *Sketches by Boz* (London: John Macrone, 1836; repr. London: Penguin Classics, 1995).

Egan, Pierce, *Life in London, or, The Day and Night Scenes of Jerry Hawthorn, Esq. and his Elegant Friend Corinthian Tom in their Rambles and Sprees though the Metropolis* (London: Chatto and Windus, 1821; repr. 1881).

Foggo, Nick, 'Fact vs. Fiction: The Early Years of the Liverpool Constabulary Force', *Transactions of the Historic Society of Lancashire and Cheshire*, 167, 1 (2018)

Forrester, Andrew, *The Female Detective* (London: Ward, Lock and Tyler, 1864; repr. London: British Library Publishing, 2012).

Fox, Warren, 'Murder in Daily Instalments: The Newspapers and the Case of Franz Müller (1864)', *Victorian Periodicals Review*, 31, 3 (1998), 271–298.

Fyfe, Paul, 'The Random Selection of Victorian New Media', *Victorian Periodicals Review*, 42, 1 (2009), 1–23.

Gatrell, Vic, *The Hanging Tree: Execution and the English People*, 1770–1868 (Oxford: Oxford University Press, 1994).

Goode, Erich, *Justifiable Conduct: Self-Vindication in Memoir* (Philadelphia: Temple University Press, 2013).

Kayman, Martin, *From Bow Street to Baker Street: Mystery. Detection and Narrative* (Basingstoke: Macmillan, 1992).

Kestner, Joseph, *Sherlock's Sisters: The British Female Detective, 1864–1913* (London: Routledge, 2003).

Klein, Kathleen Gregory, *The Woman Detective: Gender and Genre* (Illinois: University of Illinois Press, 1988).

Knight, Stephen, *Crime Fiction 1800–2000: Detection, Death, Diversity* (Basingstoke: Palgrave Macmillan, 2004).

Korte, Barbara, 'On Heroes and Hero Worship: Regimes of Emotional Investment in Mid-Victorian Popular Magazines', *Victorian Periodicals Review*, 49, 2 (2016), 181–201.

Mayhew, Henry and John Binny, *The Criminal Prisons of London and Scenes of London Life* (London: Griffin, Bohn and Co., 1862).

Miller, D. A., *The Novel and the Police* (California, University of California Press, 1988).

Mogg, Edward, *London in Miniature* (London: Edward Mogg, 1806).

Nickerson, Catherine, 'Murder as Social Criticism', *American Literary History*, 9, 4 (1997), 744–757.

Ousby, Ian *Bloodhounds of Heaven: The Detective in English Fiction from Godwin to Doyle* (Cambridge, MA: Harvard University Press, 1976).

Ousby, Ian, *The Crime and Mystery Book: A Readers Companion* (London: Thames and Hudson, 1997).

Patten, Robert, 'George Cruikshank', *Oxford Dictionary of National Biography* <http://www.oxforddnb.com/view/article/6843> [accessed 22 September 2017] (2006).

Pittard, Christopher, 'Cheap, Healthful Literature: The Strand Magazine, Fictions of Crime and Purified Reading Communities', *Victorian Periodicals Review*, 40, 1 (2007), 1–23.

Reitz, Caroline, 'Colonial "Gwilt": In and Around Wilkie Collins's Armadale', *Victorian Periodicals Review*, 33, 1 (2000), 92–103.

Reynolds, James, *Map of Modern London* (London: James Reynolds, 1862).

Richard, Isaac and George Cruikshank, 'Symptoms of the Finish of "Some Sorts of Life" in London. Tom, Jerry and Logic in the Press Yard at Newgate', in *Pierce Egan, Life in London, or, The Day and Night Scenes of Jerry Hawthorn, Esq. and his Elegant Friend Corinthian Tom in their Rambles and Sprees though the Metropolis* (London: Chatto and Windus, 1821; repr. 1881), p. 315.

'Richmond' (attrib. T. S. Surr), *Richmond, or, Scenes in the Life of a Bow Street Runner* (London: H. Colburn, 1827; repr. New York: Dover Publications, 1976).

Russell, William, *Leaves from the Diary of a Law Clerk* (London: J & C Brown and Co., 1857).

Russell, William, *Recollections of a Detective Police-Officer* (London: J & C Brown and Co., 1856).

Rzepka, Charles, *Detective Fiction* (Cambridge: Polity, 2005).

Saunders, Samuel, '"I was again passing along Leicester Square … with all my eyes about me': Mapping Popular 'Police Memoir' Detective Fiction', *Victorian Popular Fictions*, 1, 2 (2019), 100–109.

Saunders, Samuel, '"To Pry Unnecessarily into Other Men's Secrets': Crime Writing, Private Spaces and the mid-Victorian Police Memoir', *Law, Crime and History*, 8, 1 (2018), 76–90.

Shpayer-Makov, Haia, 'Explaining the Rise and Success of Detective Memoirs in Britain', in *Police Detectives in History, 1750–1950*, ed. by Clive Emsley and Haia Shpayer-Makov (Hampshire: Ashgate, 2006), pp. 103–134.

Shpayer-Makov, Haia, *The Ascent of the Detective: Police Sleuths in Victorian and Edwardian England* (Oxford: Oxford University Press, 2011).

Stephens Hayward, William, *Revelations of a Lady Detective* (London: George Vickers, 1864; repr. London: British Library Publishing, 2013).

Trodd, Anthea, 'The Policeman and the Lady: Significant Encounters in Mid-Victorian Fiction', *Victorian Studies*, 24, 4 (1984), 435–460.

Valdez, Jessica, 'Dickens's 'Pious Fraud': The Popular Press and the Moral Suasion of Fictional Narrative', *Victorian Periodicals Review*, 44, 4 (2011), 377–400.

Von Rothkirch, Alyce, '"His face was livid, dreadful, with a form at the corners of his mouth': A Typology of Villains in Classic Detective Stories', *Modern Language Review*, 108, 4 (2013), 1042–1063.

Worthington, Heather, *The Rise of the Detective in Early Nineteenth Century Popular Fiction* (Basingstoke: Palgrave Macmillan, 2005).

Zlotnick, Susan, 'The Law's a Bachelor: Oliver Twist, Bastardy and the New Poor Law', *Victorian Literature and Culture*, 34, 1 (2006), 131–146.

4 The Romance of the Detective
Police Memoir Fiction and Sensation Fiction

Introduction: From Memoir to Sensation

The preceding chapter argued that the mid-Victorian 'police memoir' constituted a legitimate yet understudied form of detective fiction that should have a stronger place in the widely-accepted chronology of the genre's evolution than it has hitherto been afforded. The microgenre has been paid only scant attention within academic discussion, at least partially because it has been generally perceived as simply cheap and common writing produced by 'hacks' seeking little more than financial gain.[1]

However, there is a second reason why police memoirs have been pushed to the rear of scholarly discourse on the evolution of detective fiction between 1855 and 1875. These years witnessed the heyday of another form of writing that *has* received extensive academic attention in this regard; the 'sensation novel', a term originally coined by Margaret Oliphant while writing for *Blackwood's Edinburgh Magazine*.[2] In an article titled 'Sensation Novels' that appeared in *Blackwood's* in 1862, Oliphant attempted to define exactly what it was that constituted this kind of writing, suggesting that it included such characteristics as

> fierce expedients of crime and violence, by *diablerie* of divers [sic] kinds, and by the wild devices of a romance which smiled at probabilities [...] Hectic rebellion against nature – frantic attempts by any kind of black art of mad psychology to get some grandeur and sacredness restored to life – or if not sacredness and grandeur, at least horror and mystery, there being nothing better in earth or heaven [...][3]

The cultural significance of 'sensation' fiction has been a popular area of exploration within the history of crime fiction for some years. Given its focus on criminality (and the efforts made by individual characters to resolve it) it has become widely accepted by those working in the field to have had a strong influence on the makeup of the modern crime story. Consequently, as a far cheaper, more formulaic, and less high-profile form of writing, mid-Victorian police memoir fiction remains relatively obscure by comparison.

However, while it is tempting, it is not my intention to argue here that sensation fiction is somehow less deserving of such focused attention than that which it has hitherto received, or even to suggest that refocusing our efforts elsewhere would immediately generate new and more complex understanding of detective fiction's development. In fact, sensation fiction's position within the academic debate on crime fiction's history is for the most part deserved, and so instead this next chapter opts for a more comparative approach, by placing the meteoric rise of sensation writing *alongside* contemporarily-published police memoir fiction. By doing so, it solidifies *both* genres' places in the wider chronology of 'detective fiction', and sidesteps the issue of having to navigate a largely unnecessary generic hierarchy.

This chapter therefore aims to highlight how the development of 'detective fiction' across the mid-Victorian era was not limited to merely one form of writing or another, but was instead the by-product of a variety of other forms of writing shifting, meshing, and evolving, with the periodical press (and its discussion of the police and crime) consistently at the core. It firstly establishes some scholarly context by looking at exactly how sensation fiction has been placed on a proverbial pedestal in the history of crime fiction – with the added implication that this has perhaps been at the expense of other kinds of potentially significant forms of writing. It then takes a step back to explore how a number of mid-Victorian journalists and critics suggested that the emergence of sensation fiction was connected to the popularity of the police memoir, which, I argue, ties the two kinds of writing together more closely than has been hitherto recognised. Indeed, in some cases, contemporary commentators argued that sensation fiction was actually a direct *evolution* of the police memoir, as it represented a literary diversification from the specific experiences of the police into broader, more imaginative narratives about 'crime'.

The chapter then switches perspective again to look more closely at the thematic connections between police memoir fiction and sensation fiction, suggesting that they were more structurally similar than it might initially seem. This particularly surrounds both genres' use of the police; both kinds of writing frequently used police officers or detectives to help 'reveal' hidden secrets that lay beneath the visible surface of society, and also naturally depicted the reader (and other characters) accompanying them as they played the 'narrative "hide and seek"' through the text.[4] These shared characteristics, naturally, also tie both forms of writing to the contemporary periodical press, as it was the press that originally created and fostered the prevalent image of the police officer as socially invulnerable and thus able to invade the private and provide protection to those who moved in their company. Thus, sensation fiction and police memoirs were not only thematically connected with each other, but were also both linked to the abundance of periodical commentary that surrounded it in precisely the same ways.

Sensation Fiction and Detective Fiction in Scholarship

From quite a high-level perspective, academic scholarship has consistently connected 'sensation fiction' with 'detective fiction'.[5] However, while this is certainly justified in most cases, and modern detective fiction does indeed owe mid-Victorian sensation novels a great deal, occasionally the way in which the connection is made is problematic. There is, for example, an observable con- sensus that situates sensation fiction within a convenient chronology of texts that emerged both before and after it, placing it in an overly-linear pathway of the evolution of detective writing across the nineteenth century. The texts placed before and after sensation fiction's mid-Victorian heyday respectively tend to be Edgar Allan Poe's 'C. Auguste Dupin' stories from the 1840s, and Arthur Conan Doyle's 'Sherlock Holmes' stories that appeared from 1887 onwards. These two pivotal moments are separated by around 50 years of history, and sensation fiction is often inserted into this chronological gap as a potential narrative carrier. In *Crime Fiction: The New Critical Idiom* (2005), for example, John Scaggs pays some brief attention to the work of Emile Gaboriau before arguing that it was Charles Dickens and Wilkie Collins who supposedly made the most important contributions to detective fiction's development in the mid-Victorian era – Dickens through Inspector Bucket in *Bleak House*, and Collins through Sergeant Cuff in *The Moonstone* (1868).[6] Scaggs then turns his attention to the 'Sherlock Holmes' stories as the next significant moment in the detective genre's evolution, and eventually sum- marises his argument when he contends that:

> [...] the line of the modern crime thriller can be traced from the Gothic novel
> (and even from revenge tragedy [...]), through the novels of Charles Dickens
> and on to the Victorian 'sensation fiction' of the 1860s and 1870s [...][7]

Other well-known historians of the crime genre have made similar claims. In his widely-cited monograph *Detective Fiction* (2005), Charles Rzepka argues that sensation fiction effectively carried the evolution of detective writing through the mid-nineteenth century, claiming that 'detective fiction' was not a distinct genre of its own, but was instead 'largely submerged in other types of [...] literature', with sensation fiction being 'particularly fertile' in this respect.[8] Rzepka does rather grudgingly admit that police memoir fiction may have been an 'exception' to this, but he does not go into detail surrounding how or why this might have been the case.[9] From another perspective, Stephen Knight suggests that 'crime and excitement' were central mechanisms to sensation fiction, and he actively characterises sensation fiction as a literary bridge between earlier Gothic writing and later detective fiction by suggesting that it brought 'both Gothic sensibility and that popular energy into the domain of conventional respectable fiction', and that it thus paved the way for the development of literary 'detection'.[10]

In addition to inserting sensation fiction into the supposed 'interregnum'[11] period between Poe's Dupin and Doyle's Sherlock Holmes, some scholars exploring detective fiction's history also tend to repeatedly home in on the pre- sence of Wilkie Collins's novel *The Moonstone*. In fact, this may itself go some way to explaining why sensation fiction has received the bulk of critical focus on the development of detective writing, as *The Moonstone* is widely considered to be a hallmark sensation text. A number of critics subscribe to the (in)famous T. S. Eliot quote where he referred to it as 'the first, the longest, and the best of modern English detective novels';[12] Scaggs, for example, argues that *The Moonstone* is 'generally identified' to be the first English detective novel,[13] while Martin Priestman asserts that *The Moonstone* was influenced by works such as those by Emile Gaboriau and Edgar Allan Poe, and that it is this that cements it as a link in a narrative chain of the genre's evolution.[14] Rzepka meanwhile, alongside Mary Elizabeth Leighton and Lisa Surridge,[15] retrospectively singles out *The Moonstone* as a pivotal moment in the genre's evolution due to its connection with modern conceptions of detective fiction, arguing that '[i]n *The Moonstone* we find, for the first time, all the essential components of the classic novel of detection deployed in proper relation to each other'.[16] These 'essential components', he argues, include a crime, clues, suspects, red herrings, victims, accomplices, professional and amateur 'detectives' who can be thematically linked to their later literary descendants,[17] and an overall solution to the mystery.

I should perhaps clarify at this stage that most of these scholarly claims regarding *The Moonstone* are actually correct – Rzepka's in particular, as the novel does indeed contain all of the supposed 'elements' that he lists. It is therefore certainly possible to read it as one of the earliest moments in detective fiction's history where the text's structure adheres to our modern expectations a detective story. Consequently, I should point out that I am not suggesting that *The Moonstone*'s prominent position in the history of detective fiction is not *justified*. Rather, I simply contend that the sustained critical focus on it has helped to obscure other writing that might also have just as tangible a connection to later iterations of detective fiction. I also suggest that the focus the novel has received has largely assisted in keeping mid-Victorian sensation fiction at the forefront of academic consciousness with regard to the detective genre's development across this period.

Still further scholarly explorations link sensation fiction with the evolution of detective fiction through their characterisation of figures within texts themselves. Martin Priestman, for example, suggests that multiple characters from sensation novels can, and should, be described as 'detectives', despite their often-amateur status, their disassociation from the police, and their often personal (as opposed to professional) motive:

> [...] guilty parties and protagonists [...] are, to a greater or lesser extent, detectives. In Walter Lester, Robert Audley and Collins's Marian Halcombe and Walter Hartright, it could be argued that we have precursors of [...] amateur detective protagonists [...][18]

Priestman goes on to link the amateur nature of these 'detective' figures with much later and widely-known lay-sleuths, including Dorothy L. Sayers's Lord Peter Wimsey, Margery Allingham's Albert Campion, or even Sherlock Holmes himself. Thus, by connecting these sensational characters with other literary detectives that appeared both before and after them, Priestman further entrenches sensation fiction within the narrative chronology of detective fiction's evolution. Indeed, this is quite a common argumentative thread; Rzepka similarly claims that protagonists in sensation novels can be considered 'amateur detectives' and he suggests that sensation novels from the 1860s and 70s were particularly abundant in such characters, including Collins's Walter Hartright from *The Woman in White* (1860) and, again, Franklin Blake from *The Moonstone*. [19]

However, some examinations of the connection between sensation fiction and detective fiction are more complex than simply using the sensation genre to bridge an observable gap between Edgar Allan Poe and Arthur Conan Doyle. Christopher Pittard, for example, offers a slightly more nuanced reading by looking retrospectively to highlight how the sensation novel underwent an observable 'transformation' into the recognisable form of detective fiction in the late-Victorian era. He uses Fergus Hume's *The Mystery of a Hansom Cab* (1887) as a representative example of a transitional text that demonstrates how the sensation genre mutated into what is now called 'detective fiction',[20] thus connecting sensation fiction and detective writing more thematically than structurally. Pittard argues that the text's themes surrounding the discovery of the secret of the Frettlby family, coupled with the ability of an hansom cab to 'cross social and geographical boundaries', mirrors the overarching themes of the earlier sensation genre of discovering hidden family secrets and exploring private, often-impenetrable and usually middle-class realms. Yet, he goes on to argue, it *also* served as the model for *later* iterations of crime fiction that appeared in periodicals such as the *Strand Magazine* – famously including the Sherlock Holmes stories that traversed labyrinthine urban landscapes.[21]

In short, then, there is an observable scholarly consensus that a connection between detective fiction and sensation fiction exists, and this has been comprehensively argued from a variety of perspectives. However, there does remain some disagreement about how the connection actually works. In his book *From Bow Street to Baker Street* (1992), for example, Martin Kayman is visibly suspicious of sensation fiction's position as part of the development of detective writing. Quite apart from consistently placing the term 'detective' in inverted commas when referring to characters in sensation novels that others have almost greedily characterised as amateur sleuths in their retrospective efforts to find concrete connections to later detective writing, Kayman more cautiously, and correctly, suggests that because sensation novels are structurally different from detective fiction (as they are more inclined to play with the expectations of the reader), they are less formulaic and thus less like detective fiction than it might initially seem.[22] He also refuses to characterise *The Moonstone* as an example of 'detective fiction' in the same way as others do. While acknowledging its presence, he instead suggests that it was an 'isolated attempt' to 'develop the genre invented by Poe' and more broadly contends that 'there is no evidence of the existence or emergence of a recognized genre of "detective fiction" between the 1840s and 1880s'.[23]

However, Kayman's most important argument in terms of the focus of the present volume stems from the fact that he connects the 'sensational' aspects of sensation fiction with what he terms 'dramatic press reports of contemporary crimes',[24] and he suggests that press-coverage of criminal activity was a 'fund for sensation'.[25] Lyn Pykett makes a similar argument, which she eloquently (and usefully) summarises:

> In the 1860s the sensation novel and the sensation debate were [...] closely intertwined with developments in the newspaper press. The growth of cheap newspapers [...] and the tendency of both the expanding penny press and the middle-class newspapers to include more crime reporting was one factor in the creation of the market for sensation novels. Real life crime, as reported in contemporary newspapers [...] also provided the plots for sensation novels.[26]

A well-known example of a true crime that visibly made its way into sensation fiction was the infamous Road Hill House murder of 1860 which, as Kate Summerscale highlights in her book *The Suspicions of Mr. Whicher; or, the Murder at Road Hill House* (2008),

> turned everyone detective. It riveted the people of England, hundreds of whom wrote to the newspapers [...] with their solutions. It helped shape the fiction of the 1860s and beyond, most obviously Wilkie Collins' *The Moonstone*, which was described by T. S. Eliot as the first and best of all English detective novels. Whicher was the inspiration for that story's cryptic Sergeant Cuff, who has influenced nearly every detective hero since. Elements of the case surfaced in Charles Dickens' last, unfinished novel, *The Mystery of Edwin Drood.* [27]

The Road Hill House case thus left the pages of contemporary press reports to reappear, in 'disguised and intensified' forms, in the pages of various pieces of popular fiction.[28] Indeed, Summerscale also goes on to convincingly argue that the murder's chief suspect, Constance Kent, was also 'refracted into every woman' in Mary Elizabeth Braddon's novel *Lady Audley's Secret* (1862), from the murderess Lady Audley herself, to her accomplice/co-conspirator in crime, her maid Phoebe Marks.[29]

The point regarding the connection between sensation fiction and popular journalism made by Kayman, Pykett, and Summerscale can be developed slightly, however. Contemporary crime reports not only appeared in sensation fiction in the form of plot-retellings of famous and popular crimes, but the genre *also* consciously capitalised on the wider sociocultural anxieties surrounding new forms of law enforcement, state surveillance, subterfuge, and detection that were similarly exacerbated by the exact same periodical crime reports.[30] As Anthea Trodd argues, encounters between police officers and (often female) characters in sensation fiction were often deliberate renderings of the anxiety surrounding the invasive presence of the police that, as we have seen, was extensively discussed in the pages of contemporary periodicals.

More importantly, however, the argument that the periodical press helped to 'feed' sensation fiction (either structurally or ideologically) actually helps to demonstrate how sensation novels were also connected to *police memoir fiction*. In simple terms, it was not only sensation fiction that was influenced by contemporary press-reportage of criminal activity; as we have seen throughout this volume, press reports of crime and periodical discussions of the police also influenced the construction of other kinds of fiction, notably including the police memoir. Thus, the periodical press remained at the core of the construction of *both* kinds of writing, providing plotlines and ideas for characters; developing the wider sociocultural anxieties against which fictional authors set their writing; and improving knowledge of the police officer as a figure that could simultaneously navigate the world of the everyday and the world of the criminal.

The final point to note is that the connection between the police memoir and sensation fiction ran even deeper than both genres utilising press reports to help construct their fiction. There is actually evidence to suggest that one kind of fiction directly influenced the appearance of the other – a fact that some contemporary commentators noticed and commented on. The next section of this chapter, therefore, explores exactly how numerous periodicals actively connected the two genres together, and argues that closer inspection of this phenomenon helps to cement both genres' places in the chronological evolution of detective fiction. Not only were crime-reports a good source of inspiration, but the periodical press *itself* made tangible connections between the two types of writing.

Contemporary Periodical Connections: Sensation and Police Memoir Fiction

A surprisingly large number of mid-Victorian periodical commentators made connections between police memoirs and sensation novels – particularly around the beginning of the 1860s when police memoir fiction was relatively well-established and sensation fiction was rapidly developing as a new cultural phenomenon. An excellent example of this in action appeared in the *London Review* in 1862, which directly referenced William Russell's detective 'Waters' to argue that the popularity of the police memoir had sparked a wider literary movement, and that sensation fiction was one of the genre's evolutions. It also contended that this was entirely predictable in retrospect, as the 'sensation' genre had a broader focus and could thus perform literary functions that police memoirs could not, thereby appealing to a much wider audience:

> It is now some years since the name of "Waters" first became familiar and welcome to readers in railway trains. [...] In fact, it was discovered that a new vein of literature was opened up. [...] [T]he policeman line of writing was found to possess an interest often sadly wanting to more decorous publications. The multitude of novel writers had worn out every conceivable theme when this welcome discovery was made. Accordingly the criminal novel is now the *mode*. The crime is, of course, a mystery; and the

plot is the statement of the means by which the mystery is detected. Mr. Wilkie Collins was perhaps the first to adopt this fashion.[31]

Put simply, police memoir fiction was characterised here as a *progenitor* of sensation fiction. The police memoir had focused literary attention onto the detection of crime, which was found to be a popular and lucrative avenue of writing. It's appeal thus naturally spawned lots of new novels and stories that were similarly interested in the depiction of criminal activity (and the fight against it), and naturally came to diversify from formulaic retellings of the police experience into wider tales of crime – moving from 'the policeman line of writing' to the 'criminal novel', exemplified here by Wilkie Collins. The same article also (slightly cynically) suggested that the diversification of the genre provided an opportunity for authors to, essentially, produce less and charge more:

> The result is that instead of a dozen criminals, discoveries, and executions from "Waters," in the space of one volume, and for the price of one shilling, we have the detection of only one criminal – without any execution at all, – extending over three volumes, and charged at the exorbitant rate of thirty-one shillings and sixpence.[32]

A variety of other pieces also commented on the apparently-observable connection between police memoir fiction and sensation fiction. Some were particularly interested in their similar narrative perspective, noting that sensation novels were often told as a series of first-person recollections in much the same way as fictional memoirs. A review of Mary Elizabeth Braddon's *Sir Jasper's Tenant* (1865) published in the *Saturday Review* complimented the novel on the way it retold 'incidents' in a linear, connected and (crucially) accurate manner, and argued that '[a] *clever detective with a literary knack* could not have reported incidents with greater accuracy or more befitting simplicity [my italics]'.[33] Similarly, a review of Braddon's more famous novel, *Lady Audley's Secret*, from the *Critic* in December 1862 shared this sentiment by suggesting that the reader's attention was kept through a linear stream of 'sensation scenes' from which their attention 'never for an instant flag[ged]'.[34]

A review of Flora Dawson's *Princes, Public Men, and Pretty Women: Episodes in Real-Life* (1864) that appeared in the *Reader* also commented on the perspective of the text, when it argued that the fact that the author wrote directly to the reader, drawing from their own experiences, was that which made the text 'sensational':

> There are some more sensation stories in the book, particularly one of a *vivandïere* [sic], who poisons her canteen in order to be revenged on the Emperor of Russia and his officers for an injury done to her husband. [...] *The author writes [...] from her personal experience* [my emphasis].[35]

In fact, this particular review was itself titled 'Sensation Recollections', which again demonstrates an implicit connection between police memoirs – which were often given titles such as 'Recollections of...' or 'Reminiscences of...' – and sensation fiction.

Elsewhere, a review of Russell's *Autobiography of an English Detective* (1863) published in the *Reader* in January 1863, also commented on the structural connection between the two genres when it suggested that the format of the novel, marketed as a series of *truthful* recollections, actually helped to make it more 'sensational' than even sensation fiction itself. In doing so, the piece consciously tied the novel to contemporary sensation fiction:

> Are these stories facts, or not? [...] If it be so, then, not only is truth stranger than fiction – [...] even than such fiction *as that of the sensation kind*, so popular just now – but stranger than any melodrama put on the Adelphi stage [...] [my italics].[36]

This focus on textual structure was actually a common perspective from which periodical commentators critiqued the connection between the two kinds of writing. Indeed, some defined sensation fiction as tales that directly followed a detective in their attempts to solve a puzzling crime or mystery, a textual construction that directly mirrored the popular police memoir that had come before it and that had essentially invented this narrative structure. In the June 1864 issue of the *Saturday Review*, for example, the author argued that 'detective literature' formed one of the most common kinds of 'sensation' writing:

> Of all forms of sensation novel-writing, none is so common as what may be called the romance of the *detective* [my italics].[37]

The deployment of the detective figure thus attracted significant attention in contemporary periodical criticism, as this was the figure around which narratives in both kinds of fiction was often constructed. An article attributed to Margaret Oliphant titled 'Novels' and published in *Blackwood's Edinburgh Magazine* in August 1863 suggested that the central pillar of a number of genres of popular mid-Victorian fiction lay in how they utilised a detective to track down criminals, and that readers consistently followed them in their wake:

> This is what fiction has come to. Yet though we laugh at it, sneer at it, patronise it, we continue to read, or somebody continues to read [...] We turn with a national instinct rather to the brutalities than to the subtleties of crime. Murder is our *cheval de bataille* [...] The horrors of our novels are crimes against life and property. The policeman is the Fate who stalks relentless, or flies with lightning steps after our favourite villain.[38]

Oliphant here argued that a variety of mid-century genres were focused on crime, murder, and detection, and her image of the policeman who 'stalks' (or 'flies') after the reader's 'favourite villain' intimated at the ways in which the reader figuratively accompanied them as they did so. Indeed, in police memoir fiction, this concept of the police officer chasing his prey was the main way of constructing the entire narrative and the reader, acting on some level as the detective's 'sidekick', followed the officer in his wake.[39] This trope of the dogged detective was naturally transposed into sensation fiction, as an article by the celebrated poet (later Poet Laureate) Alfred Austin (1825–1913) from a June 1870 issue of *Temple Bar* suggested:

> [...] in the stories we are discussing [sensation novels] there is always a wonderful detective [...] who has nothing else to do but to go about and unravel the mysterious threads [...][40]

Finally, yet *more* commentators simply felt that sensation fiction was popular because it was tied to the everyday, the familiar, or that which was concealed just beneath the surface of visible society. This, once again, mirrored the purpose of the police memoir, which was similarly designed to explore and reveal criminality that lurked beneath society's exterior and which was usually inaccessible to everyday readers. Perhaps the most interesting and convincing example of this was an article written by cleric Henry Mansel (1820–1871) titled 'Sensation Novels' from the April 1863 issue of the *Quarterly Review* argued:

> The sensation novel, be it mere trash or something worse, is usually a tale of our own times. It is necessary to be near a mine to be blown up by its explosion; and a tale which aims at electrifying the nerves of the reader is never thoroughly effective unless the scene be laid in our own days and among the people we are in the habit of meeting. [...] we are thrilled with horror [...] by the thought that such things may be going on around us and among us.[41]

There was, therefore, a variety of connections made between police memoir fiction and popular sensation novels in various pieces of mid-Victorian periodical commentary. Some made thematic connections, whilst others connected the two through their shared narrative perspective and structure. Still more noted the common role of the (sometimes amateur) 'police officer' that had a shared purpose of revealing hidden secrets and spaces, and, finally, some placed police memoirs and sensation fiction within a literary genealogy, by arguing that the sensation genre was symptomatic of the diversification of police memoir fiction away from focusing on the police officer and onto wider tales of 'crime'. This was a correct interpretation; the sensation genre was indeed a movement away from a *focus* on the police towards their *utilisation* for alternative narrative ends, and this was perhaps a natural development as fiction itself steadily became more diverse and creative across the mid-nineteenth century.[42]

From the Slum to the Stately Home: A Shift in Perspective

Contemporary periodical journalism therefore made numerous, diverse connections between police memoir fiction and sensation novels, and so it seems clear that the two forms of writing, at the very least, were aware of and influenced each other's production and consumption right from the outset. It is therefore the task of the remainder of this chapter to explore exactly how the two genres were connected, and how this operated in reality.

The first apparent connection is the fact that both genres were concerned with revealing that which was being kept hidden just beneath society's visible surface. Indeed, as the previous section highlighted, some contemporary periodical commentators noticed this. For example, Henry Mansel's 1863 article from the *Quarterly Review* that mused on sensation fiction's popularity commented directly on how the genre was centred on revealing the supposedly-hidden criminality that existed in the midst of the public:

> [...] we are thrilled with horror, even in fiction, by the thought that such things may be going on around us and among us. The man who shook our hand with a hearty English grasp half an hour ago – the woman whose beauty and grace were the charm of last night, and whose gentle words sent us home better pleased with the world and with ourselves – how exciting to think that under thee pleasing outsides may be a concealed demon in human shape, a Count Fosco or a Lady Audley![43]

As we have seen at length, the concept of revealing secrets or scandals that lurked beneath the surface of society was also the central theme of police memoir fiction, again cementing the two genres. However, there is an observable distinction in the *kinds* of secrets which texts from the two respective genres were designed to reveal (as well as in the locations on which they focused to look for them) that is worth specifically noting here. Put simply, police memoir fiction concerned itself with utilising police officers to explore and reveal criminality that existed in urban slum areas, and to allow readers to experience them alongside them under their protection. By contrast, however, sensation fiction moved away from exploring criminality contained within external urban environments and progressed (essentially) indoors, because it concerned itself with revealing a different kind of secret: that of bourgeois domesticity. Novels such as, but by no means limited to, Wilkie Collins's *The Woman in White* (1860), *No Name* (1862), *The Moonstone* (1868), and *The Law and the Lady* (1875), as well as Mary Elizabeth Braddon's *The Trail of the Serpent* (1860/61) or *Lady Audley's Secret* (1862) shifted their prying focus away from urban criminality and into the domestic sphere.

Interestingly enough, there is a slightly ironic element to this shift of literary focus into the domestic space. As we have seen already, it had originally been the progression from the exploration of indoor criminal spaces, such as court rooms or prisons, to the exploration of the hidden external urban environment that had sparked the popularity of police memoir fiction in the first place. Now however, things seemingly went back inside. As Stephen Knight correctly argues, crimes or thrilling occurrences within sensation novels were often deliberately placed within the private domestic sphere to create maximum sensationalism, because the home was tied to both familiarity and respectable safety.[44] Similarly, Christopher Pittard echoes Knight when he points out that sensation narratives had progressed from the urban spaces of the streets and criminal slums of cities, so prominently-placed in police memoirs, into the family home:

> The sensation novel [...] caused controversy not only because of a potential glamorizing of crime along the lines of the penny dreadful, but also in terms of its treatment of the middle-class family as the site of a destructive mystery. *The sensation novel marked the shift of the crime narrative from the public space of the streets and slums to the private realm of the family home* [...] [my italics].[45]

There are, however, two other observable reasons for this shift off the streets and into the home than the assertion that placing the crime in the familiar domestic space was designed to create maximum sensationalism by putting it in a setting to which every reader could relate. Firstly, as the *London Review* observed in 1862 (quoted earlier), sensation fiction was a complex diversification of the police memoir in an attempt to prevent it from becoming stagnated through lack of originality.[46] Secondly, and perhaps slightly more convincingly, the 'movement indoors' of the location of the 'secret to be discovered' in sensation fiction is symptomatic of a new focus on *female* criminality, and on that which potentially lurked within the idyllic family unit.[47] This idea has received quite extensive attention in scholarship; as Andrew Mangham suggests, mid-nineteenth century notions of femininity (influenced by widely publicised cases involving female criminals such as the trial of the Mannings or the aforementioned Road Hill House murder) 'perceived there to be a ghastly, destructive energy lurking beneath female spaces and feminine graces'.[48] Saverio Tomaiuolo agrees, and suggests that the relationship between sensation fiction and the detection of crime manifested a variety of social anxieties, including (although not limited to) the increasing independence of women.[49] This focus on feminine and family criminality, when combined with the popular mid-Victorian association between women and the interior domestic space (famously highlighted by the publication of Coventry Patmore's now-infamous poem 'The Angel in the House' between 1854 and 1862),[50] can thus help further explain why the literary focus shifted away from revealing the secrets of the urban underworld towards revealing those contained within bourgeois domesticity. As Lyn Pykett asserts, a common trope in sensation fiction was to include a police officer or detective figure that was specifically designed to root out the criminality lurking within it,[51] while Anthea Trodd also argues that 'encounter[s] between a detective policeman, intruder into the sanctuary of the home, and a young lady, representative of that home's sanctities' were a common 'feature' that was a manifestation of a variety of prevalent social anxieties.[52] Thus, a wide variety of sensation authors such as Braddon, Gaskell, Dickens, Trollope and Collins all explored new possibilities of relations between domestic and public spheres in these encounters between police officers and ladies.[53]

Naturally, the police officer was rarely a *welcome* figure in the domestic space in sensation fiction. Christopher Pittard's argument that female criminals contained within middle-class homes were often sympathetically portrayed[54] complements Trodd's correct suggestion that there was a sense of indignation at the presence of a police officer, often seen as an external 'intruder' into the idyllic domestic sphere.[55] However, she crucially argues that while police officers were seen as invaders of the domestic space, they were not truly a part of it themselves as they were not members of the bourgeoisie. This made them *ineffective* operatives within the bourgeois space, and thus most textual examples of sensational detectives, such as Wilkie Collins's Sergeant Cuff or Grimstone from Braddon's *Aurora Floyd* (1863), are left unable to solve the novel's central mystery.[56] This thematic connection helps to cement sensation fiction's connection to police memoirs, as the police officer's external position outside of the middle-class domestic space made them capable of crossing both geographical and social boundaries, just as they in both social exploration journalism and in police memoir fiction. They also had the ability to cross *social* boundaries, and were depicted as able to contradict or openly refute those of a class significantly higher than themselves, by shielding themselves with their socio-politically ascribed authority as police officers. The next section of this chapter, therefore, explores this phenomenon in detail, looking at exactly how police officers were represented in a number of sensation novels, and arguing that this was thematically identical to how they were represented in police memoirs.

'Time and place cannot bind Mr Bucket': Police Officers, Sensation Fiction, and the Police Memoir

The clearest thematic connection between sensation fiction and police memoir fiction is, quite simply, the common presence of a police officer or detective in both genres. This shared figure effectively anchors the two genres together, as their literary purpose in both forms of writing was to uncover the texts' various 'secrets' to the best of their ability, and to expose them for the reader. In both genres, the police officer was necessarily able to ignore almost all geographical and social conventions that would have otherwise restricted them from performing this task through their imbued authority as a manifestation of the law, and they therefore had the ability to move wherever they pleased and converse with whoever they wanted on all social levels without restraint. This has already received some, admittedly slightly oblique, critical attention. Again, Christopher Pittard's thoughts on Hume's *The Mystery of a Hansom Cab* centre on how the hansom itself had the ability to 'cross social and geographical boundaries',[57] while Philipp Erchinger also makes an relevant point surrounding

Wilkie Collins's *The Woman in White* (1859–60), arguing that the 'detective', Walter Hartright, is afforded the right to uncover the novel's secrets by the authority of the law itself.[58] He suggests that Hartright's investigation plays out in the same invasive way as would otherwise take place within a court of justice, and thus he, like the police, is imbued with the ability to ignore social convention in the course of his investigation.[59] Erchinger also argues that there is the potential for a 'theoretical comparison between the conduct of a legal investigation and a reader's construction of a narrative plot', and suggests that this 'legal justification' for reading itself constitutes the authority to uncover the secrets of the novel's content.[60] Additionally, from a slightly more metafictional perspective, Caroline Reitz further suggests that literary detectives also crossed *textual* borders, moving eventually from the sensation novel and into the recognisable detective novel.[61]

Charles Dickens's *Bleak House* demonstrates the connection between police memoirs and sensation fiction through their shared use of police officers who could easily ignore physical boundaries and social conventions. The novel is often cited as an early example of sensation fiction[62] as it uses many of the tropes that later came to characterise the genre. Dickens himself actually suggested that the novel 'dwelt upon the romantic side of familiar things',[63] while some contemporary critics similarly argued that his work was, at least on some level, sensational. Margaret Oliphant writing in *Blackwood's* in 1862, for example, suggested that 'Mr. Dickens rarely writes a book without an attempt at a similar effect by means of some utterly fantastic creation, set before his readers with all that detail of circumstance in which he is so successful',[64] while George Augustus Sala writing in *Belgravia* in 1868, claimed that Dickens's work was inherently sensational and labelled him 'the most persistently, "sensational" writer of the age'.[65]

Bleak House's detective, Inspector Bucket, is thus an excellent place to begin an exploration of how police officers and detectives in sensation fiction mirrored those in police memoirs in that they could cross social and geographical boundaries and could intrude upon almost anywhere at will. Indeed, the connection between Bucket and Dickens's own interest in exploring the urban criminal underworld is clear; Bucket himself was apparently based on Dickens's real-life detective friend and occasional police-collaborator[66] Charles Frederick Field (although Dickens himself always denied that this connection was actually true).[67] However, as D. A. Miller points out, it exists at least in thematic terms even if it was not conscious or deliberate; Bucket's escort of Mr Snagsby through the slum of Tom-all-Alone's directly mirrors Dickens's exploits throughout St. Giles-in-the-Fields alongside Inspectors Field and Whicher,[68] and the fact that Dickens's adventures with Field provided inspiration for *both* Inspector Bucket's character *and* early examples of police memoir fiction (see Chapter 3) certainly helps to firmly tie the two genres together. In more thematic terms, Dickens's description of Bucket in the novel immediately suggests that he continuously operates outside of rigid social constraints:

> In his fondness for society, and *his adaptability to all grades [of it]*, Mr
> Bucket is presently standing before the hall-fire [...] [my italics][69]

Bucket maintains this social 'adaptability' across the entire novel. He has a
natural tendency to ignore established social conventions and to simply go
wherever he pleases without concern of whether he should or should not. In a
strong (and quite amusing) example of this, he ignores a specifically-given
request to remain where he was standing (waiting in the hallway), but instead
follows an obviously-irritated Mr Jarndyce upstairs without invitation:

> Mr Jarndyce begs him to remain there, while he speaks to Miss Summerson.
> Mr Bucket says he will; but acting on his usual principle, does no such
> thing – following upstairs instead, and keeping his man in sight.[70]

Bucket's 'usual principle' refers to his penchant for disregarding boundaries and
entering wherever he pleases without invitation, using his authority as a police
officer in order to do so without consequence. He readily adapts himself to
occupy any space like a chameleon, and opens it up for those that accompany
him in the process. Indeed, Dickens elaborates on this idea when he directly
describes Bucket as unconstrained by almost anything when executing his duty:

> Time and place cannot bind Mr Bucket. Like man in the abstract, he is here
> today and gone tomorrow – but, very unlike man indeed, he is here again the
> next day. This evening he will be casually looking into the iron extinguishers
> at the door of Sir Leicester Dedlock's house in town; and tomorrow morning
> he will be walking on the leads at Chesney Wold [...] Drawers, desks
> pockets, all things belonging to him Mr Bucket examines.[71]

Bucket thus ties many of our previously-explored literary tropes together, and
his behaviour repeatedly highlights his connection with the liminal nature of the
police in both crime journalism and in police memoir fiction. He is a character
who is not constantly present throughout the text, but who appears only when
he is required (regardless of whether he is wanted or not) and then, as if by
magic, vanishes again when his work is done, much like police officers in crime
journalism who appeared only when they were necessary.[72] His socially
'unconstrained' characteristics also place him in a position similar to the
detectives of police memoirs such as Richmond or 'Waters', who could (and
did) perform the exact same function and had precisely the same ability to go
anywhere, see anything and converse with anyone. Bucket is, as Miller elegantly
puts it, '[a] master of disguise, who makes himself appear in as "ghostly" a
manner as, with a touch of his stick, he makes others "instantly evaporate"'.[73]

Detective characters in police memoirs and sensation fiction are also connected together in that they offer both the reader and other characters guidance
and protection, as they are temporarily covered by their authority while they
are in the detective's company. There are moments in sensation novels where

other characters accompany police officers in this way, and in these situations the characters, like the journalist in social exploration journalism, come to manifest the presence of the reader themselves.[74] *Bleak House*'s protagonist, Esther Summerson, for example, is one such a character that particularly exemplifies this. Chapter 57 (one of many titled simply 'Esther's Narrative') depicts Esther being whisked away by Bucket in pursuit of the missing Lady Dedlock, as Bucket believes Esther may be able to convince Lady Dedlock to return home. Bucket is shown flitting in and out of various areas of London's underworld; crossing bridges and passing through gates in another demonstration of how his authority affords him the ability to go anywhere, illustrated particularly well by Hablot Knight Browne (alias 'Phiz') (see Figure 4.1).[75]

Esther, under the protective cover of Bucket's authority, is temporarily imbued with the same ability as he, and ends up exploring places that she would never have entered under ordinary circumstances:

> We rattled with great rapidity through such a labyrinth of streets, that I soon lost all idea where we were; except that we had crossed and re-crossed the river, and still seems to be traversing a low-lying, waterside, dense neighbourhood of narrow thoroughfares, chequered by docks and basins, high piles of warehouses, swing-bridges, and masts of ships. At length, we stopped at the corner of a little slimy turning [...] After some [...] conference, Mr Bucket (whom everybody seemed to know and defer to) went in with the others at a door [...][76]

In this moment, therefore, Esther manifests the reader, who accompanies Bucket in just as confused a state as Esther herself. This confusion is a trope that Trodd identifies as common in sensation narratives where heroines encounter police officers, and she argues that this is to allow the female character to avoid 'possible contamination by the police habit of mind'.[77] Trodd is largely correct; the fact that Esther accompanies Bucket in a confused state, and has to trust in him to guide her through the urban underworld, cements the idea that her ability to enter this criminal space is merely temporary and does not affect her own respectability. However, it also serves to highlight how the *reader* is just as reliant on Bucket to pass through the urban underworld. Just as in social exploration journalism and in police memoir fiction, the police officer here represents a guide into the confused world of the criminal, without which the journalist, reader, or character would be completely lost.

From another perspective, Bucket's position as a police officer also allows him to bypass certain *social* boundaries, as well as the various *physical* ones that make up the urban labyrinth. This affords the reader a slightly different window into various, perhaps inaccessible social situations and an inside-view of their hierarchies to which they perhaps would not otherwise have been privy. In police memoirs, detectives are depicted interacting with characters from all walks of life in much the same way, as they operated outside of the stringent class-structure. In a scene where Bucket has gathered together various

THE NIGHT.

Figure 4.1 'Phiz' (Hablot Knight Browne), 'The Night'
Source: *Bleak House*, Victorian Web <http://www.victorianweb.org/victorian/art/illustration/phiz/bleakhouse/36.html> [accessed February 28 2018], scanned and uploaded by George P. Landow (1853, uploaded 2007).

characters, he demonstrates that he is able to converse with (and ultimately accuse) those from all social levels, ranging from shopkeeper to Baronet:

> 'Now, perhaps you may know me, ladies and gentlemen [...] I am Inspector Bucket of the Detective, I am; and this,' producing the tip of his convenient little staff from his breast-pocket, 'is my authority [...]'[78]

This concept is even further developed in a scene where Bucket informs Sir Leicester Dedlock of his suspicions surrounding Lady Dedlock and Mr Tulkinghorn's murder. Sir Leicester is angry at Bucket's suggestion that Lady Dedlock may have been involved in the death, yet he consciously remains powerless to control him:

> [Sir Leicester, to Bucket] 'Do your duty; but be careful not to overstep it. I would not suffer it. I would not endure it. You bring my Lady's name into this communication, upon your responsibility – upon your responsibility. My Lady's name is not a name for common persons to trifle with!' [...] [Bucket, in reply] 'Sir Leicester Dedlock, Baronet, I say what I must say; and no more.'[79]

Sir Leicester naturally attempts to warn Bucket not to accuse Lady Dedlock as he is used to his position of social privilege and Bucket's interference would overstep the social boundary that exists between them. This seemingly confirms Trodd's suggestion that police detectives were seen as 'unwelcome interlopers' within the domestic sphere; Bucket's presence, not to mention his accusations, upsets the typical social hierarchy, and causes Sir Leicester to now see him as an intruder.[80] However this scene also raises a further point worth briefly noting; the fact that the detective provoked an unwelcome reaction from the occupants of bourgeois domestic spaces revealed uncertain questions about their own social status, as most police officers came from working-class backgrounds.[81] The authority ascribed to 'the police' thus supersedes the social status of the person wearing the uniform, and again, as the reader acts as Bucket's companion, they too are temporarily imbued with the same authority regardless of their *own* social status.

Moving on from *Bleak House*, Mary Elizabeth Braddon's novel *Three Times Dead, or, The Secret of the Heath* (1860), republished under the name of *The Trail of the Serpent* in 1861, contains another detective figure who demonstrates one of the strongest and perhaps most striking connections between police memoirs and sensation novels. Braddon made a significant number of revisions to the text on the advice of her publisher between the novel's original publication in 1860 and the revised and re-titled edition published after 1861, and one of these changes was the name of the novel's principle detective. In the revised edition, the character's name was (and remained) Joseph Peters; however in the original 1860 text Peters's name was, in fact, Mr. *Waters*. This may simply be nothing more than coincidence, but the connection here between this character and his contemporary namesake created by William Russell is certainly noteworthy.

The character has other connections with detectives from police memoirs besides his name, however. Waters/Peters (hereafter referred to as 'Peters' simply to avoid confusion with Russell's detective) is a mute who communicates through the use of a written alphabet, and may be one of the earliest detectives with an openly-referenced disability to appear in fiction. However, far from being disadvantageous, Peters actually uses his marginal social position as both police officer and as disabled to enhance his Bucket-esque social fluidity. His muteness firstly allows him to keep certain aspects of his profession to himself more effectively than his counterparts:

> [...] there were secrets and mysteries of his art he did not trust at all times to the dirty alphabet [sic]; and perhaps his opinion on the subject of the murder of Mr. Montague Harding was one of them.[82]

Peters's secretive nature is thus *augmented* by the fact that he cannot verbally communicate, as it makes him a natural at keeping secrets from characters (whilst simultaneously revealing them to the reader). This aspect, combined with the description of his appearance and personality, helps Peters to effectively demonstrate how depictions of the police officer in sensation novels mirrored that of their ability in police memoir fiction to pass unhindered and, in many cases, unnoticed, while the reader follows along:

> He might have passed in a hundred crowds, and no one of the hundreds of people in any one of these hundred crowds would have glanced aside to look at him. [...] You could only describe him by negatives. He was neither very tall nor very short, he was neither very stout nor very thin, neither dark nor fair, neither ugly nor handsome; but just such a medium between the two extremities of each as to be utterly commonplace and unnoticeable.[83]

Peters thus fulfils a similar textual purpose to Bucket, in that he possesses the ability to go wherever he pleases unseen or unremarked, and the reader continually accompanies him as he does so. A scene that demonstrates this particularly well is a moment where he overhears a conversation in a public-house between the novel's villain and his lover. Peters notes the voices, and boldly walks directly into the scene in order to overhear this conversation better. Perhaps most interestingly, he also uses his muteness to his advantage in order to penetrate the scene more effectively than even other detectives would have been able to:

> But in I walks, past the bar; and straight afore me I sees a door as leads into the parlour – the passage was jolly dark; and this 'ere door was ajar; and inside I hears voices. [...] so I listens. [...] [I]n I walks, very quiet and quite unbeknownst. He was a-sittin' with his back to the door, and the young woman he was a-talkin' to was standin' lookin' out of the winder; so neither of 'em saw me. [...] He turned round and looked at me. [...] I says to myself, if ever there was anything certain in this world since it was

begun, I've come across the right 'un: so I sits down and takes up a newspaper. I signified to him that I was dumb, and he took it for granted I was deaf as well [...] so he went on a-talking to the girl.[84]

Interestingly enough, this scene also reads almost identically to a number of examples of police memoir fiction that depict the detective figure in the same way, both in terms of narrative structure and content. In fact, the 1860 novel *Diary of an Ex-Detective* by Charles Martel includes a very similar scene taken from inside a public house, from the first-person perspective of a detective. I am not suggesting that one text directly influenced another, but the similarities in the way the scene is retold, particularly when combined with the fact that Peters's name was originally Waters, certainly help to connect the memoir genre with sensation fiction, as both kinds of writing depict almost identical scenes acted out in almost the exact same way:

[I]n a few minutes I was drying myself before a huge fire in the kitchen of the Rising Sun. [...] There were some very rough, ill-looking fellows hanging about the room, drinking their beer. I fancied I was the subject of conversation with one group, for they conversed in whispers, and sent some very sinister, furtive glances at me from across the room.[85]

Moving on again, Braddon's *Lady Audley's Secret* (1862) provides a third example of a detective figure who performs these actions which connect the sensation and memoir genres. However, this novel's 'detective character' is not a self-identified 'detective', but is instead the barrister Robert Audley. That said, Robert is today often cited as a pseudo-detective figure, and is certainly depicted in the text as at least influenced by characters from popular detective fiction when he consciously 'turns sleuth' to discover what has happened to his friend, George Talboys, who has gone missing:

'I haven't read Alexander Dumas and Wilkie Collins for nothing,' he muttered. 'I'm up to their tricks, sneaking in at doors behind a fellow's back, and flattening their white faces against window panes, and making themselves all eyes in the twilight. [...]'[86]

Similarly to his true-detective counterparts, Robert also possesses the ability to go wherever he pleases in a comparable fashion to Bucket and Peters, and a particularly strong example of this appears when he enters Lady Audley's private dressing room through a secret passage of which she is totally unaware. However, there is a clear difference here. As Robert is not actually a detective like Bucket or Peters, his authority to invade Lady Audley's boudoir does not stem from any socially-ascribed authority like that given to police officers. Rather, it comes from the fact that he is more legitimately a family member than Lady Audley is herself. Thus, as Lyn Pykett argues, the detection of the novel's 'dreadful secret' thus comes directly from a character who 'polices the family' rather than the actual police.[87] The combination of his legitimate familial status *and* his position as the novel's 'detective' character thus means that Robert's authority to enter into Lady Audley's private boudoir supersedes her own authority to keep it concealed. As he is both legitimate family member and pseudo-'detective', the tension between these two oft-conflicting figures is resolved before it begins, leaving Lady Audley with no chance of escaping detection. Indeed, this helps to explain why the plot-driver in *Lady Audley's Secret* is not the discovery of the criminal, but is instead the fact that Robert discovers the perpetrator extremely quickly, and has to spend the remainder of the novel working out how to prove it to everyone else who does not possess the same authority as he does himself.

The invasion of Lady Audley's boudoir is thus a particularly clear example of the sensation novel's connection with the police memoir genre through their mutual depictions of detectives who invade the inaccessible, and this scene contains a number of similar ideas. The reader, again, accompanies the 'detective' into a usually-private or closed location, this time through the use of a secret passageway. The scene also reveals the fact that the boudoir does not genuinely belong to Lady Audley; and thus it was not her space to conceal in the first place:

> Robert Audley lifted a corner of the carpet [...] and disclosed a rudely-cut trapdoor in the oak flooring. [...] George, submissively following his friend, found himself, in five minutes, standing amidst the elegant disorder of Lady Audley's dressing-room.[88]

In Robert's company, the reader is allowed to enter into this very private domestic space, and again, this helps reinforce the fact that mid-Victorian sensation fiction was connected with popular police memoir fiction through their shared use of the detective figure acting as the reader's guide and protector into usually inaccessible locations. Just as Esther Summerson was temporarily imbued with the Inspector Bucket's authority to wander around wherever he went, so too is George Talboys temporarily imbued with Robert Audley's authority to accompany him into Lady Audley's boudoir:

> George Talboys saw his bearded face and tall gaunt figure reflected in the cheval-glass, and wondered to see how out of place he seemed among all these womanly luxuries.[89]

It is particularly interesting to note that Talboys feels a strong sense of displacement here, and he assumes that it is because he is occupying a 'womanly' space filled with unusual things. However, I suggest that Talboys also feels out of place because he does not enter or occupy the dressing-room through his own authority, but instead through that provided by Robert as the 'family police officer'.[90] Talboys is therefore correct in his assertion that he should feel out of place, however his interpretation of his own feelings is only partially true. Conveniently enough, throughout the remainder of the novel Talboys is replaced by the reader, who accompanies Robert Audley in his quest to find out what has happened to Talboys after he disappears. The reader therefore occupies the same space as the reader of police memoir fiction – as the direct temporary companion of the detective figure.[91]

Elsewhere, Wilkie Collins's novel *The Moonstone*, which appeared serially in *All the Year Round* before being published as a three-volume novel in 1868, is yet another important text to consider when exploring connections between sensation fiction and police memoir fiction, through their shared uses of the police officer. There are a number of useful perspectives to be examined in relation to the novel's detective, the famous Sergeant Cuff. Cuff manifests several of the elements of the sensational detective already mentioned in this chapter – he is protected by both his authority and reputation, is easily able to intrude on the Verinder's household despite his own class status, and both fails and succeeds in solving the mystery and revealing the novel's underlying secret.

Cuff, who for a variety of reasons is often lambasted for his failure to solve the mystery of the theft of the diamond,[92] further helps to demonstrate how the 'detective' in sensation novels allows readers to enter and explore a multitude of private, domestic, and bourgeois spaces. Like Bucket, who is first presented to the reader in a similar way, when the reader of *The Moonstone* is introduced to Sergeant Cuff they are immediately greeted with a demonstration of his ability to invade anywhere, domestic, private, or otherwise, without invitation, occupation or reason, thanks to his authority as a police officer:

> Asking for my lady, and hearing that she was in one of the conservatories, we went round to the gardens at the back, and sent a servant to seek her. While we were waiting, Sergeant Cuff looked through the evergreen arch on our left, spied out our rosery [sic], and walked straight in [...][93]

Cuff's rejection of etiquette as less important than his own interest in roses has been earmarked, particularly by scholars like John Scaggs, as a sign of his eccentricity and therefore his connection to later fictional sleuths who also demonstrate some form of eccentric behaviour in the name of detection.[94] However, I suggest that it is also a deliberate inclusion to highlight his ability to ignore physical barriers due to his authority as a police officer, tying him to both other examples of sensation fiction and to contemporary police memoirs. Cuff demonstrates the same disdain again when he enters the house, by inviting himself to look over the room in which the crime occurred:

> [Superintendent Seegrave] 'The Sergeant wishes to see Miss Verinder's sitting-room,' says Mr Seegrave, addressing me with great pomp and eagerness. 'The Sergeant may have some questions to ask. Attend the sergeant, if you please!' [...] While I was being ordered about in this way, I looked at the great Cuff. The great Cuff, on his side, looked at Superintendent Seegrave in that quietly expecting way which I have already noticed.[95]

As Miller argues, Cuff's presence immediately disrupts the routine and hier-archy inside the Verinder household,[96] and this is often meant to be the catalyst by which the domestic secrets of the bourgeois family are revealed to readers of sensation novels. But, the fact that Cuff does *not* make use of this disruption to notice things that are out of place, and to subsequently present the solution to the crime, often leaves readers feeling underwhelmed. Indeed, Cuff is frequently criticised for his failure to find the culprit of the Moonstone's theft, and it is often argued that his failure stems from the simple fact that he is not part of the middle-class family itself.[97] However, there are other reasons that account for Cuff's failure; Lyn Pykett suggests that Cuff is defeated by the silence of women (particularly Rosanna Spearman and Rachel Verinder), and points out argues that his eventual success stems from him eventually getting the 'family to police itself' rather than any direct effort on his part that can be attributed to him.[98] Others, such as R. P. Ashley, argue that Cuff's failure stems from the fact that he never achieves full detective-status as he his part in the novel is only minor,[99] while D. A Miller simply labels him as an 'eccentric outsider'.[100]

For my part, I suggest that it is the fact that Franklin Blake is simulta-neously positioned as a member of the middle-class family household (from which Cuff is inherently disassociated) and as the actual culprit, that causes Cuff to fail. This is, in essence, the reverse Robert Audley effect; as I suggested earlier, Robert is simultaneously a legitimate family member *and* the novel's detective, thus immediately thwarting any efforts that Lady Audley can throw at him to put him off the scent. Franklin Blake, meanwhile, is simultaneously a legitimate family member and the *villain*, which achieves the same effect of thwarting the efforts of the opposing force – in this case, Sergeant Cuff – from all perspectives.

However, there is also an alternative perspective to be uncovered here. Cuff does eventually resurface at the end of the novel, in a dramatic scene in a hos-pital ward where he reveals that Godfrey Abelwhite is the novel's true antagonist:

> [Blake] At the moment when I crossed the threshold of the door, I heard Sergeant Cuff's voice, asking where I was. He met me, as I returned into the room, and forced me to go back with him to the bedside. [...] 'Mr Blake!' he said. 'Look at the man's face. It is a face disguised – and here's a proof of it!'[101]

Miller rather conversely dismisses this moment in the novel as unimportant, arguing that Cuff's reappearance is merely an exercise in clearing up some 'incidental matters at the end' and that the mystery is largely solved without Cuff's assistance.[102] However, I suggest that Cuff (with the assistance of his unlikely 'sidekick', Gooseberry)[103] uncovers the true 'secret' of the novel more successfully than most of the other characters of the novel who have all tried to solve the mystery – namely the fact that Godfrey Abelwhite was the true crim-inal hiding behind the scenes all along:

He traced with his finger a thin line of livid white, running backward from the dead man's forehead [...] 'Let's see what's under this,' said the Sergeant ... [Cuff proceeds to remove hair, beard and face-paint] [...] 'Come back to the bed, sir!' [Cuff] began. He looked at me closer, and checked himself. 'No!' he resumed. 'Open the sealed letter first – the letter I gave you this morning.' [...] I read the name that he had written. It was – *Godfrey Abelwhite*. [...] 'Now,' said the Sergeant, 'come with me, and look at the man on the bed.' [...] I went with him, and looked at the man on the bed. [...] GODFREY ABELWHITE![104]

Here, Cuff rather undermines Trodd's argument that the police figure's existence outside of the family space in sensation fiction leaves them powerless to penetrate it and reveal its secrets. On the contrary, it is Cuff who proves that Abelwhite is the novel's true criminal, fully exonerating Blake, simply *because* of his existence outside of the family sphere, which has largely 'failed to know itself'.[105] The theft of the diamond in *The Moonstone* is arguably the central crime with which all of the detective figures, from Franklin Blake to Gabriel Betteredge to Ezra Jennings, work to resolve. However, it turns out to not be a crime at all, but simply an accident, and it is left up to Cuff to actually reveal the true 'secret underlying crime' of the novel: Godfrey Abelwhite's theft of a trust fund that was not meant for him. This places Cuff in a similar position to other sensational detectives and, I argue, actually helps to bring *The Moonstone* more closely back into the realm of hallmark 'sensation fiction' that depicted crimes such as embezzlement, identity theft, and (particularly) the appropriation of inheritance for which Collins himself was famous.[106] In more relevant terms to this chapter, however, this moment solidifies Cuff's position as the uncoverer of the novel's underlying secrets, once more tying him to earlier police memoir fiction, where the police officer used their ability to perform the exact same task.

As a final point before this chapter concludes, it is worth noting that some *criminals* presented in sensation fiction also occupy socially awkward or indistinct positions much like their detective counterparts. Aviva Briefel, for example, cites the position of Eustace Macallan (alias Woodville) in Wilkie Collins's *The Law and the Lady*, serialised in both *Harper's Weekly* and in the *Graphic* between 1874 and 1875 before being published in three volumes in 1875. Macallan is ostracised by the shadow of a 'not-proven' verdict against him, used exclusively in Scottish court proceedings and which made him neither guilty nor innocent of murdering his first wife.[107] However, the most interesting character in this novel as regards the present chapter is Macallan's second wife, Valeria Brinton, who assumes the identity of a 'detective' in order to try and uncover the secret beneath the surface of the novel and to overturn Eustace's verdict. Valeria consciously assumes this role, which effectively places her in the same position as other 'detectives' in other sensation novels before her, such as Bucket, Peters, Audley, and Cuff. As Valeria operates within the family unit she, Like Robert Audley, seems to conform to Pykett's suggestion that sensational 'detectives' were often designed to 'police the family unit'.[108] However, Valeria's position as the novel's sleuth stems from an external perspective, as she works to uncover the secret of Eustace's *previous* marriage, with which she had no involvement or knowledge. Consequently, she marginalises herself as both wife (internal) and detective (external). This is a position that Valeria herself recognises, and she proceeds to create for herself a new self-identity – the wife-detective. This combination of different social positions allows her to perform the same tasks as other sensational detectives and fluidly move between social classes, taking the reader along with her as she makes headway on the case where others before her had failed. In Valeria's response to a letter which Eustace sends her, informing her that he has fled England, she argues that the law's failed procedures can be fixed by the resolute doggedness of a devoted wife:

> How am I to help you? [...] The question is easily answered. What the Law has failed to do for you, your Wife must do for you. [...] the Law and the Lady have begun by understanding one another. [...] I mean to win you back, a man vindicated before the world, without a stain on his character or his name – thanks to his Wife.[109]

Valeria's identity as a detective has been recognised within scholarship; Ashley, for example, places her on the same level Sergeant Cuff (although he strangely labels her a 'detectivette').[110] However Ashley does not explore Valeria's position between social identities as both wife and detective, the combination of which allowed Valeria to make headway and explore places and engage with people with which she would not otherwise have been able to. Valeria uses both identities to cross a variety of social boundaries, boundaries that are especially restrictive due to her position as a woman, under the pretext of solving the mystery and uncovering the secret. When one identity (as either Eustace's troubled wife or as determined pseudo-detective) does not serve her immediate purpose, Valeria simply switches to the other or combines them depending on which suits her best. A good example of this from the novel is Valeria's attempts to obtain a meeting with the deformed eccentric Miserrimus Dexter. In this scene, Valeria is advised against meeting Dexter by Major Fitz-David who argues that, under ordinary circumstances, Valeria should not engage with such a person:

> [Fitz-David] 'In all England you could not have picked out a person more essentially unfit to be introduced to a lady – to a young lady especially – than Dexter. Have you heard of his horrible deformity? [...] Forgive me if the inquiry is impertinent. What can your motive possible be for wanting an introduction to Miserrimus Dexter?'[111]

Without her combined identities as both detective and wife of the 'accused' party, Valeria would have no response to this question. However to combat this, she utilises her position *between* wife, detective, and woman to convince

Fitz-David that the introduction is necessary in order for her to continue her inquiries into Eustace's trial. Fitz-David eventually succumbs and promises to attempt an introduction (although this is not a promise which he actually fulfils).

Valeria therefore demonstrates a final example of how detective figures in sensation novels connected with those in police memoirs, in a similar way to Dickens's Bucket, Braddon's Peters and Audley, and Collins's Cuff. Bucket utilises his politically-assigned authority as a police officer to address (and indeed, congregate) people of all different social classes in a situation where class is forgotten, and Cuff is deliberately able to pick and choose which kinds of social conventions he follows or does not follow. Valeria Macallan (alias Woodville alias Brinton) has a more complex relationship with extant social structures, assigning herself multiple identities as woman, wife, and detective, the application of which to herself allows her to transcend social conventions in much the same way as the other detective figures in both genres.

'Sensation Recollections': Chapter 4 Conclusions

Overall, it initially seems that the police memoir genre and the sensation genre were two distinct and largely separate literary moments that coexisted throughout the mid-nineteenth century but that were not related to each other. Police memoir fiction, which was designed to provide the reader with literary windows into urban criminality through figuratively accompanying the detective protagonist, seems disconnected from the sensation novel's purpose of providing a thrill to readers by depicting murder, arson, bigamy, or various other crimes that usually tend to take place within a middle-class, bourgeois or even occasionally aristocratic domestic setting.

On closer inspection, however, I suggest that they were much more connected than they initially seem. In essence, they were two sides of the 'coin' of the development of detective fiction from the 1860s and 1870s, both of which connected to earlier forms of crime, social exploration, and police-focused periodical journalism that remained at the centre of both forms of writing. When one analyses the sensation genre using a common denominator, namely the stylistic tropes that emerged in the pages of contemporary periodicals, various similarities between the two genres emerge. Police detectives in *both* memoir fiction and sensation fiction were designed to help uncover underlying secrets from a variety of settings – either urban spaces deemed to be criminalised, or the bourgeois or middle-class family home. Indeed, uncovering a 'secret' was often the purpose of sensation writing in the first place.[112]

The police-detective was therefore a character that anchored both memoir fiction and sensation fiction together. In both genres, they had (and used) the power to transcend most geographical or social boundaries that restricted the experiences of most everyday people. In both memoir and sensation fiction, police detectives were often depicted entering and exiting various private and often criminal spaces where other characters, for one reason or another, were not permitted to enter. The detective figures in both genres were also able to ignore social conventions in both the tasks that they performed and the other characters with whom they associated (such as Inspector Bucket's refusal to desist from his accusation of Lady Dedlock of murder in *Bleak House*, or Sergeant Cuff's refusal to leave when commanded by Lady Verinder in *The Moonstone*).[113] Alongside this, the reader (and occasionally other characters in the novel that manifested the reader's presence within the text) accompanied the police officer or detective in their exploits and under their protection, thus vicariously participating in and viewing the criminal underworld.

There were some differences in purpose between the genres, however. Whilst police memoir fiction was strictly focused on the experiences of the police officer and concerned itself with representing the officer's operations and methodologies, the sensation genre was more strongly concerned with revealing domestic secrets and far less interested in police procedure. It is for this reason, argues Stephen Knight that the sensation genre repeatedly places itself in *domestic* situations,[114] and as Pittard suggests, the sensation novel took the crime narrative, and moved it firmly to within the family home – deemed to be a 'safe' space – rather than keeping it on the street.[115]

These connections between sensation novels and police memoir fiction help to legitimise the police memoir genre as a moment in the development of the detective novel in a stronger fashion than has previously been granted to it. As the sensation novel has numerous similarities with the police memoir genre from the perspective of how it represented detectives and police officers, the memoir genre can perhaps be looked at from a more sympathetic perspective. However, as the next chapter will explore, the comfortable position of the police officer as a literary guide and protector for both other fictional characters and the reader was not to last. This literary relationship was built on a level of trust existing in the concept of policing at a wider social level, and this trust was to be catastrophically damaged as the mid-Victorian era gave way to the late-Victorian years and the *fin-de-siècle*.

Notes

1 Ian Ousby, *The Crime and Mystery Book: A Readers Companion* (London: Thames and Hudson, 1997), p. 34.
2 The origin of the term 'sensation novel' remains contentious. Martin Kayman in *From Bow Street to Baker Street* suggests that the term as it appears here originated in Oliphant's 'Sensation Novels' article from 1862, however as Lyn Pykett points out, the term 'sensation' was applied more broadly by critics to various pieces of writing across the 1850s. See both Martin Kayman, *From Bow Street to Baker Street: Mystery. Detection and Narrative* (Basingstoke: Macmillan, 1992), p. 173 and Lyn Pykett, 'The Newgate Novel and Sensation Fiction, 1830–1868', in *The Cambridge Companion to Crime Fiction*, ed. by Martin Priestman (Cambridge: Cambridge University Press, 2003), pp. 19–40 (p. 33).
3 Margaret Oliphant, 'Sensation Novels', *Blackwood's Edinburgh Magazine*, May 1862, p. 565.
4 Lyn Pykett, *The Nineteenth Century Sensation Novel* (Devon: Tavistock Publishing, 1994, repr. 2011), p. 57.

5   Saverio Tomaiuolo, *In Lady Audley's Shadow: Mary Elizabeth Braddon and Victorian Literary Genres* (Edinburgh: Edinburgh University Press, 2010), p. 79.

6   John Scaggs, *Crime Fiction: The New Critical Idiom* (Oxon: Routledge, 2005), pp. 22–24.

7   Scaggs, p. 106

8   Charles Rzepka, *Detective Fiction* (Cambridge: Polity, 2005), p. 99.

9   Rzepka, p. 99.

10 Stephen Knight, *Crime Fiction 1800–2000: Detection, Death, Diversity* (Basingstoke: Palgrave Macmillan, 2004), pp. 38–39.

11 Samuel Saunders, '"Always with the Inspector": The Reader as Sidekick in Mid-Victorian "Detective Literature", c. 1845–1877', in *The Detective's Companion in Crime Fiction: A Study in Sidekicks*, ed. by Samuel Saunders and Lucy Andrew (Basingstoke: Palgrave, 2021). This chapter forms part of an edited collection which is contracted for publication, but which has not yet appeared in print.

12 Rzepka, p. 101.

13 Scaggs, p. 23.

14 Martin Priestman, *Crime Fiction: From Poe to the Present* (Devon: Northcote House, 1998; repr. Devon: Northcote House, 2013), p. 13.

15 Mary Elizabeth Leighton and Lisa Surridge, 'The Transatlantic Moonstone: A study of the Illustrated Serial in *Harper's Weekly*', *Victorian Periodicals Review*, 42, 3 (2009), 207–243 (p. 207).

16 Rzepka, p. 103.

17 Scaggs, p. 24.

18 Priestman, p. 37.

19 Rzepka, p. 99.

20 Christopher Pittard, 'From Sensation to the *Strand*', in *A Companion to Crime Fiction*, ed. by Charles Rzepka and Lee Horsley (Chichester: Wiley Blackwell, 2010), p. 108.

21 Pittard, 'From Sensation to the *Strand*', in *A Companion to Crime Fiction*, ed. by Rzepka and Horsley, pp. 108–109.

22 Kayman, p. 175.

23 Kayman, p. 105.

24 Kayman, p. 175.

25 Kayman, p. 175.

26 Pykett, 'The Newgate Novel and Sensation Fiction', in *The Cambridge Companion to Crime Fiction*, ed. by Priestman, p. 35.

27 Kate Summerscale, *The Suspicions of Mr Whicher; or, the Murder at Road Hill House* (London: Bloomsbury, 2008), p. xi.

28 Summerscale, p. 217.

29 Summerscale, p. 217.

30 Anthea Trodd, 'The Policeman and the Lady: Significant Encounters in Mid-Victorian Fiction', *Victorian Studies*, 24, 4 (1984), 435–460 (p. 436).

31 'The Last Sensation Novel', *London Review*, 29 November 1862, p. 481.

32 'The Last Sensation Novel', *London Review*, 29 November 1862, p. 481.

33 'Sir Jasper's Tenant', *Saturday Review*, 21 October 1865, p. 521.

34 'Lady Audley's Secret', *Critic*, December 1862, p. 179.

35 'Sensation Recollections', *Reader*, September 1864, p. 377.

36 'Autobiography of a Detective', *Reader*, 23 January 1864, p. 104.

37 'Detectives in Fiction and in Real Life', *Saturday Review*, 11 June 1864, p. 712.

38 Margaret Oliphant, 'Novels', *Blackwood's Edinburgh Magazine*, August 1863, p. 168.

39 Saunders, '"Always with the Inspector"', in *The Detective's Companion in Crime Fiction*, ed. by Saunders and Andrew, pp. TBC.

40 Alfred Austin, 'Our Novels', *Temple Bar*, June 1870, p. 416.

41 Henry Mansel, 'Sensation Novels', *Quarterly Review*, April 1863, pp. 488–489.

42 Both Warren Fox and Jessica Valdez point out that true crime narratives originally provided writers with inspiration, but eventually lost out to completely fictional depictions of criminality as this could be more creative, imaginative, entertaining and less formulaic. See Warren Fox, 'Murder in Daily Instalments: The Newspapers and the Case of Franz Müller (1864)', *Victorian Periodicals Review*, 31, 3 (1998), 271–298 (pp. 282–283) and Jessica Valdez, 'Dickens's "Pious Fraud": The Popular Press and the Moral Suasion of Fictional Narrative', *Victorian Periodicals Review*, 44, 4 (2011), 377–400 (pp. 378–379).

43 Mansel, 'Sensation Novels', *Quarterly Review*, April 1863, pp. 488–489.

44 Knight, p. 39.

45 Pittard, 'From Sensation to the *Strand*', in *A Companion to Crime Fiction*, ed. by Rzepka and Horsley, p. 107.

46 'The Last Sensation Novel', *London Review*, 29 November 1862, p. 481.

47 Tomaiuolo, p. 79.

48 Andrew Mangham, *Violent Women and Sensation Fiction: Crime, Medicine and Victorian Popular Culture* (Basingstoke: Palgrave Macmillan, 2007), p. 9.

49 Tomaiuolo, p. 79.

50 Coventry Patmore, *The Angel in the House* (London: J. W. Parker and Son, 1854–1862).

51 Pykett, *The Nineteenth Century Sensation Novel*, p. 55 and p. 81.

52 Trodd, 435–460 (p. 435).

53 Trodd, 435–460 (pp. 435–436).

54 Pittard, 'From Sensation to the *Strand*', in *A Companion to Crime Fiction*, ed. by Rzepka and Horsley, p. 107.

55 Trodd, 435–460 (p. 436).

56 Trodd, 435–460 (pp. 446–450).

57 Pittard, 'From Sensation to the *Strand*', in *A Companion to Crime Fiction*, ed. by Rzepka and Horsley, p. 108.

58 Philipp Erchinger, 'Secrets Not Revealed: Possible Stories in Wilkie Collins's *The Woman in White*', *Connotations*, 18, 1–3 (2008/2009), 48–81 (p. 48).

59 Erchinger, 48–81 (p. 48).

60 Erchinger, 48–81 (pp. 49–50).

61 Caroline Reitz, 'Colonial "Gwilt": In and Around Wilkie Collins's Armadale, *Victorian Periodicals Review*, 33, 1 (2000), 92–103 (p. 93).

62 Pykett, 'The Newgate Novel and Sensation Fiction, 1830–1868', in *The Cambridge Companion to Crime Fiction*, ed. by Priestman, pp. 33–34.

63 Winifred Hughes, *The Maniac in the Cellar: Sensation Novels of the 1860s* (Princeton: Princeton University Press, 1980), p. 16.

64 Oliphant, 'Sensation Novels', pp. 565–566.

65 George Augustus Sala, 'On the "Sensational" in Literature and Art', *Belgravia*, February 1868, p. 454.

66 See Chapter 3.

67 Jacqueline Banerjee, 'Inspector Bucket Points the Way', *Victorian Web* <http://www.victorianweb.org/authors/dickens/bleakhouse/bucket.html> [accessed 21 May 2020] (2013).

68 D. A. Miller, *The Novel and the Police* (California, University of California Press, 1988), p. 76.

69 Charles Dickens, *Bleak House* (London: Bradbury and Evans, 1853; repr. London: Penguin Classics, 1988), p. 777.

70 Dickens, *Bleak House*, p. 823.

71 Dickens, *Bleak House*, p. 769.

72 See Chapter 2.

73 Miller, p. 79.

74   Erich Goode, *Justifiable Conduct: Self-Vindication in Memoir* (Philadelphia: Temple University Press, 2013), p. 27.

75   'Phiz' (Hablot Knight Browne), 'The Night', in *Bleak House*, Victorian Web <http://www.victorianweb.org/victorian/art/illustration/phiz/bleakhouse/36.html> [accessed February 28 2018], scanned and uploaded by George P. Landow (1853, uploaded 2007).

76   Dickens, *Bleak House*, p. 827.

77   Trodd, 435–460 (p. 437).

78   Dickens, *Bleak House*, p. 785.

79   Dickens, *Bleak House*, pp. 782–783.

80   Trodd, 435–460 (p. 436).

81   Trodd, 435–460 (pp. 435–436).

82   Mary Elizabeth Braddon, *The Trail of the Serpent* (London: Ward, Lock and Tyler, 1860; repr. London: Ward, Lock and Tyler, 1866), pp. 54–55.

83   Braddon, *The Trail of the Serpent*, pp. 29–30.

84   Braddon, *The Trail of the Serpent*, pp. 275–277.

85   Charles Martel, *Diary of an Ex-Detective* (London: Ward and Lock, 1860) pp. 139–140.

86   Mary Elizabeth Braddon, *Lady Audley's Secret* (London: William Tinsley, 1862; repr. Ware: Wordsworth Editions, 1997), p. 320.

87   Pykett, *The Nineteenth Century Sensation Novel*, p. 81.

88   Braddon, *Lady Audley's Secret*, pp. 55–56.

89   Braddon, *Lady Audley's Secret*, pp. 56.

90   Pykett, *The Nineteenth Century Sensation Novel*, p. 81.

91   Saunders, '"Always with the Inspector"…', in *The Detective's Companion in Crime Fiction*, ed. by Saunders and Andrew, p. TBC.

92   Robert P. Ashley, 'Wilkie Collins and the Detective Story', *Nineteenth Century Fiction*, 6, 1 (1951), 47–60 (p. 52).

93   Wilkie Collins, *The Moonstone* (London: Tinsley Brothers, 1868; repr. London: Penguin, 1998), p. 107.

94   Scaggs, p. 24. Scaggs briefly alludes to this tradition and does not elaborate on the purpose of detectives' often eccentric nature, which I suggest is usually in place in the genre to somehow separate the character from the reader and, by extension, from the general public, earmarking them as somehow extraordinary.

95   Collins, *The Moonstone*, pp. 108–109.

96   Miller, p. 36.

97   Trodd, pp. 435–460 (pp. 446–450).

98   Pykett, *The Nineteenth Century Sensation Novel*, p. 55.

99   Ashley, 'Wilkie Collins and the Detective Story', pp. 47–60 (pp. 52–53).

100 Miller, p. 36.

101 Collins, *The Moonstone*, p. 447.

102 Miller, p. 37

103 Oriah Amit, '"Passed by unnoticed": Surveillance and the Street Urchin in Wilkie Collins's *The Moonstone*' in *The Detective's Companion in Crime Fiction: A Study in Sidekicks*, ed. by Samuel Saunders and Lucy Andrew (Basingstoke: Palgrave, 2021). This chapter forms part of an edited collection that is currently contracted for publication, but has not yet appeared in print.

104 Collins, *The Moonstone*, pp. 447–448.

105 Miller, p. 41.

106 See Collins's *No Name* (1862) for a particularly strong example of this.

107 Aviva Briefel, 'Cosmetic Tragedies: Failed Masquerade in Wilkie Collins's *The Law and the Lady*', *Victorian Literature and Culture*, 37, 2 (2009), 463–481 (p. 466).

108 Pykett, *The Nineteenth Century Sensation Novel*, p. 55 and p. 81.

109 Wilkie Collins, *The Law and the Lady*, (London: Chatto and Windus, 1875; repr. Oxford: Oxford University Press, 1992), p. 117.

110   Ashley, 'Wilkie Collins and the Detective Story', pp. 47–60 (p. 56).
111   Collins, *The Law and the Lady*, pp. 191–192.
112   Trodd, 435–460 (pp. 435–436).
113   Collins, *The Moonstone*, p. 167.
114   Knight, p. 39.
115   Pittard, 'From Sensation to the *Strand*', in *A Companion to Crime Fiction*, ed. by Rzepka and Horsley, p. 107.

Bibliography

Primary Periodical Material

Austin, Alfred, 'Our Novels', *Temple Bar*, June 1870, pp. 410–424.
'Autobiography of a Detective', *Reader*, 23 January 1864, p. 104.
'Detectives in Fiction and in Real Life', *Saturday Review*, 11 June 1864, pp. 712–713.
'Lady Audley's Secret', *Critic*, December 1862, pp. 178–179.
Mansel, Henry, 'Sensation Novels', *Quarterly Review*, April 1863, pp. 481–514.
Sala, George Augustus, 'On the "Sensational" in Literature and Art', *Belgravia*, February 1868, pp. 449–458.
'Sensation Recollections', *Reader*, September 1864, p. 377.
'Sir Jasper's Tenant', *Saturday Review*, 21 October 1865, pp. 520–521.
'The Last Sensation Novel', *London Review*, 29 November 1862, pp. 481–482.

Secondary Material

Amit, Oriah, ' "Passed by unnoticed": Surveillance and the Street Urchin in Wilkie Collins's The Moonstone', in *The Detective's Companion in Crime Fiction: A Study in Sidekicks*, ed. by Samuel Saunders and Lucy Andrew (Basingstoke: Palgrave, 2021).
Ashley, Robert P., 'Wilkie Collins and the Detective Story', *Nineteenth Century Fiction*, 6, 1 (1951), 47–60.
Banerjee, Jacqueline, 'Inspector Bucket Points the Way', Victorian Web <http://www.victorianweb.org/authors/dickens/bleakhouse/bucket.html> [accessed 21 May 2020] (2013).
Braddon, Mary Elizabeth, *Lady Audley's Secret* (London: William Tinsley, 1862; repr. Ware: Wordsworth Editions, 1997).
Braddon, Mary Elizabeth, *The Trail of the Serpent* (London: Ward, Lock and Tyler, 1860; repr. London: Ward, Lock and Tyler, 1866), pp. 54–55.
Briefel, Aviva, 'Cosmetic Tragedies: Failed Masquerade in Wilkie Collins's The Law and the Lady', *Victorian Literature and Culture*, 37, 2 (2009), 463–481.
Collins, Wilkie, *The Law and the Lady* (London: Chatto and Windus, 1875; repr. Oxford: Oxford University Press, 1992).
Collins, Wilkie, *The Moonstone* (London: Tinsley Brothers, 1868; repr. London: Penguin, 1998).
Dickens, Charles, *Bleak House* (London: Bradbury and Evans, 1853; repr. London: Penguin Classics, 1988).
Erchinger, Philipp, 'Secrets Not Revealed: Possible Stories in Wilkie Collins's *The Woman in White*', *Connotations*, 18, 1–3 (2008/2009), 48–81 (p. 48).
Fox, Warren, 'Murder in Daily Instalments: The Newspapers and the Case of Franz Müller (1864)', *Victorian Periodicals Review*, 31, 3 (1998), 271–298.

Goode, Erich, *Justifiable Conduct: Self-Vindication in Memoir* (Philadelphia: Temple University Press, 2013).

Hughes, Winifred, *The Maniac in the Cellar: Sensation Novels of the 1860s* (Princeton: Princeton University Press, 1980).

Kayman, Martin, *From Bow Street to Baker Street: Mystery. Detection and Narrative* (Basingstoke: Macmillan, 1992).

Knight, Stephen, *Crime Fiction 1800–2000: Detection, Death, Diversity* (Basingstoke: Palgrave Macmillan, 2004).

Leighton, Mary Elizabeth, and Lisa Surridge, 'The Transatlantic Moonstone: A study of the Illustrated Serial in *Harper's Weekly*', *Victorian Periodicals Review*, 42, 3 (2009), 207–243.

Mangham, Andrew, *Violent Women and Sensation Fiction: Crime, Medicine and Victorian Popular Culture* (Basingstoke: Palgrave Macmillan, 2007).

Martel, Charles, *Diary of an Ex-Detective* (London: Ward and Lock, 1860).

Miller, D. A., *The Novel and the Police* (California, University of California Press, 1988).

Oliphant, Margaret, 'Novels', *Blackwood's Edinburgh Magazine*, August1863, p. 168.

Oliphant, Margaret, 'Sensation Novels', *Blackwood's Edinburgh Magazine*, May1862, p. 565.

Ousby, Ian, *The Crime and Mystery Book: A Readers Companion* (London: Thames and Hudson, 1997).

Patmore, Coventry, *The Angel in the House* (London: J. W. Parker and Son, 1854–1862).

'Phiz' (Hablot Knight Browne), 'The Night', in *Bleak House*, Victorian Web <http://www.victorianweb.org/victorian/art/illustration/phiz/bleakhouse/36.html>   [accessed 2018], scanned and uploaded by George P. Landow (1853, uploaded 2007).

Pittard, Christopher, 'From Sensation to the *Strand*', in *A Companion to Crime Fiction*, ed. by Charles Rzepka and Lee Horsley (Chichester: Wiley Blackwell, 2010).

Priestman, Martin, *Crime Fiction: From Poe to the Present* (Devon: Northcote House, 1998; repr. Devon: Northcote House, 2013).

Pykett, Lyn, 'The Newgate Novel and Sensation Fiction, 1830–1868', in *The Cambridge Companion to Crime Fiction*, edited by Martin Priestman (Cambridge: Cambridge University Press, 2004), pp. 33–34.

Pykett, Lyn, *The Nineteenth Century Sensation Novel* (Devon: Tavistock Publishing, 1994, repr. 2011).

Reitz, Caroline, 'Colonial "Gwilt": In and Around Wilkie Collins's *Armadale*', *Victorian Periodicals Review*, 33, 1 (2000), 92–103.

Rzepka, Charles, *Detective Fiction* (Cambridge: Polity, 2005).

Saunders, Samuel, '"Always with the Inspector': The Reader as Sidekick in Mid-Victorian "Detective Literature", c. 1845–1877', in *The Detective's Companion in Crime Fiction: A Study in Sidekicks*, ed. by Samuel Saunders and Lucy Andrew (Basingstoke: Palgrave, 2021).

Scaggs, John, *Crime Fiction: The New Critical Idiom* (Oxon: Routledge, 2005).

Summerscale, Kate, *The Suspicions of Mr Whicher; or, the Murder at Road Hill House* (London: Bloomsbury, 2008).

Tomaiuolo, Saverio, *In Lady Audley's Shadow: Mary Elizabeth Braddon and Victorian Literary Genres* (Edinburgh: Edinburgh University Press, 2010).

Trodd, Anthea, 'The Policeman and the Lady: Significant Encounters in Mid-Victorian Fiction', *Victorian Studies*, 24, 4 (1984), 435–460.

Valdez, Jessica, 'Dickens's "Pious Fraud": The Popular Press and the Moral Suasion of Fictional Narrative', *Victorian Periodicals Review*, 44, 4 (2011), 377–400.

Part III

From Scandal to the *Strand Magazine*

5 '...people are naturally distrustful of its future working'

The 1877 Detective Scandal in the Victorian Mass Media

Introduction: The 1877 Detective Scandal

Hitherto, this volume has constructed an image of the landscape of detective fiction across the mid-Victorian era as consisting of several chronologies that were interwoven through their shared connections to contemporary periodical journalism. The first strand consisted of the poplar 'police memoir', which had been influenced by both periodical criticism of the police and journalistic reports of criminality, which merged together to create a genre which appealed to the interests of readers keen to explore and safely experience criminality in the figurative company of the police officer. The second strand was 'sensation fiction', which has repeatedly been connected with the 'detective' genre due to its interest in crime, scandal, and the uncovering of a hidden secret, but which should also be connected more directly to 'police memoir fiction' through both their shared literary characteristics and largely identical links to contemporary journalistic commentary on the position of the police. Both genres utilised many of the same thematic tropes in order to drive their narratives forward, such as using police officers or detectives to invade private spaces, reveal criminal secrets, flout numerous social conventions and, of course, ultimately fight crime. This was, to summarise, the complex and multifarious literary climate of 'detective fiction' across the mid-Victorian era.

The continued existence of this climate was, however, predicated on the maintenance of a certain level of public trust in the police themselves. Throughout this period, the police force had enjoyed at least *some* support in the periodical and newspaper presses, despite the rather stark differences of largely-politicised opinion detailed in this book's first chapter. As Clive Emsley (maybe a little sweepingly) asserts, mid-Victorians were, on the whole, 'proud of their police'.[1] There is certainly some truth to this claim, although perhaps it is slightly more pragmatic to say that periodical commentary on the police in *any* guise (whether supportive or otherwise) had, at the very least, helped to cement the force as a necessary and intrinsic part of the social fabric of mid-Victorian society. It was at least universally recognised that the police existed to solve and prevent crime, even if there was disagreement about how effective they actually were at fulfilling this mandate or whether they should continue to try to do so.

However, this uneasy acceptance was to fundamentally change after around 1870, as public estimation of the police force began to steadily decline. As Charles Rzepka highlights, historical events such as the actions of the Reform League (including the notable Hyde Park demonstration of 1867) and the Clerkenwell Prison bombing (also in 1867), called into question the public's confidence in the police's ability to prevent such 'outrages'.[2] Rzepka also notes that:

> Several well-publicized [sic], unsolved murders occurred in the early years of the [1870]s, and a major corruption scandal led to the complete reorganization of Scotland Yard in 1878.[3]

The series of unsolved murders to which Rzepka refers included several widely publicised cases, notably the 1876 Charles Bravo murder, also known as the Murder at the Priory: a sensational poisoning that captured the public imagination and which remains unsolved. Press reactions to these (and various other) events resulted in the increasingly-frequent appearance of articles with frustrated and scathing titles such as 'Inefficiency of the London Police' or 'Where are the Police?', both published in the *Saturday Review* in 1870 and 1872 respectively. However, as Rzepka alludes to in the quotation above, the reputation of the police was most seriously damaged by a major corruption scandal which engulfed the detective branch of the Metropolitan Police in 1877, which was predictably publicised extensively in both the periodical and newspaper presses. As a result of this scandal, public estimation of the police force reached perhaps its lowest point of the nineteenth century.

It is worth exploring this event in some detail. In 1877, four detective inspectors from the Metropolitan Police's 'detective department' named Meiklejohn, Druscovich, Palmer, and Clarke, alongside a solicitor named Froggatt, were arrested and charged with conspiracy to defeat the ends of justice.[4] They were specifically accused of receiving bribes from convicted criminals in return for information regarding the police's movements against them. Their crime was connected to the infamous 'turf fraud' scandal, in which several criminals, among them the well-known William Kurr and Harry Benson, had illegitimately obtained £10,000 from a French noblewoman, named Madame de Goncourt, by convincing her to invest money in fraudulent horse races which they guaranteed that she would win, but which were actually completely fictitious.[5] The corrupt inspectors provided a constant stream of information to Kurr, Benson, and their associates, warning them of their impending arrests, and thus they were able to continuously elude the police's clutches. However, their luck ran out in April 1877, and both Kurr and Benson were apprehended and sentenced to penal servitude for ten and 15 years respectively.[6] In an attempt to reduce their sentences, the criminals almost immediately betrayed the informant inspectors and, as George Dilnot points out, it was likely that this had been their intention all along as they had 'carefully preserved and secreted every scrap of correspondence [they] had received from [their] detective tools'.[7] At the very least, their relationship had not been a trustworthy one, and the criminals had possessed the foresight to cover their own backs right from the off. By July 1877, Kurr and Benson's statements had been heard in court, and enough corroborating evidence had been gathered to affect an arrest.[8] The four inspectors, and Froggatt, were apprehended and a long inquiry and subsequent trial began. Inspectors Meiklejohn, Druscovich, and Palmer (as well as the solicitor Froggatt), were eventually found guilty and each sentenced to two years' imprisonment with hard labour.[9] The fourth inspector, Clarke, was acquitted.

It is difficult to overstate the public outrage this scandal caused. Indeed, Dilnot goes so far as to argue that '[e]normous and wide-world [sic] interest was taken in the trial'.[10] Consequently, it dramatically deepened public distrust of law enforcement, and also brought the detective department as a distinct entity sharply into the public spotlight, whereas it had hitherto been able to operate largely independently without a great deal of external or political scrutiny. This, combined with the fact that the public opinion of the police had already been in decline, caused the then Home Secretary, R. A. Cross, to order an immediate investigation into the operations of the department. It was subsequently restructured into the Criminal Investigations Department (CID) in 1878, which still operates today.[11]

This narrative is relatively well known amongst those who explore the history of Victorian policing, although it is rarely explored in detail except to iterate how (and perhaps why) the department was so extensively and repeatedly restructured towards the end of the nineteenth century.[12] More importantly for the purposes of this volume, however, it has almost never been explored in relation to the development of detective fiction. Rzepka and Kayman, for example, both make only brief allusions to the scandal. Rzepka notes that public estimation of the police was already falling in the early 1870s, but suggests that it peaked slightly earlier than the 1877 case and that the detective department's restructure in the wake of it was unconvincing.[13] Kayman opts for a different approach, arguing that the restructure was actually an effort to bring the British detective system more into line with the French Sûreté, perceived to be a more effective organisation.[14] Elsewhere however, Heather Worthington makes a slightly more comprehensive and useful connection between the case and detective fiction by suggesting that it may have at least contributed to the unflattering portrayal of police detectives in the early Sherlock Holmes stories that emerged in the late 1880s.[15] Perhaps the most detailed piece of scholarship which directly addresses this scandal in detail is Haia Shpayer-Makov's *The Ascent of the Detective*, in which she argues that it 'confirmed what the public had initially feared: corrupt practices, including the collusion of the police with criminals'.[16] Makov also includes an image of the detectives on trial taken from the *Illustrated London News* [17] and returns to the case periodically as her book progresses – even briefly mentioning how the case was presented to the public in popular journalism.[18] However, Makov's book is not focused on detective *fiction*, but is instead more of a history of the department itself, and so this connection between historical moment and cultural production is, again, largely omitted.

However, these brief mentions of the case are very much in the minority when it comes to scholarly criticism of the development of detective fiction across the late Victorian era. Indeed, other historians of the genre such as Stephen Knight, Martin Priestman, John Scaggs, and John Cawelti do not mention the scandal as impacting the development of detective fiction towards the end of the nineteenth century at all. The purpose of this next chapter is therefore to begin to rectify this scholarly oversight and to highlight how the case (and particularly its reportage in the press) helped fundamentally to destabilise the landscape of detective fiction which this volume has so far constructed. I explore the 1877 corruption scandal in relation to how it was presented to the public through periodicals and newspapers, and relate this to how the press perceived the police and detectives both before and after the scandal came to light. The chapter performs this task so that the next, and final, one can subsequently connect it to the appearance of late-Victorian detective fiction. Indeed, the final chapter of this volume ultimately links the deteriorated perception of the police to the emergence of the private or 'gifted amateur' detective,[19] by suggesting that the loss of trust in the official police meant that they had lost their privileged position as 'guides' into the criminal underworld, which had been so comprehensively solidified by the landscape of mid-Victorian detective writing. This shift in interest towards the amateur or private detective eventually culminated in the appearance of one of the most famous private detectives of the literary canon – Arthur Conan Doyle's Sherlock Holmes.

'Surely [...] every policeman ought to be a detective': Periodical Perceptions of *Detectives*, 1842–1877

As the opening chapter of this book extensively highlighted, the periodical press and the activities of the police were closely tied through political and socioeconomic commentary.[20] Perhaps rather surprisingly, however, periodical commentary on the force was largely inconsistent when it came to knowledge surrounding the differences between regular, uniformed police officers, and plain-clothes detectives. This lack of specific scrutiny, even within periodical commentary which was aware that the detective department existed in the first place, was later to become problematic, and so it is worth spending some time exploring it here before this chapter moves on.

As this volume's introduction briefly described, the first 'detective department' of the Metropolitan Police was established in 1842. This was, ironically, influenced at least partially by a public outcry in the popular press – just as the department's 1878 restructure was also influenced by substantial press-outrage. The uproar which led to the founding of the detective department resulted largely from the incompetence of uniformed police officers in apprehending a murderer-at-large named Daniel Good.[21] Originally under suspicion of theft, Good was convicted of murdering his girlfriend, Jane Jones, but eluded capture for several days before being apprehended by a civilian in a public house in Tonbridge Wells.[22] The mass media was naturally quick to demonise Good, with one 1842 broadside stylistically depicting him identically to an illustration of the notorious and largely detested seventeenth-century executioner Jack Ketch, from the popular *Autobiography of Jack Ketch* (1835) (Figure 5.1).[23]

The failure of the uniformed police to quickly capture Good motivated the establishment of a department dedicated to hunting wanted suspects and criminals. As is widely known, the uniformed police had originally been designed to *prevent* crime from occurring in the first place by maintaining a visible street presence, rather than to solve those that had been already committed.[24] The failure to apprehend Good embarrassingly and publicly exposed this flaw in the system, and so consequently the establishment of a detective force designed to *solve* crimes which had already been committed quickly followed.

Despite the public resentment surrounding the inefficiency of the Good investigation, the new detective department itself was both very small and established relatively quietly in terms of its press coverage. This was perhaps due to what Shpayer-Makov terms a 'lingering belief in the ability of beat officers to quell crime', combined with a latent mistrust in plain-clothes policing, which was seen as a threat to civil liberties.[25] Perhaps it was also simply because the new detective department was designed to operate secretively, and thus publicly promoting it in the press seemed slightly counterintuitive. The *Morning Post* was one of a small number of larger papers to run a short column declaring that a small force of detectives had been established, and very usefully this article declared that the reason for the detectives' establishment was directly linked to the failings of the police to apprehend criminals:

> Several cases having lately occurred, in which criminals have not been taken into custody so promptly as the public had a right to expect, the commissioners of police have arranged that a new company shall be immediately raised out of the present police, to be called the "Detective Force," [...].[26]

Figure 5.1 Original illustration of Jack Ketch reused in later material
Source: Anon. *Autobiography of Jack Ketch* (Philadelphia: Carey, Lea and Blanchard, 1835), n.p. [front matter]. Public domain.

This new 'Detective Force' was to operate in plain clothes, maintain strict secrecy at all times, and its operatives were designed to 'mingle unnoticed in mass gatherings, keep "felons" and "persons of bad character" under observation [...] and follow perpetrators once a crime was committed'.[27]

As the department had initially appeared under a cloud of relative obscurity, it was extremely slow to grow across the nineteenth century, and largely remained small and obscure well into the mid-Victorian period.[28] By 1868, the department had grown from only eight officers appointed in 1842 (six detectives and two sergeants), to around 15.[29] As a result, mid-Victorian periodical criticism of the police understandably made inconsistent distinctions between uniformed police officers and plain-clothes detectives. However, I should make it clear at the outset that this is not to suggest that there was *no* knowledge of the existence of a separate detective force in periodical criticism. In fact, some periodicals and journalists (again such as Dickens writing in the early 1850s) went out of their way to attempt to understand the distinction between uniformed police officers and plain-clothes detectives. For example, a commentator for the *Leisure Hour*, writing in October 1857, made the difference clear:

> For ordinary offences – such as shoplifting, stealing from the person, street impostures, begging letters, passing false coin, and others of a like kind – the services of the detective are rarely called into requisition. Such offenders mostly fall into the hands of the regular police, who haul them before the magistrates to be summarily dealt with. It is the practitioners who work under covert, and aim at higher game, that set the detectives on the alert and try their mettle.[30]

That said, even those with a vested interest often found it difficult to find concrete information about the detective force, even if they were aware of its separate existence. A noteworthy example of this appeared in a lengthy article titled 'The Police of London', which was published in the *Quarterly Review* in July 1870 and which extensively discussed the structure and duties of London's police. The author devoted an entire section to describing the detective department and its remit in a piece that was completely supportive of the very concept of a uniformed police force, and argued that it had provided substantial benefits with regard to high-profile cases such as the Road Hill House murder and the Irish Republican Brotherhood (IRB) 'outrages' that had occurred in the late 1860s.[31] However, in a 42-page article on the police, the section devoted to the discussion of the detective force consists of just three paragraphs across two pages, highlighting how information on it was difficult to come by even for those who actively sought it. Indeed, the author openly stated that it was difficult to actually describe what these detectives did on a daily basis due to their secretive nature, simply asserting that their job was to track and apprehend criminals:

> The duties of the detective force are of a very varied character, which it would be difficult to describe in detail. It may, however, be mentioned that

they are principally occupied in tracking the perpetrators of murder, forgery, and other crimes of a serious nature.[32]

Elsewhere in another example of knowledge-without-detail, in February 1868 the *Saturday Review* demonstrated a clear understanding of the difference between an officer and a detective:

> In addition to the ordinary force, there is a special department of detective police at Scotland Yard, consisting of once chief inspector, three inspectors and fifteen sergeants.[33]

This small line is easily overlooked, but again does serve to highlight how at least some (again, usually those with a particular interest in the structure of the police) understood that the detective department operated largely separately from the bulk of the official uniformed force. For the *Saturday Review*, this is particularly understandable, as it was one of the most engaged publications when it came to criticising the police across the mid-to-late Victorian era. However, the slightly offhand nature of this quotation, the entirety of that which the article devoted to the detective department, also suggests that some periodical commentators but did not think it worth going (or simply were unable to go) into any further detail.

By contrast however, other commentators openly rejected the notion of a distinction between police officers and detectives, suggesting that it was largely pointless. In 1860, for example, the *Examiner* rather outspokenly suggested that there shouldn't even *be* a distinction; when musing on the organisation and the administration of the Irish Constabulary, formed in 1837, the magazine indirectly questioned whether the need for a separate section of a police force to detect and apprehend offenders was necessary at all:

> We are told, indeed, that there does exist a detachment of detectives, constituting a part of the force, but this really makes the system more ridiculous, for surely, to a certain extent, every policeman ought to be a detective [...][34]

Others, with a less focused or deliberate interest in the makeup of the force, merely stuck to using the terms 'police officer' or 'detective' interchangeably, with little regard for the distinctions between them, which suggested that their understanding of the differences between the two kinds of officer was erratic at best. In October 1871, for example, the *Examiner* wrote:

> It is impossible to escape the conclusion that our metropolitan detective police force is inadequate to the work which it has to perform. [...] We may take the Camden Town murder as a typical instance. The body of a young woman is found in the canal. [...] There is nothing upon her to point out her name. The *police* are absolutely without a clue. And without a clue, the *detective* cannot work [my italics].[35]

Another good representative example of this appeared in *St. Paul's Magazine*, where an author also made the mistake of labelling a detective as a 'policeman' when discussing prospective qualities which made excellent policing in William Brighty Rands's article 'The Apotheosis of the Policeman' (1874):

> It was, therefore, all the more remarkable when, one Christmas-tide, in the dusk of the afternoon in our great metropolis, Policeman Q – one of the Detective Moralists in plain clothes [...][36]

Still other journalists simply combined the terms 'police officer' and 'detective' into the widely used and, for them, highly useful portmanteau 'police detective' or 'detective police', apparently in order to avoid the pitfalls of navigating exactly what the distinctions between the two actually were.[37] Elsewhere, some also demonstrated ignorance of the distinctions between uniformed police officers and detectives through illustration. Whilst historical accuracy was likely not its main objective, in 1869 the magazine *Fun* published a comic-strip titled 'The Idiot Detective, or, the Track! The Trial! and the Triumph!', in which the 'detective' is actually depicted as a police officer in uniform (see Figure 5.2).[38]

This example is particularly interesting, as it quite effectively highlights the lack of a contemporary stereotypical mid-Victorian image of a 'detective' for the cartoonist to utilise in order to demonstrate the character's profession clearly to the reader. In other words, a clear stereotyped image of the plain-clothes detective, as distinct from the uniformed branch of the police, had not yet permeated into public consciousness.

Overall, despite the valiant efforts of some contemporary commentators, the distinctions between uniformed officers and plain-clothes detectives was not yet widely understood by the periodical press or, by extension, the general public. Indeed, the distinctions between uniformed police officers and detectives was only really understood by those who were actually interested enough to go and

Figure 5.2 'The Idiot Detective, or, the Track! The Trial! and the Triumph!'
Source: *Fun*, 2 January 1869, p. 13. Image published with permission of ProQuest. Further reproduction is prohibited without permission.

actively find out. By 1877, the year in which the severe extent of the department's corruption had been revealed to the public, this still seemed to be the case. In December 1877, the *Saturday Review* helpfully summarised:

> [...] there does not appear to be [...] the means of knowing exactly what [detectives] are about.[39]

Reporting the 1877 Crisis

The details of the 1877 scandal, and how it progressed (firstly) through the Bow Street police court and (subsequently) the Central Criminal Court, were eagerly followed by interested journalists. In fact, the so-called 'turf frauds' were already attracting attention in the media even before the corrupt detectives themselves were implicated as having been involved. In January 1877, for example, *Bell's Life in London* wrote that Inspector Druscovich was the officer who had apprehended the criminal fraudsters who were, in fact, bribing him at the time.[40] In April 1877, when Benson and Kurr were apprehended and convicted, the *Examiner* published a lengthy (and utterly outrageous) description of the case which focused attention on the failings and pitfalls of the victim, Madame de Goncourt. The article speculated as to whether she herself might not have been at least partially to blame for being swindled out of such a large amount of money:

> It seems at first incredible that a lady of sufficient age to manage her own affairs should send cheques to the amount of 10,000*l.* to a perfect stranger upon his written assurance that he will be able to secure her an enormous profit. Women, as a rule, are supposed to be even sharper in business matters than men. [...] Greedy and credulous people like Mme. de Goncourt commit the initial mistake of fancying themselves wiser than men who have given their whole life and time to business.[41]

In an attempt to reduce their own sentences, Kurr and Benson testified against their detective informers soon after they themselves were indicted.[42] In mid-July 1877, the officers were arrested and an inquiry began at Bow Street police court. Naturally, the case's reporting immediately shifted focus away from Kurr and Benson, et. al. and onto the detectives, and quickly grew in ferocity, presenting a particularly clear example of Andrew Hobbs's process of news spreading across the entire country in provincial newspapers 'in the same way that own-brand Corn Flakes are produced in one factory but sold under many different brand names around the country'.[43] Between 13 and 15 July 1877, newspapers from all over the country published short, one or two column news pieces on the arrest and charge of the inspectors at Bow Street police court. These included larger newspapers, such as *Reynolds's Newspaper,* or the *Manchester Courier* but also smaller publications from rural areas outside of the large cities, such as the *York Herald, Sunderland Daily Echo*, and the *Sheffield and Rotherham Independent*.

Many of these newspapers eagerly and immediately reported the crisis to be 'Serious',[44] 'Grave',[45] or in some cases even 'Extraordinary',[46] hinting at the media frenzy that was to follow. Some of the reports from the time of the detectives' arrest registered unbridled astonishment (as well as occasional glee). A report from *Reynolds's Newspaper* was apparently incredulous, arguing that the detectives' colleagues could hardly believe that such a charge could be true of trustworthy police detectives who had served the force for such a lengthy amount of time:

> The order to arrest was given effect to at ten o'clock, when Druscovitch, Meiklejohn and Palmer came on duty. At that hour Superintendent Williamson entered the detective's room, and stated that it was with extreme regret he had to request the officers named to consider themselves in custody. Nothing could exceed the surprise with which the announcement was heard by their colleagues, whom many years' experience had taught to have entire confidence in the integrity and honour of the accused.[47]

This slightly unconvincing air of astonishment was echoed by the *Edinburgh Evening News*, which suggested that the accused '[...] had been known so long and so faithfully trusted [...]' that accusing them in the first place was a very 'painful' duty of the counsel for the prosecution to have to undertake.[48] However, the initial 'surprise' at the detectives' arrest quickly gave way to detailed reporting of the inquiry at Bow Street which took place between July and September 1877, after which the officers were finally committed for trial at the Old Bailey. An enormous number of newspapers from all over the country reported the progress of the inquiry, based in locations as widespread as Chelmsford, Sheffield, Edinburgh, Liverpool, Dundee, Leeds, Huddersfield, Manchester, Gloucester, and, of course, London. The *Manchester Guardian*, and its sister paper the *Observer*, published an almost daily two-to-three column feature titled 'The Charge Against Detective Officers and a Solicitor' (or variations of this name), which followed the enquiry closely. These newspaper reports surrounding the details of the proceedings became lengthy and very closely detailed.[49]

Interestingly enough, as the inquiry developed a number of publications embarked on a second, far less truthful campaign against each of the accused detectives, in a wild attempt to smear them even further in the public view. For each of the detectives arrested, the media went out of its way to source at least one sensational or scandalous story about their circumstances that cast a negative or at least a suspicious light upon them. Druscovich was a particular target for publicity-hungry publications, as there were at least two 'scandals' that surrounded him that occurred while he was in custody which were widely circulated in the papers. The first happened at the end of July 1877, when it was reported that he had attempted to commit suicide in his cell – an act that was viewed as both morally reprehensible and which was actually a criminal offence until 1961. The story was quickly revealed to have been fabricated, but not before the rumour had spread across a large number of newspapers and the damage was done. The *Standard* was suggested to have been the guilty culprit for starting the rumour; on July 24th, it published a short article titled 'Attempted Suicide of Inspector Druscovich', which read:

> It is reported that Inspector Druscovich [...] when conveyed to the House of Detention, attempted to commit suicide. A correspondent informs us that when the accused had been placed in his cell he tore up his sheet and made it into a rope. Having done this he fastened it to the bar of the window in his cell. He stood on his bed and fastened the noose round his neck. He then jumped off the bed and fell suspended within a few inches off the ground.[50]

Other newspapers immediately seized on the story. The 'correspondent' from inside the prison who informed the press of this incident had apparently contacted multiple papers, as on the same day the *Edinburgh Evening News* also reported that Druscovich had attempted to hang himself. However some of the details were different – whilst the *Standard* reported that Druscovich had made a rope from his sheet, the *Edinburgh Evening News* reported that it had actually been his *shirt.* [51]

The reports of Druscovich's attempted suicide caused enough disturbance for it to be directly mentioned in the inquiry's proceedings. Druscovich himself was forced to openly refute the claims in court, and the *Standard* was openly blamed in court as the originator of the rumour. Three days later, on 27 July, the *Leeds Mercury* wrote:

> Mr. ST. JOHN WONTNER called the attention of Sir James Ingham to a report that appeared in the *Standard* and another paper [likely the *Edinburgh Evening News*] that Druscovitch [sic] had attempted to commit suicide. It was necessary to say that it was a gross libel on Mr. Druscovitch and upon the officials of the prison, there being not the slightest foundation for it. He was quite prepared to meet this charge, and hoped to prove his innocence.[52]

Druscovich's official denial of the accusation forced papers to admit that the rumour was not true, although some attempted to hide their clarifications so that readers could potentially miss it. For example, on 25 July, the *Dundee Courier and Argus* published a small, very easily overlooked line that merely read:

> The report that Inspector Druscovitch [sic] had attempted suicide is wholly unfounded.[53]

This was the entirety of the clarification offered by the paper. It was printed with no headline, no context, and was buried amongst other, longer and headlined articles, which were all collectively published under a regular column titled 'Imperial Parliament' that usually reported proceedings from within the

House of Commons. The apparent ploy to conceal the truth worked to some extent; even after the story had been emphatically proven false, other newspapers were still reporting that Druscovich *had* attempted to kill himself, either due to their ignorance of the truth, or a desire for sensationalism that had little regard for it. The *Cheltenham Chronicle*, for example, was still reporting the attempted suicide on 31 July, days after Druscovich had publicly refuted the accusation.[54]

Mercifully for Druscovich, the rumour did not persist. However, he seemingly could not catch a break, as the brief respite was not to last. The media quickly went searching for dirt elsewhere, and in an unfortunately-timed coincidence, in August 1877 Druscovich's brother, John Vincent, was arrested and accused of conspiracy to defraud. Ordinarily, his arrest would either have not featured in the newspaper, or at most may have been included in a crime 'round-up' column. However, as he was related to an accused detective in the 'Great Detective Case', as it was later dubbed, the media seized the story and used it to further smear Inspector Druscovich himself. The *Edinburgh Evening News*, for example, headlined their report 'The Brother of Detective Druscovich Arrested', and the paper immediately stated that the accused was the brother of the corrupt detective, even before stating the crime he was accused of:

> Yesterday at the Manchester City Police Court, John Vincent Druscovich, *alias* John Vincent, aged 22 years, the brother of Nathanial Druscovich of the metropolitan police, was brought up in custody [...][55]

Other newspapers naturally followed suit. The *Citizen*, for example, echoed the *Edinburgh Evening News* by naming Inspector Druscovich in the headline of their article reporting about John Vincent's arrest, and titled it 'Serious Charge Against Inspector Druscovich's Brother'.[56] The *Huddersfield Chronicle* also mentioned Inspector Druscovich in the headline, titling their report 'Arrest of the Brother of Detective Druscovich'.[57]

Away from Druscovich, it had been Meiklejohn who had first met with Kurr and Benson in 1872, and he himself had apparently initiated their working relationship.[58] Consequently, the media had very little sympathy for him right from the start. In November 1877, a number of newspapers began to characterise him as a career criminal, and suggested that he was just as much a skilled thief as he had been a skilled thief-taker – an interesting perspective when considered alongside the history of the apparently-blurred relationship between criminals and police officers.[59] To back this up, several publications cited a story depicting Meiklejohn on a trans-Atlantic voyage, betting a fellow passenger that he could steal his watch and scarf-pin without his knowledge. The *Edinburgh Evening News* told the story in great detail:

> Meiklejohn was not only a clever thief-taker, but he could palm money, abstract a watch, or relieve a gentleman of his scarf-pin as adroitly as the most experienced thief. [...] Meiklejohn asked, "What would you say if

your watch and pin [...] were taken from you before we reach Sandy Hook [...]?" "Certainly it would be impossible," said the passenger. [...] Three days afterwards the watch was missing. [...] It had some to the last day of the voyage [...] "Pardon me," [Meiklejohn] said, "I have dropped some ash on your scarf," and he carelessly brushed it off. [...] in that movement he dexterously abstracted the diamond pin.[60]

Much like the rumour of Druscovich's attempted suicide and the arrest of his brother, this story surrounding Meiklejohn's prowess as a pickpocket permeated through other newspapers. The *Dundee Courier*, the *Derbyshire Times and Chesterfield Chronicle*, the *York Herald*, the *Sheffield and Rotherham Independent*, and the *Western Daily Press* ran identical stories denouncing Meiklejohn, citing his ability to pickpocket strangers.

On a broader scale, some newspapers began to use the case of the corrupt detectives as a springboard to further scrutinise the activities of other detectives who had not been involved at all, and also used incidents of other detectives being caught committing crimes as ammunition to further damage the reputation of those already on trial. In October 1877 another detective named George Harvey was indicted for attempting to prevent a witness from giving evidence in court for a divorce case (Gladstone v. Gladstone 1875). Despite the fact that this case had nothing whatsoever to do with the case of the 'turf fraud' detectives, and that George Harvey was actually a detective inspector serving in the Portsmouth police as opposed to the Metropolitan Police, several newspapers headlined their reporting of the Harvey case as connected to them. The *Evening Telegraph*, for example, headlined a short article as 'Another Detective in Trouble',[61] whilst the *York Herald* opted for 'Charge Against Another Detective'.[62]

As summer 1877 drew to a close, the preliminary inquiry at Bow Street was becoming drawn out, and the media were beginning to lose focus. In fact, it went on for so long, and was reported so widely by so many different publications, that in September 1877, the *Saturday Review* complained that proceedings were beginning to grow tedious:

> At last the case of the police Detectives in its first stage is over. It has occupied twenty-eight days, spread over nine weeks, and the only result – the committal of the prisoners – is one which might [...] have been arrived at in half the time [...] All parties have apparently done their best to spin out the case as much as possible [...][63]

Obviously, the inevitable full criminal trial at the Old Bailey was the key event for which many publications were waiting, and it naturally served to rejuvenate media interest. As proceedings began, *John Bull* gleefully predicted that '[t]he trial will occupy some weeks', implying the media would be there following its every stage.[64] Any remaining doubt that commentators might have had as to the detectives' guilt vanished as the case moved into its latter stages, and consequently reports became lengthier and fiercer as evidence was heard and the full extent of their collusion came to light. Newspaper commentary largely abandoned short summary pieces included in crime 'round-up' sections, and instead opted to write lengthy (though still sensationalised) descriptions of the case, the suspects, the victim, and intimate details surrounding the crime. In November 1877, for example, *John Bull* produced a lengthy article dedicated to the case, which spanned three columns, and took accounts from a wide variety of different media sources (such as the *Times* and the *Telegraph*) in order to recount the story of the embezzled funds, the bribes, and the criminals' apprehension in as much detail as possible. It also recognised and commented on the fact that there had been considerable media interest surrounding the corruption scandal. It argued that it was a case

> which has, for nearly five months, supplied the daily papers with [...] very exciting, though at the same time very questionable reading [...][65]

Perhaps naturally, the detectives' trial at the Old Bailey received probably the most detailed and in-depth reporting of all of the different aspects of the case, particularly as it was the space where journalists were in attendance and thus able to hear the evidence first hand. The above example from *John Bull* contained a highly detailed description of proceedings, which it had itself quoted from a variety of other media sources. This took up at least half of the article and went into an enormous detail, as exemplified by the highly descriptive and accurate scene in which the jury returned to the courtroom to give their verdicts:

> Back came the ladies, off went the obstinate hats, silence was emphatically pronounced, and at seventeen minutes past four the jury had returned, preceded by the young foreman, who held in his hand an ominous paper. This was the verdict. He had not returned to ask any questions, as some asserted. The fate of the prisoners was in the foreman's hands. But now there was a painful interval. The prisoners were arranged in front of the dock, all terribly distressed and nervous. But the judge had not returned.[66]

The return of the verdict itself made for particularly harrowing reading due to the sheer amount of detail, including the nervousness of the foreman, who is depicted anxious to ensure that protocol was properly followed. This, clearly, was designed to give readers the clearest possible picture as to the scene inside the court, and it almost goes without saying that this is strangely reminiscent of some older forms of crime writing which this volume has analysed in previous chapters:

> At last the names of the jurymen are called over and the Clerk of the Arraigns asks the dread question in order and in deep silence. Meiklejohn? Guilty. Druscovich? Guilty. Palmer? There is an anxious hesitation, and the

young foreman, who is terribly nervous, wishes to go back and recommend Druscovich to mercy. So Palmer's fate hangs in the balance, and the presentment of the jury is made commending Druscovich to clemency. Once more the questioning begins again. Palmer? Guilty. Once more there is hesitation. Clarke? No; the foreman wishes to do everything in order, and goes back instantly to Palmer. He, too, is recommended to mercy, because he was not bribed. And now comes Clarke's turn, and apparently the most anxious moment of all, for the silence deepens. Clarke? Not guilty. The words were scarcely uttered before a burst of cheering rang through the court [...][67]

The 'blatantly sensationalist'[68] *Illustrated Police News* also gave gleefully detailed, blow-by-blow accounts of the proceedings from inside the Central Criminal Court, and happily dubbed the scandal 'The Great Detective Case', in the apparent hope that the name would catch on and become a permanent stain on the reputation of the detective department.[69] Printed alongside the highly-detailed account of the trial proceedings was a large engraved image of the scene inside the court-room which took up approximately a third of the entire page (see Figure 5.3).[70]

This case was, then, a huge moment both in terms of the police's public perception, and also how the newspaper and periodical press helped to shape contemporary ideology surrounding the concept of law enforcement in more general terms. It is therefore worth briefly summarising the key effects of the prolific media reporting of the detectives' trial before this chapter moves on. Alongside an understandable dramatic downturn in the public opinion of detectives, some secondary and perhaps slightly unexpected effects took shape. There was a substantial improvement in the hitherto inconsistent media perception of the distinction between uniformed police officers and plain-clothes detectives as a result of the case's publicity, and this became important later in terms of the detective genre's internal demarcation between competent private sleuths and bumbling, ineffective uniformed officers. In connection to this, an equally important consequence of the scandal's reporting was the sudden realisation by both journalists and the public that the detective department had, due to its secretive nature and its quiet existence, been subject to very little administrative or public scrutiny throughout its operation. Since its inception in 1842, the detective department of the Metropolitan Police had rarely, if ever, been held to account for its actions as a separate part of the wider police force. However, this changed in the wake of the 1877 scandal, and periodical commentators seized on the case and began to use it as a springboard to present varying opinions on the detective department's freedom, and to make dramatic recommendations about its future position in late-Victorian society.

'Officers of the Committee of *Criminal* Investigation': The 1877 Scandal's Reflections on the Police and Detectives

It had been the newspaper press, as opposed to the *periodical* press, which had largely focused on daily reporting the progress of the scandal through Bow

TRIAL OF THE DETECTIVES: SCENE IN THE CENTRAL CRIMINAL COURT.

Figure 5.3 'The Great Detective Case – Trial at the Central Criminal Court'
Source: *Illustrated Police News*, 3 November 1877, p. 4. Copyright The British Library Board.

Street and subsequently through the Old Bailey. The relation of the case's facts in a linear and informative fashion was a job for newspaper reporters and journalists writing in daily papers, which suited the quick-fire reporting of current events. By contrast, the weekly and monthly periodical press, suited more to a lengthier form of socio-political commentary, took a much broader approach to discussion surrounding the case, and used it to explore the wider impacts of the case on the concepts of policing and the detection of crime.

Perhaps the most obvious effect of the case's publicity was an immediate, dramatic downturn in the reputation of the police and detective forces. Once the detectives had been tried and convicted, periodical discussion shifted quickly in this direction, and critics began to question the police's overall competence and trustworthiness. This helped to fundamentally change the way that both police officers and detectives were seen by the 'mass-reading public' towards the end of the nineteenth century.[71] These figures which had previously been perceived as trusted protectors of middle-class values such as commerce, wealth, family, and property,[72] increasingly began to be depicted as stupid, untrustworthy, incompetent, and corrupt.

Perhaps understandably, a variety of satirical magazines particularly seized the case in this respect. The magazine *Fun* was very active, in fact, its attacks on the police had predated the scandal itself. As Rzepka notes, public estimation in the police force was already declining prior to the scandal, and in January 1877 *Fun* detailed the story of a man arrested for attempting to assist a lost child by taking her to the police station.[73] An incompetent officer, tellingly named 'Sergeant Cuff', is depicted as both incompetent and almost illiterate:

> Police officer 09 B. U. Z.: [detailing the reasons for arresting the innocent bystander] "[...] his conduct vasint fatherly a bit, that is, not tsackly what I would call a fatherly kind o' way; 'e voz a patting 'er werry gently on the ed, 'e voz, then 'e went and wiped the child's hies with 'is hown 'ankerchief an' then 'e took 'old of her 'and an' [sic] led 'er away, 'e did, quite kind like, as I considered the proceeding altogether werry suspicious and irreg'lar [...] hif 'e'd a guv 'er a good cuff o' the 'ead ven she voz a-cryin', I shouldn't a took no notice of 'em, hi shouldn't.[74]

The officer's peculiar, supposedly Cockney dialect is designed to connote both idiocy and a working-class background, highlighting his inability to understand middle-class relationships such as the relationship shown between the gentleman and the lost child. The police officer's 'working-class background' is a point also raised by Anthea Trodd, who quotes the *Saturday Review*[75] to claim that Victorian commentators struggled with the concept of police officers solving 'crime involving middle-class participants' as constables themselves came mostly from working-class backgrounds.[76] These snippets attacking the police's trustworthiness and competence in satirical magazines became extremely common in 1877–1878. In October 1877, *Fun* published a poem starkly criticising the operations of the police force and how they responded to the public as they performed their duties:

Such lots of burglars gets away
Scot free with all their booty,
I think it's very wrong to say
A man exceeds his dooty
Because he goes and takes a chap
Whose head is broke and bleeding –
As if a peeler cares a rap
For wounds and surgeon's pleading!
I says as Allingham was right,
Although the go's a rum one.
The public mind was in a fright,
And so he collared someone.
The majesty of Henglish law,
With which he was invested,
Demanded that the first he saw,
At once should be arrested.[77]

In April 1878, *Fun* argued that R. A. Cross's restructure of the detective department begun in the immediate aftermath of the 1877 case was likely to be ineffective, and sarcastically suggested in its 'Unfounded Rumours' section that:

> There is no foundation for the statement contained in some of our contemporaries that detectives will in future be styled, "Officers of the Committee of *Criminal* Investigation." They never catch any to investigate. Now Messrs. Meiklejohn and Co. *were* criminal investigators.

The magazine did not temper its attacks as the reorganisation of the detective department took shape. In December 1878, *Fun* was still drawing readers' attention to the 'turf fraud' case, and directly named the corrupt Inspectors as examples of why detectives could no longer be taken at their word. In a rare departure from open comedy, the magazine quoted a short poem which stated that Inspectors or detectives could always be trustworthy, before half-mockingly, half-seriously asking whether the conviction of the three detectives did not openly prove this assertion wrong:

The Test of Truth

"Who has a doubt should scout it:
Doubt here is quite absurd;
I have no 'doubt' about it
When I've an INSPECTOR's word."
London Magistrate

What about the "word" of such inspectors as Druscovitch, Meiklejohn, and Palmer?[78]

Other satirical magazines than *Fun* also engaged with the case, and further implied that the public opinion of detectives had declined as a direct result of the scandal. Whilst not mentioning any specific names, the magazine *Judy, or, the London Serio-Comic Journal* referenced the corruption scandal with an article titled 'The Mechanical Detective' in September 1877:

> In consequence of the recent theft of antique gems from the British Museum, a system of protection for the future [...] is under the considera- tion of the Trustees. Its main feature is that thieves shall detect themselves; which, *considering recent disclosures*, seems to suggest the only means likely to be successful [my italics].[79]

Whilst police officers and detectives were increasingly portrayed as idiotic in the pages of satirical magazines (which was perhaps predictable), in other publica- tions they were presented as both incompetent and corrupt with a far more serious tone. Earlier positive assertions regarding the skills and competence of the police made by periodical journalism which had appeared across the mid- century were now largely diminished, replaced by assertions that they were largely untrustworthy, undesirable, and dishonest.[80]

The *Saturday Review*, particularly, became one of the most virulent publications in terms of presenting criticism of the police through the lens of the 'turf fraud' scandal across the late 1870s and beyond. Indeed, given its robust engagement with socio-political debates which had led to its nickname 'the *Saturday Reviler*', this is hardly surprising.[81] As a result of the trial, it commented that the detective department's lack of supervision and administrative scrutiny was to blame for its corruption, and it targeted the operational freedom that the department had previously enjoyed:

> [...] the main questions which the Commissioners will have to decide will therefore be [...] whether its organization and discipline can be improved by more direct and minute supervision of the officers who are employed in such exceptional work. [...] The recent trial seems to show that at present the supervision over the Detectives is not sufficient.[82]

The corruption in the detective department which *had* been revealed also led concerned periodical commentators to speculate on that which had *not*. In the immediate aftermath of the trial, the *Saturday Review* also raised the concern that this case may only have been the tip of the iceberg, and that there may be much worse problems that had not yet been revealed:

> It is not the mere conviction of these prominent members of the Detective force that gives rise to uneasiness; it is the possibility thereby raised that many

crimes may have hitherto remained undetected or unpunished through similar dereliction of duty.[83]

On the same day as this article from the *Saturday Review*, the *Examiner* also commented on the case from an almost identical perspective. It expressed that this 'case of dishonesty' in the detective department was unlikely to be either the first or last to be revealed, and augmented this point by suggesting that it was the nature of the detective as a profession which had made it so difficult for the detectives themselves to be discovered as criminal or corrupt:

> It is hardly likely that the first case of proved dishonesty should actually be the first case of dishonesty, and the treachery of detectives is of course particularly difficult to prove.[84]

This concept of the dishonesty specifically of detectives was a point of anxiety for many periodical commentators. The secretive nature of the detective, the historic mistrust in plain-clothes policing which Shpayer-Makov argues contributed to the detective department's lack of growth,[85] and the close proximity they were professionally required to have with those who were already criminals and therefore used to attempting to evade capture, made detectives particularly difficult to 'detect' themselves. The police had hitherto been trusted guardians of law and order, as well as protectors of middle-class values such as property, family, and economic wealth, however now this trust had broken down. Indeed, the police's occupation of a space between respectability and criminality had hitherto been seen as an advantage for others wishing to experience it, to those who wished to speculatively write about what it would be like to be a police officer, and to those who wished to keep the criminal classes isolated. Now, it had seemingly contributed to their downfall.

The downturn in perceptions of the detective department and of individual detective officers did not quickly dissipate. In fact, their tarnished reputation looked as though it was going to last for a significant time. At the time of the trial, the *Saturday Review* predicted that the scandal would stop the general public from ever trusting the detectives again, given the privileged position that the department had thoughtlessly squandered:

> When a department has once seriously broken down people are naturally distrustful of its future working.[86]

A further article published in December 1878, highlighted how the enormous shift in the perception of detectives had caused the mistrust felt by periodical journalists and commentators to become almost permanent:

> [...] it must be said that distrust now to a great extent replaced the confidence which was once felt in this branch of the police. Of course this is in part due to the effect produced by the trial and conviction of the three men who are now

undergoing punishment for aiding criminals [...] Policemen are not now habitually spoken of as "skilful" or as "active and intelligent," and this is a sad proof of the extent to which they have fallen in popular estimation.[87]

Interestingly, the scandal ignited a debate surrounding the socio-political positions of criminals. This had been quite a fierce discussion throughout the mid-Victorian era in periodical commentary,[88] however the 1877 scandal added a new dimension to it and further emphasised the depths to which the detective had fallen in popular opinion. In August 1877, during the height of the trial, *Punch* pointed out that the court audience's support for the criminals as 'lovable rogues' stemmed not merely from the fact that they were criminals, but also from the fact that they were party to convicting detectives, who were now seen as worse due to their position of trust which they had abused. Ordinary criminals were at least honest in their criminality, but the criminal detectives had betrayed the (admittedly rather grudging) confidence which the public had once placed in them:

> Mr. Kurr [one of the criminals who had bribed the Inspectors] got cheered not only as a criminal, but as an accuser of Detectives.[89]

Other commentators were horrified at the idea that criminals were receiving support for convicting members of the police force. In November 1877, *John Bull* wrote that rapt admiration for the criminals who were assisting in convicting the corrupted detectives was both unhealthy, and not merely limited to only those of a social class who expected to react in this way, but that the middle classes were also just as appreciative:

> We cannot, however, but trust that there is one feature of the recent trial which will not soon be repeated, and that the unhealthy admiration excited by the hardened and reckless criminals whose revelations led to the recent prosecution will not receive fresh fuel. The development of such convict-hero worship [...] is not a wholesome sign of the times [...][90]

Finally, while a significant number of periodicals used the scandal to criticise the police, there were a few who approached it from alternative perspectives which are worth briefly mentioning, such as Dickens's *All the Year Round*. Rather than commenting on the corrupt or inept nature of detectives from the Metropolitan Police, the magazine positioned itself as a rare voice of reason. As Dickens himself had died in 1870 and had therefore not lived to see the scandal, it was left to Charles Dickens Jr. (1837–1896) to undertake the editorship of the magazine. Perhaps in some part due to the earlier admiration for detectives for which Dickens Sr. had been famous, *All the Year Round* remained pragmatic when discussing the falling estimation of the detective force by suggesting that critics of detectives had been rather too quick to criticise:

Nevertheless a considerable amount of injustice has been done. Many of those who have "rushed in" as critics, have evidently written without knowledge of their subject, have apparently gone upon the principle of the reviewer who did not read the books he had to notice lest he be prejudiced. That our detectives have not been particularly successful in apprehending the perpetrators of such dynamite outrages as have become accomplished facts is no doubt true; but they have probably done much more in the way of preventing purposed crimes of this kind than could be safely made known, or than their adverse critics would be prepared to give them credit for.[91]

Whilst perhaps an admirable sentiment and a rare example of journalistic pragmatism, it is probably worth saying that the argument presented here, that the public probably did not see the bulk of the good work being done by the police, was thin at best.

The final consequence of the scandal and its reporting was that the largely inconsistent understanding of the differences between uniformed officers and plain-clothes detectives improved in the wake of the reporting of the 1877 detective scandal, and the detective department's distinct existence was thrown sharply into the spotlight. Whilst the police had been a subject of interest for journalists across the early to mid-nineteenth century, the concept of a difference between police officers and plain-clothes detectives had not always been clear. However, the crisis and subsequent restructure of the Detective Department into the Criminal Investigations Department (CID) and the wide media reaction surrounding these events caused the development of a greater understanding of how the police force was separated into its uniformed and detective elements, and thus understood much better in general. This, as we will see in the next and final chapter of this volume, had extensive ramifications for the development of detective fiction as a literary genre across the late nineteenth century.

'[…] little, if at all, better': Chapter 5 Conclusions

In short, the 1877 'trial of the detectives' was no small incident, yet it has been largely overlooked in scholarly discourse. The media attention it was given was immense, and had attracted considerable interest from all over the country. It was also not an isolated moment which was quickly allowed to be forgotten; two years later, as the detectives were released, the solicitor Froggatt was immediately rearrested and charged with conspiracy to defraud his wife of over £8,000 and promptly sent back to prison which reignited these discussions in the national newspaper and periodical media.[92]

The scandal changed the public's perception of both the Metropolitan Police and its detective department permanently, and the police suffered greatly in the public view across periodical criticism of the 1880s. The Home Secretary's restructure of the detective department had not had the desired effect to restore faith in the police, and it was quickly followed by a series of reorganisations which were also viewed as largely ineffective. This prompted the *Saturday*

Review in 1885 to suggest that the new department was 'talkative, indolent and unintelligent',[93] and in September 1878 the *Examiner* argued that:

> [...] there are grave reasons for supposing that the new Criminal Investigation Department is little, if at all, better than the old and corrupt Detective Department.[94]

It did not help that the police also had their proverbial hands full with a series of other embarrassing incidents which took place across the 1880s, such as the sustained Irish Republican Brotherhood bombing campaign and the infamous Whitechapel murders of 1888. Consequently, as the nineteenth century approached its end, police officers and detectives were seen very differently from the way they had been in the mid-Victorian era. It is worth mentioning, however, that even at this stage the police were still a relatively new institution on a nationwide scale, and had only been in existence in its current form for 21 years by the time the 1877 scandal occurred. Despite its youth, the outraged reaction to the police's corruption reinforces how the police had entrenched itself as part of the Victorian social fabric remarkably quickly.

Finally, the scandal had an observable and corresponding impact on the use of detectives in crime and detective fiction. This volume has so far identified the fact that police officers and detectives were viewed as protectors, guardians, and (occasionally) interlopers in private realms of criminality in fiction, who the reader could accompany and therefore experience the thrilling sensation of criminality and detection from a place of complete safety. However, as police officers and detectives were now seen as corrupt and ineffective, this was far less sustainable. Consequently, the late Victorian era saw the rise of the private detective, culminating in the appearance of perhaps the most famous private investigator of them all.

Notes

1 Clive Emsley, 'A Typology of Nineteenth-Century Police', *Crime, Histoire et Sociétés/ Crime, History and Societies*, 3, 1 (1999), 29–44 (p. 30).
2 'Outrages': The use of this term here comes from 'Detectives and their Work', *All the Year Round*, 25 April 1885, p. 135.
3 Charles Rzepka, *Detective Fiction* (Cambridge: Polity, 2005), p. 111.
4 George Dilnot, *The Trial of the Detectives* (New York: Charles Scribner's Sons, 1928), pp. 51–52.
5 The actual method through which the criminals managed to obtain money from Madame de Goncourt is highly interesting, but is sadly rather too complex to detail in this all-too brief summary of the case. For a comprehensive account of the criminals' methodology, consult p. 28 of Dilnot's *Trial of the Detectives* which recounts it in detail.
6 Dilnot, p. 51.
7 Dilnot, p. 51.
8 Dilnot, pp. 51–52.
9 Dilnot, pp. 301–302.

10 Dilnot, p. 52.

11 Sarah Manwaring-White, *The Policing Revolution: Police Technology, Democracy and Liberty in Britain* (Brighton: Harvester, 1983), p. 8.

12 Manwaring-White, p. 8.

13 Rzepka, p. 111.

14 Martin Kayman, *From Bow Street to Baker Street: Mystery. Detection and Narrative* (Basingstoke: Macmillan, 1992), p. 95.

15 Heather Worthington, *Key Concepts in Crime Fiction* (Basingstoke: Palgrave Macmillan, 2011), p. 65.

16 Haia Shpayer-Makov, *The Ascent of the Detective: Police Sleuths in Victorian and Edwardian England* (Oxford: Oxford University Press, 2011), p. 38.

17 Shpayer-Makov, p. 39.

18 Shpayer-Makov, pp. 202–203.

19 Rzepka, p. 111.

20 See Chapter 1 for full details.

21 Shpayer-Makov, p. 32.

22 Shpayer-Makov, p. 32.

23 'Apprehension of Good for the Barbarous Murder of Jane Jones', British Library <https://www.bl.uk/collection-items/broadside-apprehension-of-good-for-the-barbarous-murder-of-jane-jones> [accessed August 2018] (c. 1842) and Anon., *Autobiography of Jack Ketch* (Philadelphia: Carey, Lea and Blanchard, 1835), n.p. [front matter]. Both images are in the public domain.

24 Clive Emsley, *The Great British Bobby: A History of British Policing from the 18th Century to the Present* (London: Quercus, 2009), p. 40.

25 Shpayer-Makov, p. 33.

26 'New Police Arrangement', *Morning Post*, 12 July 1842, p. 7.

27 Shpayer-Makov, p. 33.

28 Shpayer-Makov, p. 33.

29 Shpayer-Makov, p. 34. See also Anthea Trodd, 'The Policeman and the Lady: Significant Encounters in Mid-Victorian Fiction', *Victorian Studies*, 24, 4 (1984), 435–460 (p. 438).

30 'Police Detectives', *Leisure Hour*, 29 October 1857, p. 692.

31 'The Police of London', *Quarterly Review*, July 1870, pp. 87–129 (p. 99).

32 'The Police of London', *Quarterly Review*, July 1870, pp. 87–129 (p. 99).

33 'The Police and Mr. Speke', *Saturday Review*, 8 February 1868, p. 172.

34 'The Irish Constabulary', *Examiner*, 3 March 1860, p. 131.

35 'Murderers and Detectives', *Examiner*, 28 October 1871, p. 1063.

36 William Brighty Rands, 'The Apotheosis of the Policeman', *St. Paul's Magazine*, February 1874, p. 240.

37 The title of the article 'Police Detectives' from the *Leisure Hour* from 1857 helpfully demonstrates this, though this was by no means the only example of this in action.

38 'The Idiot Detective, or, the Track! The Trial! and the Triumph!', *Fun*, 2 January 1869, p. 13. Image produced by ProQuest as part of *British Periodicals*. www.proquest.com.

39 'The Detective System', *Saturday Review*, 1 December 1877, p. 682.

40 'The Alleged Frauds on a French Lady', *Bell's Life in London*, 20 January 1877, p. 4.

41 'Sworn Bookmakers', *Examiner*, 28 April 1877, pp. 522–523.

42 Dilnot, p. 51.

43 Andrew Hobbs, 'When the Provincial Press was the National Press (c. 1836–1900)', *International Journal of Regional and Local Studies*, 5, 1 (2009), 16–43 (p. 25).

44 'Serious' was a term used in several headlines between 13 and 15 July 1877 – for example, 'Serious Charge Against London Detectives', *Sheffield and Rotherham Independent*, 13 July 1877, p. 4.

45 'Grave Charge Against Detectives', *Citizen*, 13 July 1877, p. 3.

46 'Extraordinary Charge Against Detectives', *York Herald*, 13 July 1877, p. 8.

47 'Charge Against Detective Officers', *Reynolds's Newspaper*, 15 July 1877, n.p.

48 'Serious Charge Against Detective Officers', *Edinburgh Evening News,* 13 July 1877, p. 4.

49 For a representative example of the minute detail, see 'The Charge Against Detective Officers', *Manchester Courier*, 30 July 1877, p. 3.

50 'Attempted Suicide of Inspector Druscovich', *Standard,* 24 July 1877, p. 5.

51 'Attempted Suicide of Inspector Druscovitch', *Edinburgh Evening News*, 24 July 1877, p. 2.

52 'The Charge Against Detective Officers', *Leeds Mercury*, 27 July 1877, n.p.

53 'Imperial Parliament', *Dundee Courier and Argus,* 25 July 1877, n.p.

54 'Attempted Suicide of Detective Druscovich', *Cheltenham Chronicle,* 31 July 1877, p. 3.

55 'The Brother of Detective Druscovich Arrested', *Edinburgh Evening News*, 14 August 1877, p. 3.

56 'Serious Charge Against Inspector Druscovich's Brother', *Citizen*, 14 August 14 1877, p. 2.

57 'Arrest of the Brother of Detective Druscovich', *Huddersfield Chronicle and West Yorkshire Advertiser*, 18 August 1877, p. 3.

58 Dilnot, p. 14.

59 I refer here, of course, to the idea that many early police officers or officials, famously such as Eugene Francois Vidocq, among others, were originally career criminals who were offered leniency if they turned against their former comrades. The line between criminal and police officer was famously quite close – and this was even reflected in fiction. See the opening issue of 'Recollections of a Police Officer', cited in Chapter 3, for example, where it is strongly implied that the new officer 'Waters' was actually a former criminal.

60 'Meiklejohn as a Thief-Taker', *Edinburgh Evening News*, 27 November 1877, p. 4.

61 'Another Detective in Trouble', *Evening Telegraph*, 29 September 1877, p. 2.

62 'Charge Against Another Detective', *York Herald*, 1 October 1877, p. 6.

63 'Nine Weeks of Preliminary Enquiry', *Saturday Review*, 29 September 1877, pp. 382–383.

64 'Law and Police', *John Bull*, 27 October 1877, p. 694.

65 'The Charge Against Detectives', *John Bull*, 24 November 1877, p. 748.

66 'The Charge Against Detectives', *John Bull*, 24 November 1877, p. 748.

67 'The Charge Against Detectives', *John Bull*, 24 November 1877, p. 748.

68 Judith Knelman, *Twisting in the Wind: The Murderess and the English Press* (Toronto: University of Toronto Press, 1998), p. 37.

69 'The Great Detective Case – Trial at the Central Criminal Court', *Illustrated Police News*, 3 November 1877, p. 4. The name 'the Great Detective Case' seemingly *did* catch on, as it was reused in a number of other publications. The article from *John Bull* (November 24 1877) used this designation to ends its reporting of the trial. Other magazines such as *Funny Folks* (November 3 1877) made use of the name, and a dedicated account of the detectives' trial published separately in December 1877 also used it. This was advertised in the *Illustrated Police News* as a 'full account of the Magistraterial [sic] Enquiry [and the] Trial at the Central Criminal Court', and which included '[...] interesting matter never before published' as well as illustrations of the detectives themselves.

70 'The Great Detective Case – Trial at the Central Criminal Court', *Illustrated Police News*, 3 November 1877, p. 4. Copyright The British Library Board.

71 'Mass-reading public': Altick usefully defines what is meant by this term on pp. 6–7 of his seminal work *The English Common Reader* (1957).

72 See Chapter 1 for full details.

73 Rzepka, p. 111.

74 'Unreported Police News', *Fun*, 3 January 1877, p. 271.

75 'Detectives in Fiction and in Real Life', *Saturday Review*, 11 June 1864, pp. 712–713.

76 Trodd, 435–460 (pp. 449–450).
77 'Our Detective System', *Fun*, 31 October 1877, p. 184.
78 'The Test of Truth', *Fun*, 4 December 1878, p. 229.
79 'The Mechanical Detective', *Judy, or, the London Serio-Comic Journal*, 5 September 1877, p. 205.
80 A good example of this positive portrayal of the police made by earlier mid-Victorian periodical articles could include an 1857 piece titled 'Police Detectives' published in the *Leisure Hour*.
81 Elizabeth Tilley, '*Saturday Review of Politics, Literature, Science, and Art* (1855–1938)', in *Dictionary of Nineteenth Century Journalism*, ed. by Laurel Brake and Marysa Demoor (London and Ghent: Academia Press, 2009), p. 558.
82 'The Detective System', *Saturday Review*, 1 December 1877, pp. 682–683.
83 'The Detectives', *Saturday Review*, 24 November 1877, p. 650.
84 'The End of the Detectives', *Examiner*, 24 November 1877, p. 1484.
85 Shpayer-Makov, pp. 33–34.
86 'The Detectives', *Saturday Review*, 24 November 1877, p. 650.
87 'Detectives', *Saturday Review*, 21 December 1878, p. 780.
88 For example, see John Ruskin, 'Essays on Political Economy', *Fraser's Magazine*, April 1863, p. 442.
89 Percival Leigh, 'Crowds and Criminals', *Punch, or, the London Charivari*, 11 August 1877, p. 53.
90 'The Detectives and Mr. Froggatt', *John Bull*, 24 November 1877, p. 753.
91 'Detectives and their Work', *All the Year Round*, 25 April 1885, p. 136.
92 A large number of national newspapers reported that Froggatt was rearrested almost immediately after his release in 1879. Froggatt had been a trustee of a fund set up as part of a marriage settlement, but when he was implicated in the 'turf fraud' scandal it caused alarm in his wife, who employed another solicitor to look into the state of the funds. The solicitor found that all of the money was gone.
93 'The Detectives', *Saturday Review*, 31 January 1885, p. 132.
94 'Our Police System', *Examiner*, 7 September 1878, p. 1133.

Bibliography

Primary Periodical Material

'Another Detective in Trouble', *Evening Telegraph*, 29 September 1877, p. 2.
'Apprehension of Good for the Barbarous Murder of Jane Jones', *British Library* <http s://www.bl.uk/collection-items/broadside-apprehension-of-good-for-the-barbarous-m urder-of-jane-jones> [accessed August 2018] (c. 1842).
'Arrest of the Brother of Detective Druscovich', *Huddersfield Chronicle and West Yorkshire Advertiser*, 18 August 1877, p. 3.
'Attempted Suicide of Detective Druscovich', *Cheltenham Chronicle*, 31 July 1877, p. 3.
'Attempted Suicide of Inspector Druscovich', *Standard*, 24 July 1877, p. 5.
'Attempted Suicide of Inspector Druscovitch', *Edinburgh Evening News*, 24 July 1877, p. 2.
'Charge Against Another Detective', *York Herald*, 1 October 1877, p. 6.
'Charge Against Detective Officers', *Reynolds's Newspaper*, 15 July 1877, n.p.
'Detectives and their Work', *All the Year Round*, 25 April 1885, pp. 135–139.
'Detectives in Fiction and in Real Life', *Saturday Review*, 11 June 1864, pp. 712–713.
'Detectives', *Saturday Review*, 21 December 1878, pp. 780–781.
'Extraordinary Charge Against Detectives', *York Herald*, 13 July 1877, p. 8.
'Grave Charge Against Detectives', *Citizen*, 13 July 1877, p. 3.

'Imperial Parliament', *Dundee Courier and Argus*, 25 July 1877, n.p.

'Law and Police', *John Bull*, 27 October 1877, p. 694.

Leigh, Percival, 'Crowds and Criminals', *Punch, or, the London Charivari*, 11 August 1877, p. 53.

'Meiklejohn as a Thief-Taker', *Edinburgh Evening News*, 27 November 1877, p. 4.

'Murderers and Detectives', *Examiner*, 28 October 1871, pp. 1062–1064.

'New Police Arrangement', *Morning Post*, 12 July 1842, p. 7.

'Nine Weeks of Preliminary Enquiry', *Saturday Review*, 29 September 1877, pp. 382–383.

'Our Detective System', *Fun*, 31 October 1877, p. 184.

'Our Police System', *Examiner*, 7 September 1878, pp. 1132–1133.

'Police Detectives', *Leisure Hour*, 29 October 1857, pp. 691–695.

Rands, William Brighty, 'The Apotheosis of the Policeman', *St. Paul's Magazine*, February 1874, pp. 232–241.

Ruskin, John, 'Essays on Political Economy', *Fraser's Magazine*, April 1863, pp. 441–462.

'Serious Charge Against Detective Officers', *Edinburgh Evening News*, 13 July 1877, p. 4.

'Serious Charge Against Inspector Druscovich's Brother', *Citizen*, 14 August 1877, p. 2.

'Serious Charge Against London Detectives', *Sheffield and Rotherham Independent*, 13 July 1877, p. 4.

'Sworn Bookmakers', *Examiner*, 28 April 1877, pp. 522–523.

'The Alleged Frauds on a French Lady', *Bell's Life in London*, 20 January 1877, p. 4.

'The Brother of Detective Druscovich Arrested', *Edinburgh Evening News*, 14 August 1877, p. 3.

'The Charge Against Detective Officers', *Leeds Mercury*, 27 July 1877, n.p.

'The Charge Against Detective Officers', *Manchester Courier*, 30 July 1877, p. 3.

'The Charge Against Detectives', *John Bull*, 24 November 1877, p. 748.

'The Detective System', *Saturday Review*, 1 December 1877, pp. 681–683.

'The Detectives and Mr. Froggatt', *John Bull*, 24 November 1877, p. 753.

'The Detectives', *Saturday Review*, 24 November 1877, pp. 648–650.

'The Detectives', *Saturday Review*, 31 January 1885, pp. 132–133.

'The End of the Detectives', *Examiner*, 24 November 1877, p. 1484.

'The Great Detective Case – Trial at the Central Criminal Court', *Illustrated Police News*, 3 November 1877, p. 4.

'The Idiot Detective, or, the Track! The Trial! and the Triumph!', *Fun*, 2 January 1869.

'The Irish Constabulary', *Examiner*, 3 March 1860, pp. 130–131.

'The Mechanical Detective', *Judy, or, the London Serio-Comic Journal*, 5 September 1877, p. 205.

'The Police and Mr. Speke', *Saturday Review*, 8 February 1868, pp. 171–173.

'The Police of London', *Quarterly Review*, July 1870, pp. 87–129.

'The Test of Truth', *Fun*, 4 December 1878, p. 229.

'Unreported Police News', *Fun*, 3 January 1877, p. 271.

Secondary Material

Altick, Richard, *The English Common Reader: A Social History of the Mass Reading Public 1800–1900* (Ohio: Ohio State University Press, 1957).

Anon., *Autobiography of Jack Ketch* (Philadelphia: Carey, Lea and Blanchard, 1835).

Dilnot, George, *The Trial of the Detectives* (New York: Charles Scribner's Sons, 1928).

Emsley, Clive, 'A Typology of Nineteenth-Century Police', *Crime, Histoire et Sociétés (Crime, History and Societies)*, 3, 1 (1999), 29–44.

Emsley, Clive, *The Great British Bobby: A History of British Policing from the 18th Century to the Present* (London: Quercus, 2009).

Hobbs, Andrew, 'When the Provincial Press was the National Press (c. 1836–1900)', *International Journal of Regional and Local Studies*, 5, 1 (2009), 16–43.

Kayman, Martin, *From Bow Street to Baker Street: Mystery. Detection and Narrative* (Basingstoke: Macmillan, 1992).

Knelman, Judith, *Twisting in the Wind: The Murderess and the English Press* (Toronto: University of Toronto Press, 1998).

Manwaring-White, Sarah, *The Policing Revolution: Police Technology, Democracy and Liberty in Britain* (Brighton: Harvester, 1983).

Rzepka, Charles, *Detective Fiction* (Cambridge: Polity, 2005).

Shpayer-Makov, Haia, *The Ascent of the Detective: Police Sleuths in Victorian and Edwardian England* (Oxford: Oxford University Press, 2011)

Tilley, Elizabeth, 'Saturday Review of Politics, Literature, Science, and Art (1855–1938)', in *Dictionary of Nineteenth Century Journalism*, ed. by Laurel Brake and Marysa Demoor (London and Ghent: Academia Press, 2009), p. 558.

Trodd, Anthea, 'The Policeman and the Lady: Significant Encounters in Mid-Victorian Fiction', *Victorian Studies*, 24, 4 (1984), 435–460.

Worthington, Heather, *Key Concepts in Crime Fiction* (Basingstoke: Palgrave Macmillan, 2011).

6   From 'Handsaw' to Holmes

Police Officers and Detectives in Late Victorian Journalism

Introduction: Turf Frauds, Torsos, and *Tit-Bits*

Just as both the periodical press and the police had experienced simultaneous fundamental changes across the mid-Victorian era,[1] a similar event was about to occur again as the era entered the 1880s. As the previous chapter detailed, the 1877 'turf fraud' scandal, resulting in the conviction of three of its chief detectives, marked a turning point in public perceptions of the police, led to a more sustained public focus on the force's operations than had hitherto existed, and largely eliminated the prevalent lack of understanding of the distinctions between plain-clothes detectives and uniformed police officers.

However, unfortunately for the force, a series of other incidents that were perceived to be embarrassing followed 1877 and persisted into the next decade, such as the prolonged Irish Republican Brotherhood bombing campaign across the 1880s, the infamous Whitechapel murders of 1888, and the discovery of a torso at Scotland Yard also in 1888 (known in many newspapers as the 'White-hall Mystery', although today more commonly referred to as the 'Thames Torso' murder). A combination of the fact that these events were allowed to occur in the first place, and the fact that the police had largely failed to catch the perpetrators, meant that the police's efforts to recover its reputation were severely hampered, and public opinion of the force turned strongly downwards. On top of this, the constant police failings also led to a poorly-received series of government-led inquiries into the state of the force, which in turn led to a variety of restructures, reorganisations, and numerous leadership replacements that took place in 1879, 1883, 1884, 1886, and 1887. Far from helping to improve the public's perception of the police force, however, they instead exacerbated the wider frustration with the police's perceived inefficiencies, as the restructures were perceived as both obstructions in of themselves, and as a gateway for further corruption.

This final chapter therefore explores these changes in the perceptions of the police as represented in the periodical press, and comments on how they affected the way that detectives and police officers were represented in fiction, leading to dramatic changes within the fledgling 'detective' genre. In short, the 1880s were characterised by the emergence of a literary climate where fiction began to focus on the exploits of private, amateur or somehow reluctant detectives.

However, it is important to note that there were also broader changes occurring simultaneously within periodical publishing itself. Experimental publishers such as George Newnes (1851–1910) paved the way for a new kind of periodical market, which pioneered innovative styles of publication and thorough market-led testing of what Kate Jackson refers to as a 'diverse range of journalistic prototypes', including penny weeklies, sixpenny illustrated magazines, evening newspapers, true-story magazines, and children's magazines.[2] Newnes, alongside other innovative late-Victorian publishers such as W. T. Stead (1849–1912), Alfred Harmsworth (1865–1922), and C. Arthur Pearson (1866–1921), cultivated a significant shift in the periodical market across the late 1880s and 1890s. This was characterised by a focus on value for money, wide reader appeal, and a strong preference for short fiction over the lengthy serialised novel.[3] For his part, Newnes managed to balance the growing appetite for this new kind of publishing, with the success of his first magazine, *Tit-Bits*, in 1881 and his flagship publication the *Strand Magazine* in 1891, which Mike Ashley argues was the magazine that 'defined the era'.[4]

These new cultural trends spectacularly collided as the Victorian era approached its end. The poor journalistic perception of the police led to the rise of private detectives in periodical detective fiction, while changes in the periodical landscape created a new focus on short, digestible, and consumable fiction. Thus, this ultimately led to the appearance and enduring popularity of Arthur Conan Doyle's Sherlock Holmes.

Periodical Perceptions of the Police in the 1880s

It is firstly important to get a sense of now largely aggressive journalistic perceptions of the police in the aftermath of the 'turf fraud' scandal. The conviction of three of its detective inspectors severely damaged the Metropolitan Police's reputation, and the downturn in public opinion was catastrophic and immediate. However, it was also long-lasting; the shadow of 1877 was not allowed to dissipate and the case was still being discussed well into the 1880s. A number of magazines, especially the malevolent *Saturday Review*, repeatedly brought up the convicted inspectors for years even after they had been released. In 1884, for example, it wrote:

> Since the time of the late Inspector Field there has been but one man known to fame at Scotland Yard [...] and that was the luckless Druscowitch [sic] [...][5]

The 1880s were therefore not an easy decade for the Metropolitan Police. The new Director of Criminal Investigations appointed after the 'turf fraud' crisis, Sir (Charles Edward) Howard Vincent (1849–1908) had the already-difficult task of building the rebranded 'detective department', now known as the Criminal Investigations Department (CID), further complicated by a number of other embarrassing incidents. The first to note was the extended dynamiting campaign by the Irish Republican Brotherhood.[6] This was a sustained operation that took place between 1881 and 1885, and included explosions at Whitehall and on the London Underground in 1883, at London Bridge, Scotland Yard, and Trafalgar Square in 1884 and attempts on Parliament and the Tower of London in 1885, although this bombing took place after Vincent had resigned in 1884. Other explosions also occurred outside of the capital, notably in Liverpool and Chester in 1881, and in Glasgow in 1883.

The police's failure to prevent or capture those responsible for these attacks helped to maintain its already-damaged reputation. A number of periodicals frustratedly reported that the police had been inefficient in both stopping them occurring and catching those who had carried them out. In 1881, for example, the *Examiner* argued that the state of the Metropolitan Police was in desperate need of critical attention, lest its inefficiency lead to innocent casualties:

> At the present time, when London is threatened with a repetition of the Fenian outrages of 1867, the lamentably inefficient condition of the Metropolitan Police is a matter of very serious moment.[7]

Similarly, in January 1885 the *Saturday Review*, which had begun its campaign against the police in the 1870s and happily kept it up across the 1880s, made its opinion of the police's efforts to halt the bombing campaign quite clear:

> Dynamite outrages follow one another, and differ more or less; but there is one point they have in common. They are all carried out with fair success as far as the police are concerned. [...] They have also one pretty uniform consequence. For days after they have happened we hear of "clues" in the hands of the Criminal Investigation Department, that remarkable Government office which investigates with untiring zeal [...] but which somehow finds out so little. There is much running to and fro, or show of running to and fro, and wonderful vigilance is displayed. Then the hubbub dies down, and nobody has been caught. [...] we are only too likely to see another instance of useless police activity.[8]

However, it was not only the IRB bombings that caused the police trouble in the press. The situation was worsened further with the Bloody Sunday riots of 1887, and the Whitechapel murders of 1888. Naturally, these events were also widely commented on, generating what seemed to be an endless stream of negative press coverage which often commented on the police's lack of zeal and lack of tangible results. The Whitechapel murders, in particular, drew concentrated fire from journalists. In September 1888 the *Saturday Review* reported on the murder which took place in Hanbury Street,[9] and complained:

> Unfortunately there is another fault to be found with Scotland Yard besides its lack of numerical strength. The quality of the English detective has

seriously declined. [...] in the detection of criminals they have fallen below their old standard [...][10]

As already mentioned, the constant police failings and their accompanying negative press coverage across the 1880s resulted in a lengthy series of inquiries into the state of the police force. It underwent a variety of restructures and/or leadership replacements in 1879 as a direct result of the 'turf fraud' scandal, as well as in 1883, 1884, 1886, and 1887. However, instead of reassuring commentators that the matter was under control (or at least under review) these measures merely exacerbated periodical frustration with the police's inefficiencies. In February 1880, for example, the venerable *Examiner* wrote that the 1879 restructure had been at best superficial and at worst totally ineffective, before concluding that nothing less than a complete revolution would solve the problem:

> Something more than a mere departmental inquiry, such as was held in 1877 after the conviction of three of the detective for complicity in the Turf Frauds, is now required in order to allay the feeling of insecurity that the recent arbitrary conduct of the police has aroused in public mind. The Criminal Investigation Department was created in order to remedy the abuses that had crept into the Detective Department. [...] The new system, indeed, appears to be a much less efficient one than the old plan of employing the most intelligent of the ordinary constables as detectives as occasion required.[11]

The *Examiner* returned to this subject in July 1880 to also suggest that the restructure of the Detective Department into the Criminal Investigations Department had been nothing less than a 'miserable failure',[12] and suggested, quite simply, that 'the Metropolitan Police is rotten to the very core' [...].[13]

As the new Director of the Criminal Investigations Department, Howard Vincent himself came under direct public scrutiny in a substantial amount of periodical criticism. A number of publications openly questioned his effectiveness at creating an effective new department, including the *Nineteenth Century*, which initially seemed pragmatic towards him in May 1883 when it suggested that his reforms had caused a 'great improvement' in the department.[14] However, the same article, attributed to Malcolm Laing Meason, went on to argue that Vincent's reforms to the detective department had, despite meaning well, been largely ineffectual:

> [...] it is a curious fact that as regards a detective force we are very little if at all better off than our grandfathers were half a century ago [...] the detection of crime seems to be a problem which our so-called detectives have not the capacity in most cases to solve. And it is the same with the great as with smaller affairs. Is there a capital in Europe where the Hatton Garden robbery and the attempt to blow up the Government Offices in Westminster would have remained mysteries of which it seems impossible to discover the sources?[15]

The 'attempt to blow up Government Offices' refers to the IRB attempt to destroy Government buildings in Whitehall, as well as the office of the *Times* newspaper, in March 1883.[16] The piece argued that if this had taken place in any other European capital, the police would surely have quickly apprehended the culprits. However, as the crimes had taken place in London (which, it perceived, had an underperforming police force) there was little to no chance of the criminals' discovery. Similarly, in February 1884 the venomous *Saturday Review* also targeted Vincent by producing a hostile response to a comment that he himself had made regarding his efforts in restructuring the department:

> Mr Howard Vincent lately told us that, as regards life and property, London under his guardianship has become the "safest capital in the world." [...] he not only forgets that it is a comparatively easy business to make it safe, our criminal classes being of a low type of intellect; but he also forgets that the precincts of the Savoy, the Thames Embankment are not even now, with all his precautions, much safer than Hounslow Heath in the days of Jonathan Wild [...] Does he not also ignore the 124 persons who disappeared in London last year, of whom all traces are lost? What allowance does he make for the number of dead bodies in the river, technically known to the Rogue Riderhood and his fellow-fishermen as "stiff uns,"[...]?[17]

Alongside its rhetorical questions surrounding Vincent's claims of success, this piece also turned the blame on those detectives that Vincent had appointed in place of the old, now disbanded, detective department. It suggested that the new were simply no better than the old, and that the only scenario where they were likely to catch a criminal was where the criminal's intellect was sufficiently inferior to the detectives' own:

> The plain truth is that the business of detecting crime is very badly done in London, save when the criminal is a dull-witted brutal rough or a reckless dissipated rogue "so loose of soul" that in his cups he will talk incautiously about his affairs in the hearing of associates, especially female associates, who can betray him at will. [...] In attempting to discover a murder or a burglary committed by an intelligent person, Mr. Howard Vincent's "staff" are pretty nearly impotent.[18]

Vincent's public claim to London now being the 'safest capital in the world' was also derisively quoted in a similar piece that appeared in *Chambers's Journal*. In May 1884, it argued that the latest criminal statistics actually suggested otherwise:

> The number of murders that have taken place, and the very few murderers that have been brought to justice in and about London during the last few months, must go far towards contradicting the assertion to the effect that the metropolis of England is 'the safest city in the world' to live in. [...]

And if to the list of crimes against life which have not been, and never are likely to be, brought home to the perpetrators, we add the innumerable thefts, burglaries, and other offences against property which go unpunished because the criminals are never found out, it can hardly be denied that we require a new departure in the system of our Detective Police, for the simple reason that, as at present constituted, the practical results of the same are very much the reverse of satisfactory.[19]

Elsewhere, various commentators also took issue with Vincent's individual reforms designed to centralise of all of the force's detectives. Previously, the detective department had consisted of disjointed local operatives, based at local stations and who were known by local residents. Vincent's reforms had removed this structure and instead the department was operated centrally out of the new Criminal Investigations Department. Somewhat ironically, resistance to the idea of centralising areas of policing had been prominent in the mid-nineteenth century discussion on law enforcement, when the 1856 County and Borough Police Act had forced individual communities to establish county-wide police forces that mirrored the Metropolitan Police. At that time, a desire to maintain the tried-and-tested system of local volunteer constables and night-watchmen who 'knew the area' had fuelled the reluctance for change. In the 1880s this desire was echoed; as the *Saturday Review* exemplified in February 1884:

The system of detective crime by means of "the policeman's nose" was one which depended for its efficiency on its localization [sic]. At each police-court there is usually a local detective, who knows the district, as he himself will tell you, "like a book."[20]

The issues with Vincent's sweeping reforms to local detection were also commented upon by the ever-sceptical *Examiner*, which in February 1880 argued that centralising the detective department was an unwise move:

It seems probable that the centralisation has been carried too far in the case of the new Detective Department; at any rate, it is indisputable that during the last eighteen months burglars have enjoyed an immunity from capture to an extent almost unknown since the establishment of the Metropolitan Police fifty years ago.[21]

In July 1880 the *Examiner* added, perhaps in slightly alarmist terms, that the centralisation of the detective department was actually an exercise in further corruption, as the changes had been sneakily used to grant officers higher salaries than that they had previously received. It also emphatically called for the department to be totally disbanded:

The inquiry into the organisation of the detective branch of the Metropolitan Police, after the conviction of three of its chief officers, for being concerned in the Turf Fraud case, led to a much higher scale of pay being granted, and to the placing of the whole body under the control of one officer at Scotland Yard. This was undoubtedly a serious mistake. The detective department should have been disbanded altogether [...][22]

Vincent himself resigned his post as Director of Criminal Investigations in 1884, and was replaced by James Monro (1838–1920), who was actually appointed as an Assistant Commissioner of the Metropolitan Police (as opposed to the Director of CID).[23] But despite his best efforts, Vincent's sweeping changes had done little to improve journalistic perceptions of the police, and even his resignation prompted yet another inquiry into the department's operation. Predictably the press reacted, with the ever-militant *Saturday Review* exasperatedly reporting:

> Already the effect of the latest experiment in the political uses of dynamite has become manifest. There is to be another overhauling of Scotland Yard, and once more the rude hand of reform is to be laid on the Criminal Investigation Department.[24]

Even after Vincent had gone, the *Saturday Review* continued its campaign against the force, essentially summarising its view in January 1885 by stating that '[o]ur Criminal Investigation Department [...] is talkative, indolent and unintelligent',[25] and in March 1886 that '[...] the police force is too weak, ill organised, ill supplied with information, and ill lodged'.[26]

Across this difficult period, even those magazines that had hitherto been supportive of the force struggled to maintain their positive view, though some tried valiantly to do so. In February 1886, for example, the *National Review* published an article by Robert Gregory, titled 'Is Crime Increasing or Diminishing with the Spread of Education?', which measured changes in the police force since the passage of the Education Act in 1870. It attempted to highlight the immense (and still increasing) expense of the police as a positive change, because it meant that there were more police officers per person. It was, however, forced to grudgingly admit that, despite the increased public spending on the police, it had not been as effective in its mandate as it perhaps should have been:

> In 1870 there were 26,441 men in the various grades of the Constabulary force, and they cost the country £2,182,521; in 1884, the Police Force numbered 34,999 men, who were employed at an expense of £3,476,000. It will be seen at a glance that this preventative and detective force has grown at a much more rapid rate than the population; and whilst it has probably done much in preventing crime, it is a matter for surprise that it has not been more successful in detecting greater criminals.[27]

In 1886 *Blackwood's Edinburgh Magazine* (which, as we have seen already, had previously afforded the police substantial support) produced a lengthy article by barrister Alexander Innes Shand (1832–1907), which both praised the police and pointedly referenced the stream of criticism stemming from other, less charitable periodicals – particularly the *Saturday Review*:

> The 'Saturday Review' [sic] does not always sin on the side of charity, where it is a question of criticising our public institutions.[28]

The piece continued by suggesting that the police could perhaps be forgiven their shortcomings due to the fact that their continued existence was, at least, preferable to their abolition. It argued that readers should count themselves lucky to have a police force at all, as 100 years previously the state of law and order had been much less comfortable:

> We are apt to take present mercies as a matter of course; while we are slow to appreciate the advances and reforms which have made life far easier and infinitely more agreeable. There are grumblers always ready to swear by "the good old times," though as Dickens showed in one of the brightest of his articles in 'Household Words,' those good old times, being phantoms of the fancy, fade into the myth before the philosophical inquirer. [...] Criminals were strung up of a Monday by batches before Newgate; and there was much pocket-picking in the crowds gathered under the gallows. But it is by looking back on that disgraceful state of things, that we find much to be grateful to the present guardians of public safety.[29]

Elsewhere, in July 1882 *Macmillan's Magazine* published a piece by Malcolm Laing Meason which attempted to present a supportive attitude towards London's police force but, similarly to *Blackwood's*, struggled to find a convincing argument. The best it could manage was to suggest that any failing on the part of the force was not due to incompetence, but was instead down to the fact that the large and complex jurisdiction of the force itself was difficult for them to constantly manage, and that the public too easily forgot this fact:

> We are all far too apt not to make allowances for the police when a constable is wanted and is not to be found. But we ought to remember that however good the qualities of the force may be, it is impossible for any one of them to be in two places at the same time. The suburbs of this vast wilderness of bricks are every day increasing, and are spreading every day in a manner which it is wonderful to contemplate. [...] To keep even a partially effective supervision of the houses in these places would require an increase of at least a hundred per cent of our present police force.[30]

In short, then, the uniformed police force struggled to maintain a credible image in the periodical press in the aftermath of the 1877 corruption scandal. However, from another perspective, the 'turf fraud' case and the successive debates that had followed it did have at least one positive outcome – both the press itself and, consequently, the public now far better understood the distinction between plain-clothes detectives and uniformed police officers than they had done previously. A variety of periodical commentators began to demonstrate open knowledge of the fact that the detective department (or Criminal Investigation Department) was a distinct entity from the rest of the Metropolitan Police with its own remit, image, and structure. This was evident in much criticism of the police across the late 1870s and 80s, though it is worth reiterating that it was almost always contained within a larger article which, overall, attacked the force's supposed lack of efficiency. For example, in May 1883, the *Nineteenth Century* wrote that the only difference between a police officer and a detective was their attire:

> It is very true that we have, both in London and the provinces, a considerable number of what are called detective officers; but except that these individuals wear plain clothes instead of uniform, they differ very little or nothing from the ordinary constable of the force.[31]

The article thus rejected the distinction between police officer and detective as nothing more than an illusion, and went on to suggest that further, far more drastic reforms were needed to improve the detective department to a point where it could credibly operate. The focus on uniform was also echoed by *Chambers's Journal*, which in May 1884 wrote:

> Our English detective [...] does not wear uniform, but he might just as well do so, for his appearance and dress proclaim him to be what he is quite as plainly as if he was clad like X142 of the force.[32]

Aside from the claim that the detectives' methodologies of avoiding recognition through disguise were apparently useless, the assertion here that criminals recognised plain-clothes detectives from their attire is interesting. It firstly seems to suggest that the police's uniform was a reassuring feature of the force, and that the lack of it on the part of detectives actually detracted from their trustworthiness. Secondly however, it also suggests that a stereotypical image of the 'detective' was beginning to form in the public consciousness. Prior to the 1880s, and especially prior to the 'turf fraud' scandal, the concept of the plain-clothes detective had not really had a stereotyped public image attached to it, demonstrated by features such as the illustration of the 'idiot detective' published in the satirical magazine *Fun* in January 1869.[33] However, this began to change in the 1880s, and a growing image of a stereotypical 'detective' permeating though public consciousness can begin to be observed. To demonstrate the change which had taken place, it is useful to return to *Fun*. In 1885, it published a short tale titled 'Violet's Valentine, or, the Undetected Detective', which included an illustration of what the magazine took to be a stereotypical 'detective' (see Figure 6.1):[34]

Figure 6.1 'Violet's Valentine, or, the Undetected Detective'
Source: *Fun*, 11 February 1885, p. 60. Image published with permission of ProQuest. Further reproduction is prohibited without permission.

In 1888, the same image of the stereotypical detective can be observed again. In October, *Fun* published another comic-strip which can highlight again how much the awareness of the distinctions between police officers and detectives had changed. Titled 'Adventures of our Own Private Detective', the strip demonstrates a hapless private investigator arresting a disguised policeman in error (see Figure 6.2):[35]

The storyline of this comic-strip bears remarkable similarity to that of *Fun*'s 1869 piece 'The Idiot Detective', which showed a police officer arresting several innocent bystanders – including another policeman. However, the key difference here is that the distinction between uniformed officers and plain-clothes detectives is much clearer and far more sophisticated.

Dress and appearance remained a key point for periodicals concerned with discussing the distinctions between officers and detectives. As we have seen, the lack of uniform worn by plain-clothes detectives was not enough for some to accept that detectives were distinct from police officers. However, others went slightly further than this; in 1880, the *Examiner* went as far as to suggest that employing permanent detectives *at all* was the problem, as they were recognisable by intelligent criminals no matter what they did or did not wear:

> The employment of the same men day after day as detectives tells very much against the detection of crime, since there is probably not a detective officer in any division with whose appearance the criminal classes are not intimately acquainted.[36]

To summarise very briefly, then, across the 1880s the police and detective forces experienced a sustained assault in periodical criticism. The 1877 'turf fraud' scandal, the IRB bombings, and numerous widely-publicised unsolved murders

Figure 6.2 'Adventures of our Own Private Detective'
Source: Fun, 24 October 1888, p. 181. Image published with permission of ProQuest. Further reproduction is prohibited without permission.

all caused the public to broadly question the police's efficiency, and meant that it was not until well into the twentieth century that they were able to begin to recover and regain their former status as guardians and protectors of social values and property. Subsequent waves of new kinds of periodical detective *fiction* reflected these shifts in values, launching a style of recognisable detective fiction which endures to this day.

The Bumbling Bobby and the Private Detective: 1880s Periodical Detective Fiction

According to Clare Clarke, the term 'detective fiction' first appeared (at least in a periodical setting) in December 1886 in the *Saturday Review*. [37] She argues that this was the moment where the genre became entrenched, self-aware and solidified in its recognisable form:

> These were the years in which detective fiction established itself as a genre and sealed its popularity with the reading public.[38]

Whilst this is certainly true, it is perhaps a little more accurate in the context of the present volume's arguments to say that the genre was actually undergoing a fundamental transformation away from its obscure and multi-layered mid-Victorian incarnations into what is recognised today as 'detective fiction'. As this volume has argued at length, mid-Victorian conceptions of detective fiction had been centred on the idea that its purpose was to relate the supposed 'true experiences' of police officers and detectives. It utilised the figure of the police officer as a trustworthy guide for readers to experience criminality in a variety of locations that were often inaccessible to them in reality. Indeed, this historic purpose of the established genre was actually recognised by some contemporary late-Victorian critics. In May 1883, for example, the *Saturday Review* suggested that, up to the beginning of the 1880s, the retelling of the real experiences of police officers had been the primary purpose of 'detective literature':

> For a long time past fictitious detectives and their achievements have more or less interested the readers of novels; and it is not superfluous to note that some of the later descriptions which have appeared have not been altogether imaginary, but, though mingled with much that was extravagant, *have been to some extent based on fact*. Thirty years ago Charles Dickens gratified the public taste in this respect, and endeavoured to describe the doings of a policeman of extraordinary acuteness [...] After Inspector Bucket had made his appearance, and gained what was at best a *succès d'estine,* other writers of less note than Dickens tried to invent detectives for the benefit of their readers [...] [my emphasis].[39]

In fact, this quotation provides quite a useful, contemporaneous summary of the precise narrative that this volume has endeavoured to reveal. Dickens's experiences with detectives, which he recounted to readers in *Household Words* in 1850 and 1851, had inspired the creation of the infamous Inspector Bucket in *Bleak House*. The article suggests that Bucket's character directly inspired 'other writers of less note than Dickens' to come up with their own police-detective characters 'for the benefit of their readers', such as authors of police memoirs like William Russell. Detective fiction published in the mid-Victorian era was therefore *characterised* by the presence of a detective designed to reveal that which readers could not usually access, and to act as their literary guide and protector.

However, the loss of trust in the police across the 1870s and 80s, permeated by the extensive and vicious criticism of the police that appeared in contemporary periodical writing, made the position of the police officer as trustworthy guardian for readers and characters largely untenable. Thus, two main changes therefore took place in periodical-based detective fiction in the 1880s. Firstly, official police officers and detectives were now often represented as stupid, untrustworthy, inefficient and (occasionally) corrupt. Indeed, this idea of the ineffective police officer was to become (and remains) a stereotype within the genre, as evidenced by *Punch,* which in June 1897 wrote in its 'Literary Recipes' section:

> *The Detective Story.* – Take one part of GABORIAU and fifty parts of water. Add a lady of title, *a comic official from Scotland Yard*, and a diamond bracelet [my emphasis].[40]

Secondly, there was a corresponding increase in the use of private or amateur detectives as the protagonist of detective stories. Let us explore each of these two changes in turn. The perceived idiocy of official police officers is observable in a large amount of periodical crime fiction published throughout the 1880s, and was, understandably, particularly clear in satirical magazines. In March 1881, for example, *Judy* published 'Handsaw, the Detective', a short one-page fictional story about a member of the police ('Handsaw') who demonstrates considerable ineptitude. The piece depicted him as both incompetent in his methodology, and apparently questionable in his morals:

> [...] as I was shaving, I saw the man by whose talents we expected to recover our lost silver, in a suit of rusty black, a white tie round his neck, and a tall hat upon his distinguished head, leaning, in what in any other person I should have called a drunken attitude, against an opposite lamp-post.[41]

When questioned as to what he is doing leaning drunkenly on a lamp-post, instead of working to recover the narrator's stolen property, Handsaw's response suggests the attitude that *all* detectives work as inefficiently as he does himself:

> As I left the road he crossed to meet me, his finger to his lips. [...] "In this disguise," hissed he, "you fail to recognise – HANDSAW, the detective?"

[...] I hadn't the heart to tell him the contrary. [...] "Bless me!" I cried, endeavouring to simulate surprise. "And what are you doing here?" [...] "Detecting," he answered, and went back to lean against his lamp-post.[42]

In 1888 the magazine *Fun* published a story titled 'Mr. Clumper', in which a plain-clothes detective was shown to not possess the knack for secrecy that was usually required of a successful detective:

> We were engaged at that time in seeking a specimen of the London detective, and casually asked a constable at a street corner if he could introduce us to one. [...] "Detective?" he repeated; and at the sound of his voice three loafers a quarter of a mile away started, and the echoes rolled along both sides of the street; then, sinking his voice to a mysterious whisper which shook the pavement, he continued – "Follow me! Hush! Secrecy is everything in our department." [...] We followed him round to the secluded side of a lamp-post; then, placing his mouth to our ear, he whispered, "I'm a detective. I'm Detective Clumper [...]"[43]

Clumper's failure at remaining hidden despite the fact that it is the very purpose of a detective to operate in secret again evidences how the negative stereotypes caused by the downturn of public opinion of the police were replicated (or satirised) in periodical fiction. Interestingly, though, Clumper's 'disguise' as a detective here seems to be the uniform of a regular police officer, and so the question surrounding the usefulness of plain-clothes detectives is indirectly raised again. The narrative continues after the narrator later meets Clumper, no longer dressed as a constable, and subsequently questions whether he thought himself likely to be recognised:

> "[...] we suppose you are never *recognised* [original italics] [...] as a member of the force – by the criminal classes?" [...] "Eh? No fear of that!" replied Mr. Clumper, in his awe-inspiring whisper. "I'm in plain clothes, don't you see? Why, that alone's enough to put 'em off the scent [...]"[44]

The concept of plain-clothes detectives operating separately from the uniformed police is therefore under attack again, as the idea that the non-uniformed disguise of the detective was seen as a flawed concept in of itself. Criminals, the story argues, would recognise the detective no matter what clothes they were wearing. The most damning part of this story, however, appears at the end, where it broadly questions the overall competence of detectives. The narrator, curious about law enforcement, questions Clumper with respect to the 'criminal classes', and Clumper responds most unsatisfactorily:

> "Now, tell me candidly," we said, "as a member of the Detective Department, what are your opinions, in a general way, with respect to the criminal classes?" [...] Mr. Clumper scratched his nose reflectively, then

he said decidedly, "Well, I don't believe there *are* any criminal classes. *I've* never come across 'em yet."[45]

The narrator, reassured by Clumper's confidence that there was no such thing as a 'criminal class', walks home with a new-found sense of confidence, only to be pickpocketed of his watch and chain, and 'casually garrotted, and the gold stopping abstracted from our teeth'.[46] Upon reaching home, the narrator proclaims:

> [...] on reaching our villa we discovered seven burglars in the act of removing the last load of our furniture and plate in a van.[47]

Away from satire, other periodical titles began to publish fiction that demonstrated the changed perception of police detectives. These attacks were often subtler, but their underlying general scepticism remained clear. In 1879, for example the magazine *Every Week* published a story titled 'The Defeated Detective', which depicted a Scotland Yard officer tricked into being committed into an asylum under suspicion of mental instability, before an attempt on his life is made and he is rescued by his colleagues at the last minute.[48] In other cases, these pieces of short fiction showed detectives failing to solve cases, or confidently performing their duties, assured of success, only for the outcomes of their efforts to fall short of their expectations. Another story published in *Every Week* in March 1881 portrayed two officers confident that they had quickly and successfully apprehended a criminal, only for them to discover that she had immediately escaped:

> "Still, we are lucky in finding out the truth so early in the game." [...] As the inspector made this remark he procured the necessary keys, and the two men proceeded below stairs, carefully locking themselves into the corridor [...] It seldom happens that policemen are taken by surprise, but the discovery which followed startled the perspiration on even the veteran detective's face. [...] The woman had escaped.[49]

The prisoner, a woman who tricked the detectives into thinking she was insane, is not recaptured, and interestingly it transpires that she escaped not through her own prowess as a criminal, but instead due to the police officer's incompetence as he failed to properly lock her in and she simply walked out:

> [...] when the officer supposed he had locked up the cell, he had only secured the padlock to the staple, and in order to escape it was necessary for the woman simply to lift the bar as though it were a latch, and push open the door.[50]

Another inept police officer emerged in *Chambers's Journal* in 1880, in a story titled 'Recollections of an Equestrial Manager' included an eager yet incompetent detective being somewhat cruelly tricked by a group of local residents into believing he had found something of consequence to a case at the bottom of a river, whilst it was actually just a box of detritus:

> An old box was obtained, and filled with brick-ends and other rubbish; the lid was securely fastened down [...] [T]he box was thrown over the parapet, falling with a loud splash into the water below. The passers-by who witnessed the affair [...] at once communicated the mysterious occurrence to Detective Blank, knowing full well he would spare no pains to ferret the matter out.[51]

Blank retrieves the box from the river, and a group of curious local residents (all in on the joke) gather around to witness his reaction upon finding nothing of consequence inside:

> At last the lid is free, and Blank hurriedly lifts it from the box, exposing the contents to view. The reader can imagine the scene which followed much better than I can describe it. Indeed, I should only weaken the effect in the reader's mind by attempting to depict the blank speechless consternation of all present, the utter confusion that fell upon poor Blank![52]

As the official police and detectives were falling in public estimation and had become the butt of jokes in cheap periodical fiction, authors naturally turned to private or amateur sleuths to take their place as serious protagonists. Indeed, some authors had already picked up on this at a much earlier point than the dramatic downshift in public opinion of the police which characterised the 1880s, and had already begun to use it in their writing. A story titled 'From a Detective's Note-Book' published in the *Argosy* in 1872, for example, argued that private detectives were useful specifically because of their disassociation with Scotland Yard:

> It was not the first time that I, a private detective, had been summoned by the authorities at Scotland Yard to inquire into matters they had not themselves succeeded in unravelling. An appeal to me was always a last resource with them. They did not like doing it; it was a confession of weakness [...][53]

In other cases, the shift away from recounting the activities of official police and towards the exploits of private detectives was performed quite subtly. Sometimes, stories quietly rejected the police force, or simply removed any assertion that the main detective protagonist was an official police detective working for Scotland Yard at all. In November 1881, for example, *Chambers's Journal* published a short tale titled 'My Last Detective Case', in which the detective-protagonist asserted that he had been 'thinking of getting out' of the police force for a long time, to create narrative distance.[54] In September 1882, *Every Week* published 'A

Detective's Story', which related a detective's campaign to capture a well-known burglar who had disappeared into the western part of England. The narrator-detective states that the case had 'defied the utmost skill of the [official] police to apprehend him', and thus the case had been referred to him in his private capacity.[55]

As the public opinion of the police deteriorated, the rejection of official detectives and the corresponding use of private ones became increasingly overt. Private detectives were seen as figures that could be called in to solve crimes where the official police force had already failed. An example which illustrates this appeared in *Chambers's Journal* in 1886, titled 'The Great Jewel Robbery'. This, like the story from the *Argosy*, suggested that the private investigator was called in when official channels had failed to solve the mystery, and further argued that official police detectives were hampered by the fact that they were obliged to take on so many different cases simultaneously. The author suggested that, as a private detective, he was free from the kind of administrative and complex external influences from other cases that the police themselves had to cope with:

> These robberies defied [official police] detection. A clue in one case was upset by the facts in another. When my aid as private detective was called in, I resolved to confine m attention to three distinct cases, though, of course, if useful information came in my way concerning other matters, I should know how to take advantage of it.[56]

The private detective figure in fiction was seen to be a figure in possession of more professional freedom to operate than officers under the bureaucratic umbrella of Scotland Yard, which had a professional obligation to attempt to solve *all* crimes. Private detectives, by contrast, could pick and choose the cases which they wished to work on, and could opt to accept only those which they felt confident enough to be able to solve successfully. This more flexible way of working also meant that private sleuths could opt to be more independent and discreet in terms of the discovery and subsequent punishment of offenders. Whilst official police detectives had an obligation to prosecute those that they apprehended, a private detective allowed much more creative freedom in this respect. This is a point which John Greenfield makes succinctly regarding late Victorian crime fiction:

> [...] sometimes these resolutions vary from standard "Scotland Yard" solutions in which the perpetrator is caught and punished. Such resolutions, which are most likely to occur in cases of justified revenge, place the detective in a position of being a dispenser of justice that seems right to readers, even though it is not strictly legal.[57]

Greenfield is specifically referring to the 'Martin Hewitt' stories by Arthur Morrison, a series published in the *Strand* after Sherlock Holmes's 'death' and which were apparently intended to replace Holmes. However, the idea that private detectives were freer to dispense their own form of justice is evidenced in earlier fiction. Indeed, there is even evidence of this in the Holmes stories themselves.[58] Additionally, a story attributed to F. G. Walters titled 'A Private Detective's Story' published in *Belgravia* in September 1886 gives an example of this tactful freedom of the private sleuth. In this, an investigator is called in to solve the mystery of the theft of bank notes from a bank's safe at night. The thief ultimately proves to be the bank-manager's wife, who stole the notes in order to fund her long-lost brother's hidden gambling habit. However, far from reporting her to the police, the private detective chooses to let the case go:

> [...] the kneeling, shivering, sobbing, miserable woman told all. She had robbed the safe, and no one else knew of it. The notes were sent to her only brother – a thorough scamp – supposed to be dead, recently turned up, but idolised by his sister, and a mere gambler [...] I left husband and wife together. [...] No one knew the secret but myself, and I didn't need his entreaties, when he gave me my handsome fee, to respect it. And he and she sailed for Australia [...][59]

Across the 1880s, then, the relationship between the police, the periodical press, and the detective fiction had fundamentally transformed from that which had characterised the mid-Victorian period. Gone were the days of the trustworthy fictional police officer, who retold their experiences directly to the reader and who allowed the reader to accompany them as they went about their duties apprehending criminal rogues and solving mysteries. Instead, the police officer was now often a character designed to provide comic relief in periodical fiction, and authors subsequently turned to the amateur or private detective to replace the police officer as central protagonist in detective narratives.

However, there was another change occurring simultaneously within the nature of periodical publishing itself, which was to have one final dramatic effect on the relationship between periodicals and detective fiction. The emergence of George Newnes's the *Strand Magazine* in 1891 was to drastically alter both the landscape of the periodicals market and its connection with detective fiction, and this marks the point at which this volume ends its exploration into this relationship.

From *Tit-Bits* to the *Strand Magazine*: George Newnes, Periodical Publishing, and the Short Story

Alongside the drastic overhaul of journalistic perceptions of policing and detection in both periodical criticism and periodical fiction, it is worth noting that the 1880s also witnessed major shifts in the landscape of periodical publishing itself. Throughout the 1880s and 1890s, a variety of new styles of magazine, designed to cater for a rapidly-expanding lower-middle class readership permanently altered the face of the popular periodical press. Kate Jackson suggests that these fundamental transformations were also a result of technological innovation, specifically the 'introduction of the telegraph, telephone, typewriter, high speed rotary press and the half-tone photographic block'.[60] Thus began an age which Mike Ashley dubs 'peculiarly modern', characterised by mass production of storytelling in the sole form of the printed word, modernised but which existed before the invention of mass-consumed film, television and radio.[61]

George Newnes was one of the best-remembered late nineteenth-century publishers whose contributions to the development of periodical publishing exemplify the shift in the landscape of the popular press in this era. Enormously ambitious and wildly inventive, Newnes established a publishing empire that was to last in various forms until the mid-twentieth century. Newnes was driven by the desire for innovation and to reach as many 'everyday' readers as possible, and this is what makes him such a prominent figure in the history of late Victorian publishing. In fact, Kate Jackson quotes Newnes himself answering a question as to the reason for his success:

> Most people have no idea of doing anything beyond what they may have seen done before, and what they are told to do. They are frightened by originality, lest it might be dangerous. I supposed I have been inclined to do things differently from, rather than the same way as, other people, and I have always struck while the iron was hot. That, I think, to put it briefly, is the cause of any success which has attended my efforts.[62]

Newnes's metaphor of 'striking while the *iron was hot*' is particularly apt. A new wave of industrialisation took place in the late-nineteenth century beginning at around 1870, and this had sped up mechanised production and changed the way ordinary people were living and working. The 1880s and 90s thus saw a dramatic rise in commuter culture, mass-transportation, and in general living standards. The 1870 Education Act was also simultaneously beginning to show its effects, as the first generation to benefit from it were beginning to mature as the end of the nineteenth century approached, and public literacy increased. This was the backdrop against which Newnes's journalism was set, and as Jackson eloquently puts it:

> The 'growing millions' were members of the expanding lower middle class: a commuting, educated, urban, increasingly enfranchised and consumerist public, with access to leisure time. To George Newnes, with the advantage of commercial training and a knowledge of the tastes of the lower middle classes, they represented a vast pool of potential periodical readers.[63]

Newnes recognised that both the production of, and the appetites for, magazines and reading material were changing. During the 1880s and 90s he experimented with 'diverse journalistic prototypes' in attempts to both cater for this new and increasingly large readership and to improve the quality of material which these readers were absorbing.[64] Christopher Pittard argues that Newnes was 'aware of the potential for his publications to improve his readers' cultural health',[65] and A.

J. A. Morris also suggests that Newnes sought not only to cater for the 'literary diet of the masses', but also to improve it.[66]

Newnes's first magazine, *Tit-Bits*, appeared in October 1881 and was a journal designed to be entirely made up of 'entertaining and interesting anecdotes', and was a 'carefully calculated play for the periodical market'.[67] According to Newnes's biographer, Hulda Friederichs, *Tit-Bits* was designed to cater for the rising lower-middle classes, after he became sceptical about the quantity and quality of material available to this steadily growing readership.[68] Newnes consciously recognised that the effects of the 1870 Education Act were soon to be realised, and sought to cater for maturing, literate young people in a publication which avoided that which Newnes thought to be either salacious, mawkish or simply too expensive.[69]

Despite being unable to achieve financial backing for the magazine after several attempts, Newnes managed to produce the first issue using the profits from a vegetarian restaurant he opened in Manchester.[70] Within two hours of the first issue going on sale, also in Manchester, it had reportedly sold 5,000 copies.[71] *Tit-Bits* encapsulated the changing face of Victorian journalism, and became wildly successful, though it attracted fierce criticism from contemporaries such as George Gissing for being too light hearted and frivolous.[72] It achieved its aim of catering for the rapidly expanding lower-middle classes, with uncanny perception of reader's interests and tastes. By 1891 it provided Newnes with an annual income of £30,000, and had reached a circulation of 900,000 copies per week, superseded only by Alfred Harmsworth's *Daily Mail*. [73] His financial success from this magazine left Newnes free to experiment with other journalistic endeavours, some of which have become slightly obscured by the famous *Strand Magazine*. These included *The Million* (1892), the *Westminster Gazette* (1893), the *New World Magazine* (1898), and *The Captain* (1899).[74]

In 1890, Newnes formed a partnership with his school friend W. T. Stead, and together they founded the *Review of Reviews* (originally to be titled the *Sixpenny Monthly*), which was designed to provide a collection of reviews and comment. The magazine was immediately successful, but the partnership between Stead and Newnes was short-lived as profound disagreements sprang up between them almost immediately. Newnes became uncomfortable with Stead's overzealous enthusiasm for publishing politically inflammatory material, and famously argued that Stead's idea of journalism was far different from his own. Friederichs provides the famous passage which summarises the consciously-felt differences between Stead and Newnes:

> Mr. Newnes [...] preaches a short homily on the subject of two kinds of journalism as observed by the practical man of affairs. "There is one kind of journalism," he said, "which directs the affairs of nations; it makes and unmakes Cabinets; it upsets governments, builds up Navies and does many other great things. It is magnificent. This is your journalism. There is another kind of journalism which has no such great ambitions. It is content to plod on, year after year, giving wholesome and harmless entertainment

to crowds of hard-working people, craving for a little fun and amusement. It is quite humble and unpretentious. That is my journalism.'[75]

The arrangement between Stead and Newnes was dissolved after three months due to these fundamental differences of opinion. Stead bought out Newnes's share of the business for, according to Jackson, £10,000,[76] and left Newnes 'high and dry', with a complete staff but nothing for them to work on.[77] Newnes's concern for his staff, coupled with his wealth from the success of *Tit-Bits* and *The Million*, led him to immediately begin to pursue a '"long cherished" project to start a sixpenny monthly which combined popular illustration with popular literary matter'.[78] The first issue of the *Strand Magazine* thus appeared in January 1891 and which has been argued was magazine which came to both 'define the era',[79] and to 'single-handedly changed the landscape of British fiction'.[80] It was an immediate success – the first issue's entire print run of 300,000 copies sold out, and monthly sales quickly began to exceed 500,000.[81] The emergence of Arthur Conan Doyle's Sherlock Holmes stories served to make this already-successful publication almost unstoppable.[82] As Friederichs puts it:

> The *Strand* had leapt into popularity with its first number; with the arrival of Sherlock Holmes it entered upon the period when it had to be sent to press a month before the date of publication, keeping the machines working till the day it was put in the bookstalls.[83]

Aside from Holmes, the *Strand*'s popularity also stemmed from the fact that it highlighted a popular sense of 'newness' across the 1890s. It manifested a motion away from high-Victorianism and captured a sense of progression towards the new century. As Jackson points out, 'Victorianism, traditionally associated with social and economic stability, was [...] in retreat' as society changed, and therefore late-Victorian cultural developments (of which the *Strand* was a major part) were often "habitually nominated 'new'".[84] These developments included New Drama, New Criticism, New Journalism, New Hedonism, New Paganism, and the New Woman.[85] As a result, the *Strand*'s popularity stemmed from the fact that it occupied a highly charged and popular space between declining Victorianism and rising Modernism, leading the charge into the twentieth century.[86] It captured the attention of what Winnie Chan labels the 'increasingly heterogeneous reading public',[87] and echoed the purpose of Newnes's earlier publication, *Tit-Bits*, in providing entertaining reading material for the developing middle-classes. In short, it offered 'something for everyone'.[88]

That said, the *Strand* played its hand cleverly with respect to its progressive tendencies. Whilst it effectively marketed itself as 'new', it also remained sufficiently familiar to those who were used to reading older, venerable publications such as *Blackwoods*, the *Cornhill* or the *Edinburgh Review*. Indeed, Chan suggests that other publications that were perhaps jealous of the *Strand*'s success, such as the *Yellow Book* or the *Savoy*, published hard-covered, book-like publications and made a mockery of the light-blue paper cover of the *Strand* which physically linked it to older periodicals such as *Household Words*.[89] However, this did not detract from the *Strand*'s success, and if anything is an apt metaphor for how the magazine was designed to occupy a niche between 'old' and 'new'. As Chan also suggests, the magazine was eventually emulated widely by other publications, and its success meant that it became a publication where writers strove to publish their work.[90]

Crucially, the *Strand* also managed to cater for a fundamental shift in readers' tastes in periodical fiction. Ashley offers a succinct evolutionary narrative which can help explain this, where he suggests that interest in fiction throughout the late nineteenth century was characterised by the decline of the high-Victorian 'triple decker' and by the consequent rise of the more quickly produced and consumed short story.[91] Ashley argues that this interest in shorter fiction helped to iron out solid generic distinctions, suggesting that they played a significant role in 'developing popular writers establishing the popular categories of fiction'.[92] Naturally, one of these new 'popular categories of fiction' was the recognisable form of 'detective fiction' which we know today.

Ashley suggests that Robert Louis Stevenson's success with short stories such as *New Arabian Nights* (1882) and *Treasure Island* (1883), coupled with the 'large impact [Stevenson] had on other writers', sparked this shift towards short fiction.[93] Stevenson's success with short fiction inspired new publishers to market what Ashley terms 'crowd-pleasing' fiction.[94] Bristol-based publisher Arrowsmith enjoyed marked success with its 'shilling-shockers' – sensational short stories priced at a shilling each (a bargain when compared to the three-guinea (63 shillings) price tag of a traditional triple-decker).[95] One of the most successful of these shockers was Fergus Hume's infamous *The Mystery of a Hansom Cab*, published in 1886 in Australia and then the following year in Britain. Clare Clarke quotes Fergus Hume himself in suggesting that *Hansom Cab* was written to provide a 'description of low life', which certainly connects it to earlier kinds of crime writing that was designed to perform the same task.[96] *Hansom Cab*'s wild success inspired a number of other authors to write their own short stories, including a young author named Arthur Conan Doyle, who submitted a short novel titled *A Study in Scarlet* to Arrowsmith in May 1886, though it was rejected.[97] Two months later, the story was accepted by Ward, Lock and Co., who published it as part of their 1887 *Beeton's Christmas Annual*.

The period after 1880 was therefore marked by an increasing number of short, sensational, and cheaply-produced short stories in the style of *A Study in Scarlet*, *Strange Case of Dr Jekyll and Mr Hyde* (1886) or *The Mystery of a Hansom Cab*.[98] It was not just cultural interests which made the short story an appealing form of publication for magazines. As Chan argues, short-story publishing was convenient, excellent for filling tight spaces in magazines, and, above all, lucrative.[99] Crucially, the growth in interest in producing short fiction was a simultaneous development alongside the changes in reader interests for which Newnes sought to cater, and it is perhaps therefore natural that it Newnes's the *Strand Magazine* became 'the central periodical of the Age of the Storytellers'.[100] The *Strand* perfectly blended affordability with appeal to the changing cultural interests and habits of readers, and as Winnie Chan puts it, 'the *Strand* shaped the short story as a mass-cultural form'.[101] Ashley argues that the *Strand* was a magazine which was perhaps most effectively tuned-in to this growing cultural interest in the short story, and argues that this literary form was the most common form of publication in the magazine: '[a]bove all, there are short stories, and plenty of them [in the *Strand*]'.[102]

The *Strand Magazine* therefore keenly adopted the increasingly popular short-story format, which helps further characterise it as the epitome of late Victorian periodical publishing. It was the magazine which most effectively blended the greatest number of cultural changes which took place in the periodicals market after 1880, yet which also retained a curious and perhaps slightly cursory reminiscence of older periodicals which in turn made it simultaneously both 'new' and 'familiar' to readers looking for entertaining and affordable reading material. Perhaps naturally, then, the *Strand* was the magazine where the intertwined and complex relationship between periodical publishing, journalistic perceptions of police officers and detectives, and the evolution of the fictional detective story were to finally reach their zenith.

Perceptions of the Police in the *Strand Magazine*, 1891–1900

True to the idea of occupying a literary space between 'old' and 'new', as well as providing entertainment (as opposed to producing the kind of journalism which 'upsets governments'),[103] the police received quite complex treatment in the *Strand* in comparison to some of its periodical counterparts such as the militant *Saturday Review* or *Examiner*. To put it simply, the magazine did its best to present a more politically-flattened view of the police than some of its contemporaries, in line with the idea that the magazine was designed to be entertaining, and thus tried to avoid politics as much as possible. But, it must be noted that it ultimately could not escape the force's poor public reputation which had been exacerbated by a huge number of articles and periodical commentary from other publications throughout the 1880s.

The *Strand*'s attitude towards the police as a social institution is eloquently summarised by Jonathan Cranfield. The magazine frequently published portraits of different kinds of social institutions which repeatedly 'displayed a naive faith in the ability of institutions to provide and maintain the conditions under which the safe, unchallenging world of the magazine's fiction was possible'.[104] In other words, the *Strand* attempted to present a non-threatening portrait of society to readers, in order to provide a satisfactory and 'safe' backdrop against which to set equally non-threatening fiction. These institutions included the fire-brigade, the hospitals and even central government itself, through the long-running series of popular articles titled 'From Behind the Speaker's Chair' by Henry Lucy.

However, the *Strand* could not escape the poor public perception of the police, and the desire to present this 'safe' social backdrop did not mesh with the police's damaged reputation. Consequently, and with the exception of a few solitary articles such as one featuring the small Thames Police force, the police could not easily receive the same comfortable treatment as various other social institutions in the pages of the *Strand*. It therefore opted for a subtler approach, and presented much more gentle representations of policing across the 1890s designed to either bypass the police's poor reputation, or to entice readers back towards a perhaps uneasy sense of trust in the force. As Christopher Pittard suggests, Newnes was cautious of engaging with law enforcement as he 'did not want to fuel crime scares', but the *Strand* was also meant to represent the everyday, and to connect with those readers Newnes himself identified as the 'crowds of hard-working people'.[105] This 'everyday' was naturally required to include discussion on crime and law enforcement, as the magazine was designed to be a 'sampling of the tide of life Newnes perceived in the geographical Strand, [and] its journalistic counterpart could therefore not afford to ignore criminality'.[106]

The *Strand* therefore presented a rather variable view of the police. Some articles, such as 'A Night with the Thames Police' from July 1891 were relatively sympathetic and occasionally positive. This article interestingly hearkened to earlier forms of police journalism from the mid-Victorian era, nicely recalling the kind of writing in which a journalist accompanied a police officer on their nightly duties and documented their behaviour for the reader:

> It is a quarter to six o'clock. At six we are to start for our journey up the river as far as Waterloo and back again to Greenwich; but there is time to take a hasty survey of the interior of the station, where accommodation is provided for sixteen single men, with a library, reading-room, and billiard-room at their disposal.[107]

This scene is strikingly reminiscent of the opening lines of Dickens's article 'On Duty with Inspector Field', published in *Household Words* in 1850. Additionally, as Cranfield suggests, the river itself historically afforded the possibility of unauthorised entrances and exits, and thus the Thames Police offered a 'suture to cover the whole network of anxieties that attend to the role of the river'.[108] Building on this idea, the article becomes another demonstration of how the police occupied a transitional or threshold space, similarly to mid-Victorian periodical representations of the police where they existed somewhere between criminality and respectability. The river is in of itself an uncertain space; quite literally cutting through the centre of the city yet belonging really to nobody in particular, and the police here are seen to physically occupy and in some ways 'own' it, to prevent it from becoming lawless:

> [...] a sudden "Yo-ho" from the inspector breaks the quietude. [...] "Yo-ho!" replies the man in charge of the other boat. [...] These river police know every man who has any business on the water at night. If the occupant of a boat was questioned, and his "Yo-ho" did not sound familiar, he would be "towed" to the station.[109]

'A Night with the Thames Police' was written carefully, 'collated with gloved hands and put before the readers with a genteel regard for their susceptibilities', and was thus rather sympathetic to the difficulties the police faced.[110] It praised their efficiency at preventing crimes such as smuggling and, as Cranfield also suggests, highlighted the police as a solidified and 'purified' community of men, working together efficiently as a bonded unit.[111]

Other articles were less overtly supportive, but any criticism the police received still remained largely moderate and tempered with good humour. The ninth issue of the rather silly series 'Animal Actualities', titled 'Sauce for the Goose, Sauce for the Gander' can help to demonstrate this. It was illustrated by James Affleck Shepherd, the caricaturist who had also drawn for *Judy, or, the London Serio-Comic Journal*, and this instalment tells the story of a bumbling police officer, who mistakenly feeds a group of geese some biscuits whilst out on patrol. The officer quickly comes to regret this generous act:

> [...] a policeman whose notions of official dignity did not prevent him munching a biscuit as he went. There were a few loose crumbs and pieces in his hand, and in an evil moment he caught sight of the birds. Little suspecting what would be the terrible consequences to the Force, that unlucky policeman bestowed the broken pieces on the gander and his consorts, and went placidly on his beat, unconscious of ill. [...] on the following day that policeman passed again [...] and the geese knew him, and rushed at him without outstretched necks, flapping wings, and wild screeches. And not at this policeman alone, but at every other policeman who ventured to perform his duty in New Road, Mile End.[112]

The piece was accompanied by several caricatured illustrations, depicting the unfortunate police officer beset by the hungry geese (see Figure 6.3):[113]

Figure 6.3 'Animal Actualities, IX: Sauce for the Goose, Sauce for the Gander'
Source: *Strand Magazine*, March 1899, p. 304. Image published with permission of ProQuest. Further reproduction is prohibited without permission.

The police officer does not manage to extricate himself from this situation; in fact, it deteriorates until the sound of angry geese becomes an amusing signal to the local residents that a police officer is on his way through the area:

> [...] every policeman who ventured into New Road in uniform was an equal sufferer. People in the interiors of their houses heard a burst of quacks and flaps, and said to one another, "Here comes a policeman."[114]

The police officer is presented as foolish and bumbling, in a fashion not dissimilar to a number of satirical magazines such as *Fun* or indeed *Judy* – though it was substantially gentler than in the more overtly satirical magazines. Indeed, this was designed to use soft mockery to playfully encourage the reader to remember that the police were actually a part of the local community through having the local population come to the officer's rescue, rather than to display any open hostility. The officer only escapes from the geese after the local population band together and usher them back into the local dairy yard, 'rescuing' the police and leaving them free to go about their duties. This scene is also illustrated in the article, where the local people have surrounded the unfortunate police officer, and who are clearly enjoying the episode (see Figure 6.4):[115]

Other articles which specifically focused on the police were remarkably few and far between in the *Strand*, with non-fictional explorations of this world preferring to focus on *crime* as opposed to law enforcement. Harry How's series 'Crime and Criminals', published in January 1894, highlighted four unique perspectives on criminality – dynamite and dynamiters, burglars and burgling, coiners and coining, and forgers and begging-letter writers. None of these articles focused on the ways in which the police managed the crime, but rather they did present a politically-flattened view of the police by indirectly suggesting that they had an excellent record of engaging with criminal activity, evidenced by the amount of material contained within Scotland Yard's archive:

> At New Scotland Yard a large apartment is devoted to the exhibit of ten thousand and one records of crime, in the shape of the actual weapons, and what not, associated with particularly notorious, and, in some instances, almost historic, deeds.[116]

How consistently returns to this point across the series:

> New Scotland Yard has every reason to be proud of its counterfeit collection – it certainly has real and original samples of everything associated with this glittering profession [...][117]

Others amongst the few articles which *did* focus on the police often deliberately presented disconnected or individualised perspectives on the force, rather than opting to focus on the organisation as a whole. Focusing on small aspects of the police force was a clever move on the *Strand*'s part, as articles such as this

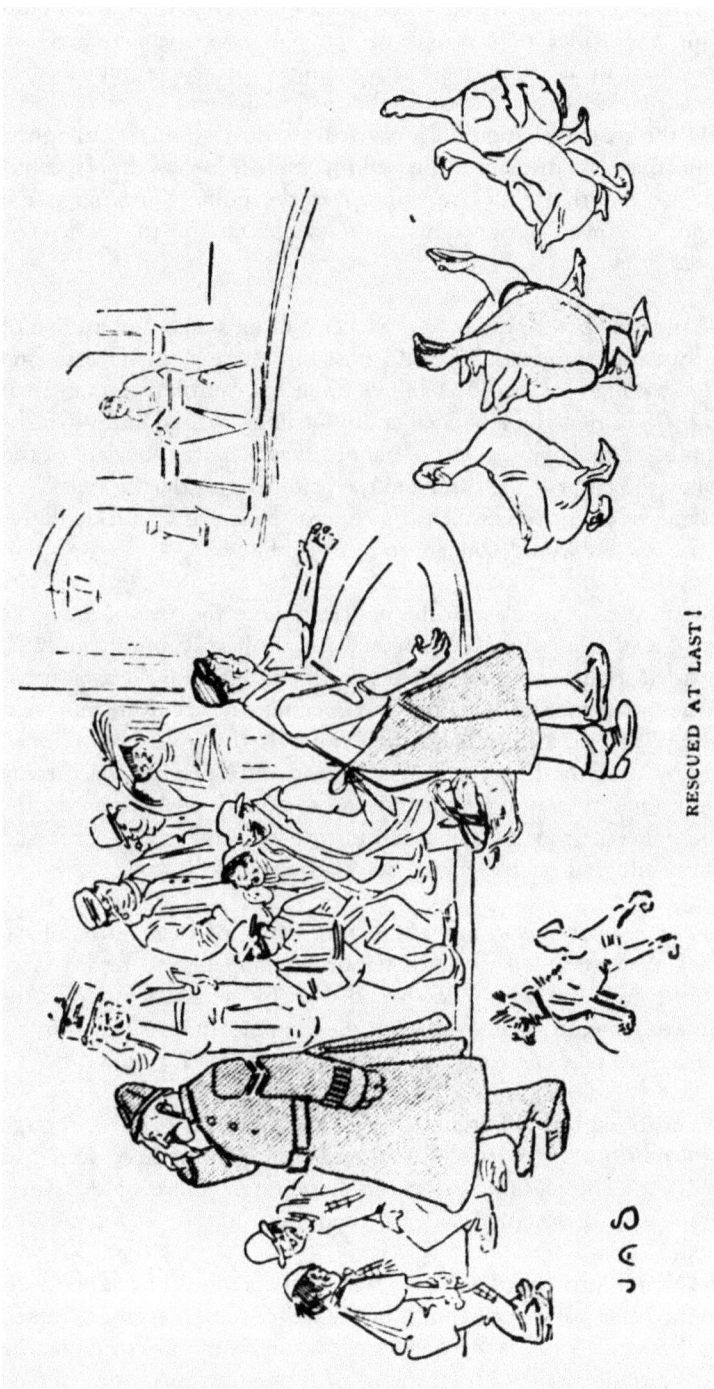

RESCUED AT LAST!

Figure 6.4 'Animal Actualities, IX: Sauce for the Goose, Sauce for the Gander'
Source: *Strand Magazine*, March 1899, p. 304. Image published with permission of ProQuest. Further reproduction is prohibited without permission.

could highlight particular areas of police efficiency or ingenuity, whilst simultaneously avoiding the wider perceptions of the police as ineffective which proliferated throughout other magazines. For example, an article published in the *Strand* in January 1894 focused specifically on the different styles of handcuffs, which drew the reader's attention away from a discussion regarding the police's overall effectiveness. Instead, it focused on a small, localised perspective which gently encouraged the reader to appreciate the police's ingenuity and responsibility, and was even designed to instil sympathy for the difficulties police officers faced:

> Even when handcuffed, we present to a clever and muscular ruffian one of the most formidable weapons he could possibly possess, as he can, and frequently does, inflict the deadliest blows upon his captor. Another great drawback is the fact that these handcuffs do not fit all wrists, and often the officer is nonplussed by having a pair of handcuffs which are too small or too large; and when the latter is the case, and the prisoner gets the "bracelets" in his hands instead of on his wrists, he is then in possession of a knuckle-duster from which the bravest would not care to receive a blow.[118]

In some cases, these specific articles on the police force in the *Strand* drew the reader's attention away from the UK's force. C. S. Pelham-Clinton, in 1897, wrote an article titled 'Policemen of the World' which, naturally, draws attention away from the 'policemen of Britain'. The opening paragraph of this piece perhaps best exemplifies the *Strand*'s attitude towards the police as a social institution as mildly pragmatic towards its existence and generally accepting that it should continue to work. It also denotes a mild push towards the restoration of the police as a necessary social institution required, as Cranfield puts it, to maintain safe and unchallenging social conditions:[119]

> *Policemen are a necessary evil, and the world is full of them* [my italics]. Every civilized, educated, and dignified nation is compelled to feed a large number in order to hunt rascals down and to help the women across the street; and in every country where law is a thing unknown, every man in his own policeman, and takes care of the above-named things for himself.[120]

The article goes on to explore different nations' police forces in turn, though it does not pay attention to the force at home. The subtext here seems to suggest that, whilst the police had experienced their fair share of difficulty, they should be socially re-accepted despite their poor public perception in other printed media.

As a result, the *Strand* proceeded carefully with its depictions of the police. It could not escape the poor public perception of the police force, but it attempted to present a light-hearted social background against which to publish its fiction without overly concerning itself with engaging with pressing social or political issues. The tension between these two perspectives was manifested in the

Sherlock Holmes short stories in the *Strand* and, as the final part of this volume concludes, the Sherlock Holmes stories represent the pinnacle of the relationship between periodical publishing and detective fiction which had developed and evolved across the entire nineteenth century.

'I am not retained by the police to supply their deficiencies': The *Strand Magazine* and Sherlock Holmes, c. 1891–1900

As previous sections of this chapter have highlighted, the poor perception of the police in late Victorian periodicals had created a literary atmosphere where 'detective fiction' had become focused on effective private detectives set alongside somewhat incompetent official police officers. This, I suggest, was eventually exemplified by the relationship between the almost superhuman private investigator, Sherlock Holmes, and the bumbling police officer, Inspector Lestrade. Additionally, the new kind of journalism favoured by George Newnes, which focused on presenting comfortable views of social institutions alongside entertaining short fiction, is exemplified by a number of factors contained within the stories themselves. These include the ways in which the Holmes and Lestrade interact, the fact that Lestrade himself consistently seeks approval from the press as he performs his duties, and also the very form of the Holmes stories' publication as a serial short story, easy to read very quickly and not predicated on continuity between issues. The relationship between Holmes and Lestrade, and also between George Newnes and Arthur Conan Doyle himself, therefore represents the final literary moment which this volume explores in this section. The Sherlock Holmes stories came to represent the epitome of the intertwined relationship between periodical journalism and the development of detective fiction which, as this book has shown, developed steadily across the entire nineteenth century.

The first of the Sherlock Holmes short stories appeared in the *Strand* in July 1891, and their publication format as a serial short story in the pages of a popular magazine was certainly a significant factor in their enormous success. Mike Ashley argues that Doyle 'essentially invented' this publication method;[121] however this is not necessarily the case. Instead, we might view the Holmes stories as connected to older examples of periodical-based 'detective literature', which helps to cement the Holmes stories as the final milestone in the development of this kind of writing which had evolved across the mid-Victorian era. The 'Waters' detective stories, for example, written by William Russell and published in a number of periodicals throughout the mid-nineteenth century had also followed this serial short story publication method. Like the Holmes stories, the 'Waters' stories were self-contained, individual tales which almost always returned to the status quo at their end. Yet they were also loosely connected, occasionally referencing events which had taken place in previous stories and utilising a number of recurring characters.[122] Additionally, it is important to note that the fact that publishing the Sherlock Holmes stories serially in a magazine which was also consciously designed to cater for a steadily-growing readership contributed to their success. Just as the *Strand Magazine* itself had successfully managed to blend the 'old' with the 'new' to make itself popular, the Sherlock Holmes stories successfully fused 'the short story with the serial' to achieve the same goal.[123] As Winnie Chan argues:

> The appeal of Doyle's famous series of short stories lay in its continuity without cumulative effect. The result, a set of connected stories, forged a community of readers without necessitating a cohesive, loyal readership – which, paradoxically, the *Strand* attracted anyhow.[124]

It is also worth noting that there was a marked difference in commercial success between Arthur Conan Doyle's original Sherlock Holmes novellas and the serial short stories published in the *Strand*. The original novellas were *A Study in Scarlet* (1887) and *The Sign of the Four* (1890), both published as novellas in less-successful periodicals and, as is common knowledge, neither novel brought Doyle significant commercial success. *A Study in Scarlet* had appeared in *Beeton's Christmas Annual* in 1887, and publishing the story in what was normally a once-a-year purchase was not likely to inspire significant sales for the rest of the year. *The Sign of the Four* was published first in *Lippincott's Monthly Magazine*, which was based overseas in the USA, in Philadelphia (as *The Sign of Four*). It was the stories' serial short-story format, coupled with the accessibility and monumental success of the *Strand* itself, which helped make Sherlock Holmes successful.[125]

However, there are a number of reasons other than the success of the *Strand* and the use of the serial short story as to why the Holmes stories came to manifest the epitome of the intertwined connection between periodical journalism and the development of detective fiction. In connection with that which this chapter has already discussed, the Holmes stories also perfectly encapsulated the growth in interest in the amateur or private detective that which had been evolving in cheap, periodical-based crime fiction across the 1880s in the wake of the changed attitudes towards the police and detective forces.

Firstly, the Sherlock Holmes stories present a character that manifests the lack of confidence in the official police, in the same way as Holmes himself represents public trust in the private investigator. Inspector Lestrade of Scotland Yard is presented as a slightly foolish, incompetent, and occasionally helpless police detective, who consults Holmes when he himself is in need of assistance in solving cases. Holmes himself suggests in *A Study in Scarlet* that Lestrade, along with his rival colleague Tobias Gregson are the 'pick of a bad lot', which seems again to intimate that Scotland Yard itself was entirely rotten.[126] In 'The Boscombe Valley Mystery' (1891), Holmes remarks:

> "[...] Lestrade, whom you may remember in connection with the Study in Scarlet, [has been retained] to work out the case in his interest. Lestrade, being rather puzzled, has referred the case to me, and hence it is that two middle aged gentlemen are flying westward at fifty mile an hour [...]"[127]

Lestrade's requests for help from Holmes tellingly echo the 'call for help' from the police to other private investigators, notably the story published in the *Argosy* in 1872 titled 'From a Detective's Note-Book' which suggested that the official police grudgingly utilised private detectives to help solve mysteries which they themselves could not figure out. Lestrade thus comes to represent the police force as a whole, still struggling to recover from the damage to its reputation that it had suffered in the wake of the 1877 'turf fraud' scandal and the series of other public 'outrages' that had so severely diminished it in the public eye. Even more tellingly, Lestrade also often seeks acceptance and praise from the *press*, which Holmes himself is often happy to provide. Holmes presents an indirectly sanctimonious attitude towards the perceived public reputation of Lestrade and his fellow officers by allowing him to take public credit for some of his own successes, catering for Lestrade's desire for redemption in the public view. In 'The Adventure of the Cardboard Box' (1893), Holmes declares that Lestrade should be able to take credit for making the arrest of the criminal himself, as he considers the solution to be beneath his own abilities:

> Holmes scribbled a few words upon the back of one of his visiting cards and threw it over to Lestrade. [...] "That is it," he said; "you cannot effect an arrest until to-morrow night at the earlier. I should prefer that you would not mention my name at all in connection with the case, as I choose to be associated only with those crimes which present some difficulty in their solution [...]"[128]

This was also echoed in both 'The Adventure of the Empty House', (1903) when Holmes drily declares:

> "To you, and you only, belongs the credit of the remarkable arrest which you have effected. Yes, Lestrade, I congratulate you! With your usual happy mixture of cunning and audacity you have got him!"[129]

Holmes's slightly cruel reference to Lestrade's 'audacity and cunning' (neither of which he believes Lestrade actually possesses) indirectly emphasises his own superior abilities, and also highlights how it is not Holmes as a private investigator who needs to try to regain the public's trust, but Lestrade who represents the official police (which *does* need to try and regain public trust). Perhaps the clearest example of this appeared in 'The Adventure of the Norwood Builder' (1903), when Holmes explicitly states that the credit for solving the case should go to Lestrade because he needs it more urgently:

> "Instead of being ruined, my good sir, you will find that your reputation has been enormously enhanced. Just make a few alterations in that report which you were writing, and they will all understand how hard it is to throw dust in the eyes of Inspector Lestrade."[130]

By contrast, Holmes himself manifests the absolute epitome of the private investigator juxtaposed with the perceived incompetence of official police detectives. The first is in terms of Holmes's overall effectiveness as a detective. In 'The Adventure of the Empty House', it is telling that Dr John Watson believes that he is able to pick out a 'plain-clothes detective' from a crowd of people, whilst maintaining a state of complete obliviousness to Holmes's own presence in the crowd:

> A group of loafers upon the pavements [...] directed me to the house which I had come to see. A tall, thin man with coloured glasses, whom I strongly suspected of being a plain-clothes detective, was pointing out some theory of his own [...] I struck against an elderly deformed man, who had been behind me, and I knocked down several books which he was carrying. [...] I retracted my steps to Kensington. I had not been in my study five minutes when the maid entered to say that a person desired to see me. To my astonishment it was none other than my strange old book collector [...] I moved my head to look at the cabinet behind me. When I turned again Sherlock Holmes was standing smiling at me across my study table.[131]

This juxtaposition of Holmes in disguise next to an apparent official police detective in disguise is certainly suggestive of the contemporary relationship between official and private sleuths in both reality and in fiction. Both Holmes and the plain-clothes detective are in disguise here, yet only one of them is immediately recognisable to Watson. The plain clothes detective, representing the official police presence in this scene, merely draws attention to himself by dressing so stereotypically like a plain-clothes detective that his disguise is largely useless. This seemingly gestures towards earlier commentary presented in a number of periodicals on the concept of plain-clothes detectives (and how the clothes actually reveal, rather than hide, the detective themselves).

Secondly, Holmes is able to pick and chooses the cases he can take on, much in the same way as the private detective from the 'Great Jewel Robbery'. For example, in 'The Adventure of the Noble Bachelor', Holmes is initially reluctant to look at a letter which he perceives to contain no case of interest to him, although he quickly changes his mind:

> "[...] my correspondence has certainly the charm of variety," he answered, smiling, "and the humbler are usually the more interesting. This looks like one of those unwelcome social summonses which call upon a man either to be bored or to lie." [...] He broke the seal, and glanced over the contents. [...] "Oh, come, it may prove to be something of interest after all."[132]

As Holmes operates outside of official police constraints, he has the ability to show sympathy or understanding for the perpetrators of some crimes, much in the same way as the unnamed detective protagonist in 'A Private Detective's Story' from *Belgravia*, published in September 1886. In 'The Man with the

Twisted Lip' (1891), for example, Holmes (along with the official police) agrees to keep Neville St. Clair's double-identity as a beggar named Hugh Boone a secret. Boone was accused of murdering St. Clair, but Holmes reveals that they are in fact one and the same person. St. Clair/Boone was willing to face the gallows rather than be exposed to his family, and consequently the authorities agree to suppress the details:

> "It must stop here, however," said Bradstreet. "If the police are to hush this thing up, there must be no more of Hugh Boone." [...] [Boone] "I have sworn it by the most solemn oaths which a man can take." [...] [Bradstreet] "In that case I think that it is probable that no further steps may be taken. But if you are found again, then all must come out. I am sure, Mr Holmes, that we are very much indebted to you for having cleared the matter up [...]"[133]

Holmes also opts to neglect to report a guilty criminal to the police in 'The Adventure of the Blue Carbuncle' (1892), where he (albeit sternly) allows James Ryder to escape justice, despite having been responsible for the theft of the Blue Carbuncle itself:

> [Ryder] burst into convulsive sobbing, with his face buried in his hands. There was a long silence, broken only by his heavy breathing, and by the measured tapping of Sherlock Holmes' fingers-tips upon the edge of the table. Then my friend rose, and threw open the door. [...] "Get out!" said he.[134]

Holmes himself details the reasons for his generous move to not report the young offender to the police, by sagely arguing:

> [Holmes] "I am not retained by the police to supply their deficiencies [...] I suppose that I am committing a felony, but it is just possible that I am saving a soul. This young fellow will not go wrong again. He is too terribly frightened. Send him to gaol now, and you make him a gaolbird for life. Besides, it is the season of forgiveness [...]"[135]

Crucially, Holmes reiterates his solid disconnection from the police here, citing them simply as 'deficient'.

In an indirect connection to Holmes's discretion at letting Ryder go, Cranfield suggests that he diverges from his predecessors in that he becomes invested in the 'emotional and psychological well-being of his clients and their worldview'.[136] This helps to reveal another connection between Holmes and other private investigators, as the relationship between Holmes and that which Cranfield terms the 'client-characters' is predicated on a certain level of trust. This was, in turn, further sanctified by the bonds of a financial transaction which would otherwise have not existed between a member of the public and an official police officer. A client literally pays Holmes for his services, which causes their relationship to move beyond a simple public/police to one of employer/employee. In this instance, 'trust' no longer matters as the relationship between detective and victim is now based on money, which is far more tangible than ethics. The rise of the private detective (and their emotional investment in their clients' cases coupled with the fact that they are paid by them) thus signifies the corresponding decrease of trust in the official police force and detective systems. The 'client-characters' often seek out Holmes's assistance as they cannot (or will not) approach the official authorities due to a lack of trust – or in some cases, the official police authorities have already failed the client, directly sending them to Holmes, who can *always* be trusted, since he is being paid. In 'The Adventure of the Beryl Coronet', Alexander Holder states this fact quite plainly to Holmes and Watson when relating his story:

> "I feel that time is of value," said [Holder], "that is why I hastened here when the police inspector suggested that I should secure your co-operation."[137]

The Sherlock Holmes stories also have another, final connection to earlier periodical crime fiction in terms of format. In some ways, they indirectly reflected some of the interests of the mid-Victorian police-memoir. Clearly, the stories are recounted in the past tense, by someone who has direct access to the details of the case and who can reveal them for the reader – Dr John Watson. However, the stories themselves also blur the lines between fiction and reality, much like their earlier memoir counterparts. Mid-Victorian crime fiction published in periodicals, especially police memoir fiction, was characterised by the desire to at least attempt to represent the real exploits of real police officers, detectives, and criminals. Much of the fiction published between 1850 and 1875 was marketed in this fashion, and this appetite for realism could still be seen in the Sherlock Holmes stories. Holmes himself famously received innumerable letters requesting advice or assistance on cases, and as Cranfield suggests this phenomenon continued well into the twentieth century.[138] Even today, letters are still written to the famous '221b Baker Street' address, highlighting that the Holmes stories have always occupied (and continue to occupy) a blurred line between fact and fiction, in much the same way as mid-Victorian police memoirs designed to convince the reader that the tales they were reading were the actual experiences of real detectives and police officers.[139]

Looking Ahead to the 'Golden Age': Chapter 6 Conclusions

The success and the enduring popularity of the Sherlock Holmes stories was therefore due to a perfect storm of fortuitous coincidences, circumstances, and intelligent decisions made by both author and publisher. George Newnes's desire was largely to create a new style of magazine disassociated from political discussion, filled with short fiction, illustrations, and priced at a reasonable amount to appeal to (and entertain) the quickly-expanding lower middle classes and commuters living in the suburbs but working in the city. Detective fiction, as John Greenfield suggests, was a way to help the magazine actually perform this task more effectively, as it helped to 'provide a stop-gap against threats from within and without' and embodied the ideological assumptions of the intended readership – the middle class.[140] The *Strand Magazine* also sat at a crossroads of periodical publishing in that it successfully managed to blend together the 'old' and the 'new', and began a new era of periodical production which looked both back to the mid-Victorian era in terms of the magazine's physicality and also ahead to the twentieth century.[141]

For Arthur Conan Doyle, the desire was to create a loosely-connected series of short stories which reflected both the growing interest in private detectives and investigators (and specifically their scientific methods) in the wake of the changed perception of the police by the public as a result of their widely-broadcast failings.[142] The corresponding lack of trust and poor perception of the official police force, which was still struggling to recover its reputation after 1877 and the chaos of the Jack the Ripper murders of 1888, helped Sherlock Holmes as a character to become the manifestation of the ultimate private consulting detective, and to achieve and maintain widespread popularity. The serial short-story format of the Sherlock Holmes stories also borrowed their publication style from older forms of periodical-based detective fiction, such as the 'Waters' stories authors by William Russell in the 1850s and 60s. Additionally, the relationship between Sherlock Holmes and Inspector Lestrade characterises the contemporary tension between official police officers and detectives, and manifests the rise of the private detective. Like the *Strand Magazine* itself, the Sherlock Holmes stories themselves also sit at a crossroads between the 'old' and the 'new', with new scientific techniques in detection being developed in the stories as well as a growth in the use of technology like telegraphy, and photography and even forensic science.

These two perspectives therefore manifest the epitome of the relationship between the periodical press and the development of detective fiction across the entire Victorian era. The publication style of the *Strand* and its politically-flattened ideologies surrounding law enforcement were a perfect arena for Arthur Conan Doyle to publish his innovative serial short-story form of detective fiction, which utilised the motif of the successful private detective offset against the bungling official police officer. These ideas of the private vs. the public detective had also been brought about by journalistic commentary, cementing the relationship between genre and periodical publishing even further.

This symbiotic relationship was to have long-lasting effects which continued well into the new century. Even after Holmes's apparent 'death' in 'The Adventure of the Final Problem', his successor detective characters continued the trend. In the *Strand* itself, Holmes's supposed replacement detective character (Martin Hewitt) operated in a similar fashion to Holmes.[143] John Greenfield, when discussing the 'Martin Hewitt' stories suggests that Hewitt manifested a closer representation of the *Strand*'s intended audience than Holmes himself, and that the relationship between Hewitt and the official police is perhaps more representative of the magazine's opinion on law enforcement epitomised by its delicate treatment of the police in articles such as 'A Night with the Thames Police':

[…] even if one concedes that Holmes's disdain for Lestrade in particular and Scotland Yard in general […] may lend some credence to this point of view, the same could not be said for Hewitt, who works as a professional for hire, often works cooperatively with Scotland Yard […] and he is not critical of Brett or other bourgeois figures.[144]

Whilst this may be true, and that Hewitt's relationship with Scotland Yard is perhaps more genial than Holmes's, there is no ignoring the fact that Hewitt is *not* a police officer but is instead a private investigator. Hewitt owed his existence to Holmes as he was designed as Holmes's replacement, and consequently private investigators had thus become the standard figure of the 'classical detective story', even in those which did not reject police officers. The popularity of the literary private detective, which Holmes so successfully manifested, continued well into the next century. Many detectives from the supposed 'Golden Age of Detective Fiction', famously such as Hercule Poirot, Lord Peter Wimsey, Albert Campion, Father Brown, Roger Sheringham, Dr John Thorndyke, Miles Bredon, Philip Marlowe, Richard Hannay, or Gervase Fen, operated privately and often engaged with largely incompetent official police officers. These characters, I argue, owed this formulaic construction to the continued legacy of the intertwined and observable connection which existed between the nineteenth-century periodical press and the generic construction of detective fiction.

Notes

1   See the earlier chapters of this volume for more information.
2   Kate Jackson, *George Newnes and the New Journalism in Britain: 1880–1910* (London: Routledge, 2001), p. 1.
3   Mike Ashley, *The Age of the Storytellers: British Popular Fiction Magazines 1880–1950* (London: British Library Publishing, 2006), pp. 4–5.
4   Ashley, p. 1.
5   'Detectives', *Saturday Review*, 9 February 1884, p. 179.
6   Clive Emsley and Reginald Lucas, 'Vincent, Sir (Charles Edward) Howard', *Oxford Dictionary of National Biography*, <http://www.oxforddnb.com/view/10.1093/ref:odnb/9780198614128.001.0001/odnb-9780198614128-e-36660?rskey=kUWBG6&result=1> [accessed 20 February 2018] (2004).
7   'The Metropolitan Police', *Examiner*, 12 February 1881, p. 151.
8   'The Detectives', *Saturday Review*, 31 January 1885, p. 132.
9   Hanbury Street murder: the second killing believed to have been committed by Jack the Ripper. Annie Chapman was murdered on 8 September 1888, and her body found in a yard behind 29 Hanbury Street, Spitalfields.
10 'The Murder in Hanbury Street', *Saturday Review*, 15 September 1888, p. 311.
11 'Police Mistakes' *Examiner*, 7 February 1880, p. 172.
12 'The Metropolitan Police', *Examiner*, 3 July 1880, p. 799.
13 'The Metropolitan Police', *Examiner*, 3 July 1880, p. 798.
14 Malcolm Laing Meason, 'Detective Police', *Nineteenth Century: A Monthly Review*, May 1883, p. 772.
15 Meason, 'Detective Police', pp. 765–766.

16 Bernard Porter, *The Origins of the Vigilant State: The London Metropolitan Police Special Branch before the First World War* (Suffolk: Boydell & Brewer, 1991), pp. 27–28.

17 'Detectives', *Saturday Review*, 9 February 1884, pp. 177–178.

18 'Detectives', *Saturday Review*, 9 February 1884, p. 178.

19 'Our Detective Police', *Chambers's Journal*, 31 May 1884, p. 337.

20 'Detectives', *Saturday Review*, 9 February 1884, pp. 178–179.

21 'Police Mistakes' *Examiner*, 7 February 1880, p. 172.

22 'The Metropolitan Police', *Examiner*, 3 July 1880, p. 799.

23 Clive Emsley and Reginald Lucas, 'Vincent, Sir (Charles Edward) Howard', *Oxford Dictionary of National Biography* <http://www.oxforddnb.com/view/10. 1093/ref:odnb/9780198614128.001.0001/odnb-9780198614128-e-36660?rskey=kUWB G6&result=1> [accessed 20 February 2018] (2004).

24 'Scotland Yard', *Saturday Review*, 14 June 1884, p. 776.

25 'The Detectives', *Saturday Review*, 31 January 1885, p. 132.

26 'Our Hopeful Mr. Childers', *Saturday Review*, 6 March 1886, p. 319.

27 Robert Gregory, 'Is Crime Increasing or Diminishing with the Spread of Education?', *National Review*, February 1886, p. 774.

28 Alexander Innes Shand, 'The City of London Police', *Blackwood's Edinburgh Magazine*, November 1886, p. 594.

29 Shand, pp. 594–596.

30 Malcolm Laing Meason, 'The London Police', *Macmillan's Magazine*, July 1882, p. 194.

31 Meason, 'Detective Police', p. 765.

32 'Our Detective Police', *Chambers's Journal*, 31 May 1884, p. 338.

33 See Chapter 5.

34 'Violet's Valentine, or, the Undetected Detective', *Fun*, 11 February 1885, p. 60. Image produced by ProQuest as part of *British Periodicals*. www.proquest.com.

35 'Adventures of our Own Private Detective', *Fun*, 24 October 1888, p. 181. Image produced by ProQuest as part of *British Periodicals*. www.proquest.com.

36 'The Metropolitan Police', *Examiner*, 3 July 1880, p. 799.

37 Clare Clarke, *Late Victorian Crime Fiction in the Shadows of Sherlock* (Basingstoke: Palgrave Macmillan, 2014), p. 1. See also 'Detective Fiction', *Saturday Review*, 4 December 1886, p. 749.

38 Clarke, p. 1.

39 'Detectives', *Saturday Review*, 5 May 1883, p. 558.

40 'Literary Recipes', *Punch, or, the London Charivari*, 12 June 1897, p. 277.

41 'Handsaw, The Detective', *Judy, or, the London Serio-Comic Journal*, 30 March 1881, p. 153.

42 'Handsaw, The Detective', *Judy, or, the London Serio-Comic Journal*, 30 March 1881, p. 153.

43 'Mr. Clumper, D.D.', *Fun*, 5 December 1888, p. 242.

44 'Mr. Clumper, D.D.', *Fun*, 5 December 1888, p. 242.

45 'Mr. Clumper, D.D.', *Fun*, 5 December 1888, p. 242.

46 'Mr. Clumper, D.D.', *Fun*, 5 December 1888, p. 242.

47 'Mr. Clumper, D.D.', *Fun*, 5 December 1888, p. 242.

48 'The Defeated Detective, *Every Week*, 9 April 1879, pp. 226–228.

49 'Every Trade has its Tricks', *Every Week*, 3 March 1881, p. 157.

50 'Every Trade has its Tricks', *Every Week*, 3 March 1881, p. 157.

51 C. W. Montague, 'Recollections of an Equestrian Manager', *Chambers's Journal*, 24 April 1880, p. 263.

52 Montague, p. 263.

53 'From a Detective's Note-Book', *Argosy*, February 1872, p. 116.

54 'My Last Detective Case', *Chambers's Journal*, 5 November 1881, p. 712.

55　'A Detective's Story', *Every Week*, 20 September 1882, p. 180.

56　'The Great Jewel Robbery', *Chambers's Journal,* 20 March 1886, p. 188.

57　John Greenfield, 'Arthur Morrison's Sherlock Clone: Martin Hewitt, Victorian Values and London Magazine Culture, 1894–1903', *Victorian Periodicals Review*, 35, 1 (2002), 18–36 (p. 19).

58　See, for example, *The Adventure of the Blue Carbuncle*, where Holmes allows the perpetrator to go free despite being caught.

59　F. G. Walters, 'A Private Detective's Story', *Belgravia*, September 1886, pp. 353–354.

60　Jackson, p. 43.

61　Ashley, p. 3.

62　Jackson, p. 1.

63　Jackson, p. 41.

64　Jackson, p. 1.

65　Christopher Pittard, 'Cheap, Healthful Literature: *The Strand Magazine*, Fictions of Crime and Purified Reading Communities', *Victorian Periodicals Review*, 40, 1 (2007), 1–23 (p. 2).

66　A. J. A. Morris, 'Newnes, Sir George, first baronet', *Oxford Dictionary of National Biography* <http://www.oxforddnb.com/view/10.1093/ref:odnb/9780198614128.001. 0001/odnb-9780198614128-e-35218?rskey=CNmNik&result=2> [accessed 22 February 2018] (2004).

67　Jackson, p. 48.

68　Hulda Friederichs, *The Life of Sir George Newnes* (London: Hodder and Stoughton, 1911), pp. 50–51.

69　Friederichs, p. 53.

70　Friederichs, pp. 61–66.

71　A. J. A. Morris, 'Newnes, Sir George, first baronet', *Oxford Dictionary of National Biography* <http://www.oxforddnb.com/view/10.1093/ref:odnb/9780198614128.001. 0001/odnb-9780198614128-e-35218?rskey=CNmNik&result=2> [accessed 22 February 2018] (2004).

72　Winnie Chan, *The Economy of the Short Story in British Periodicals of the 1890s* (New York: Routledge, 2007), p. 10.

73　Ann K. McClellan, '*Tit-Bits,* New Journalism and Early Sherlock Holmes Fandom', in *Transformative Works and Cultures*, 23, 1 (2017), n.p.

74　A. J. A. Morris, 'Newnes, Sir George, first baronet', *Oxford Dictionary of National Biography* <http://www.oxforddnb.com/view/10.1093/ref:odnb/9780198614128.001. 0001/odnb-9780198614128-e-35218?rskey=CNmNik&result=2> [accessed 22 February 2018] (2004).

75　Friederichs, pp. 116–117.

76　This figure is taken from Jackson, p. 49. However, others have disputed the amount paid to Newnes by Stead in order to dissolve the partnership. David Reed, for example, suggests that Stead paid Newnes £3,000 to extricate his share of the business, before transposing the *Review of Reviews* across to a new publisher.

77　David Reed, 'Rise and Shine!: The Birth of the Glossy Magazine', in *The British Library Journal*, 24, 2 (1998), 256–268 (p. 260).

78　Friederichs, pp. 117.

79　Ashley, p. 1.

80　Chan, p. 10.

81　A. J. A. Morris, 'Newnes, Sir George, first baronet', *Oxford Dictionary of National Biography* <http://www.oxforddnb.com/view/10.1093/ref:odnb/9780198614128.001. 0001/odnb-9780198614128-e-35218?rskey=CNmNik&result=2> [accessed 22 February 2018] (2004).

82　Clarke, p. 2.

83　Friederichs, p. 122.

84　Jackson, pp. 89–90.

85 Jackson, pp. 89–90.
86 Jackson, pp. 90.
87 Chan, p. 13.
88 Chan, p. 13.
89 Chan, p. 2.
90 Chan, p. 10.
91 Ashley, p. 4.
92 Ashley, p. 1.
93 Ashley, p. 5.
94 Ashley, p. 5.
95 Ashley, p. 5.
96 Clarke, p. 44. See the earlier chapters in this volume for extended commentary and examples of both fiction and journalism which perform the task of 'revealing the low-haunts' of criminality.
97 Ashley, p. 6.
98 Ashley, p. 7.
99 Chan, p. 2.
100 Ashley, p. 10.
101 Chan, p. 2.
102 Ashley, p. 11.
103 Friederichs, pp. 116–117.
104 Jonathan Cranfield., *Twentieth-Century Victorian: Arthur Conan Doyle and the Strand Magazine, 1891–1930* (Edinburgh: Edinburgh University Press, 2016), p. 36.
105 Pittard, 1–23 (p. 4).
106 Pittard, 1–23 (p. 4).
107 'A Night with the Thames Police', *Strand Magazine*, January 1891, p. 125.
108 Cranfield, *Twentieth-Century Victorian*, p. 37.
109 'A Night with the Thames Police', *Strand Magazine*, January 1891, p. 125.
110 Pittard, 1–23 (pp. 4–5).
111 Cranfield, *Twentieth-Century Victorian*, p. 37.
112 'Animal Actualities, IX: Sauce for the Goose, Sauce for the Gander', *Strand Magazine*, March 1899, pp. 302–303.
113 'Animal Actualities, IX: Sauce for the Goose, Sauce for the Gander', *Strand Magazine*, March 1899, p. 304. Images produced by ProQuest as part of British Periodicals. www.proquest.com.
114 'Animal Actualities, IX: Sauce for the Goose, Sauce for the Gander', *Strand Magazine*, March 1899, p. 304.
115 'Animal Actualities, IX: Sauce for the Goose, Sauce for the Gander', *Strand Magazine*, March 1899, p. 304. Images produced by ProQuest as part of British Periodicals. www.proquest.com.
116 Harry How, 'Crime and Criminals, I: Dynamite and Dynamiters', *Strand Magazine*, January 1894, p. 119.
117 Harry How, 'Crime and Criminals, III: Coiners and Coining', *Strand Magazine*, January 1894, pp. 416–417.
118 Moser Maurice, 'Handcuffs', *Strand Magazine*, January 1894, p. 96.
119 Cranfield, *Twentieth-Century Victorian*, p. 36.
120 C. S. Pelham-Clinton, 'Policemen of the World', *Strand Magazine*, February 1897, p. 214.
121 Ashley, p. 11.
122 Samuel Saunders, '"I was again passing along Leicester Square … with all my eyes about me": Mapping Popular "Police Memoir" Detective Fiction', *Victorian Popular Fictions*, 1, 2, 100–109 (p. 101).
123 Chan, p. 5.
124 Chan, p. 5.
125 Cranfield, *Twentieth-Century Victorian*, p. 23.

126   Arthur Conan Doyle, 'A Study in Scarlet', in *Beeton's Christmas Annual* (London: Ward, Lock and Co., 1887; repr. in *The Complete Illustrated Sherlock Holmes* (London: CRW Publishing, 2009)), p. 17.

127   Arthur Conan Doyle, 'The Boscombe Valley Mystery', *Strand Magazine*, October 1891 (repr. in *The Adventures of Sherlock Holmes* (London: Chancellor Press, 1985)), p. 62.

128   Arthur Conan Doyle, 'The Adventure of the Cardboard Box', *Strand Magazine*, January 1893 (repr. in *The Memoirs of Sherlock Holmes* (London: Chancellor Press, 1985)), p. 260.

129   Arthur Conan Doyle, 'The Adventure of the Empty House', *Strand Magazine*, September 1903 (repr. in *The Complete Illustrated Sherlock Holmes* (London: CRW Publishing, 2009)), p. 517.

130   Arthur Conan Doyle, 'The Adventure of the Norwood Builder', *Strand Magazine*, November 1903 (repr. in *The Complete Illustrated Sherlock Holmes* (London: CRW Publishing, 2009)), p. 530.

131   Doyle, 'The Adventure of the Empty House', in *The Complete Illustrated Sherlock Holmes*, pp. 510–511.

132   Arthur Conan Doyle, 'The Adventure of the Noble Bachelor', *Strand Magazine*, April 1892 (repr. in *The Adventures of Sherlock Holmes* (London: Chancellor Press, 1985)), p. 168.

133   Arthur Conan Doyle, 'The Man with the Twisted Lip', *Strand Magazine*, December 1891 (repr. in *The Adventures of Sherlock Holmes* (London: Chancellor Press, 1985)), p. 112.

134   Doyle, 'The Adventure of the Blue Carbuncle', in *The Adventures of Sherlock Holmes*, p. 129.

135   Doyle, 'The Adventure of the Blue Carbuncle', in *The Adventures of Sherlock Holmes*, p. 130.

136   Jonathan Cranfield, 'Sherlock Holmes, Fan Culture and Fan Letters' in *Fan Phenomena: Sherlock Holmes*, ed. by Jonathan Cranfield and Tom Ue (Bristol: Intellect, 2014), pp. 66–79 (p. 73).

137   Arthur Conan Doyle, 'The Adventure of the Beryl Coronet', *Strand Magazine*, May 1892 (repr. in *The Adventures of Sherlock Holmes* (London: Chancellor Press, 1985)), p. 187.

138   Cranfield, 'Sherlock Holmes, Fan Culture and Fan Letters' in *Fan Phenomena: Sherlock Holmes*, ed. by Cranfield and Ue, pp. 66–79 (pp. 70–71).

139   Cranfield, 'Sherlock Holmes, Fan Culture and Fan Letters' in *Fan Phenomena: Sherlock Holmes*, ed. by Cranfield and Ue, pp. 66–79 (p. 69).

140   Greenfield, 18–36 (pp. 19–20).

141   Chan, p. 2.

142   'Sir Arthur Conan Doyle 1927 Interview', YouTube, <https://www.youtube.com/watch?v=9Pf3tw2TfNo> [accessed 11 May 2018] (uploaded 29 October 2014) (1927).

143   Greenfield, 18–36 (p. 18).

144   Greenfield, 18–36 (p. 20).

Bibliography

Primary Periodical Material

'A Detective's Story', *Every Week*, 20 September 1882, pp. 180–181.

'A Night with the Thames Police', *Strand Magazine*, January 1891, pp. 124–132.

'Adventures of our Own Private Detective', *Fun*, 24 October 1888, p. 181.

'Animal Actualities, IX: Sauce for the Goose, Sauce for the Gander', *Strand Magazine*, March 1899, pp. 301–304.

'Detective Fiction', *Saturday Review*, 4 December 1886, pp. 749–750.

'Detectives', *Saturday Review*, 5 May 1883, pp. 558–559.

'Detectives', *Saturday Review*, 9 February 1884, pp. 177–179.

'Every Trade has its Tricks', *Every Week*, 3 March 1881, pp. 157–158.

'From a Detective's Note-Book', *Argosy*, February 1872, pp. 116–130.

Gregory, Robert, 'Is Crime Increasing or Diminishing with the Spread of Education?', *National Review*, February 1886, pp. 772–783.

'Handsaw, The Detective', *Judy, or, the London Serio-Comic Journal*, 30 March 1881, p. 153.

How, Harry, 'Crime and Criminals, I: Dynamite and Dynamiters', *Strand Magazine*, January 1894, pp. 119–132.

How, Harry, 'Crime and Criminals, III: Coiners and Coining', *Strand Magazine*, January 1894, pp. 416–425.

'Literary Recipes', *Punch, or, the London Charivari*, 12 June 1897, p. 277.

Meason, Malcolm Laing, 'Detective Police', *Nineteenth Century: A Monthly Review*, May 1883, pp. 765–778.

Meason, Malcolm Laing, 'The London Police', *Macmillan's Magazine*, July 1882, pp. 192–202.

Montague, C. W., 'Recollections of an Equestrian Manager', *Chambers's Journal*, 24 April 1880, pp. 263–266.

Moser, Maurice, 'Handcuffs', *Strand Magazine*, January 1894, pp. 94–98.

'Mr. Clumper, D.D.', *Fun*, 5 December 1888, p. 242.

'My Last Detective Case', *Chambers's Journal*, 5 November 1881, pp. 712–716.

'Our Detective Police', *Chambers's Journal*, 31 May 1884, pp. 337–339.

'Our Hopeful Mr. Childers', *Saturday Review*, 6 March 1886, pp. 319–320.

Pelham-Clinton, C. S., 'Policemen of the World', *Strand Magazine*, February 1897, pp. 214–224.

'Police Mistakes,' *Examiner*, 7 February 1880, pp. 171–172.

'Scotland Yard', *Saturday Review*, 14 June 1884, pp. 776–777.

'The Defeated Detective', *Every Week*, 9 April 1879, pp. 226–228.

'The Detectives', *Saturday Review*, 31 January 1885, pp. 132–133.

'The Great Jewel Robbery', *Chambers's Journal*, 20 March 1886, pp. 188–192.

'The Metropolitan Police', *Examiner*, 12 February 1881, pp. 151–152.

'The Murder in Hanbury Street', *Saturday Review*, 15 September 1888, p. 311.

'Violet's Valentine, or, the Undetected Detective', *Fun*, 11 February 1885, p. 60.

Walters, F. G., 'APrivate Detective's Story', *Belgravia*, September 1886, pp. 347–354.

Shand, Alexander Innes, 'The City of London Police', *Blackwood's Edinburgh Magazine*, November 1886, pp. 594–608.

Secondary Material

'Sir Arthur Conan Doyle 1927 Interview', YouTube, <https://www.youtube.com/watch?v=9Pf3tw2TfNo> [accessed 11 May 2018] (uploaded 29 October 2014) (1927).

Ashley, Mike, *The Age of the Storytellers: British Popular Fiction Magazines 1880–1950* (London: British Library Publishing, 2006).

Chan, Winnie, *The Economy of the Short Story in British Periodicals of the 1890s* (New York: Routledge, 2007).

Clarke, Clare, *Late Victorian Crime Fiction in the Shadows of Sherlock* (Basingstoke: Palgrave Macmillan, 2014).

Cranfield, Jonathan and Tom Ue (eds.), *Fan Phenomena: Sherlock Holmes* (Bristol: Intellect, 2014).

Cranfield, Jonathan, 'Sherlock Holmes, Fan Culture and Fan Letters,' in *Fan Phenomena: Sherlock Holmes*, ed. by Jonathan Cranfield and Tom Ue (Bristol: Intellect, 2014), pp. 66–79.

Cranfield, Jonathan, *Twentieth-Century Victorian: Arthur Conan Doyle and the Strand Magazine, 1891–1930* (Edinburgh: Edinburgh University Press, 2016).

Doyle Arthur Conan, 'The Adventure of the Beryl Coronet', Strand Magazine, May1892 (repr. in *The Adventures of Sherlock Holmes* (London: Chancellor Press, 1985)).

Doyle, Arthur Conan, 'A Study in Scarlet', in *Beeton's Christmas Annual* (London: Ward, Lock and Co., 1887; repr. in *The Complete Illustrated Sherlock Holmes* (London: CRW Publishing, 2009)).

Doyle, Arthur Conan, 'The Adventure of the Blue Carbuncle', *Strand Magazine*, January1892 (repr. in *The Adventures of Sherlock Holmes* (London: Chancellor Press, 1985)).

Doyle, Arthur Conan, 'The Adventure of the Cardboard Box', *Strand Magazine*, January1893 (repr. in *The Memoirs of Sherlock Holmes* (London: Chancellor Press, 1985)), p. 260.

Doyle, Arthur Conan, 'The Adventure of the Empty House', *Strand Magazine*, September1903 (repr. in *The Complete Illustrated Sherlock Holmes* (London: CRW Publishing, 2009)).

Doyle, Arthur Conan, 'The Adventure of the Noble Bachelor', *Strand Magazine*, April1892 (repr. in *The Adventures of Sherlock Holmes* (London: Chancellor Press, 1985)).

Doyle, Arthur Conan, 'The Adventure of the Norwood Builder', *Strand Magazine*, November 1903 (repr. in *The Complete Illustrated Sherlock Holmes* (London: CRW Publishing, 2009)).

Doyle, Arthur Conan, 'The Boscombe Valley Mystery', *Strand Magazine*, October1891 (repr. in *The Adventures of Sherlock Holmes* (London: Chancellor Press, 1985)).

Doyle, Arthur Conan, 'The Man with the Twisted Lip', *Strand Magazine*, December1891 (repr. in *The Adventures of Sherlock Holmes* (London: Chancellor Press, 1985)).

Emsley, Clive and Reginald Lucas, 'Vincent, Sir (Charles Edward) Howard', *Oxford Dictionary of National Biography*, <http://www.oxforddnb.com/view/10.1093/ref:odnb/9780198614128.001.0001/odnb-9780198614128-e-36660?rskey=kUWBG6&result=1> [accessed 20 February 2018] (2004).

Friederichs, Hulda, *The Life of Sir George Newnes* (London: Hodder and Stoughton, 1911).

Greenfield, John, 'Arthur Morrison's Sherlock Clone: Martin Hewitt, Victorian Values and London Magazine Culture, 1894–1903', *Victorian Periodicals Review*, 35, 1 (2002), 18–36.

Jackson, Kate, *George Newnes and the New Journalism in Britain: 1880–1910* (London: Routledge, 2001).

McClellan, Ann K., 'Tit-Bits, New Journalism and Early Sherlock Holmes Fandom', in *Transformative Works and Cultures*, 23, 1 (2017), n.p..

Morris, A. J. A., 'Newnes, Sir George, first baronet', *Oxford Dictionary of National Biography* <http://www.oxforddnb.com/view/10.1093/ref:odnb/9780198614128.001.0001/odnb-9780198614128-e-35218?rskey=CNmNik&result=2> [accessed 22 February 2018] (2004).

Pittard, Christopher, 'Cheap, Healthful Literature: The Strand Magazine, Fictions of Crime and Purified Reading Communities', *Victorian Periodicals Review*, 40, 1 (2007), 1–23.

Porter, Bernard, *The Origins of the Vigilant State: The London Metropolitan Police Special Branch before the First World War* (Suffolk: Boydell & Brewer, 1991).

Reed, David, 'Rise and Shine!: The Birth of the Glossy Magazine', *The British Library Journal*, 24, 2 (1998), 256–268.

Saunders, Samuel, '"I was again passing along Leicester Square … with all my eyes about me': Mapping Popular "Police Memoir" Detective Fiction', *Victorian Popular Fictions*, 1, 2 (2019), 100–109.

Conclusion

There are no further points that need to be made at this final stage of this book, save one: this volume is merely a first, and very tentative, step into the wider study of the connections between Victorian popular journalism and the growth of detective fiction. A great deal of further study is needed into this connection in order to explore it more fully, and to extend our understanding of the ways in which the detective genre evolved outwardly, rather than in a linear fashion.

In broad terms, this book has argued that the mid to late nineteenth-century periodical and newspaper presses, and their engagement with the concept of policing and detection, had a hitherto undisclosed impact on the development of detective fiction as a recognisable genre. This relationship was initially based on a public trust in the police that was itself fostered by extensive periodical discussion, leading to police officers holding a tentative, yet certainly observable position as literary guides and protectors for journalists, authors, and readers to explore criminality from a position of complete safety. This ideology was manifested both in journalism itself, and in a number of different fictional genres of writing, such as the popular police memoir and well-known sensation fiction. However, as the nineteenth century progressed, this trust in the police's ability to both physically and ideologically protect the public was steadily broken down by a variety of cataclysmic events (and the often vicious corresponding journalistic reactions to them). This, I argue, directly led to the rise of the private or amateur detective as the lead character in fiction interested in the detection of crime, and also correspondingly influenced the rise of the image of the bumbling, ineffective police officer that is still widely recognised (and indeed present) in the genre today.

It should also be remembered, however, that this volume has presented only one of the many potential narrative strands which connect the evolution of the detective genre with the depictions of police officers, detectives, criminals, and the authorities of criminal justice in nineteenth-century periodicals and newspapers. In essence, it has simply scratched the surface of available periodical material, and has revealed only one of many potential narratives that could be explored if the approach to the available resources was to change ever so slightly in any direction. The addition of new periodical titles, articles, authors, primary texts, and individual perspectives (potentially, for example, a more 'regional' or 'provincial' press focus, or a greater focus on the ways in which individual periodical titles with individual interests engaged with the concept of law enforcement) could all be employed to change, extend, or augment the broad narrative that has been presented by this volume. Indeed, any number of small changes to the book's approach to its field of study could serve to more comprehensively highlight how the periodical press is closely linked to the development of detective fiction as a distinct, formulaic literary genre.

Additionally, this book is also a mere first step from a more *methodological* perspective. The use of periodical and newspaper material to study the development of crime fiction means that not only are 'periodicals' and other journalistic content under study as an object in and of themselves, but they are also being used to study wider textual developments and the impacts that journalism had on other forms of cultural production. This therefore has the effect of blurring several critical fields together, such as genre history, periodical studies, the history of policing, the history of journalism, and the development of detective fiction, and also of further augmenting our reading and understanding of a huge amount of primary texts.

However, perhaps the most important next step for any further project than this one is the extension of this project's new historicist-based methodological explorations of the connections between nineteenth-century journalism and *other* fictional genres. For this initial study into the relationship between periodical journalism and the rise of genre fiction, 'detective fiction' was particularly fertile ground for exploration as it was connected with another nineteenth-century British innovation – the inception of a nationwide form of standardised uniformed law enforcement. However, as Paul Fyfe argues, the mid-nineteenth century experienced an enormous boom in the production of *other* genres of popular fiction, all seemingly benefiting from the abolition of the punitive 'taxes on knowledge':

> Confronted with the spectacle of popular literature, a cohort of Victorian commentators set out to explore its byways. Their curiosity about its mushroom-like profusion and spontaneity manifests in their very approach to this material: each takes random samples to investigate and *classify* [my italics]. They grab handfuls of ballads or pick any new miscellany to read through, reporting their findings in essays that adopt the classificatory rhetoric of natural history.[1]

Consequently, the natural next step for any number of further projects would be to perform an exploration of the development of *other* literary genres which formed part of this mid-century explosion of newly-categorised material, and their connection with the growth of popular mid to late Victorian journalism. These other genres could potentially include science fiction, horror fiction, gothic fiction, romance fiction, or even (post)colonial writing, given the looming presence of the expansive British Empire across this era, and the corresponding growth of journalism which concerned Britain's imperial entanglements. In fact, a further project could potentially explore the connection between periodical journalism and the rise of 'genre' fiction as a wider concept, as this was certainly a 'nineteenth-century' phenomenon, again particularly after the repeal of the 'taxes on knowledge'. One thing is particularly certain, then; the nineteenth-century periodical press had an enormous, palpable, observable, yet still underexplored link with the development of almost all mid to late Victorian popular fiction, and this is a connection which certainly warrants further, and extensive, study in the future.

Note

1 Paul Fyfe, 'The Random Selection of Victorian New Media', *Victorian Periodicals Review*, 42, 1 (2009), 1–23 (pp. 2–5). (p. 3).

Bibliography

Fyfe, Paul, 'The Random Selection of Victorian New Media', *Victorian Periodicals Review*, 42, 1 (2009), 1–23.

Index

For Product Safety Concerns and Information please contact our EU representative GPSR@taylorandfrancis.com
Taylor & Francis Verlag GmbH, Kaufingerstraße 24, 80331 München, Germany

www.ingramcontent.com/pod-product-compliance
Lightning Source LLC
Chambersburg PA
CBHW071557110726
47908CB00007B/2138